MW00453590

Abandonment to Divine Providence

J. P. de Caussade

Alpha Editions

This Edition Published in 2020

ISBN: 9789354212468

Design and Setting By
Alpha Editions
www.alphaedis.com
Email – info@alphaedis.com

As per information held with us this book is in Public Domain.
This book is a reproduction of an important historical work. Alpha Editions
uses the best technology to reproduce historical work in the same manner
it was first published to preserve its original nature. Any marks or number
seen are left intentionally to preserve its true form.

DEDICATED TO ST. JOSEPH

" the one chosen shadow of God upon earth."—*Fr. Faber.*

> " *Thou hast hid these things from the wise and prudent,
> and hast revealed them to little ones.
> Yea Father, for so hath it seemed good in thy sight.*"
>
> Matt. xi, 25, 26.

INTRODUCTION.

The Rev. Jean Pierre de Caussade was one of the most remarkable spiritual writers of the Society of Jesus in France in the 18th Century. His death took place at Toulouse in 1751. His works have gone through many editions and have been republished, and translated into several foreign languages.

The present book gives an English translation of the tenth French Edition of Fr. de Caussade's "Abandon à la Providence Divine," edited, to the great benefit of many souls, by Fr. H. Ramière, S.J.

A portion of this remarkable work in English has already appeared in America; but many readers, to whom this precious little book has become a favourite, will welcome a complete translation, especially as what has already appeared in the English version may be considered as merely the *theoretical* part, whilst the "Letters of Direction" which form the greater portion of the present work give the *practical* part. They answer objections, solve difficulties, and give practical advice. The book thus gains considerably in value and utility.

It is divided into two unequal parts, the first containing a treatise on total abandonment to Divine Providence, and the second, letters of direction for persons leading a spiritual life.

The "Treatise" comprises two different aspects of Abandonment to Divine Providence; one as a *virtue*, common and necessary to all Christians, the other as a state, proper to souls who have made a special practice of abandonment to the holy will of God.

The "Letters of Direction," now for the first time translated into English, were addressed to Nuns of the Visitation at Nancy. Fr. de Caussade had been stationed in this town for some time, and when later he was called away, his letters to the Nuns carried on the powerful influence he had exercised over them. They were treasured and preserved with religious care, and thus have come down to our own days. Fr. de Ramière, S.J., collected these letters, and edited them with painstaking labour.

i

These " Spiritual Letters " are completely suited to the present time ; Catholic spiritual life being ever the same, there is nothing in them which might require alteration or revision. Directors of souls will find them an answer to the daily and constantly recurring difficulties and trials of the interior life, from the initial difficulties of beginners to the hidden trials of souls of great sanctity. Whilst the " Letters," from the fact that they were originally written for the direction of Nuns, are chiefly intended for Religious, yet earnest people living in the world will derive from their perusal a most efficacious means for the attainment of resignation and peace in the midst of the worries and anxieties of life.

The leading idea in the letters of Fr. de Caussade is abandonment, complete and absolute, to Divine Providence. This was the mainspring of his own spiritual life, and the key-note of his direction of souls. He promises peace and holiness to every soul, however simple, that follows his counsel, if it has an upright intention, and a good will.

The following extract is from Fr. H. Ramière's preface to the Letters :

" That which renders Dr. de Caussade's letters especially valuable, and makes them useful in an eminently practical manner, is the circumstance that they are, for the most part, addressed to persons suffering under different kinds of darkness, desolation and trials ; in a word, to those whom God designs for a high degree of sanctity. To all the doubts submitted to him, and to all the sufferings exposed to him by his correspondents, the holy Director applied but one and the same solution and remedy—abandonment ; but, with perfect tact he adapts this practice to the particular nature of the trial, and proportions its exercise to the degree of perfection to which each soul has attained. The same method of direction he applies in a hundred different ways, and therefore this correspondence can be justly compared to a ladder by which the soul ascends by successive degrees from a still very imperfect state, to one of the most intimate union with God, and to the most heroic abandonment. To whatever degree a soul has attained we can safely promise that it will find in these letters suitable advice and a solution of the difficulties by which it is beset. Even those who look upon the spiritual life as an inextricable labyrinth will receive from the hands of Fr. de Caussade the clue which will enable them to escape from the darkness that envelopes them, and to enjoy peace in the midst of their uneasiness. May it prove this to all those poor souls who are troubled, and who ' tremble for fear where there is nothing to fear.' (Ps. 13). May this book realise the message of the Angels, and bring peace to souls of a good will."

The " Abandonment to Divine Providence " of Fr. de Caussade is as far removed from the false inactivity of the Quietists, as true Christian resignation is distinct from the fatalism of Mahommedans. It is a trusting, childlike, peaceful abandonment to the guidance of grace, and of the Holy Spirit; an unquestioning and undoubting submission to the holy will of God in all things that may befall us, be they due to the action of man, or to the direct permission of God. To Fr. de Caussade, abandonment to God, the " Ita Pater " of our Divine Lord, the " Fiat " of our Blessed Lady, is the shortest, surest, and easiest way to holiness and peace. Fr. de Caussade's work must be read with a certain amount of discretion, as naturally every advice he gives does not apply to all readers indiscriminately. Some of his counsels may be appropriate for beginners; others for souls of a more advanced degree of spirituality. No one, however, can fail to recognise in his writings the sure tone of a " Master," who has united practical to theoretical knowledge of his subject.

Every page is redolent with the unction of the Spirit of God, and readers will find in his doctrine a heavenly manna, a food of unfailing strength for their souls. The present work has been carefully translated into readable English, and more regard has been paid to the meaning than to the literal exactness of the sentences. The elevated, noble style of the author has been preserved throughout. It is a real contribution to the spiritual literature of England.

I am aware that our English word " Abandonment " does not adequately render the meaning of the French word " Abandon," but we have no better expression. The translation has been undertaken solely for the purpose of helping souls to follow the hidden paths of the spiritual life, and to surrender themselves entirely to the guidance of the Holy Spirit.

DOM ARNOLD, O.S.B.,
Buckfast Abbey.

(Feast of All Saints, 1921).

CONTENTS.

BOOK I.

ON THE VIRTUE OF ABANDONMENT TO DIVINE PROVIDENCE.
ITS NATURE AND EXCELLENCE.

CHAPTER I.

SANCTITY CONSISTS IN FIDELITY TO THE ORDER OF GOD, AND
IN SUBMISSION TO ALL HIS OPERATIONS.

CHAPTER II.

THE DIVINE ACTION WORKS UNCEASINGLY FOR THE
SANCTIFICATION OF SOULS

BOOK II.

CHAPTER I.

CHAPTER II.

CHAPTER III.

CHAPTER IV.

CONCERNING THE ASSISTANCE RENDERED BY THE FATHERLY
PROVIDENCE OF GOD TO THOSE SOULS WHO HAVE
ABANDONED THEMSELVES TO HIM.

SPIRITUAL COUNSELS
OF PÈRE DE CAUSSADE.

Part I.

Second Part.

FIRST BOOK.

SECOND BOOK.

THIRD BOOK.

ON THE OBSTACLES TO ABANDONMENT.

FOURTH BOOK.

THE FIRST TRIALS OF SOULS CALLED TO THE STATE OF ABANDONMENT. ARIDITIES, WEAKNESSES, AND WEARINESS.

FIFTH BOOK.

FRESH TRIALS, SUFFERINGS, AND PRIVATIONS.

SIXTH BOOK.

ON THE CONTINUATION OF TRIALS AND FEAR OF THE ANGER OF GOD.

SEVENTH BOOK.

THE LAST TRIALS. AGONY AND MYSTICAL DEATH. THE FRUIT THEREOF.

xii

BOOK I.

CHAPTER I.

SANCTITY CONSISTS IN FIDELITY TO THE ORDER ESTABLISHED BY
GOD, AND IN SUBMISSION TO ALL HIS OPERATIONS.

SECTION I.—*Hidden Operations of God.*

Fidelity to the order established by God comprehended the whole sanctity of the righteous under the old law ; even that of St. Joseph, and of Mary herself.

God continues to speak to-day as He spoke in former times to our fathers when there were no directors as at present, nor any regular method of direction. Then all spirituality was comprised in fidelity to the designs of God, for there was no regular system of guidance in the spiritual life to explain it in detail, nor so many instructions, precepts and examples as there are now. Doubtless our present difficulties render this necessary, but it was not so in the first ages when souls were more simple and straightforward. Then, for those who led a spiritual life, each moment brought some duty to be faithfully accomplished. Their whole attention was thus concentrated consecutively like a hand that marks the hours which, at each moment, traverses the space allotted to it. Their minds, incessantly animated by the impulsion of divine grace, turned imperceptibly to each new duty that presented itself by the permission of God at different hours of the day. Such were the hidden springs by which the conduct of Mary was actuated. Mary was the most simple of all creatures, and the most closely united to God. Her answer to the angel when she said : " Fiat mihi secundum verbum tuum " : contained all the mystic theology of her ancestors to whom everything was reduced, as it is now, to the purest, simplest submission of the soul to the will of God, under whatever form it presents itself. This beautiful and exalted state, which was the basis of the spiritual life of Mary, shines conspicuously in these simple words, " Fiat mihi " (Luke i, 38). Take notice that they are in complete harmony with those which Our Lord desires that we should have always on our lips and in our hearts : " Fiat voluntas tua." It is true that what was required of Mary at this great moment, was for her very great glory, but the magnificence of this glory would have made no impression on her if she had not seen in it the fulfilment of the will of God. In all things was she ruled by the divine will. Were her occupations ordinary, or of an elevated nature, they were to her but the manifestation, sometimes obscure, sometimes clear, of the operations of the most High, in which she found alike subject matter for the glory of God. Her spirit, transported with joy, looked upon all that she had to do or to suffer at each moment as the gift of Him who fills with good things the hearts of those who hunger and thirst for Him alone, and have no desire for created things.

SECTION II.

The duties of each moment are the shadows beneath which hides the divine operation.

" The power of the most High shall over-shadow thee " (Luke i, 35), said the angel to Mary. This shadow, beneath which is hidden the power of God for the purpose of bringing forth Jesus Christ in the soul, is the duty, the attraction, or the cross that is presented to us at each moment. These are, in fact, but shadows like those in the order of nature which, like a veil, cover sensible objects and hide them from us. Therefore in the moral and supernatural order the duties of each moment conceal, under the semblance of dark shadows, the truth of their divine character which alone should rivet the attention. It was in this light that Mary beheld them. Also these shadows diffused over her faculties, far from creating illusion, did but increase her faith in Him who is unchanging and unchangeable. The archangel may depart. He has delivered his message, and his moment has passed. Mary advances without ceasing, and is already far beyond him. The Holy Spirit, who comes to take possession of her under the shadow of the angel's words, will never abandon her.

There are remarkably few extraordinary characteristics in the outward events of the life of the most holy Virgin, at least there are none recorded in holy Scripture. Her exterior life is represented as very ordinary and simple. She did and suffered the same things that anyone in a similar state of life might do or suffer. She goes to visit her cousin Elizabeth as her other relatives did. She took shelter in a stable in consequence of her poverty. She returned to Nazareth from whence she had been driven by the persecution of Herod, and lived there with Jesus and Joseph, supporting themselves by the work of their hands. It was in this way that the holy family gained their daily bread. But what a divine nourishment Mary and Joseph received from this daily bread for the strengthening of their faith! It is like a sacrament to sanctify all their moments. What treasures of grace lie concealed in these moments filled, apparently, by the most ordinary events. That which is visible might happen to anyone, but the invisible, discerned by faith, is no less than God operating very great things. O Bread of Angels! heavenly manna! pearl of the Gospel! Sacrament of the present moment! thou givest God under as lowly a form as the manger, the hay, or the straw. And to whom dost thou give Him? " Esurientes implevit bonis " (Luke i, 53). God reveals Himself to the humble under the most lowly forms, but the proud, attaching themselves entirely to that which is extrinsic, do not discover Him hidden beneath, and are sent empty away.

SECTION III.—*The Work of our Sanctification.*

How much more easily sanctity appears when regarded from this point of view.

If the work of our sanctification presents, apparently, the most insurmountable difficulties, it is because we do not know how to form a just idea of it. In reality sanctity can be reduced to one single practice, fidelity to the duties appointed by God. Now this fidelity is equally within each one's power whether in its active practice, or passive exercise.

The active practice of fidelity consists in accomplishing the duties which devolve upon us whether imposed by the general laws of God and of the Church, or by the particular state that we may have embraced. Its passive exercise consists in the loving acceptance of all that God sends us at each moment.

Are either of these practices of sanctity above our strength?
Certainly not the active fidelity, since the duties it imposes
cease to be duties when we have no longer the power to fulfil
them. If the state of your health does not permit you to go
to Mass you are not obliged to go. The same rule holds good
for all the precepts laid down ; that is to say for all those which
prescribe certain duties. Only those which forbid things
evil in themselves are absolute, because it is never allowable
to commit sin. Can there, then, be anything more reasonable ?
What excuse can be made ? Yet this is all that God requires
of the soul for the work of its sanctification. He exacts it from
both high and low, from the strong and the weak, in a word
from all, always and everywhere. It is true then that He
requires on our part only simple and easy things since it is only
necessary to employ this simple method to attain to an eminent
degree of sanctity. If, over and above the Commandments,
He shows us the counsels as a more perfect aim, He always
takes care to suit the practice of them to our position and character. He bestows on us, as the principal sign of our vocation
to follow them, the attractions of grace which make them easy.
He never impels anyone beyond his strength, nor in any way
beyond his aptitude. Again, what could be more just ? All
you who strive after perfection and who are tempted to discouragement at the remembrance of what you have read in
the lives of the saints, and of what certain pious books prescribe ; O you who are appalled by the terrible ideas of perfection
that you have formed for yourselves ; it is for your consolation
that God has willed me to write this. Learn that of which
you seem to be ignorant. This God of all goodness has made
those things easy which are common and necessary in the order
of nature, such as breathing, eating, and sleeping. No less
necessary in the supernatural order are love and fidelity, therefore
it must needs be that the difficulty of acquiring them is by no
means so great as is generally represented. Review your life.
Is it not composed of innumerable actions of very little importance ? Well, God is quite satisfied with these. They are the
share that the soul must take in the work of its perfection.
This is so clearly explained in Holy Scripture that there can be
no doubt about it : " Fear God and keep the commandments,
this is the whole duty of man " (Ecclesiastes xii, 13), that is to
say—this is all that is required on the part of man, and it is
in this that active fidelity consists. If man fulfils his part
God will do the rest. Grace being bestowed only on this condition the marvels it effects are beyond the comprehension
of man. For neither ear has heard nor eye seen, nor has it
entered the mind what things God has planned in His omni-

science, determined in His will, and carried out by His power in the souls given up entirely to Him. The passive part of sanctity is still more easy since it only consists in accepting that which we very often have no power to prevent, and in suffering lovingly, that is to say with sweetness and consolation, those things that too often cause weariness and disgust. Once more I repeat, in this consists sanctity. This is the grain of mustard seed which is the smallest of all the seeds, the fruits of which can neither be recognised nor gathered. It is the drachma of the Gospel, the treasure that none discover because they suppose it to be too far away to be sought. Do not ask me how this treasure can be found. It is no secret. The treasure is everywhere, it is offered to us at all times and wherever we may be. All creatures, both friends and enemies, pour it out with prodigality, and it flows like a fountain through every faculty of body and soul even to the very centre of our hearts. If we open our mouths they will be filled. The divine activity permeates the whole universe, it pervades every creature ; wherever they are it is there ; it goes before them, with them, and it follows them ; all they have to do is to let the waves bear them on.

Would to God that kings and their ministers, princes of the Church and of the world, priests and soldiers, the peasantry and labourers, in a word, all men could know how very easy it would be for them to arrive at a high degree of sanctity. They would only have to fulfil the simple duties of Christianity and of their state of life ; to embrace with submission the crosses belonging to that state, and to submit with faith and love to the designs of Providence in all those things that have to be done or suffered without going out of their way to seek occasions for themselves. This is the spirit by which the patriarchs and prophets were animated and sanctified before there were so many systems or so many masters of the spiritual life.* This is the spirituality of all ages and of every state. No state of life can, assuredly, be sanctified in a more exalted manner, nor in a more wonderful and easy way than by the simple use of the means that God, the sovereign director of souls, gives them to do or to suffer at each moment.

---

* It would be a mistaken idea of the meaning of the author to imagine that he would urge anyone to undertake to lead a spiritual life without the guidance of a director. He explains expressly elsewhere that in order to be able to do without a director one must have been habitually and for a long time under direction. Less still does he endeavour to bring into disrepute the means made use of by the Church for the extirpation of vice and the acquisition of virtue. His meaning, of which Christians cannot be too often reminded, is, that of all direction the best is that of divine Providence, and that the most necessary and the most sanctifying of all practices is that of fulfilling faithfully and accepting lovingly whatever this paternal Providence ordains that we should do or suffer.

SECTION IV.—*In what Perfection Consists.*

Perfection consists in doing the will of God, not in understanding His designs.

———

The designs of God, the good pleasure of God, the will of God, the operation of God and the gift of His grace are all one and the same thing in the spiritual life. It is God working in the soul to make it like unto Himself. Perfection is neither more nor less than the faithful co-operation of the soul with this work of God, and is begun, grows, and is consummated in the soul unperceived and in secret. The science of theology is full of theories and explanations of the wonders of this state in each soul according to its capacity. One may be conversant with all these speculations, speak and write about them admirably, instruct others and guide souls ; yet, if these theories are only in the mind, one is, compared with those who, without any knowledge of these theories, receive the meaning of the designs of God and do His holy will, like a sick physician compared to simple people in perfect health. The designs of God and His divine will accepted by a faithful soul with simplicity produces this divine state in it without its knowledge, just as a medicine taken obediently will produce health, although the sick person neither knows nor wishes to know anything about medicine. As fire gives out heat, and not philosophical discussions about it, nor knowledge of its effects, so the designs of God and His holy will work in the soul for its sanctification, and not speculations of curiosity as to this principle and this state. When one is thirsty one quenches one's thirst by drinking, not by reading books which treat of this condition. The desire to know does but increase this thirst. Therefore when one thirsts after sanctity, the desire to know about it only drives it further away. Speculation must be laid aside, and everything arranged by God as regards actions and sufferings must be accepted with simplicity, for those things that happen at each moment by the divine command or permission are always the most holy, the best and the most divine for us.

———

SECTION V.—*The Divine Influence alone can Sanctify Us.*

No reading, nor any other exercise can sanctify us except in so far as they are the channels of the divine influence.

———

Our whole science consists in recognising the designs of God for the present moment. All reading not intended for us by God is dangerous. It is by doing the will of God and obeying His holy inspirations that we obtain grace, and this grace works in our hearts through our reading or any other employment. Apart from God reading is empty and vain and, being deprived for us of the life-giving power of the action of God, only succeeds in emptying the heart by the very fulness it gives to the mind.

This divine will, working in the soul of a simple ignorant girl by means of sufferings and actions of a very ordinary nature, produces a state of supernatural life without the mind being filled with self-exalting ideas; whereas the proud man who studies spiritual books merely out of curiosity receives no more than the dead letter into his mind, and the will of God having no connexion with his reading his heart becomes ever harder and more withered.

The order established by God and His divine will are the life of the soul no matter in what way they work, or are obeyed. Whatever connexion the divine will has with the mind, it nourishes the soul, and continually enlarges it by giving it what is best for it at every moment. It is neither one thing nor another which produces these happy effects, but what God has willed for each moment. What was best for the moment that has passed is so no longer because it is no longer the will of God which, becoming apparent through other circumstances, brings to light the duty of the present moment. It is this duty under whatever guise it presents itself which is precisely that which is the most sanctifying for the soul. If, by the divine will, it is a present duty to read, then reading will produce the destined effect in the soul. If it is the divine will that reading be relinquished for contemplation, then this will perform the work of God in the soul and reading would become useless and prejudicial. Should the divine will withdraw the soul from contemplation for the hearing of confessions, etc., and that even for some considerable time, this duty becomes the means of uniting the soul with Jesus Christ and all the sweetness of contemplation would only serve to destroy this union. Our moments are made fruitful by our fulfilment of the will of God. This is presented to us in countless different ways by the present duty which forms, increases, and consummates in us the new man until we attain the plenitude destined for us by the divine wisdom. This mysterious attainment of the age of Jesus Christ in our souls is the end ordained by God and the fruit of His grace and of His divine goodness.

This fruit, as we have already said, is produced, nourished and increased by the performance of those duties which become successively present, and which are made fruitful by the same divine will.

In fulfilling these duties we are always sure of possessing the " better part " because this holy will is itself the better part, it only requires to be allowed to act and that we should abandon ourselves blindly to it with perfect confidence. It is infinitely wise, powerful and amiable to those who trust themselves unreservedly to it, who love and seek it alone, and who believe with an unshaken faith and confidence that what it arranges for each moment is best, without seeking elsewhere for more or less, and without pausing to consider the connexion of these exterior works with the plans of God. This would be the refinement of self-love.

Nothing is essential, real, or of any value unless ordained by God who arranges all things and makes them useful to the soul. Apart from this divine will all is hollow, empty, null, there is nothing but falsehood, vanity, nothingness, death. The will of God is the salvation, health and life of body and soul, no matter to what subject it is applied. One must not, therefore, scrutinize too closely the suitability of things to mind or body in order to form a judgement of their value, because this is of little importance. It is the will of God which bestows through these things, no matter what they may be, an efficacious grace by which the image of Jesus Christ is renewed in our souls. One must not lay down the law nor impose limits on this divine will since it is all-powerful.

Whatever ideas may fill the mind, whatever feelings afflict the body ; even if the mind should be tormented with distractions and troubles, and the body with sickness and pain, nevertheless the divine will is ever for the present moment the life of the soul and of the body ; in fact, neither the one nor the other, no matter in what condition it may be, can be sustained by any other power.

The divine influence alone can sanctify us. Without it bread may be poison, and poison a salutary remedy. Without it reading only darkens the mind ; with it darkness is made light. It is everything that is good and true in all things, and in all things it unites us to God, who, being infinite in all perfections, leaves nothing to be desired by the soul that possesses Him.

Section VI.—*On the Use of Mental Faculties.*

The exercise of mental and other faculties is only useful when instrumental of the divine action.

―――――――

The mind with all the consequences of its activity might take the foremost rank among the tools employed by God, but has to be deputed to the lowest as a dangerous slave. It might be of great service if made use of in a right manner, but is a danger if not kept in subjection. When the soul longs for outward help it is made to understand that the divine action is sufficient for it. When without reason it would disclaim this outward help, the divine action shows it that such help should be received and adapted with simplicity in obedience to the order established by God, and that we should use it as a tool, not for its own sake but as though we used it not, and when deprived of all help as though we wanted nothing.

The divine action although of infinite power can only take full possession of the soul in so far as it is void of all confidence in its own action; for this confidence, being founded on a false idea of its own capacity, excludes the divine action. This is the obstacle most likely to arrest it, being in the soul itself; for, as regards obstacles that are exterior, God can change them if He so pleases into means for making progress. All is alike to Him, equally useful, or equally useless. Without the divine action all things are as nothing, and with it the veriest nothing can be turned to account.

Whether it be meditation, contemplation, vocal prayer, interior silence, or the active use of any of the faculties, either sensible and distinct, or almost imperceptible; quiet retreat, or active employment, whatever it may be in itself, even if very desirable, that which God wills for the present moment is best and all else must be regarded by the soul as being nothing at all. Thus, beholding God in all things it must take or leave them all as He pleases, and neither desire to live, nor to improve, nor to hope, except as He ordains, and never by the help of things which have neither power nor virtue except from Him. It ought, at every moment and on all occasions, to say with St. Paul, "Lord, what wilt thou have me to do?" (Acts ix, 6) without choosing this thing or that, but " whatsoever You will. The mind prefers one thing, the body another, but, Lord, I desire nothing but to accomplish Your holy will. Work, contemplation or prayer whether vocal or mental, active or passive;

the prayer of faith or of understanding; that which is distinguished in kind, or gifted with universal grace : it is all nothing
Lord unless made real and useful by Your will.   It is to Your
holy will that I devote myself and not to any of these things,
however high and sublime they may be, because it is the perfection of the heart for which grace is given, and not for that of
the mind."

The presence of God which sanctifies our souls is the dwelling
of the Holy Trinity in the depths of our hearts when they submit
to His holy will.   The act of the presence of God made in contemplation effects this intimate union only like other acts that
are according to the order of God.

There is, therefore, nothing unlawful in the love and esteem
we have for contemplation and other pious exercises, if this
love and esteem are directed entirely to the God of all goodness
who willingly makes use of these means to unite our souls to
Himself.

In entertaining the suite of a prince, one entertains the prince
himself, and he would consider any discourtesy shown to his
officers under pretence of wishing for him alone as an insult to
himself.

SECTION VII.—*On the Attainment of Peace.*
There is no solid peace except in submission to the divine
action.

The soul that does not attach itself solely to the will of God
will find neither satisfaction nor sanctification in any other means
however excellent by which it may attempt to gain them.   If
that which God Himself chooses for you does not content you,
from whom do you expect to obtain what you desire ?   If
you are disgusted with the meat prepared for you by the divine
will itself, what food would not be insipid to so depraved a taste ?
No soul can be really nourished, fortified, purified, enriched,
and sanctified except in fulfilling the duties of the present
moment.   What more would you have ?   As in this you can
find all good, why seek it elsewhere ?   Do you know better than
God ?   As He ordains it thus why do you desire it differently ?
Can His wisdom and goodness be deceived ?   When you find
something to be in accordance with this divine wisdom and
goodness ought you not to conclude that it must needs be excellent ?   Do you imagine you will find peace in resisting the

Almighty? Is it not, on the contrary, this resistance which we too often continue without owning it even to ourselves which is the cause of all our troubles? It is only just, therefore, that the soul that is dissatisfied with the divine action for each present moment should be punished by being unable to find happiness in anything else. If books, the example of the saints, and spiritual conversations deprive the soul of peace; if they fill the mind without satisfying it; it is a sign that one had strayed from the path of pure abandonment to the divine action, and that one is only seeking to please oneself. To be employed in this way is to prevent God from finding an entrance. All this must be got rid of because of being an obstacle to grace. But if the divine will ordains the use of these things the soul may receive them like the rest—that is to say—as the means ordained by God which it accepts simply to use, and leaves afterwards when their moment has passed for the duties of the moment that follows. There is, in fact, nothing really good that does not emanate from the ordinance of God, and nothing, however good in itself, can be better adapted for the sanctification of the soul and the attainment of peace.

Section VIII.—*To Estimate Degrees of Excellence.*

The perfection of souls, and the degree of excellence to which they have attained can be gauged by their fidelity to the order established by God.

The will of God gives to all things a supernatural and divine value for the soul submitting to it. The duties it imposes, and those it contains, with all the matters over which it is diffused, become holy and perfect, because, being unlimited in power, everything it touches shares its divine character. But in order not to stray either to the right or to the left the soul should only attend to those inspirations which it believes it has received from God, by the fact that these inspirations do not withdraw it from the duties of its state. These duties are the most clear manifestation of the will of God, and nothing should take their place; in them there is nothing to fear, nothing to exclude, nor anything to be chosen. The time occupied in the fulfilment of these duties is very precious and very salutary for the soul by the indubitable fact that it is spent in accomplishing this holy will. The entire virtue of all that is called holy is in its approximation to this order established by God ; therefore nothing should be rejected, nothing sought after, but everything accepted that is ordained and nothing attempted contrary to the will of God.

Books and wise counsels, vocal prayer and interior affections if they are in accordance with the will of God are instructive, and all help to guide and to unify. In contemning all sensible means to this end quietism is greatly to blame, for there are souls that are intended by God to keep always to this way. Their state of life and their attraction show this clearly enough. It is vain to picture any kind of abandonment from which all personal activity is excluded. When God requires action, sanctity is to be found in activity. Besides the duties imposed on everyone by their state of life God may require certain actions which are not included in these duties, although they may not be in any way opposed to them. An attraction and inspiration are then the signs of the divine approval. Souls conducted by God in this way will find a greater perfection in adding the things inspired to those that are commanded, taking the necessary precautions required in such cases, that the duties of their state may not clash with those things arranged by Providence.

God makes saints as He pleases, but they are made always according to His plan, and in submission to His will. This submission is true and most perfect abandonment.

Duties imposed by the state of life and by divine Providence are common to all the saints and are what God arranges for all in general. They live hidden from the world which is so evil that they are obliged to avoid its dangers ; but it is not on this account that they are saints, but only on account of their submission to the will of God. The more absolute this submission becomes the higher becomes their sanctity. We must not imagine that those whose virtue is shown in wonderful and singular ways, and by unquestionable attractions and inspirations, advance less on that account in the way of abandonment. From the moment that these acts become duties by the will of God, then to be content only to fulfil the duties of a state of life, or the ordinary inspirations of Providence would be to resist God, whose holy will would no longer retain the mastery of the passing moments, and to cease practising the virtue of abandonment. Our duties must be so arranged as to be commensurate with the designs of God, and to follow the path designated by our attraction. To carry out our inspirations will then become a duty to which we must be faithful. As there are souls whose whole duty is defined by exterior laws, and who should not go beyond them because restricted by the will of God ; so also there are others who, besides exterior duties, are obliged to carry out faithfully that interior rule imprinted on their hearts. It would be a foolish and frivolous curiosity to try to discover which is the most holy. Each has to follow the appointed path. Perfection consists in submitting unreservedly to the designs of God, and in fulfilling the duties of one's state in the most perfect manner possible. To compare the different states as they are in themselves can do nothing to improve us since it is neither in the amount of work, nor in the sort of duties given to us that perfection is to be found. If self-love is the motive power of our acts, or if it be not immediately crushed when discovered, our supposed abundance will be in truth absolute poverty because it is not supplied by obedience to the will of God. However, to decide the question in some way, I think that holiness can be measured by the love one has for God, and the desire to please Him, and that the more His will is the guiding principle, and His plans conformed to and loved, the greater will be the holiness, no matter what may be the means made use of. It is this that we notice in Jesus, Mary and Joseph. In their separate lives there is more of love than of greatness, and more of the spirit than of the matter. It is not written that they sought holiness in things themselves, but only in the motive with which they used them. It must therefore be concluded that one way is not more perfect than another, but that the most perfect is that which is most closely in conformity with the order established by God, whether by the accomplishment of exterior duties, or by interior dispositions.

SECTION IX.—*Sanctity Made Easy.*

Conclusion of the first chapter. How easy sanctity becomes when this doctrine is properly understood.

I believe that if those souls that tend towards sanctity were instructed as to the conduct they ought to follow, they would be spared a good deal of trouble. I speak as much of people in the world as of others. If they could realise the merit concealed in the actions of each moment of the day; I mean in each of the daily duties of their state of life, and if they could be persuaded that sanctity is founded on that to which they give no heed as being altogether irrelevant, they would indeed be happy. If, besides, they understood that to attain the utmost height of perfection, the safest and surest way is to accept the crosses sent them by Providence at every moment, that the true philosopher's stone is submission to the will of God which changes into divine gold all their occupations, troubles, and sufferings, what consolation would be theirs! What courage would they not derive from the thought that to acquire the friendship of God, and to arrive at eternal glory, they had but to do what they were doing, but to suffer what they were suffering, and that what they wasted and counted as nothing would suffice to enable them to arrive at eminent sanctity: far more so than extraordinary states and wonderful works. O my God! how much I long to be the missionary of Your holy will, and to teach all men that there is nothing more easy, more attainable, more within reach, and in the power of everyone, than sanctity. How I wish that I could make them understand that just as the good and the bad thief had the same things to do and to suffer; so also two persons, one of whom is worldly and the other leading an interior and wholly spiritual life have, neither of them, anything different to do or to suffer; but that one is sanctified and attains eternal happiness by submission to Your holy will in those very things by which the other is damned because he does them to please himself, or endures them with reluctance and rebellion. This proves that it is only the heart that is different. Oh! all you that read this, it will cost you no more than to do what you are doing, to suffer what you are suffering, only act and suffer in a holy manner. It is the heart that must be changed. When I say heart, I mean will. Sanctity, then, consists in willing all that God wills for us. Yes! sanctity of heart is a simple " fiat," a conformity of will with the will of God.

What could be more easy, and who could refuse to love a will so kind and so good? Let us love it then, and this love alone will make everything in us divine.

———

CHAPTER II.

THE DIVINE ACTION WORKS UNCEASINGLY FOR THE SANCTIFICATION OF SOULS.

SECTION I.

The divine action, although only visible to the eye of faith, is everywhere, and always present.

All creatures that exist are in the hands of God. The action of the creature can only be perceived by the senses, but faith sees in all things the action of the Creator. It believes that in Jesus Christ all things live, and that His divine operation continues to the end of time, embracing the passing moment and the smallest created atom in its hidden life and mysterious action. The action of the creature is a veil which covers the profound mysteries of the divine operation. After the Resurrection Jesus Christ took His disciples by surprise in His various apparitions. He showed Himself to them under various disguises and, in the act of making Himself known to them, disappeared. This same Jesus, ever living, ever working, still takes by surprise those souls whose faith is weak and wavering.

There is not a moment in which God does not present Himself under the cover of some pain to be endured, of some consolation to be enjoyed, or of some duty to be performed. All that takes place within us, around us, or through us, contains and conceals His divine action.

It is really and truly there present, but invisibly present, so that we are always surprised and do not recognise His operation until it has ceased. If we could lift the veil, and if we were attentive and watchful God would continually reveal Himself to us, and we should see His divine action in everything that happened to us, and rejoice in it. At each successive occurrence we should exclaim : " It is the Lord," and we should accept every fresh circumstance as a gift of God. We should look upon creatures as feeble tools in the hands of an able workman, and should discover easily that nothing was wanting to us, and that the constant providence of God disposed Him to bestow

c

upon us at every moment whatever we required. If only we had faith we should show good-will to all creatures; we should cherish them and be interiorly grateful to them as serving, by God's will, for our perfection. If we lived the life of faith without intermission we should have an uninterrupted commerce with God and a constant familiar intercourse with Him. What the air is for the transmission of our thoughts and words, such would be our actions and sufferings for those of God. They would be as the substance of His words, and in all external events we should see nothing but what was excellent and holy. This union is effected on earth by faith, in Heaven by glory; the only difference is in the method of its working. God is interpreted by faith. Without the light of faith creation would speak to us in vain. It is a writing in cypher in which we find nothing but confusion, an entangled mesh from which no one would expect to hear the voice of God. But as Moses saw the fire of divine charity in the burning bush, so faith gives us the clue to the cypher, and reveals to us, in this mass of confusion, marvels of divine wisdom. Faith changes the face of the earth; by it the heart is raised, entranced and becomes conversant with heavenly things. Faith is our light in this life. By it we possess the truth without seeing it; we touch what we cannot feel, and see what is not evident to the senses. By it we view the world as though it did not exist. It is the key of the treasure house, the key of the abyss of the science of God. It is faith that teaches us the hollowness of created things; by it God reveals and manifests Himself in all things. By faith the veil is torn aside to reveal the eternal truth.

All that we see is nothing but vanity and deceit; truth can be found only in God. What a difference between the thoughts of God and the illusions of man! How is it that although continually warned that everything that happens in the world is but a shadow, a figure, a mystery of faith, we look at the outside only and do not perceive the enigma they contain?

We fall into this trap like men without sense instead of raising our eyes to the principle, source and origin of all things, in which they all have their right name and just proportions, in which everything is supernatural, divine, and sanctifying; in which all is part of the plenitude of Jesus Christ, and each circumstance is as a stone towards the construction of the heavenly Jerusalem, and all helps to build a dwelling for us in that marvellous city.

We live according to what we see and feel and wander like madmen in a labyrinth of darkness and illusion for want of the light of faith which would guide us safely through it. By means of faith we should be able to aspire after God and to live for Him alone, forsaking and going beyond mere figures.

SECTION II.—*By Faith the Operation of God is recognised.*
The more hidden the divine operation beneath an outwardly
repulsive appearance, the more visible it is to the eye of faith.

The soul, enlightened by faith, judges of things in a very
different way to those who, having only the standard of the
senses by which to measure them, ignore the inestimable treasure
they contain.   He who knows that a certain person in disguise
is the king, behaves towards him very differently to another
who, only perceiving an ordinary man, treats him accordingly.
In the same way the soul that recognises the will of God in every
smallest event, and also in those that are most distressing and
direful, receives all with an equal joy, pleasure and respect.
It throws open all its doors to receive with honour what others
fear and fly from with horror.   The outward appearance may
be mean and contemptible, but beneath this abject garb the
heart discovers and honours the majesty of the king.   The
deeper the abasement of his entry in such a guise and in secret
the more does the heart become filled with love.   I cannot describe what the heart feels when it accepts the divine will in such
humble, poor, and mean disguises.   Ah !   how the sight of God,
poor and humble, lodged in a stable, lying on straw, weeping
and trembling, pierced the loving heart of Mary !   Ask the in-
habitants of Bethlehem what they thought of the Child.   You
know what answer they gave, and how they would have paid
court to Him had He been lodged in a palace surrounded by the
state due to princes.
Then ask Mary and Joseph, the Magi and the Shepherds.
They will tell you that they found in this extreme poverty an
indescribable tenderness, and an infinite dignity worthy of the
majesty of God.   Faith is strengthened, increased and enriched
by those things that escape the senses ; the less there is to see,
the more there is to believe.   To adore Jesus on Thabor, to
accept the will of God in extraordinary circumstances does not
indicate a life animated by such great faith as to love the will of
God in ordinary things and to adore Jesus on the Cross ; for faith
cannot be said to be real, living faith until it is tried, and has
triumphed over every effort for its destruction.   War with the
senses enables faith to obtain a more glorious victory.   To
consider God equally good in things that are petty and ordinary
as in those that are great and uncommon is to have a faith that
is not ordinary, but great and extraordinary.
To be satisfied with the present moment is to delight in, and
to adore the divine will in all that has to be done or suffered in

all that succession of events that fill, as they pass, each present moment. Those souls that have this disposition adore God with redoubled love and respect in each consecutive humiliating condition ; nothing can hide Him from the piercing eye of faith. The louder the senses proclaim that in this, or that, there is no God ; the more firmly do these souls clasp and embrace their " bundle of myrrh." Nothing daunts them, nothing disgusts them.

Mary, when the apostles fled, remained steadfast at the foot of the Cross. She owned Jesus as her Son when He was disfigured with wounds, and covered with mud and spittle. The wounds that disfigured Him made Him only more lovable and adorable in the eyes of this tender Mother. The more awful were the blasphemies uttered against Him, so much the deeper became her veneration and respect.

The life of faith is nothing less than the continued pursuit of God through all that disguises, disfigures, destroys and, so to say, annihilates Him. It is in very truth a reproduction of the life of Mary who, from the Stable to the Cross, remained unalterably united to that God whom all the world misunderstood, abandoned, and persecuted. In like manner faithful souls endure a constant succession of trials. God hides beneath veils of darkness and illusive appearances which make His will difficult to recognise ; but in spite of every obstacle these souls follow Him and love Him even to the death of the Cross. They know that, leaving the darkness, they must run after the light of this divine Sun which, from its rising to its setting, however dark and thick may be the clouds that obscure it, enlightens, warms, and inflames the faithful hearts that bless, praise and contemplate it during the whole circle of its mysterious course.

Pursue then without ceasing, ye faithful souls, this beloved Spouse who with giant strides passes from one extremity of the heavens to the other. If you be content and untiring nothing will have power to hide Him from you. He moves above the smallest blades of grass as above the mighty cedar. The grains of sand are under His feet as well as the huge mountains. Wherever you may turn, there you will find His footprints, and in following them perseveringly you will find Him wherever you may be.

Oh ! what delightful peace we enjoy when we have learnt by faith to find God thus in all His creatures ! Then is darkness luminous, and bitterness sweet. Faith, while showing us things as they are, changes their ugliness into beauty, and their malice into virtue. Faith is the mother of sweetness, confidence and joy. It cannot help feeling tenderness and compassion for its enemies by whose means it is so immeasurably enriched. The greater the harshness and severity of the creature, the greater by the operation of God, is the advantage to the soul. While the human instrument strives to do harm, the divine Workman in whose hands it is, makes use of its very malice to remove from the soul all that might be prejudicial to it.

The will of God has nothing but sweetness, favours and treasures for submissive souls; it is impossible to repose too much confidence in it, nor to abandon oneself to it too utterly. It always acts for, and desires that which is most conducive to our perfection, provided we allow it to act. Faith does not doubt. The more unfaithful, uncertain, and rebellious are the senses, the louder faith cries : " all is well, it is the will of God." There is nothing that the eye of faith does not penetrate, nothing that the power of faith does not overcome. It passes through the thick darkness, and, no matter what clouds may gather, it goes straight to the truth, and holding to it firmly will never let it go.

Section III.—*How to Discover what is the Will of God.*

The divine action places before us at every moment things of infinite value, and gives them to us according to the measure of our faith and love.

If we understood how to see in each moment some manifestation of the will of God we should find therein also all that our hearts could desire. In fact there could be nothing more reasonable, more perfect, more divine than the will of God. Could any change of time, place, or circumstance alter or increase its infinite value ? If you possess the secret of discovering it at every moment and in everything, then you possess all that is most precious, and most worthy to be desired. What is it that you desire, you who aim at perfection ? Give yourselves full scope. Your wishes need have no measure, no limit. However much you may desire I can show you how to attain it, even though it be infinite. There is never a moment in which I cannot enable you to obtain all that you can desire. The present is ever filled with infinite treasure, it contains more than you have capacity to hold. Faith is the measure. Believe, and it will be done to you accordingly. Love also is the measure. The more the heart loves, the more it desires ; and the more it desires, so much the more will it receive. The will of God is at each moment before us like an immense, inexhaustible ocean that no human heart can fathom ; but none can receive from it more than he has capacity to contain, it is necessary to enlarge this capacity by faith, confidence, and love.

The whole creation cannot fill the human heart, for it is greater than all that is not God. It is on a higher plane than the material creation, and for this reason nothing material can satisfy it. The divine will is a deep abyss of which the present moment is the entrance. If you plunge into this abyss you will find it infinitely more vast than your desires. Do not flatter anyone, nor worship your own illusions, they can neither give you anything nor receive anything from you. Receive your fulness from the will of God alone, it will not leave you empty. Adore it, put it first, before all things ; tear all disguises from vain pretences and forsake them all going straight to the sole reality. The reign of faith is death to the senses ; it is their spoliation, their destruction. The senses worship creatures ; faith adores the divine will. Destroy the idols of the senses and they will rebel and lament, but faith must triumph because the will of God is indestructible. When the senses are terrified, or famished, despoiled, or crushed, then it is that faith is nourished, enriched and enlivened. Faith laughs at these calamities as a governor of an impregnable fortress laughs at the useless attacks of an impotent foe. When a soul recognises the will of God and shows a readiness to submit to it entirely, then God gives Himself to such a soul and renders it most powerful succour under all circumstances. Thus it experiences a great happiness in this coming of God, and enjoys it the more, the more it has learnt to abandon itself at every moment to His adorable will.

Section IV.—*The Revelations of God.*

God reveals Himself to us in as mysterious a manner in the most ordinary circumstances, and as truly and adorably as in the great events of History or of Holy Scripture.

The written word of God is full of mystery ; and no less so His word fulfilled in the events of the world. These are two sealed books, and of both it can be said " the letter killeth." God is the centre of faith ; all that emanates from this centre is hidden in the deepest mystery. This word and these events are, so to say, but feeble rays from a sun obscured by clouds. It is vain to expect to see with our mortal eyes the rays of this sun ; even the eyes of our soul are blind to God and His works. Darkness takes the place of light, ignorance of knowledge, and one neither sees nor understands. The sacred Scripture is the mysterious utterance of a God yet more mysterious ; and the events of the world are the obscure language of this same hidden and unknown God. They are mere drops from an ocean of midnight darkness, and partake of the nature of their source. The fall of the angels and of Adam ; the impiety and idolatry of men before and after the Deluge up to the time of the Patriarchs who knew, and related to their children the history of the Creation, and of the still recent preservation from the universal deluge ; these are, indeed, very obscure words of holy Scripture. That, at the coming of the Messiah, only a handful of men should be preserved from idolatry in the general ruin and overthrow of faith throughout the world : that impiety should prove always dominant, always powerful, and the small numbers of the upholders of truth should be ever persecuted and maltreated, seems incredible ! Consider the treatment of Jesus Christ. Think of the plagues of the Apocalypse, yet these are the words of God. They are what He has revealed ! He has dictated them ! And the effect of these terrible, mysteries which will continue till the end of time is still the living word, teaching us His wisdom, power, and goodness. All the events which form the world's history show forth these divine attributes ; all teach the same adorable word. We cannot doubt it, although we do not see. What is meant by the existence of Turks, heretics, and all the other enemies of the Church ? Surely they all proclaim loudly the divine perfections. Pharaoh and the impious men who follow his example are allowed to exist only for that purpose, but assuredly, unless beheld with the eye of faith, it would all have the exactly contrary appearance. To behold divine mysteries it is necessary to shut the eyes to what is external, and to cease to reason. You speak, Lord, to the generality of men by great public events. Every revolution is as a wave from the sea of Your providence, raising storms and tempests in the minds of those who question Your mysterious action. You speak also to each individual soul by the circumstances occurring at every moment of life. Instead, however, of hearing Your voice in these events, and receiving with awe what is obscure and mysterious in these Your words, men see in them only the outward aspect, or chance, or the caprice of others, and censure everything. They would like to add, or diminish, or reform, and to allow themselves absolute liberty to commit any excess, the least of which would be a criminal and unheard-of outrage. They respect the holy Scriptures, however, and will not permit the addition of even a single comma. " It is the word of God " say they, " and is altogether holy and true. If we cannot understand it, it is all the more wonderful and we must give glory to God, and render justice to the depths of His wisdom." All this is perfectly true, but when you read God's word from moment to moment, not written with ink on paper, but on your soul with suffering, and the daily actions that you have to perform, does it not merit some attention on your part? How is it that you cannot see the will of God in all this? Instead you find fault with everything that happens, nothing pleases you. Do you not see that you are gauging everything by the senses, and by reason, not by faith the only true standard; and that when you read the word of God in the sacred Scriptures with the eye of faith, you do wrong to make use only of your reason in reading the word in His marvellous operations.

———

SECTION V.—*The action of Jesus Christ in the Souls of Men.*

The divine action continues to write in the hearts of men the work begun by the holy Scriptures, but the characters made use of in this writing will not be visible till the day of judgment.

———

" Jesus Christ yesterday, to-day, and for ever " (Heb. xiii, 8), says the Apostle. From the beginning of the world He was, as God, the first cause of the existence of souls. He has participated as man from the first instant of His incarnation, in this prerogative of His divinity. During the whole course of our life He acts within our souls. The time that will elapse till the end of the world is but as a day; and this day abounds with His action. Jesus Christ has lived and lives still. He began from Himself and will continue in His Saints a life that will never end. O life of Jesus! comprehending and extending beyond all the centuries of time, life effecting new operations of grace at every moment; if no one is capable of understanding all that could be written of the actual life of Jesus, all that He did and said while He was on earth; if the Gospel merely outlines a few of its features; how many Gospels would have to be written to record the history of all the moments of this mystical life of Jesus Christ in which miracles are multiplied to infinity and eternity. If the beginning of His natural life is so hidden yet so fruitful, what can be said of the divine action of that life of which every age of the world is the history?

The Holy Spirit has pointed out in infallible and incontestable characters, some moments in that ocean of time, in the Sacred Scriptures. In them we see by what secret and mysterious ways

He has brought Jesus before the world. Amidst the confusion of the races of men can be distinguished the origin, race, and genealogy of this, the first-born. The whole of the Old Testament is but an outline of the profound mystery of this divine work; it contains only what is necessary to relate concerning the advent of Jesus Christ. The Holy Spirit has kept all the rest hidden among the treasures of His wisdom. From this ocean of the divine activity He only allows a tiny stream to escape, and this stream having gained its way to Jesus is lost in the Apostles, and has been engulfed in the Apocalypse; so that the history of this divine activity consisting of the life of Jesus in the souls of the just to the end of time, can only be divined by faith. As the truth of God has been made known by word of mouth, so His charity is manifested by action. The Holy Spirit continues to carry on the work of our Saviour. While helping the Church to preach the Gospel of Jesus Christ, He writes His own Gospel in the hearts of the just. All their actions, every moment of their lives, are the Gospel of the Holy Spirit. The souls of the saints are the paper, the sufferings and actions the ink. The Holy Spirit with the pen of His power writes a living Gospel, but a Gospel that cannot be read until it has left the press of this life, and has been published on the day of eternity. Oh! great history! grand book written by the Holy Spirit in this present time! It is still in the press. There is never a day when the type is not arranged, when the ink is not applied, or the pages are not printed. We are still in the dark night of faith. The paper is blacker than the ink, and there is great confusion in the type. It is written in characters of another world and there is no understanding it except in Heaven. If we could see the life of God, and behold all creatures, not as they are in themselves, but as they exist in their first cause; and if again we could see the life of God in all His creatures, and could understand how the divine action animates them, and impels them all to press forward by different ways to the same goal, we should realize that all has a meaning, a measure, a connexion in this divine work. But how can we read a book the characters of which are foreign to us, the letters innumerable, the type reversed, and the pages blotted with ink? If the transposition of twenty-five letters is incomprehensible as sufficing for the composition of a well-nigh infinite number of different volumes, each admirable of its kind, who can explain the works of God in the universe? Who can read and understand the meaning of so vast a book in which there is no letter but has its particular character, and encloses in its apparent insignificance the most profound mysteries? Mysteries can neither be seen nor felt, they are objects of faith. Faith judges of their virtue and truth only by their origin, for they are so obscure in themselves that all that they show only serves to hide them and to blind those who judge only by reason.

"Teach me, divine Spirit, to read in this book of life. I desire to become Your disciple and, like a little child, to believe what I cannot understand, and cannot see. Sufficient for me that it is my Master who speaks. He says that! He pronounces this! He arranges the letters in such a fashion! He makes Himself heard in such a manner! That is enough. I decide that all is exactly as He says. I do not see the reason, but He is the infallible truth, therefore all that He says, all that He does is true. He groups His letters to form a word, and different letters again to form another word. There may be three only, or six; then no more are necessary, and fewer would destroy the sense. He who reads the thoughts of men is the only one who can bring these letters together, and write the words. All has meaning, all has perfect sense. This line ends here because He makes it do so. Not a comma is missing, and there is no unnecessary full-stop. At present I believe, but in the glory to come when so many mysteries will be revealed, I shall see plainly what now I so little understand.

Then what appears to me at present so intricate, so perplexing, so foolish, so inconsistent, so imaginary, will all be entrancing and will delight me eternally by the beauty, order, knowledge, wisdom, and the incomprehensible wonders it will all display."

———

SECTION VI.—*The Treatment of the Divine Action.*

The divine action as manifested in daily events is treated by many Christians in as unworthy a manner as the Jews treated the Sacred Body of Jesus.

———

The world is full of infidelity. How unworthy are its thoughts of God! It complains continually of the divine action in a way that it would not dare to use towards the lowest workman about his trade. It would reduce God to act only within the limits, and following the rules of its feeble reason. It presumes to imagine it can improve upon His acts. These are nothing but complaints and murmurings. We are surprised at the treatment endured by Jesus Christ at the hands of the Jews, but, O divine love! adorable will! infallible truth! in what way are you treated? Can the divine will ever be inopportune? Can it be mistaken? "But there is this business of mine! I require such a thing! The necessary helps have been taken from me. That man thwarts all my good works, is it not most unreasonable ? This illness comes on just when my health is most necessary to me." To all this there is but one answer—that the will of God is the only thing necessary, therefore what it does not grant must be useless. My good souls ! nothing is wanting to you. If you only knew what these events really are that you call misfortunes, accidents, and disappointments, and in which you can see nothing but what is irrelevant, or unreasonable, you would be deeply ashamed and excuse yourselves of your complainings as of blasphemies ; but you never think of them as being the will of God, and His adorable will is blasphemed by His own children who refuse to acknowledge it. When You were on earth, O my Jesus, the Jews treated You as a demoniac, and called You a Samaritan ; and now, although it is acknow ledged that You live and work through all the centuries of time, how is Your adorable will received ? that will worthy of all benediction and praise for ever. Has one moment passed from the creation to the present time, and will one moment pass even to the day of judgment in which the holy name of God will not deserve praise ; that name which fills all the ages, and every-thing which takes place in the ages, that name by which every-thing is sanctified ? What ! can the will of God do me harm ? Shall I fear, or fly from the will of God ? And where shall I find anything better if I dread the divine action in my regard, or regret the effect of His divine will ? We ought to listen attentively to the words uttered in the depths of our heart at every moment. If our sense and reason do not understand nor enter into the truth and goodness of these words, is it not because they are incapable of appreciating divine truths ? Ought I to wonder that my reason is bewildered by mysteries ? When God speaks it is a mystery, and therefore a death-blow to my senses and reason, for it is the nature of mysteries to compel the sacrifice of both. Mystery makes the soul live by faith ; for all the rest there is nothing but contradiction. The divine action by one and the same stroke kills and gives life ; the more one feels the death to the senses and reason, the more convinced should one become that it gives life to the soul. The more ob-scure the mystery to us, the more light it contains in itself. This is why a simple soul will discover a more divine meaning in that which has the least appearance of having any.

The life of faith is a continual struggle against the senses.

SECTION VII.—*The Hidden Work of Divine Love.*

The divine love is communicated to us through every creature under veils, like the Eucharistic species.

———

What great truths are hidden even from Christians who imagine themselves most enlightened! How many are there amongst them who understand that every cross, every action, every attraction according to the designs of God, give God to us in a way that nothing can better explain than a comparison with the most august mystery? Nevertheless there is nothing more certain. Does not reason as well as faith reveal to us the real presence of divine love in all creatures, and in all the events of life, as indubitably as the words of Jesus Christ and of the Church reveal the real presence of the sacred flesh of our Saviour under the Eucharistic species? Do we not know that by all creatures, and by every event the divine love desires to unite us to Himself, that He has ordained, arranged, or permitted everything about us, everything that happens to us with a view to this union? This is the ultimate object of all His designs to attain which He makes use of the worst of His creatures as well as of the best, and of the most distressing events as well as of those which are pleasant and agreeable. Our communion with Him is even more meritorious when the means that serve to make it closer are repugnant to nature. If this be true, every moment of our lives may be a kind of communion with the divine love, and this communion of every moment may produce as much fruit in our souls as that which we receive in the Communion of the Body and Blood of the Son of God. This latter, it is true, is efficacious sacramentally which the former cannot be, but on the other hand, how much more frequently can it not be renewed, and what great increase of merit it can acquire by the more perfect dispositions with which it may be accomplished. Consequently how true it is that the more holy the life the more mysterious it becomes by its apparent simplicity and littleness. O great feast! O perpetual festival! God! given and received under all that is most feeble, foolish and worthless upon earth! God chooses that which nature abhors, and human prudence rejects. Of these He makes mysteries, sacraments of love, and by that which seems as if it would do most harm to souls, He gives Himself to them as often and as much as they desire to possess Him.

SECTION VIII.—*Experimental Science.*

That which is sent us at the present moment is the most useful because it is intended especially for us.

We can only be well instructed by the words which God utters expressly for us. No one becomes learned in the science of God either by the reading of books, or by the inquisitive investigation of history. The science that is acquired by such means is vain and confused, producing much pride. That which instructs us is what happens from one moment to another producing in us that experimental science which Jesus Christ Himself willed to acquire before instructing others. In fact this was the only science in which He could grow, according to the expression of the holy Gospel; because being God there was no degree of speculative science which He did not possess. Therefore if this experimental science was useful to the Word incarnate Himself, to us it is absolutely necessary if we wish to touch the hearts of those whom God sends to us. It is impossible perfectly to understand anything that experience has not taught us by suffering or by action. This is the school of the Holy Spirit who in this way speaks life-giving words to the soul, and those which He speaks to us through others come from the same source.

Reading and seeing become fruitful and possess virtue and light only by the acquisition of this divine science, otherwise they are like dough to which leaven is necessary, and the salt of experience to season it. And since without this salt we have only vague ideas to act upon, we are like visionaries, who, though knowing the roads that lead to all the towns, yet lose their way going to their own house.

We must listen to God from moment to moment to become learned in the theology of virtue which is entirely practical and experimental. Do not attend therefore to what is said to others, but listen to that which is said to you and for you; there will be enough to exercise your faith because this interior language of God exercises, purifies, and increases it by its very obscurity.

SECTION IX.—*The Will of God in the Present Moment is the Source of Sanctity.*

O, all you who thirst, learn that you have not far to go to find the fountain of living waters; it flows quite close to you in the present moment; therefore hasten to find it. Why, with the fountain so near, do you tire yourselves with running about

after every little rill ?   These only increase your thirst by giving
only a few drops, whereas the source is inexhaustible.   If you
desire to think, to write, and to speak like the Prophets, the
Apostles, and the Saints, you must give yourself up, as they did,
to the inspirations of God.   O unknown Love !   it seems as if
Your wonders were finished and nothing remained but to copy
Your ancient works, and to quote Your past discourses !   And
no one sees that Your inexhaustible activity is a source of new
thoughts, of fresh sufferings and further actions :   of new Patriarchs, Apostles, Prophets, and Saints who have no need to copy
the lives and writings of the others, but only to live in perpetual
abandonment to Your secret operations.   We hear of nothing
on all sides but " the first centuries," " the time of the Saints."
What a strange way of talking !   Is not all time a succession of
the effects of the divine operation, working at every instant,
filling, sanctifying, and supernaturalising them all ?   Has there
ever been an ancient method of abandonment to this operation
which is now out of season ?   Had the Saints of the first ages
any other secret than that of becoming from moment to moment
whatever the divine power willed to make them ?   And will this
power cease to pour forth its glory on the souls which abandon
themselves to it without reserve.

O Love eternal, adorable, ever fruitful, and ever marvellous !
May the divine operation of my God be my book, my doctrine,
my science.   In it are my thoughts, my words, my actions,
and my sufferings.   Not by consulting Your former works shall
I become what You would have me to be ; but by receiving You
in everything.   By that ancient road, the only royal road, the
road of our fathers shall I be enlightened, and shall speak as
they spoke.   It is thus that I would imitate them all, quote
them all, copy them all.

SECTION X.—*God Makes Known His Will Through Creatures.*

In the present moment are made manifest the name of God,
and the coming of His Kingdom.

The present moment is the ambassador of God to declare His
mandates.   The heart listens and pronounces its " fiat."   Thus
the soul advances by all these things and flows out from its
centre to its goal.   It never stops but sails with every wind.
Any and every direction leads equally to the shore of infinity.
Everything is a help to it, and is, without exception, an instrument of sanctity.   The one thing necessary can always be found
for it in the present moment.   It is no longer a choice between

prayer and silence, seclusion and society, reading and writing, meditation and cessation of thought, flight from and seeking after spiritual consolations, abundance and dearth, feebleness and health, life and death, but it is all that each moment presents by the will of God.   In this is despoilment, abnegation, renunciation of all things created, either in reality or affectively, in order to retain nothing of self, or for self, to be in all things submissive to the will of God and to please Him ; making it our sole satisfaction to sustain the present moment as though there were nothing else to hope for in the world.

If all that happens to a soul abandoned to God is all that is necessary for it, then we can understand that nothing can be wanting to it, and that it should never pity itself, for this would be a want of faith and living according to reason and the senses which are never satisfied, as they cannot perceive the sufficiency of grace possessed by the soul.   To hallow the name of God, is according to the meaning of the holy Scripture, to recognise His sanctity in all things and to love and adore Him in them. Things, in fact, proceed from the mouth of God like words.   That which God does at each moment is a divine thought expressed by a created thing, therefore all those things by which He intimates His will to us are so many names and words by which He makes known His wishes.   His will is unity and has but one name, unknown, and ineffable ; but it is infinitely diverse in its effects, which are, as it were, so many different characters which it assumes.   To hallow the Name of God is to know, to adore, and to love the ineffable Being whom this name designates. It is also to know, to adore and to love His adorable will at every moment and in all its decrees, regarding them all as so many veils, shadows and names of this holy and everlasting will.

It is holy in all its works, holy in all its words, holy in all its diverse characters, holy in all the names it bears.

It was for this reason that Job blessed the name of God in his utter desolation.   Instead of looking upon his condition as ruin, he called it the name of God and by blessing it he protested that the divine will under whatever name or form it might appear, even though expressed by the most terrible catastrophes, was holy.   David also blessed it at all times, and in all places.   It is then, by this continual recognition of the will of God as manifested and revealed in all things, that He reigns in us, that His will is done on earth as it is in Heaven, and that our souls obtain nourishment.   The whole matter of that incomparable prayer prescribed by Jesus Christ is comprised and contained in abandonment to the divine will.   Many times daily is it recited vocally, by the command of God and of Holy Church, but we repeat it at every moment in the centre of our hearts when we love to do, or to suffer whatever this holy will ordains. That which takes time to repeat in words, the heart pronounces at every moment, and it is in this way that simple-minded souls are called to bless God. Nevertheless they cannot bless Him as much as they desire, and this inability is a subject of grief to them ; so true is it that by the very means that seem like privations, God bestows graces and favours on faithful souls. To enrich the soul at the expense of the senses, filling it by so much the more as they experience the more terrible emptiness, is a secret of the divine wisdom.

The events of every moment bear the impress of the will of God, and of His adorable Name. How holy is this name ! It is right, therefore, to bless it, to treat it as a kind of sacrament which by its own virtue sanctifies those souls which place no obstacles in its way.

Everything bearing the impress of this august Name should be held in the most profound veneration. It is a divine manna from Heaven, and imparts a constant increase of grace. It is the reign of holiness in the soul, the bread of angels eaten on earth as well as in Heaven. We can no longer consider our moments as trifles since in them is a whole kingdom of sanctity and food for angels.

" Yes, Lord, may your kingdom come in my heart to sanctify it, to nourish it, to purify it, and to render it victorious over all its enemies. Moment most precious ! How insignificant in the eyes of the vulgar, but how great in those enlightened by faith. If it is great also in the eyes of my Father who is in Heaven, how can I regard it as insignificant ? All that comes from His hand is essentially good and bears the impress of its origin."

SECTION XI.—*Everything is Supernaturalised by the Divine Action.*

The divine action incites souls to aim at the most eminent sanctity ; all that is required on the part of the soul is abandonment to this action.

It is only from want of knowing how to make use of the divine action that so many Christians pass their lives in anxiously pursuing a multitude of methods which might prove useful if ordained by this divine action, but which by preventing a simple union with it, become positively harmful. All this multiplicity fails to impart that which can only be found in the principle of all life, that which is continually present with us, and which stamps each of its tools with a character of its own and makes it work

with an incomparable fitness.   Jesus is sent to us as a Master to
whom we do not sufficiently attend.   He speaks to every heart,
and to each He utters the word of life, the only word applicable
to us, but we do not hear it.   We want to know what He has
said to others and do not listen when He speaks to ourselves.
We do not sufficiently regard things as having been supernaturalised by the divine action.   We should always accept them
with the perfect confidence they merit ; with an open mind and
with generosity, and be sure that nothing will harm those who
act thus.   This vast activity, which is in itself ever the same
from the beginning to the end of time, is employed with every
moment, pouring out its immensity and virtue on the souls
which adore it, love it, and rejoice in it alone.

You say you would be delighted to find an opportunity of
dying for God, and would be completely satisfied with some such
action, or with a life leading to the same result.   To lose all,
to die forsaken, to sacrifice your life for others, these are indeed
charming ideas !   But as for me, Lord, I glorify in all things
the might of Your will in which I find all the happiness of
martyrdom, austerities, and good works for others.   Your will
is enough, and I am content to live and to die as it decrees.   In
itself it is more pleasing to me than all the attributes of the
instruments of which it makes use, or than their effects, because
it pervades all, makes all divine, and changes all into itself.
It is all heavenly to me, and every one of my moments is a
genuine divine action, and living or dying I shall always be
satisfied with it.   Yes, divine Love, I shall no longer single out
times or ways, but shall welcome You always and in any fashion.
It seems to me, O divine Will, as if You had revealed Your immensity to me ; I will therefore take no steps save in the bosom
of Your infinity, You who are the same yesterday, to-day, and
for ever.   The unceasing torrent of graces has its rise in You.
It is from You that it flows, is carried on, and made active.
Therefore it is not within the narrow limits of a book, or the life
of a saint, or in some sublime idea that I ought to seek You.
These are but drops of that ocean which is poured out over
every creature and in which they are all immersed.   They are
mere atoms that disappear in this deep abyss.   I will no longer
seek this action in the thoughts of spiritual persons.   I will
no longer beg my bread from door to door, nor pay court to
creatures, but I will live as the child of an infinitely good, wise,
and powerful father whom I desire to please, and to make happy.
I wish to live according to my faith, and since the divine action
is applied by every single thing and at every moment for my
perfection, I will live on this immense fortune, this certain
income, and in the most profitable manner.

D

Is there any creature whose action can equal that of God? Why then should I go to creatures for help since all that happens to me is the work of His uncreated hand? Creatures are powerless, ignorant, and without affection and I should die of thirst rushing like this from one fountain to another, from one stream to another when there is a sea at hand, the waters of which encompass me on every side. All that happens to me therefore will be food for my nourishment, water for my cleansing, fire for my purification, and a channel of grace for all my needs. That which I might endeavour to find in other ways seeks me incessantly and gives itself to me through all creatures.

O Love of God! how is it that all creatures do not know how freely you lavish Yourself and Your favours on them while they are seeking You in byways and corners where You are not to be found? How foolish to refuse to breathe the open air! to search for a spot on which to place the foot when there is the whole countryside before you; to be unable to find water when there is a whole deluge at your service, nor to possess and enjoy God, nor to recognise His action when it is present in all things. You search for hidden ways of belonging to God, good people, but the only way is that of making use of whatever He sends you. All leads to union, to perfection, except what is sinful or not a duty. All that is necessary is to accept everything, placing no obstacle in the way of its action but letting it accomplish its work. All things are intended to guide, raise, and support you, and are in the hand of God whose action is vaster and more present than the elements of earth, air, and water. Even by means of the senses God will enter, provided they are used only as He ordains, because everything contrary to His will must be resisted. There is not a single atom that goes to form part of your being, even to the marrow of the bones, that is not formed by the divine power. From it all things proceed, by it all things are made. Your very life-blood flows through your veins by the movement this power imparts to it, and all the fluctuations that exist between strength and weakness, languor and liveliness, life and death, are divine instruments put in motion to effect your sanctification. Under its influence all bodily states become operations of grace. From this invisible hand come all your opinions, all your ideas on whatever subject they may be formed. What this action will effect in you, you will learn by successive experiences, for there is no created heart or mind that can teach it to you. Your life flows on uninterruptedly in this unsounded abyss in which each present moment contains all that is best for you, and as such must be loved and esteemed. It is necessary to have a perfect confidence in this action which of itself can do nothing but what is good.

Yes, divine Love ! to what heights of supernatural, sublime, admirable and incomparable virtue would all souls arrive if they would but be satisfied with Your action !

Yes, if they would leave the matter in this divine hand they would attain to an eminent degree of perfection ! Everyone would arrive at it because it is offered to all. No effort is required because the work accomplishes itself. Every soul possesses in You an infinitely perfect model, and by your action which works ceaselessly to this end, is rendered like this model. If all souls were faithful copies of this divine example they would all speak, act, and live divinely. They would not require to copy each other, but would be singled out by the divine influence, and each would be rendered unique by the most simple and ordinary things.

By what means, O my God, can I make your creatures appreciate what is offered to them ? Must I who possess so great a treasure with which I could enrich the whole world, see souls perish in poverty ? Must I behold them withering like plants in a desert when I can show them the source of living waters ?

Come, foolish souls, you who have not an atom of sensible devotion, you too who possess no talent nor even the rudiments of education, you who cannot understand a single spiritual term, who stand astonished at the eloquence of the learned whom you admire ; come, and I will teach you a secret which will place you far beyond these clever minds. I will make perfection so easy to you that you will find it everywhere and in everything. I will unite you to God, and make you walk hand in hand with Him from the moment that you begin practising what I will teach you. Come, not to study the map of the spiritual country, but to possess it, to walk in it at your ease without fear of losing your way. Come, not to study the theory of divine grace, nor to find out what it has accomplished in the past and still continues to accomplish ; but to become simply subject to its operations. It is not necessary that you should understand what it has said to others, nor to repeat the words intended only for them and which you have overheard, but you, yourself, will receive from it what is best for you.

———

SECTION XII.—*The Divine Word our Model.*

The divine action alone can sanctify us, for that alone can make us imitate the divine Example of our perfection.

———

In course of time the idea formed by the Eternal Wisdom of all things is carried out by divine action. All things have, in God, their likeness, and are recognised and known by the divine Wisdom. Should you know all those things that are not for you, such knowledge would be no guide to you in any way. The divine action beholds in the Word the idea after which you ought to be formed and this example is always before it. It sees in the Word all that is necessary for the sanctification of every soul. The holy Scriptures contain one part, and the workings of the divine action in the interior of the soul, after the example set forth by the Word, complete the work. We must understand that the only way of receiving the impression of this eternal idea is to remain quietly amenable to it; and that neither efforts, nor mental speculations can do anything to that end. It is obvious that a work such as this cannot be effected by cleverness, intelligence, nor subtlety of mind, but only by the passive way of abandonment to its reception, and by yielding to it like metal in a mould, or canvas under the pencil, or stone in the hands of the sculptor. It is evident that to know all the divine mysteries of God is by no means the way in which by His will we are made to resemble His image, that image which the Word has formed of us; that our resemblance to the divine type can only be formed in us by the impression of the seal of the divine action, and that this impression is not produced in the mind by ideas, but in the will by abandonment. The wisdom of the just soul consists in being content with what is intended for it! in confining itself within the boundary of its path, and not trespassing beyond its limit. It is not inquisitive about God's ways of acting, but is content as regards itself with the arrangements of His will, making no effort to discover its meaning by comparisons or conjectures, but only desiring to understand what each moment reveals. It listens to the voice of the Word when it sounds in the depths of the heart, it does not inquire as to what the divine Spouse has said to others, but is satisfied with what it receives for itself, so that moment by moment it becomes, in this way, divinised without its knowledge. It is thus that the divine Word converses with His spouse, by the solid effects of His action which the spouse without scrutinising curiously, accepts with loving gratitude. Thus the spirituality of such a soul is perfectly simple, absolutely solid, and thoroughly diffused throughout its entire being. Its actions are not determined by ideas nor by a confusion of words which by themselves would only serve to excite pride. Pious people make a great use of the mind, whereas mental exertion is of very little use, and is even antagonistic to true piety. We must make use only of that which God sends us to do or to suffer, and not forsake this divine reality to occupy our minds with the historical wonders of the divine work instead of gaining an increase of grace by our fidelity.

The marvels of this work, of which we read for the purpose of satisfying our curiosity, often only tend to disgust us with things that seem trifling but by which, if we do not despise them, the divine love effects very great things in us. Fools that we are! We admire and bless this divine action in the writings relating its history, and when it is ready to continue this writing on our hearts, we keep moving the paper and prevent it writing by our curiosity, to see what it is doing in and around us. Pardon, divine love, these defects; I can see them all in myself, for I am not yet able to understand how to let You act. So far I have not allowed myself to be cast into the mould. I have run through all Your workshops and have admired all Your works, but have not as yet, by abandonment, received even the bare outlines of Your pencil. Nevertheless I have found in You a kind Master, a Physician, a Father, a beloved Friend.

I will now become Your disciple, and will frequent no other school than Yours. Like the Prodigal Son I return hungering for Your bread. I relinquish the ideas which tend only to the satisfaction of mental curiosity; I will no longer run after masters and books but will only make use of them as of other things that present themselves, not for my own satisfaction, but in dependence on the divine action and in obedience to You. For love of You and to discharge my debts I will confine myself to the one essential business, that of the present moment, and thus enable You to act.

BOOK II.

CHAPTER I.

ON THE NATURE AND EXCELLENCE OF THE STATE OF ABANDONMENT.

SECTION I.—*The life of God in the soul.*

There is a time when the soul lives in God, and a time when God lives in the soul. What is appropriate to one state is inconsistent with the other. When God lives in the soul it ought to abandon itself entirely to His providence. When the soul lives in God it is obliged to procure for itself carefully and very regularly, every means it can devise by which to arrive at the divine union. The whole procedure is marked out ; the readings, the examinations, the resolutions. The guide is always at hand and everything is by rule, even the hours for conversation. When God lives in the soul it has nothing left of self, but only that which the spirit which actuates it imparts to it at each moment. Nothing is provided for the future, no road is marked out, but it is like a child which can be led wherever one pleases, and has only feeling to distinguish what is presented to it. No more books with marked passages for such a soul ; often enough it is even deprived of a regular director, for God allows it no other support than that which He gives it Himself. Its dwelling is in darkness, forgetfulness, abandonment, death and nothingness. It feels keenly its wants and miseries without knowing from whence or when will come its relief. With eyes fixed on Heaven it waits peacefully and without anxiety for someone to come to its assistance. God, who finds no purer disposition in His spouse than this entire self-renunciation for the sake of living the life of grace according to the divine operation, provides her with necessary books, thoughts, insight into her own soul, advice and counsel, and the examples of the wise. Everything that others discover with great difficulty this soul finds in abandonment, and what they guard with care in order to be able to find it again, this soul receives at the moment there is occasion for it, and afterwards relinquishes so as to admit nothing but exactly what God desires it to have in order to live by Him alone. The former soul undertakes an infinity of good works for the glory of God, the latter is often cast aside in a corner of the world like a bit of broken crockery, apparently of no use to anyone. There, this soul, forsaken by creatures but in the enjoyment of God by a very real, true, and active love (active although infused in repose), does not attempt anything by its own impulse ; it only knows that it has to abandon itself and to remain in the hands of God to be used by Him as He pleases. Often it is ignorant of its use, but God knows well. The world thinks it is useless, and appearances give colour to this judgment, but nevertheless it is very certain that in mysterious ways and by unknown channels, it spreads abroad an infinite amount of grace on persons who often have no idea of it, and of whom it never thinks. In souls abandoned to God everything is efficacious, everything is a sermon and apostolic. God imparts to their silence, to their repose, to their detachment, to their words, gestures, etc., a certain virtue which, unknown to them, works in the hearts of those around them ; and, as they are guided by the occasional actions of others who are made use of by grace to instruct them without their knowledge, in the same way, they, in their turn, are made use of for the support and guidance of others without any direct acquaintance with them, or understanding to that effect.

God it is who works in them, by unexpected and often unknown impulses, so that these souls are like to Jesus, from whom proceeded a secret virtue for the healing of others. There is this difference between Him and them, that often they do not perceive the outflow of this virtue and even contribute nothing by co-operation : it is like a hidden balm, the perfume of which is exhaled without being recognised, and which knows not its own virtue.

SECTION II.—*The most perfect way.*

In this state the soul is guided by the divine action through every kind of obscurity.

When the soul is moved by the divine influence, it forsakes all works, practices, methods, means, books, ideas, and spiritual persons in order to be guided by God alone by abandoning itself to that moving power which becomes the sole source of its perfection. It remains in His hands like all the saints, understanding that the divine action alone can guide it in the right path, and that if it were to seek other means it would inevitably go astray in that unknown country which God compels it to traverse. It is, therefore, the action of God which guides and conducts souls by ways which it alone understands. It is, with these souls, like the changes of the wind. The direction is only known in the present moment, and the effects follow their causes by

the will of God, which is only explained by these effects because
it acts in these souls and makes them act either by hidden undoubted instincts, or by the duties of their state. This is all the
spirituality they know ; these are their visions and revelations,
this is the whole of their wisdom and counsel insomuch that
nothing is ever wanting to them. Faith makes them certain
that what they do is well, whether they read, speak, or write ;
and if they take counsel it is only to be able to distinguish more
clearly the divine action. All this is laid down for them and they
receive it like the rest, beholding beneath these things the divine
motive power and not fastening on the things presented, but
using or leaving them, always leaning by faith on the infallible,
unruffled, immutable and ever efficacious action of God at each
moment. This they perceive and enjoy in all things, the least
as well as the greatest, for it is entirely at their service at every
moment. Thus they make use of things not because they have
any confidence in them, or for their own sake, but in submission
to the divine ordinance, and to that interior operation which,
even under contrary appearances, they discover with equal
facility and certitude. Their life, therefore, is spent, not in
investigations or desires, weariness or sighs, but in a settled
assurance of being in the most perfect way.

Every state of body or soul, and whatever happens interiorly
or exteriorly as revealed at each moment to these souls is, to
them, the fulness of the divine action, and the fulness of their
joy. Created things are, to them, nothing but misery and dearth ;
the only true and just measure is in the working of the divine
action. Thus, if it take away thoughts, words, books, food,
persons, health, even life itself, it is exactly the same as if it did
the contrary. The soul loves the divine action and finds it
equally sanctifying under whatever shape it presents itself. It
does not reason about the way it acts ; it suffices for its approval
that whatever comes is from this source.

SECTION III.—*Abandonment a Pledge of Predestination.*

The state of abandonment contains in itself pure faith, hope,
and charity.

The state of abandonment is a certain mixture of faith, hope,
and charity in one single act, which unites the soul to God and
to His action. United, these three virtues together form but
one in a single act, the raising of the heart to God, and abandonment to His action. But how can this divine mingling, this
spiritual oneness be explained ? How can a name be found to

convey an idea of its nature, and to make the unity of this trinity intelligible ? It can be explained thus. It is only by means of these three virtues that the possession and enjoyment of God and of His will can be attained. This adorable object is seen, is loved, and all things are hoped for from it. Either virtue can with equal justice be called pure love, pure hope, or pure faith, and if the state of which we are speaking is more frequently designated by the last name, it is not that the other theological virtues are excluded, but rather that they may be understood to subsist and to be practised in this state in obscurity.

There can be nothing more secure than this state in the things that are of God ; nothing more disinterested than the character of the heart. On the side of God is the absolute certitude of faith, and on that of the heart is the same certitude tempered with fear and hope. O most desirable unity of the trinity of these holy virtues ! Believe then, hope and love, but by a simple feeling which the Holy Spirit who is given you by God will produce in your soul. It is there that the unction of the name of God is diffused by the Holy Spirit in the centre of the heart. This is the word, this is the mystical revelation, and a pledge of predestination with all its happy results. " Quam bonus Israel Deus his qui recto sunt corde " (Psalm 72, i). This impress of the Holy Spirit in souls inflamed with His love, is called pure love on account of the torrent of delight overflowing every faculty, accompanied by a fulness of confidence and light ; but in souls that are plunged in bitterness it is called pure faith because the darkness and obscurity of night are without alleviation. Pure love sees, feels, and believes. Pure faith believes without either seeing or feeling. In this is shown the difference between these two states, but this difference is only apparent, not real. The appearances are dissimilar, but in reality as the state of pure faith is not lacking in charity, neither is the state of pure love lacking in faith nor in abandonment ; the terms being applied according to which virtue prevails. The different gradations of these virtues under the touch of the Holy Spirit form the variety of all supernatural and lofty states. And since God can rearrange them in an endless variety there is not a single soul that does not receive this priceless impress in a character suitable to it. The difference is nothing, there are the same faith, hope, and charity in all. Abandonment is a general means of receiving special virtues in every variety of different impresses. Souls cannot all lay claim to the same sort, nor to a similar state, but all can be united to God, all can be abandoned to His action, all can receive the impress that is best suited to them, all in fact can live under the reign of God and enjoy a share in His justice with all its advantages. In this kingdom every soul can aspire to a crown, and whether a crown of love, or a crown of faith, it is always a crown, always the kingdom of God. There is this difference, it is true—the one is in light, the other in darkness; but again what does this signify if the soul belongs to God and obeys His will ? We do not seek to know the name of this state, its characteristics, nor excellence, but we seek God alone and His action. The manner of it ought to be a matter of indifference to the soul. Let us therefore no longer preach to souls about either the state of pure love, or of perfect faith, the way of delights, or of the Cross, for these cannot be imparted to all in the same degree nor in the same manner ; but let us preach abandonment in general to the divine action, to all simple souls who fear God, and let us make them all understand that by these means they will attain to that particular state chosen and destined for them by the divine action from all eternity. Let us not dishearten, nor rebuff, nor drive away anyone from that most eminent perfection to which Jesus calls everyone, exacting from them submission to the will of His heavenly Father and thus making them members of His mystical body. He is their head only in so far as their will is in accordance with His. Let us continually repeat to all souls that the invitation of this sweet and loving Saviour does not exact anything very difficult from them, nor very extraordinary. He does not ask for talent and ingenuity, all He desires is that they have a good will and desire to be united to Him so that He could guide, direct and befriend them in proportion as they are so united.

SECTION IV.—*Abandonment a Source of Joy.*

The state of abandonment comprises the most heroic generosity.

There is nothing more generous than the way in which a soul having faith, accepts the most deadly perils and troubles, beholding in them something divine of the spiritual life. When it is a question of swallowing poison, of filling a breach, of slaving for the plague-stricken ; in all this they find a plenitude of divine life, not given to them drop by drop, but in floods which inundate and engulf the soul in an instant.

If an army were animated by the same ideals it would be invincible. This is because the instinct of faith is an elevation and enlargement of the heart above and beyond all that is presented to the senses.

The life of faith, and the instinct of faith are one and the same. It is an enjoyment of the goods of God, and a confidence founded

on the expectation of His protection, making everything pleasant
and received with a good grace. It is indifference to, and at the
same time a preparation for every place, state, or person. Faith
is never unhappy even when the senses are most desolate. This
lively faith is always in God, always in His action above contrary
appearances by which the senses are darkened. The senses,
in terror, suddenly cry to the soul, " Unhappy one ! You have
now no resource, you are lost," and instantly faith with a stronger
voice answers : " Keep firm, go on, and fear nothing."

SECTION V.—*The Great Merit of Pure Faith.*

By the state of abandonment and of pure faith the soul gains
more merit than by the most eminent good works.

Whatever we find extraordinary in the lives of the saints,
such as revelations, visions and interior locutions, is but a
glimpse of that excellence of their state which is contained and
hidden in the exercise of faith ; because faith possesses all this
by knowing how to see and hear God in that which happens from
moment to moment. When these favours are manifested visibly ·
it does not mean that by faith they have not been already
possessed, but in order to make the excellence of faith visible for
the purpose of attracting souls to the practice of it ; just as the
glory of Thabor, and the miracles of Jesus Christ were not from
any increase of His intrinsic excellence, but from the light which
from time to time escaped from the dark cloud of His humanity
to make it an object of veneration and love to others.

That which is wonderful in the saints is the constancy of their
faith under every circumstance ; without this there would be
no sanctity. In the loving faith which makes them rejoice in
God for everything, their sanctity has no need of any extraordinary manifestation ; this could only prove useful to others
who might require the testimony of such signs ; but the soul
in this state, happy in its obscurity, does in no way rely on these
brilliant manifestations ; it allows them to. show outwardly
for the profit of others, but keeps for itself what all have in
common, the will of God, and His good pleasure. Its faith is
proved in hiding, and not in manifesting itself, and those who
require more proof have less faith.

Those who live by faith receive proofs, not as such, but as
favours from the hand of God, and in this sense things that are
extraordinary are not in contradiction to the state of pure faith.

But there are many saints whom God sets up for the salvation
of souls, and from whose faces He causes rays of glory to stream

for the enlightenment of the most blind.   Of such were the
Prophets and the Apostles and all those saints chosen by God
to be set in the candlestick of the Church.   There will ever be
such, as there ever have been.

There is also an infinity of others who, having been created to
shine in the heavens give no light in this world, but live and die
in profound obscurity.

Section VI.—*Submission a Free Gift to God.*

The state of abandonment includes the merit of every separate
operation.

Abandonment as practised interiorly contains every possible
variety of operation, because, the soul giving itself up to the good
pleasure of God, this surrender, effected by pure love, extends
to all the operations of this good pleasure.   Thus the soul
practises at each moment an abandonment without limit, and
in its virtue are comprehended all possible qualities and every
method.   It is, therefore, by no means the business of the
soul to decide what is the object of the submission it owes to
God ; its sole occupation is to submit at all times and for all
things.

What God requires of the soul is the essential part of abandonment.   The free gifts He asks are abnegation, obedience, and
love, the rest is His business.   Provided that the soul carefully
fulfils the duties of its state ; provided it quietly follows the
attraction given to it, and submits peacefully to the dealings of
grace as to body and soul, it is in this way exercising interiorly
one general and universal act, that of abandonment.   This act
is by no means limited by time, nor by the special duty of the
moment, but possesses in the main all the merit and efficacy
which a sincere good will always has, although the result does
not depend upon it.   What it desired to do is done, in the sight
of God.

If God's good pleasure sets a limit to the exercise of particular
faculties, it sets none to that of the will.   The good pleasures of
God, the being and essence of God are the objects of the will,
and by the exercise of charity its union with God has neither
limit, distinction, nor measure.   If this charity ends in the
exercise of the faculties for certain objects, it is because the will
of God only goes so far ; it contracts itself, so to speak, restricting
itself to the exigencies of the present moment from whence
it passes to the faculties, and then to the heart.   Finding the

heart pure, free, and without reserve, it communicates itself
fully to it on account of the infinite capacity which charity has
effected, by emptying it of all created things, thus rendering it
capable of union with God. O heavenly purity! O blessed
annihilation! O unreserved submission! through you is God
drawn into the centre of the heart. Let the faculties then be
what they will, provided, Lord, that I possess You. Do what
You will with this insignificant creature; whether it works,
becomes inspired, or becomes the subject of Your impressions,
it is all one. All is Yours, all is from You and for You. I have
no longer anything to look after, anything to do. I have no
hand in the arrangement of one single moment of my life, all is
Yours. I ought neither to add to, nor to diminish anything,
neither to seek after, nor to reflect upon, anything. It is for
You to regulate everything. Direction, mortification, sanctity,
perfection, and salvation are all Your business, Lord; mine is
to be satisfied with Your work, and not to appropriate any
action, or any state, but to leave all to Your good pleasure.

Section VII.—*Divine Favours Offered to All.*

Every soul is called to enjoy the infinite benefits contained
in this state.

Therefore do I preach abandonment, and not any particular
state. Every state in which souls are placed by Your grace is
the same to me. I teach a general method by which all can
attain the state which You have marked out for them. I do
not exact more than the will to abandon themselves to Your
guidance. You will make them arrive infallibly at the state
which is best for them.

It is faith that I preach; abandonment, confidence, and faith;
the will to be subject to, and to be the tool of the divine action,
and to believe that at every moment this action is working in
every circumstance, provided that the soul has more or less
good-will. This is the faith that I preach. It is not a special
kind of faith, nor of charity, but a general state by which all souls
can find God under the different conditions which He assumes;
and can take that form which divine grace has marked out for
them. I have spoken to souls in trouble, and now I am speaking
to all kinds of souls. It is the genuine instinct of my heart to care
for all, to announce the saving secret far and wide, and to make
myself all to all. In this happy disposition I make it a duty
which I fulfil without difficulty, to weep with those who weep,
to rejoice with those who rejoice, to speak foolishly with the

foolish, and with the learned to make use of more learned and more scholastic terms. I wish to make all understand that although they cannot aspire to the same distinct favours, they can attain to the same love, the same abnegation, the same God and His work, and thence it follows naturally, to the highest sanctity. Those graces which are called extraordinary and are given as privileges to certain souls, are only so called because there are so few sufficiently faithful to become worthy of receiving them. This will be made manifest at the day of judgment. Alas! it will then be seen that instead of these divine favours having been withheld by God, it has been entirely by their own fault that these souls have been deprived of them. What untold blessings they would have received through the complete submission of a steadfast good-will.

It is the same with regard to Jesus as with the divine action. If those who have no confidence in Him, nor respect for Him, do not receive any of the favours He offers to all, they have only their own bad disposition to thank for it. It is true that all cannot aspire to the same sublime states, to the same gifts, to the same degree of perfection; yet if, faithful to grace, they corresponded to it, each according to his degree, they would all be satisfied because they would all attain that degree of grace and of perfection which would fully satisfy their desires. They would be happy according to nature, and according to grace, because nature and grace share equally in the ardent desire for this priceless advantage.

Section VIII.—*God Reigns in a Pure Heart.*

All the treasures of grace are the fruit of purity of heart and perfect abandonment.

He, therefore, who wishes to enjoy an abundance of all blessings had but one thing to do; to purify his heart by detaching it from creatures, and to abandon himself entirely to God. In this purity and abandonment he will find all that he desires. "May others, Lord, ask You for all sorts of gifts, may they multiply their words and prayers; as for me, my God, I only ask one single gift, I have only one prayer to make—give me a pure heart." O pure heart! how happy you are; for by the liveliness of your faith you see God as He is in Himself. You see Him in all things and at every moment working within you and around you. In all things you are His subject and His instrument. He rules you and leads you. You have not to think because He thinks for you. Whatever happens to you, or may happen by His will, it is enough for Him that you will it also. He understands your readiness. In your salutary blindness you try to discover in yourself this desire, but you cannot see it, nevertheless He sees it quite clearly. How foolish you are! a well-disposed heart is a heart in which God dwells. Seeing therefore the good inclinations in this heart God well knows that it will remain always submissive to His will; He knows also that you are ignorant of what would be useful to you and therefore He makes it His business to give you what is necessary.

It matters very little to Him whether you are thwarted or not. You imagine you are going East, He makes you go West. You are about to strike against a rock, He pushes the tiller and brings you into port. Without either a map or a compass, wind or tide, the voyages you make are always fortunate. If you encounter pirates, an unexpected puff of wind instantly wafts you beyond their reach.

O good will! O pure heart! Jesus well knew where to place you when He ranked you among the Beatitudes. What greater happiness can there be than to possess God, if He mutually possesses you? It is a state full of charm and of joy, in which the soul reposes peacefully in the bosom of divine Providence where it sports innocently with the divine Wisdom, feeling no anxiety about the journey which suffers no interruption, but in spite of rocks and pirates and constant storms, ever continues as happy as possible.

O pure heart! O good will! the sole foundation of every spiritual state, to you are granted the gifts of firm faith, holy hope, perfect confidence and pure love, and by you are they made profitable.

On your stem are grafted the flowers of the desert; in other words, from you spring those priceless graces which blossom in souls entirely detached, where God, as in an uninhabited dwelling, takes up His abode to the exclusion of all else. You are the faithful source from whence flow those streams that water the flower garden of the divine Spouse, and of His chosen one. Your voice calls all the souls of men saying to them, " Look well at me; it is I who impart fair love, that love which chooses the better part and lays hold of it. It is I who give birth to that fear, so gentle and efficacious, which produces a horror of evil, and makes it easy to avoid; I, who bring to light those fine perceptions by which are discovered the greatness of God and the value of virtue ; in fine it is from me that those ardent desires take their rise, enkindled by holy hope. It is I who cause virtue to be practised in expectation of the promised reward—

that divine Object of our love, the possession of Whom will one day form the happiness of faithful souls. Invite them all to come to you to be enriched with your inexhaustible treasures. All spiritual states and paths lead back to you. It is from you that they derive all that is beautiful, attractive, and charming, for all is drawn from your depths. Those marvellous fruits of grace, and of every kind of virtue that helps to nourish the soul, and that abounds on every side, are produced by you. Milk and honey flow in your land. Your breasts distil milk, and on your bosom is the bouquet of myrrh from which, under the pressure of your fingers, the aromatic liquid flows abundantly.

Let us go, then, let us run and fly to that ocean of love by which we are attracted! What are we waiting for? Let us start at once, let us lose ourselves in God, even in His heart, to become inebriated with the wine of His charity. We shall find in His heart the key of heavenly treasures. Let us begin at once our journey to Heaven. There is no passage that we cannot discover, nothing is shut against us, neither the garden, nor the cellar, nor the vineyard. If we desire to breathe the fresh country air, we can go on our own feet and return when we please. With this key of David we can enter and depart; it is the key of science, and of that abyss in which are contained all the hidden treasures of divine Wisdom. With this heavenly key we also open the gates of mystical death with its sacred darkness. By it also we descend into the deep pools and into the den of lions. By it souls are thrust into those obscure prisons from whence they emerge unscathed. By it we are introduced into that joyful place where light and understanding have their dwelling, where the Spouse takes the midday rest in the open air, and where He reveals the secrets of His love to faithful souls. O divine incommunicable secrets that no mortal tongue can describe! Since every good thing that it is possible to possess is given to those who love, let us love then, in order to be enriched with them; for love produces sanctity with all that accompanies it. It flows on every side, on the right hand and on the left, into those hearts open to receive this divine outpouring. O divine harvest for eternity! it is not possible to praise you sufficiently. And why speak so much about you? How much better to possess you in silence than to praise you with mere words. But what am I saying? You must be praised but only because you take possession of us, for, from the moment you enter into possession of a heart, then reading, writing, speaking or silence are matters of complete indifference. One can take or leave anything, live in solitude, or as an apostle; one is well or ill, dull or eloquent, in fact anything that you will. That which you dictate, your faithful echo, the heart, repeats to all the faculties. In that compound of matter and spirit, the heart, which you regard as your kingdom, you reign supreme, and as it has no other instincts than those which you inspire, all the things that you present are equally agreeable. Those things that nature, or the devil wish to substitute, cause nothing but disgust and horror. If you allow it to be occasionally overcome, it is only to make it wiser and more humble ; but from the moment it realises its mistake it returns to you with renewed love, and clings to you with greater tenacity.

CHAPTER II.

THE DUTIES OF THOSE SOULS CALLED BY GOD TO THE STATE OF ABANDONMENT.

SECTION I.—*Sacrifice, the Foundation of Sanctity.*

The first great duty of souls called by God to this state is the absolute and entire surrender of themselves to Him.

" Sacrificate sacrificium, et sperate in Domino." That is to say that the great and solid foundation of the spiritual life is the sacrifice of oneself to God, subjecting oneself to His good pleasure in all things, both interior and exterior, and becoming so completely forgetful of self thereafter as to regard oneself as a chattel, sold and delivered, to which one no longer has any right. In this way the good pleasure of God forms one's whole felicity; and His happiness, glory and existence one's sole good. This foundation laid, the soul has nothing else to do but to rejoice that God is God, and to abandon itself so entirely to His good pleasure that it feels an equal satisfaction in whatever it does, nor ever reflects on the uses to which it is applied by the arrangements of this good pleasure. To abandon oneself, therefore, is the principal duty to be fulfilled, involving, as it does, the faithful discharge of all the obligations of one's state. The perfection with which these duties are accomplished will be the measure of the sanctity of each individual soul. A saintly soul is a soul freely submissive, with the help of grace, to the divine will. All that follows on this free consent is the work of God, and not of man. The soul should blindly abandon itself and be indifferent about everything. This is all that God requires of it, and as to the rest He determines and chooses according to His own plans, as an architect selects and arranges the stones for the building he is about to construct. It is therefore of the first importance to love God and His will, and to love this will in whatever way it is made manifest to us, without desiring anything else. The soul has no concern in the choice of different objects, that is God's affair, and whatever He gives is best for the soul. The whole of spirituality is an abridgment of this maxim, " Abandon yourself entirely to the over-ruling of God, and by self-oblivion be eternally occupied in loving and serving Him without any of those fears, reflexions, examens, and anxieties which the affair of our salvation, and perfection sometimes occasion." Since God wishes to do all for us, let us place everything in His hands once and for all, leaving them to His infinite wisdom; and trouble no more about anything but what concerns Him. On then, my soul, on with head uplifted above earthly things, always satisfied with God, with everything He does, or makes you do. Take good care not to imprudently entertain a crowd of anxious reflexions which, like so many trackless ways, carry our footsteps far and wide until we are hopelessly astray. Let us go through that labyrinth of self-love by leaping over it, instead of traversing its interminable windings.

On, my soul, through despondency, illness, aridity, uncertain tempers, weakness of disposition, snares of the devil and of men; through suspicions, jealousies, evil imaginations and prejudices. Let us soar like the eagle above all these clouds with eyes always fixed on the sun, and on its ways, which represent our obligations. All this we must needs feel, but we must, at the same time, remember that ours is not a life of mere sentiment, and that it does not depend upon us either to feel, or to be callous. Let us live in the higher regions of the soul in which God and His will form an eternity ever equal, ever the same, ever unchanging. In this dwelling entirely spiritual, wherein the uncreated, immeasurable and ineffable holds the soul at an infinite distance from all that is specific in shadows and created atoms, it remains calm, even when the senses are tossed about by tempests. It has become independent of the senses; their troubles and agitations and innumerable vicissitudes no more affect it, than the clouds that obscure the sky for a moment and then fade away, affect the sun. We know that all passes away like clouds blown along by the wind, and nothing is consecutive nor ordered, but everything is in a state of perpetual change. In the state of faith, as in that of glory, God and His will is the eternal object that captivates the heart, and will one day form its true happiness, and this glorious state of the soul will influence the material part which at present is the prey of monsters and savage beasts. Beneath these appearances, terrible though they be, the divine action will so work on this material part as to make it partake of a heavenly power which will render it brilliant as the sun; for the faculties of the sensitive soul, and those of the body are prepared here below like gold or iron, or like canvas for a picture, or stones for a building. Like the matter of which these different materials are composed they will not attain their brilliance and purity of form until they have passed through many alterations, have endured many deprivations, and survived many destructions. Whatever they suffer here below under the hand of God serves to that end.

The soul, in the state of faith, which knows the secret of God, dwells always in peace. All that takes place interiorly, instead of alarming, reassures it. Deeply convinced that it is guided by God, it takes all that happens as so much grace, and over-looking the instrument with which God works, it thinks only of the work that He is doing.

It is actuated by love to fulfil faithfully and exactly all its duties. All that is distinct in a soul abandoned to God, is the work of grace, with the exception of those defects which are slight, and which the action of grace even turns to good account. I call that distinct of which a soul receives a sensible impression either of sorrow or consolation through those things applied to it unceasingly by the divine will for its improvement. I call it distinct because it is more clearly distinguished by the soul from all else that takes place within it. In all these things faith sees only God, and applies itself solely to become conformed to His will.

SECTION II.—*The Pains and Consolations of Abandonment.*

The soul ought to strip itself of all things created in order to arrive at the state of abandonment.

This state is full of consolation for those who have attained it ; but to do so it is necessary to pass through much anguish. The doctrine concerning pure love can only be taught by the action of God, and not by any effort of the mind. God teaches the soul by pains and obstacles, not by ideas.

This science is a practical knowledge by which God is enjoyed as the only good. In order to master this science it is necessary to be detached from all personal possessions, to gain this detachment, to be really deprived of them. Therefore it is only by constant crosses, and by a long succession of all kinds of mortifications, trials, and deprivations, that pure love becomes established in the soul. This must continue until all things created become as though they did not exist, and God becomes all in all. To effect this God combats all the personal affections of the soul, so that when these take any especial shape, such as some pious notion, some help to devotion ; or when there is any idea of being able to attain perfection by some such method, or such a path or way, or by the guidance of some particular person ; in fine to whatever the soul attaches itself, God upsets its plans, and allows it to find, instead of success in these pro-jects, nothing but confusion, trouble, emptiness, and folly.

Hardly has it said "I must go this way, I must consult this person, or, I must act in such a manner," than God immediately says the exact contrary, and withdraws all the virtue usual in the means adopted by the soul. Thus, finding only deception and emptiness in everything, the soul is compelled to have recourse to God Himself, and to be content with Him.

Happy the soul that understands this lovingly severe conduct of God, and that corresponds faithfully with it. It is raised above all that passes away to repose in the immutable and the infinite. It is no longer dissipated among created things by giving them love and confidence, but allows them only when it becomes a duty to do so, or when enjoined by God, and when His will is made especially manifest in the matter. It inhabits a region above earthly abundance or dearth, in the fulness of God who is its permanent good. God finds this soul quite empty of its own inclinations, of its own movements, of its own choice. It is a dead subject, and shrouded in universal indifference. The whole of the divine Being, coming thus to fill the heart, casts over all created things a shadow, as of nothingness, absorbing all their distinctions and all their varieties. Thus there remains neither efficacy, nor virtue in anything created, and the heart is neither drawn towards, nor has any inclination for created things, because the majesty of God fills it to its utmost extent. Living in God in this way, the heart becomes dead to all else, and all is dead to it. It is for God, who gives life to all things, to revive the soul with regard to His creation, and to give a different aspect to all things in the eyes of the soul. It is the order of God which is this life. By this order the heart goes out towards the creature as far as is necessary or useful, and it is also by this order that the creature is carried towards the soul and is accepted by it. Without this divine virtue of the good pleasure of God, things created are not admitted by the soul, neither is the soul at all inclined towards them. This dissolution of all things as far as the soul is concerned, and then, by the will of God, their being brought once more into existence, compels the soul at each moment to see God in all things, for each moment is spent for the satisfaction of God only, and in an unreserved self-abandonment with regard to its relations to all possible created things, or rather to those created, or possibly to be created by the order of God. Therefore each moment contains all.

———

SECTION III.—*The Different Duties of Abandonment.*

The active exercise of abandonment either in relation to precept, or to inspiration.

———

Although souls called by God to a state of abandonment are much more passive than active, yet they cannot expect to be exempted from all activity. This state being nothing else but the virtue of abandonment exercised more habitually, and with greater perfection, should, like this virtue, be composed of two kinds of duty; the active accomplishment of the divine will, and the passive acceptance of all that this will pleases to send. It consists essentially, as we have already said, in the gift of our whole self to God to be used as He thinks fit. Well! the good pleasure of God makes use of us in two ways; either it compels us to perform certain actions, or it simply works within us. We, therefore, submit also in two ways, either by the faithful accomplishment of its clearly defined orders, or else by a simple and passive submission to its impressions of either pleasure or pain. Abandonment implies all this, being nothing else but a perfect submission to the order of God as made manifest at the present moment. It matters little to the soul in what manner it is obliged to abandon itself, and what the present moment contains; all that is absolutely necessary is that it should abandon itself unreservedly. There are, then, prescribed duties to be fulfilled, and necessary duties to be accepted, and further there is a third kind which also forms part of active fidelity, although it does not properly belong to works of precept. In this are comprised inspired duties; those to which the spirit of God inclines the hearts that are submissive to Him. The accomplishment of this kind of duty requires a great simplicity, a gentle and cheerful heartiness, a soul easily moved by every breath of directing grace; for there is nothing else to do but to give oneself up, and to obey its inspirations simply and freely. So that souls may not be deceived, God never fails to give them wise guides to indicate with what liberty or reserve these inspirations should be made use of. The third kind of duty takes precedence of all law, formalities, or marked-out rules. It is what, in saints, appears singular and extraordinary; it is what regulates their vocal prayer, interior words, the perception of their faculties, and also all that makes their lives noble, such as austerities, zeal, and the prodigality of their self-devotion for others. As all this belongs to the interior rule of the Holy Spirit, no one ought to try to obtain it, to imagine that they have it, to desire it, nor to regret that they do not possess the grace to undertake this kind of work, and to practise these uncommon virtues, because they are only really meritorious when practised according to the direction of God. If one is not content with this reserve one lays oneself open to the influence of one's own ideas, and will become exposed to illusion.

It is necessary to remark that there are souls that God keeps hidden and little in their own eyes, and in the eyes of others. Far from giving them striking qualities, His design for them is that they should remain in obscurity. They would be deceived if they desired to attempt a different way. If they are well instructed they will recognise that fidelity to their nothingness is their right path, and they will find peace in their lowliness. The only difference, therefore, in their way and that of, apparently, more favoured souls, is the difference they make for themselves by the amount of their love and submission to the will of God; for, if they surpass in these virtues the souls that appear to work more than they exteriorly, their sanctity is, without doubt, so much the greater. This shows that each soul ought to content itself with the duties of its state, and the over-ruling of Providence; clearly God exacts this equally from all. As to attraction and the impressions received by the soul, these are given by God alone to whom He pleases. One must not try to produce them oneself, nor to make efforts to increase them. Natural effort is in direct opposition and quite contrary to infused inspirations, which should come in peace. The voice of the divine Spouse will awaken the soul, which should only proceed according to the inspirations of the Holy Spirit, for, if it were to act according to its own ideas it would make no progress.

Therefore, if it should feel neither attraction nor grace to do those things that make the saints so much admired, it must, in justice to itself, say, " God has willed it thus for the saints, but not for me."

SECTION IV.—*God Does All for a Soul of Good-Will.*

The conduct of a soul raised to a state of abandonment with regard to this two-fold manifestation of the good pleasure of God.

Souls called by God to a life of perfect abandonment resemble in this respect our Lord, His holy Mother, and St. Joseph. The will of God was, to them, the fulness of life. Submitting entirely to this will as to precept and inspiration directly it was made manifest to them, they were always in complete depend

ence on, what we might call, the purely providential will of God.
From this it follows that their lives, although extraordinary in
perfection, showed outwardly nothing that is not common to
all, and quite ordinary. They fulfilled the duties of religion,
and of their state as others do, and in, apparently, the same way.
For the rest, if one scrutinizes their conduct, nothing can be
discovered either striking or peculiar; all follows the same
course of ordinary events. That which might single them out
is not discernible; it is that dependence on the supreme will
which arranges all things for them, and in which they habitually
live. The divine will confers on them a complete self-mastery
on account of the habitual submission of their hearts.

Therefore the souls in question are, by their state, both solitary
and free; detached from all things in order to belong to God,
to love Him in peace, and to fulfil faithfully the present duty
according to His expressed will. They do not allow themselves
to reflect, to neglect, nor to think of consequences, causes or
reasons; it is enough for them to go on simply, accomplishing
their plain duties just as if there did not exist for them anything
but their present obligation, and their duty to God. The present
moment, then, is like a desert in which the soul sees only God
whom it enjoys; and is only occupied about those things which
He requires of it, leaving and forgetting all else, and abandoning
it to Providence. This soul, like an instrument, neither receives
interiorly more than the operation of God effects passively, nor
gives exteriorly more than this same operation applies actively.

This interior application is accompanied by a free and active
co-operation which is, at the same time, infused and mystical;
that is to say that God, finding in this soul all the necessary
qualifications for acting according to His laws, and satisfied
with its good-will, spares it the trouble of doing so, by bestowing
all that would otherwise be the fruit of its efforts, or of its effectual
good-will. It is as though someone, seeing a friend preparing
for a troublesome journey, would go in his stead, so that the friend
would have the intention of going, but be spared the trouble
of the journey; yet by this impersonation he would have gone
himself, at least virtually. This journey would be free because
it would be the result of a free determination taken beforehand
to please the friend who then takes upon himself the trouble and
expense; it would also be active because it will be a real advance;
and it will be interior because effected without outward activity;
and, finally, it will be mystical because of the hidden principle
it contains. But to return to that kind of co-operation that we
have explained by this imaginary journey; you will observe that
it is entirely different from fidelity in the fulfilment of obligations.
The work of fulfilling these is neither mystical nor infused, but

free and active as commonly understood. Therefore abandonment to the good pleasure of God contains activity as well as
passivity. In it there is nothing of self, but an habitual general
goodwill, which like an instrument, has no action of itself, but
responds to the touch of the master. While in his hands it
fulfils all the purposes for which it was formed. Intentional
and determined obedience to the will of God is, in the ordinary
order of vigilance, care, attention, prudence, and discretion;
although ordinary efforts are sensibly aided, or begun by grace.
Leaving God, then, to act for all the rest, reserve for yourself
at the present moment, only love and obedience, which virtues
the soul will practise eternally. This love, infused into the soul
in silence, is a real action of which it makes a perpetual obligation.
It ought, in fact, to preserve it faithfully, and to maintain itself
constantly in those dispositions resulting from it, all of which,
it is evident, cannot be done without action. The action, however, is quite different to obedience to the present duty, by which
the soul so disposes its faculties as to fulfil perfectly the will of
God made manifest to it exteriorly, without expecting anything
extraordinary.

This divine will is to the soul in all things its method, its rule,
and its direct and safe way. It is an unalterable law which is of
all times, of all places, and of all states. It is a straight line
which the soul must follow with courage and fidelity, neither
diverging to the right, nor to the left, nor overstepping the bounds.
Whatever is over and above must be received passively, as it
carries on its work in abandonment. In a word, the soul is active
in all that the present duty requires, but passive and submissive
in all the rest, about which there should be no self-will, but
patient waiting for the divine motion.

SECTION V.—*The Common Way of all Souls.*

The soul that aims at union with God should value all the
operations of His grace, but should only attach itself to that of
the present moment.

It is by union with the will of God that we enjoy and possess
Him; and it is an illusion to endeavour to obtain this divine
enjoyment by any other means. Union with the will of God is
the universal means. It does not act by one method only, but
all methods and all ways are, by its virtue, sanctified. The divine
will unites God to our souls in many different ways, and that
which suits us is always best for us. All ways should be esteemed

and loved, because in each we should behold that which is ordained by God accommodating itself to each individual soul, and
selecting the most suitable method of effecting by it the divine
union.   The duty of the soul is to submit to this choice, and to
make none for itself; and this without dispensing itself from
esteeming and loving this adorable will in its work in others.
For instance, if this divine will should prevent me saying vocal
prayers, having sensible devotion, or receiving lights on mysteries, I should still love and esteem the silence and bareness
induced by the sight of the faith of others ; while for myself I
should make use of the present moment, and by it should become
united to God.   I should not, as the Quietists do, reduce all
religion to personal inaction despising all other means ; because
what makes perfection is obedience to the law of God which
always renders the means it applies suitable to the soul.   No !
I should not admit of obstacles or bounds to the will of God,
neither should I take anything in place of it, but should welcome
it in whatever way it was made manifest to me, and should revere
it in whatever way it was pleased to unite itself to others.   Thus
all ordinary souls have but one common way in which each is
distinct and different in order to form the variety of the mystical
robe of the Church.   All these souls mutually approve of, and
esteem each other, and all say " We are going to the same goal by
different paths, and are all united in the same way, and by the
same means in the ordinance of God, which is so different in
each."   It is in this sense that we must read the lives of the saints,
and other spiritual books, without ever making a change, and
forsaking our own path.   For this reason it is necessary that we
should neither read spiritual books, nor hold spiritual conversation unless God so will; for, if He makes it the duty of the
present moment, the soul, far from making any change, will be
strengthened in its way, either by what it finds in conformity wit h
its own method, or even by that in which it differs.   But if the w:ll
of God does not make this reading, or spiritual intercourse a
present duty it will cause nothing but trouble, and a confusion of
ideas ; and a succession of changes will ensue; because without the
concurrence of God's will there cannot be order in anything.

Since when, therefore, have we busied ourselves with the pains
and anxieties of our souls which have nothing to do with our
present duty ?   When will God be all in all to us ?   Let creatures
act according to their nature, but let nothing hinder us, let us
go beyond all created things and live entirely for God.

SECTION VI.—*The Duty of the Present Moment the Only Rule.*

From souls in this state God exacts the most perfect docility to the action of His grace.

It is necessary to be detached from all that one feels, and from all that one does, to follow this method, by which one subsists in God alone, and in the present duty. All regard to what is beyond this should be cut off as superfluous. One must restrict oneself to the present duty without thinking of the preceding one, or of the one which is to follow. I imagine the law of God to be always before you, and that the practice of abandonment has rendered your soul docile to the divine action. You feel some impulse that makes you say, " I have a drawing towards this person " ; or " I have an inclination to read a certain book, to receive, or to give certain advice, to complain of certain things, to open my mind to another, or to receive confidence ; to give away something, or to perform some action." Well! obey this impulse according to the inspiration of grace without stopping to reflect, to reason, or to make efforts. Give yourself up to these things for as long as God wishes without doing so through any self-will. In the state in question the will of God is shown to us because He dwells within us. This will ought to supplant all our usual supports. At each moment we have to practise some virtue. To this the obedient soul is faithful ; nothing of what it has learnt by reading or hearing is forgotten, and the most mortified novice could not fulfil her duties better. It is for this that these souls are attracted sometimes to one book, sometimes to another ; or else to make some remark, some re-flexion on what may seem but a trifling circumstance. At one time God gives them the attraction to learn something that at some future time will encourage them in the practice of virtue. Whatever these souls do, they do because they feel an attraction for it, without knowing why. All they can explain on the subject can be reduced to this : " I feel myself drawn to write, to read, to ask, to examine this ; I follow this attraction, and God who gives it to me keeps these particular things in reserve in my faculties to become in future the nucleus of other attractions which will become useful to myself and others." This is what makes it necessary for these souls to be simple, gentle, yielding, and submissive to the faintest breath of these scarcely perceptible impressions.

In the state of abandonment the only rule is the duty of the present moment. In this the soul is light as a feather, liquid as water, simple as a child, active as a ball in receiving and following all the inspirations of grace. Such souls have no more consistence and rigidity than molten metal. As this takes any form according to the mould into which it is poured, so these souls are pliant and easily receptive of any form that God chooses to give them. In a word, their disposition resembles the atmosphere, which is affected by every breeze; or water, which flows into any shaped vessel exactly filling every crevice. They are before God like a perfectly woven fabric with a clear surface; and neither think, nor seek to know what God will be pleased to trace thereon, because they have confidence in Him, they abandon themselves to Him, and, entirely absorbed by their duty, they think not of themselves, nor of what may be necessary for them, nor of how to obtain it. The more assiduously do they apply themselves to their little work, so simple, so hidden, so secret, and outwardly contemptible, the more does God embroider and embellish it with brilliant colours. On the surface of this simple canvas of love and obedience His hand traces the most beautiful design, the most delicate and intricate pattern, the most divine figures. " Mirificavit Dominus sanctum suum." "The Lord hath made His holy one wonderful." (Psalm iv.) It is true that a canvas simply and blindly given up to the work of the pencil only feels its movement at each moment. Each blow of the hammer on the chisel can only produce one cruel mark at a time, and the stone struck by repeated blows cannot know, nor see the form produced by them. It only feels that it is being diminished, filed, cut, and altered by the chisel. And a stone that is destined to become a crucifix or a statue without knowing it, if it were asked, " What is happening to you ? " would reply if it could speak, " Do not ask me, I only know one thing, and that is, to remain immovable in the hands of my master, to love him, and to endure all that he inflicts upon me. As for the end for which I am destined, it is his business to understand how it is to be accomplished; I am as ignorant of what he is doing as of what I am destined to become ; all I know is that his work is the best, and the most perfect that could be, and I receive each blow of the chisel as the most excellent thing that could happen to me, although, truth to tell, each blow, in my opinion, causes the idea of ruin, destruction, and disfigurement. But that is not my affair ; content with the present moment, I think of nothing but my duty, and I endure the work of this clever master without knowing, or occupying myself about it."

Yes ! give to God what belongs to Him, and remain lovingly passive in His hands. Hold for certain that what takes place either exteriorly or interiorly is best for you.

Allow God to act, and abandon yourself to Him. Let the chisel perform its office, the needle do its work. Let the brush of the artist cover the canvas with many tints which only have the appearance of daubs. Correspond with all these divine operations by a simple and constant submission, a forgetfulness of self, and an assiduous application to duty. Continue thus in your own groove without studying the way, the ins and outs, and surroundings, the names or particulars of the places ; go on blindly pursuing this path, and you will be shown what is to follow. Seek only the kingdom of God and His justice by love and obedience, and all the rest will be added to you. We meet with many souls who are distressed about themselves, and inquire anxiously, " Who will direct us so that we may become mortified and holy, and attain perfection ? " Let them search in books for the description and characteristics of this marvellous work, its nature and qualities ; but as for you, do you remain peacefully united to God by love, and follow blindly the clear straight path of duty. The angels are at your side during this time of darkness, and they will bear you up. If God requires more of you, He will make it known to you by His inspirations.

SECTION VII.—*Trust in the Guidance of God.*

The docile soul will not seek to learn by what road God is conducting it.

When God makes Himself the guide of a soul He exacts from it an absolute confidence in Him, and a freedom from any sort of disquietude as to the way in which He conducts it. This soul, therefore, is urged on without perceiving the path traced out before it. It does not imitate either what it has seen, or what it has read, but proceeds by its own action, and cannot do otherwise without grave risk. The divine action is ever fresh, it never retraces its steps, but always marks out new ways. Souls that are conducted by it never know where they are going ; their ways are neither to be found in books, nor in their own minds ; the divine action carries them step by step, and they progress only according to its movement.

When you are conducted by a guide who takes you through an unknown country at night across fields where there are no tracks, by his own skill, without asking advice from anyone, or giving you any inkling of his plans ; how can you choose but abandon yourself ? Of what use is it looking about to find out where you are, to ask the passers-by, or to consult maps and travellers ? The plans or fancies of a guide who insists on being trusted would not allow of this. He would take pleasure in overcoming the anxiety and distrust of the soul, and would insist on an entire surrender to his guidance. If one is convinced that he is a good guide one must have faith in him, and abandon oneself to his care.

The divine action is essentially good; it does not need to be reformed or controlled. It began at the creation of the world, and to the present time has manifested ever fresh energy. Its operations are without limit, its fecundity inexhaustible. It acted in one way yesterday, to-day it acts differently. It is the same action applied at each moment to produce ever new effects, and it will extend from eternity to eternity. It has produced Abel, Noah, Abraham, all different types; Isaac, also original, and Jacob from no copy; neither does Joseph follow any prefigure. Moses has no prototype among his progenitors. David and the Prophets are quite apart from the Patriarchs. St. John the Baptist stands alone. Jesus Christ is the first-born; the Apostles act more by the guidance of His spirit than in imitation of His works.

Jesus Christ did not set a limit for Himself, neither did He follow all His own maxims to the letter. The Holy Spirit ever inspired His holy soul, and, being entirely abandoned to its every breath, it had no need to consult the moment that had passed, to know how to act in that which was coming. The breath of grace shaped every moment according to the eternal truths subsisting in the invisible and unfathomable wisdom of the Blessed Trinity. The soul of Jesus Christ received these directions at every moment, and acted upon them externally. The Gospel shows in the life of Jesus Christ a succession of these truths; and this same Jesus who lives and works always, continues to live and work in the souls of His saints.

If you would live according to the Gospel, abandon yourself simply and entirely to the action of God. Jesus Christ is its supreme mouthpiece. "He was yesterday, is to-day, and will be for ever" (Hebr. xiii, 8); continuing, not recommencing His life. What He has done is finished; what remains to be done is being carried on at every moment. Each saint receives a share in this divine life, and in each, Jesus Christ is different, although the same in Himself. The life of each saint is the life of Jesus Christ; it is a new gospel. The cheeks of the spouse are compared to beds of flowers, to gardens filled with fragrant blossoms. The divine action is the gardener, admirably arranging the flower beds. This garden resembles no other, for among all the flowers there are no two alike, or that can be described as being of the same species, except in the fidelity with which they respond to the action of the Creator, in leaving Him free to do as He pleases, and, on their side, obeying the laws imposed on them by their nature. Let God act, and let us do what He requires of us ; this is the Gospel ; this is the general Scripture, and the common law.

Section VIII.—*Great Faith is Necessary.*

This total abandonment is as simple as its effects are marvellous.

Such then is the straight path to sanctity. Such is the state of perfection, and of the duties imposed by it ; such the great and incomparable secret of abandonment ; a secret that is, in reality, no secret, an art without art.

God, who exacts it of all, has explained it clearly, and made it intelligible, and quite simple. What is obscure in the way of pure faith is not necessary for the soul in that way, to practise ; there is, in fact, nothing more easy to understand, nor more luminous ; the mystery is only in what is done by God.

This is what takes place in the Blessed Eucharist. That which is necessary to change bread into the Body of Jesus Christ, is so clear and so easy that the most ignorant priest is capable of doing it ; yet it is the mystery of mysteries, where all is so hidden, so obscure, so incomprehensible that the more spiritual and enlightened one is, the more faith is required to believe it. The way of pure faith presents much that is similar. Its effect is to enable one to find God at each moment ; it is this that makes it so exalted, so mystical, so blessed. It is an inexhaustible fund of thought, of discourse, of writing, it is a whole collection, and source of wonders. To produce so prodigious an effect but one thing is necessary ; to let God act, and to do all that He wills according to one's state. Nothing in the spiritual life could be easier, nor more within the power of everyone ; and yet nothing could be more wonderful, nor any path more obscure. To walk in it the soul has need of great faith, all the more so, as reason is always suspicious, and has always some argument against it. All its ideas are confused. There is nothing in it that reason has ever known or read about, or been accustomed to admire ; it is something quite new. " The Prophets were saints, but this Jesus is a sorcerer," said the Jews. If the soul following their example, is scandalised, it shows but little faith, and well deserves to be deprived of those wonderful things that God is so ready to work in the faithful soul.

CHAPTER III.

THE TRIALS CONNECTED WITH THE STATE OF ABANDONMENT.

SECTION I.—*Unwise Interference.*

The first trial : the obloquy and unreasonable exactions of persons with a reputation for wisdom and piety.

There is no way more secure than that of abandonment, and none more easy, sweet, clear, and less subject to illusion and error. In it God is loved and all Christian duties fulfilled ; the Sacraments are frequented, and all the exterior acts of religion which are binding to all are performed.   Superiors are obeyed, and the duties of the state of life are discharged ; temptations of the flesh, the world, and the devil are continually resisted ; for none are more on guard, or more vigilant in acquitting themselves of all their obligations, than those who follow this way.

If this is the case, why is it that they should be subject to so many contradictions ? The most usual of these is, that when they, like other Christians, have accomplished all that the most strict theologian could exact, they are expected also to be bound to inconvenient practices to which the Church by no means obliges them ; and if they do not comply they are charged with labouring under illusion.   But I ask, can a Christian who confines himself to the observance of God's commandments, and those of the Church, and who, besides, without practising meditation, contemplation, or spiritual reading, and without being attached to any particular form of devotion, yet attends to worldly business, and to other affairs of private life—can he be wrong ? One cannot presume to accuse, or even to suspect him of error. One must admit this to oneself, and while leaving the Christian of whom I am speaking in peace, it is but justice not to trouble a soul that not only fulfils the precepts at least as well as one does oneself, but who, in addition, practises exterior acts of piety that are even unknown to others, or, if known, are treated with indifference.   Prejudice goes so far as to affirm that this soul deceives itself, and deludes itself because, after having submitted to all that the Church prescribes, it holds itself free to be in the condition to give itself without hindrance to the interior operations of God, and to attend to the impressions of His grace at times when no other duty intervenes to expressly compel them. In a word they are condemned because they employ that time

which others give to amusements and temporal affairs, in loving
God. Is not this a crying injustice ? This cannot be too strongly insisted upon. If anyone keeps the ordinary course, goes to
confession once a year, nothing is said about it, he is left in peace
with an occasional injunction, not pressed with too much im-
portunity, nor making it an obligation, to do a little more. If
he should change his ways and try to improve them, then he is overwhelmed with counsels for his conduct, and with different
methods ; and if he does nòt follow these pious rules diligently,
then he is done for, he is a subject of suspicion, and nothing is
too bad to predict of him.

Are they not aware that these practices, however good and
holy they may be, are, after all, only a way leading to divine
union ? Is it necessary, then, to be always on the road when one
has already arrived at the goal.

Nevertheless, it is this that is exacted of a soul which is supposed to be labouring under illusion. This soul has made its
way, like others, at the beginning ; like them it knew what to
do, and did it faithfully ; it would be vain now to attempt to
keep it bound to the same practices. Since God, moved by the
efforts it has made to advance with these helps, has taken it
on Himself to lead it to this happy union, from the time it arrived
at the state of abandonment, and by love possessed God ; in
fine,f from the time that the God of all goodness, relieving
it o all its trouble and industry, made Himself the principle
of its operations, these first methods lost all their value and were
but the road it had traversed. To insist upon these methods
being resumed and constantly followed, would be to make
the soul forsake the end at which it had arrived to re-enter
the way which led to it. But, if this soul has any experience,
their time and trouble will be thrown away. In vain will they
pursue it with noisy clamours ; turning a deaf ear it will remain
untroubled and unmoved in that intimate peace in which it so
advantageously exercises its love. This is the centre in which
it reposes, or, if you prefer it, it is the straight line traced by
the hand of God. It will continue to walk therein, for all its
duties are plainly marked out in it and by following this line
it fulfils them without confusion or haste as they present themselves. For all else it holds itself in perfect liberty, always
ready to obey every movement of grace directly it perceives it,
and to abandon itself to the care of Providence. God makes
known to this soul that He intends to be its Master, and to direct
it by His grace ; and makes it understand that it cannot, without
attacking the sovereign rights of its Creator, allow its own liberty
to be fettered. It feels that, if it tied itself down to the rules
of those who live by their own efforts and industry, instead of

F

acting according to the attraction of grace, it would be deprived of many things necessary in order to be able to fulfil future duties. But, as no one knows this, it is judged and condemned for its simplicity, and, though it does not find fault with others but approves of every state, and well knows how to discern every degree of progress, it is despised by pretended wiseacres who cannot appreciate this sweet and hearty submission to divine Providence.

Worldly wisdom cannot understand the perpetual wanderings of the Apostles, who did not settle anywhere. Ordinary spirituality also cannot endure that souls should depend for their action on divine Providence. There are but few in this state who approve of them, but God, who instructs men by means of their fellow creatures, never fails to make such souls encounter those who abandon themselves to Him with simplicity and fidelity. Besides, these latter require less direction than others in consequence of having attained to this state with the help of very good directors. If they find that they are occasionally left to themselves, it is because divine Providence removes by death, or banishes by some event, the guides who have led them in this way. Even then, they are always willing to be guided, and only wait in peace the moment arranged by Providence. During the time of privation also, they meet from time to time persons in whom they feel they can repose a confidence inspired by God, although they know nothing about them. This is a sign that He makes use of them to communicate certain lights, even if these are only temporary. These souls ask advice, therefore, and when it is given they follow it with the greatest docility. In default of such assistance however, they have recourse to the maxims supplied to them by their first directors. Thus they are always very well directed, either by the old principles formerly received, or by the advice of those directors they encounter, and they make use of all until God sends them persons in whom they can confide, and who will show them His will.

Section II.—*Unjust Judgments.*

Second trial of the state of abandonment. The apparent uselessness and exterior defects allowed by God in the souls He wills to raise to this state.

The second trial of souls conducted by God in this way is the result of their apparent uselessness, and of their exterior defects. There can be neither honour nor reward in a service hidden, often enough, under the most utter incapacity and uselessness, as far as the world is concerned. Doubtless those who are given more important posts, are not, on this account, necessarily precluded from the state of abandonment. Less still is this state incompatible with striking virtue, and that sanctity which attracts universal veneration. Nevertheless there is a far greater number of souls raised to this sublime state whose virtue is known only to God. By their state these souls are free from nearly every outward obligation. They are little suited for worldly business or affairs, for complicated concerns, or for putting their mind into the conducting of industries. It seems as though they were quite useless; nothing is noticeable in them but feebleness of body, mind, imagination and passions. They take no notice of anything. They are, so to say, quite stupid, and possess nothing of that culture, study, or reflexion which go to the making of a man. They are like children of nature before they are placed in the hands of masters to be formed. They have noticeable faults which, without rendering them more guilty than children, cause more offence. God takes away everything but innocence in order that they should have nothing to rely upon but Him alone. The world, being in ignorance of this mystery can only judge by appearance, and can find nothing in them to its taste, nor anything that it values. It, therefore, rejects and despises them, and they seem to be exposed to censure from all. The more closely they are observed, the less is thought of them and the more opposition do they encounter; no one knows what to make of them. Although some hidden voice seems to speak in their favour, yet people prefer to adhere to their own malignant prepossessions rather than to follow this instinct, or at least to suspend their judgment. Their actions are pried into to find out their opinions, and like the Pharisees who could not endure the actions of Jesus, they are regarded with such prejudice that everything they do appears either ridiculous or criminal.

SECTION III.—*Self-Contempt.*

The third trial : interior humiliations.

Contemptible as they are in the eyes of others, the souls raised by God to this state are far more contemptible in their own. There is nothing either in what they do, or in what they suffer that is not altogether paltry and humiliating; there is nothing striking in anything about them, all is quite ordinary, nothing but troubles and afflictions interiorly, and contradictions and disappointments exteriorly. With a feeble body requiring many alleviations and comforts, the very reverse one would think of that spirit of poverty and austerity so much admired in the saints. Neither heroic undertakings, nor fasts, large alms, nor ardent and far-reaching zeal can be discerned in them; but united to God by faith and love they behold in themselves nothing but disorder. They despise themselves still more by comparison with those who pass for saints, and who, besides adapting themselves with facility to rules and methods show nothing irregular either in their persons or actions. Therefore their own short-comings in this respect fill them with confusion, and are unbearable to them. It is on this account that they give way to sighs and tears, marking the grief with which they are oppressed. Let us remember that Jesus Christ was both God and man; as man He was destroyed, and as God He remained full of glory. These souls have no participation in His glory, but they share in the sadness and misery of His sufferings. Men regard them in the same way as Herod and his court regarded Jesus Christ. These poor souls, therefore, are nourished as to their senses and mind, with a most disgusting food, in which they can find no pleasure. They aspire to something quite different, but all the avenues leading to the sanctity they so much desire, remain closed to them. They must live on this bread of suffering, on this bread mingled with ashes, with a continual shrinking both exterior and interior. They have formed an idea of saintliness which gives them constant and irremediable torment. The will hungers for it, but is powerless to practise it. Why should this be, except to mortify the soul in that which is its most spiritual and intimate part, which, finding no satisfaction or pleasure in anything that happens to it, must needs place all its affection in God who conducts it this way for the express purpose of preventing it taking pleasure in anything but Him alone.

It seems to me that it is easy to conclude from all this that souls abandoned to God cannot occupy themselves, as others do, with desires, examinations, cares, or attachments to certain persons. Neither can they form plans, nor lay down methodical rules for their actions, or for reading. This would imply that they still had power to dispose of themselves, which would entirely exclude the state of abandonment in which they are placed. In this state they give up to God all their rights over themselves, over their words, actions, thoughts, and proceedings; over the employment of their time and everything connected with it. There remains only one desire, to satisfy the Master they have chosen, to listen unceasingly to the expression of His will in order to execute it immediately. No condition can better represent this state than tha of a servant who obeys every order he receives, and does not occupy his time in attending to his own affairs ; these he neglects in order to serve His Master at every moment. These souls then should not be distressed at their powerlessness ; they are able to do much in being able to give themselves entirely to a Master who is all-powerful, and able to work wonders with the feeblest of instruments if they offer no resistance.

Let us, then, endure without annoyance the humiliations entailed on us in our own eyes, and in the eyes of others, by what shows outwardly in our lives ; or rather, let us conceal ourselves behind these outward appearances and enjoy God who is all ours. Let us profit by this apparent failure, by these requirements, by this care-taking and the necessity of constant nourishment, and of comfort ; of our ill-success, of the contempt of others, of these fears, uncertainties, troubles, etc., to find all our wealth and happiness in God, who, by these means, gives Himself entirely to us as our only good. God wishes to be ours in a poor way, without all those accessories of sanctity which make others to be admired, and this is because God would have Himself to be the sole food of our souls, the only object of our desires. We are so weak that if we displayed the virtues of zeal, almsgiving, poverty, and austerity, we should make them subjects for vainglory. But as it is, everything is disagreeable in order that God may be our whole sanctification, our whole support, so that the world despises us, and leaves us to enjoy our treasure in peace. God desires to be the principle of all that is holy in us, and therefore what depends on ourselves and on our active fidelity is very small, and appears quite contrary to sanctity. There cannot be anything great in us in the sight of God except our passive 'endurance. Therefore let us think of it no more, let us leave the care of our sanctification to God who well knows how to effect it. It all depends on the watchful care, and particular operation of divine Providence, and is accomplished in a great measure without our knowledge, and even in a way that is unexpected, and disagreeable to us. Let us fulfil peacefully the little duties of our active fidelity, without aspiring to those that are greater, because God does not give Himself to us by reason of our own efforts. We shall become saints of God, of His grace, and of His special providence. He knows what rank to give us, let us leave it to Him, and without forming to ourselves false ideas, and empty systems of sanctity, let us content ourselves with loving Him unceasingly, and in pursuing with simplicity the path He has marked out for us, where all is so mean and paltry in our eyes, and in the estimation of the world

SECTION IV.—*Distrust of Self.*

The fourth trial of souls in the state of abandonment; the obscurity of their state, and their apparent opposition to the will of God.

For a soul that desires nothing else but the will of God, what could be more miserable than the impossibility of being certain of loving Him? Formerly it was mentally enlightened to perceive in what consisted the plan for its perfection, but it is no longer able to do so in its present state. Perfection is given to it contrary to all preconceived ideas, to all light, to all feeling. It is given by all the crosses sent by Providence, by the action of present duties, by certain attractions which have in them no good beyond that of not leading to sin; but seem very far from the dazzling sublimity of sanctity, and all that is unusual in virtue. God and His grace are given in a hidden and strange manner, for the soul feels too weak to bear the weight of its crosses, and disgusted with its obligations. Its attractions are only for quite ordinary exercises. The ideal it has formed of sanctity reproaches it interiorly for its mean and contemptible disposition. All books treating of the lives of the saints condemn it, it can find nothing in vindication of its conduct; it beholds a brilliant sanctity which renders it disconsolate because it has not strength sufficient to attain to it, and it does not see that its weakness is divinely ordered, but looks upon it as cowardice. Those whom it knows to be distinguished for striking virtue, of sublime contemplation regard it only with contempt. " What a strange saint," say they; and the soul, believing this, and confused by its countless useless efforts to raise itself from this low condition, is overwhelmed with opprobrium, and has nothing to advance in its own favour either to itself or to others. The soul in this state feels as if it were lost. Its reflexions afford it no help for its guidance, or enlightenment, and divine grace seems to have failed it. It is, however, through this loss that it finds again that same grace substituted under a different form, and restoring a hundredfold more than it took away by the purity of its hidden impressions.

This is, without doubt, a death-blow to the soul, for it loses sight of the divine will which, so to speak, withdraws itself from observation to stand behind it and push it on, becoming thus its invisible principle, and no longer its clearly defined object. Experience proves that nothing kindles the desire more than this apparent loss; therefore the soul vehemently desires to be united to the divine will, and gives vent to the most profound sighs, finding no possible consolation anywhere. A heart that has no other wish but to possess God must attract Him to itself, and this secret of love is a very great one since by this way alone are established in the soul sure faith and firm hope. It is then that we believe what we cannot see, and expect to possess what we cannot feel. Oh! how much does this incomprehensible conduct of an action, of which one is both subject and instrument, tend to one's perfection without any visible sign of appearance. Everything that one does seems done by chance, or natural inclination, and is very humiliating to the soul. When inspired to speak, it seems as if one spoke only from oneself. One never sees by what spirit one is impelled; the most divine inspiration is a terror, and whatever one does or feels is a source of constant self-contempt, as though it were all faulty and imperfect. Others are always admired, and one feels very inferior to them, while their whole way of acting causes confusion. The soul distrusts its own judgment, and cannot be certain about any of its thoughts; it pays excessive submission to the least advice given by a respectable authority, and the divine action in thus keeping it apart from striking virtue seems to plunge it into deeperhumiliation. This humiliation has no appearance of virtue to the soul; according to its own idea it is pure justice. The most admirable thing about it is, that in the eyes of others whom God does not enlighten, and even in its own eyes, the soul appears actuated by feelings absolutely contrary to virtue, such as pure obstinacy, disobedience, troublesomeness, contempt, and indignation, for which there seems no remedy. The more earnestly the soul strives to overcome these defects the more do they increase, because they form part of the design of God as being the most suitable means of detaching the soul from itself to prepare it for the divine union.

It is from this sad trial that the principal merit of the state of abandonment is gained. Now all is of a nature to withdraw the soul from its narrow path of love and simple obedience and it requires heroic virtue and courage to keep firm in plain active fidelity, and to sing its part in a song that seems to express in its tones that the soul is mistaken and lost; while grace sings a second. It does not hear this, however, and if it has courage to let the thunder roll, the lightning flash, and the tempest roar, and to walk with a firm tread in the path of love and obedience, of duty, and of the present attraction, it can be compared to the soul of Jesus during His passion, when our divine Saviour walked steadfastly in the fulfilling of the will of His Father, and in His love which imposed upon Him a task apparently quite inconsistent with the dignity of a soul of such sanctity as His.

The hearts of Jesus and Mary, bearing the fury of that darkest of nights, let the clouds gather, and the storm rage. A multitude of things in appearance most opposed to the designs of God and of His order, overwhelmed their faculties; but though deprived of all sensible support they walked without faltering in the path of love and obedience. Their eyes were fixed only on what they had to do, and leaving God to act as He pleased with all that concerned them, they endured the whole weight of that divine action. They groaned under the burden, but not for a single instant did they waver or pause. They believed that all would be well, provided that they kept on their way and let God act.

———

SECTION V.—*The Life of Faith.*

The fruit of these trials. The conduct of the submissive soul·

———

It results from all that has just been described that, in the path of pure faith, all that takes place spiritually, physically, and temporarily, has the aspect of death. This is not to be wondered at. What else could be expected? It is natural to this state. God has His plans for souls, and under this disguise He carries them out very successfully. Under the name of " disguise " I include ill-success, corporal infirmities, and spiritual weakness. All succeeds, and turns to good in the hands of God. It is by those things that are a trouble to nature that He prepares for the accomplishment of His greatest designs. "Omnia co-operantur in bonum iis qui secundum propositum vocati sunt sancti." " All things work together unto good to such as according to His purpose are called to be saints." (Rom. viii, 28). He brings life out of the shadow of death ; therefore, when nature is afraid, faith, which takes everything in a good sense, is full of courage and confidence. To live by faith is to live by joy, confidence, and certainty about all that has to be done or suffered at each moment according to the designs of God. It is in order to animate and to maintain this life of faith that God allows the soul to be plunged into and carried away by the rough waters of so many pains, troubles, difficulties, fatigues and overthrows ; for it requires faith to find God in all these things. The divine life is given at every moment in a hidden but very sure manner, under different appearances, such as the death of the body, the supposed loss of the soul, and the confusion of all earthly affairs. In all these, faith finds its food and support. It pierces through all, and clings to the hand of God, the giver of life.

Through all that does not partake of the nature of sin, the faithful soul should proceed with confidence, taking it all as a veil, or disguise of God whose immediate presence alarms and at the same time reassures the faculties of the soul. In fact this great God who consoles the humble, gives the soul in the midst of its greatest desolation an interior assurance that it has nothing to fear, provided it allows Him to act, and abandons itself entirely to Him. It is grieved because it has lost its Well-beloved, and yet something assures it that it possesses Him. It is troubled and disturbed, yet nevertheless has in its depths I know not what important grounds for attaching itself steadfastly to God. " Truly," said Jacob, " God is in this place, and I knew it not " (Gen. xxviii, 16). You seek God and He is everywhere; everything proclaims Him, everything gives Him to you. He walks by your side, is around you and within you : there He lives, and yet you seek Him. You seek your own idea of God while all the time you possess Him substantially. You seek perfection, and it is in everything that presents itself to you. Your sufferings, your actions, your attractions are the species under which God gives Himself to you, while you are vainly striving after sublime ideas which He by no means assumes in order to dwell in you.

Martha tried to please Jesus by cooking nice dishes, but Mary was content to be with Jesus in any way that He wished to give Himself to her ; but when Mary sought Him in the garden according to the idea she had formed of Him, He eluded her by presenting Himself in the form of a gardener. The Apostles saw Jesus, but mistook Him for a phantom. God disguises Himself, therefore, to raise the soul to the state of pure faith, to teach it to find Him under every kind of appearance ; for, when it has discovered this secret of God, it is in vain for Him to disguise Himself ; it says, " He is there, behind the wall, He is looking through the lattice, looking from the windows " (Cant. ii, 9). Oh ! divine Love, hide yourself, proceed from one trial to another, bind by attractions, blend, confuse, or break like threads all the ideas and methods of the soul. May it stray hither and thither for want of light, and be unable to see or understand in what path it should walk ; formerly it found You dwelling in Your ordinary guise, in the peaceful repose of solitude and prayer, or in suffering ; even in the consolations You give to others, in the course of conversation, or in business ; but now after having tried every method known to please you, it has to stand aside not seeing You in any of these things as in former times. May the uselessness of its efforts teach it to seek You henceforth in Yourself, which means to seek You everywhere, in all things without distinction and without reflexion ; for, oh divine Love ! what a mistake it is, not to find you in all that is good, and in every creature. Why then seek You in any other way than that by which You desire to give Yourself? Why, divine Love, seek You under any other species than those which You have chosen for Your Sacrament? The less there is to be seen or felt so much the more scope for faith and obedience. Do You not give fecundity to the root hidden underground, and can You not, if You so will, make this darkness in which You are pleased to keep me, fruitful? Live then, little root of my heart, in the deep, invisible heart of God ; and by its power, send forth branches, leaves, flowers and fruits, which, although invisible to yourself, are a pure joy and nourishment to others. Without consulting your own taste give of your shade, flowers, and fruit to others. May all that is grafted on you receive that indeterminate sap which will be known only by the growth and appearance of those same grafts. Become all to all, but as to yourself remain abandoned and indifferent. Remain in the dark and narrow prison of your miserable cocoon, little worm, until the warmth of grace forms you, and sets you free. Then feed upon whatever leaves it offers you, and do not regret, in the activity of abandonment, the peace you have lost. Stop directly the divine action would have you stop, and be content to lose, in the alternations of repose and activity, in incomprehensible changes, all your old formulas, methods and ways, to take upon you those designed for you by the divine action. Thus you will spin your silk in secret, doing what you can neither see nor feel. You will condemn in yourself a secret envy of your companions who are apparently dead and motionless, because they have not yet arrived at the point that you have attained ; you continue to admire them although you have surpassed them. May your affliction in your abandonment continue while you spin a silk in which the princes of the Church and of the world and all sorts of souls will glory to be attired.

After that what will become of you, little worm ? by what outlet will you come forth ? Oh ! marvel of grace by which souls are moulded in so many different shapes ! Who can guess in what direction grace will guide it ? And who could guess either, what nature does with a silkworm if he had not seen it working ? It is only necessary to provide it with leaves, and nature does the rest.

Therefore no soul can tell from whence it came, nor whither it is going ; neither from what thought of God the divine wisdom drew it, nor to what end it tends. Nothing is left but an entire passive abandonment, and to allow this divine Wisdom to act without interfering by our own reflexions, examples and methods.

We must act when the time to act comes, and cease when it is time to stop; if necessary letting all be lost, and thus, acting or remaining passive according to attraction and abandonment we, insensibly, do, or leave undone without knowing what will be the result; and after many changes the formed soul receives wings and flies up to Heaven, leaving a plentiful harvest on earth for other souls to gather.

CHAPTER IV.

CONCERNING THE ASSISTANCE RENDERED BY THE FATHERLY
PROVIDENCE OF GOD TO THOSE SOULS WHO HAVE ABANDONED
THEMSELVES TO HIM.

SECTION I.—*Confidence in God.*

The less the soul in the state of abandonment feels the help
it receives from God, the more efficaciously does He sustain it.

There is a kind of sanctity in which all the communications
of God are luminous and distinct; but in the passive state of
pure faith all that God communicates partakes of the nature
of that inaccessible darkness that surrounds His throne, and
all ideas are confused and indistinct. The soul, in this state of
obscurity is often afraid, like the Prophet, of running headlong
against a rock. " Fear not, faithful soul, for this is your right
path, and the way by which God conducts you. There is no
way more safe and sure than this dark way of faith." " But
it is so dark that I cannot tell which way to go." " Go wherever
you please; you cannot lose the way where there is no path;
every way looks the same in the dark, you cannot see the end
because nothing is visible." " But I am afraid of everything.
I feel as if, at any moment, I might fall over a precipice. Everything is an affliction to me; I well know that I am acting according to abandonment, but it seems to me that there are things I
cannot do without acting contrary to virtue. I seem to be so
far from all the virtues. The more I wish to practise them the
more remote they seem. I love virtue, but the obscure impressions by which I am attracted seem to keep virtue far from me.
I always give in to this attraction, and although I cannot perceive that it guides me well, I cannot help following it. The
spirit seeks light; but the heart is in darkness. Enlightened
persons, and those with lucid minds are congenial to my spirit,
but when I hear conversations and listen to discourses, my heart
understands nothing; its whole state and way is simply an
impression of the gift of faith, which makes it love and appreciate those principles, truths, and paths wherein the spirit has
neither object nor idea, and in which it trembles, shudders, and
falters. I have an assurance, I do not know how, in the depths
of my heart, that this way is right; not by the evidence of my
senses, but by a feeling inspired by faith." This is because it

is impossible for God to lead a soul without persuading it that the path is a right one, and this with a certainty all the greater the less it is perceived. And this certainty is victorious over all censures, fears, efforts, and all imaginations. The mind vainly cries out and seeks some better way. The bride recognises the Bridegroom unconsciously, but when she stretches out her hand to hold Him, He disappears. She understands that the Spouse to whom she belongs has rights over her, and she prefers to wander without order or method in abandoning herself to His guidance rather than to endeavour to gain confidence by following the beaten tracks of virtue.

Let us go to God, then, my soul, in abandonment, and let us acknowledge that we are incapable of acquiring virtue by our own industry or effort; but let us not allow this absence of particular virtues to diminish our confidence. Our divine Guide would not have reduced us to the necessity of walking if He had not intended to carry us in His arms. What need have we of lights and certainties, ideas and reflexions ? Of what use would it be to us to see, to know, and to feel, when we are no longer walking but being carried in the arms of divine Providence. The more we have to suffer from darkness, and the more rocks, precipices, and deserts there are in our way ; the more we have to endure from fears, dryness, weariness of mind, anguish of soul, and even despair, and the sight of purgatory and hell, the greater must be our confidence and faith. One glance at Him who carries us is sufficient to restore our courage in the greatest peril. We will forget the paths and what they are like ; we will forget ourselves, and abandoning ourselves entirely to the wisdom, goodness, and power of our Guide we will think only of loving Him, and avoiding all sin, not only that which is evident, however venial it may be, but even the appearance of evil, and of fulfilling all the duties and obligations of our state.

This is the only charge You lay upon Your children, O divine Love ! all the rest You take upon Yourself. The more terrible this may be, the more surely can Your presence be felt and recognised. Your children have only to love You without ceasing, and to fulfil their small duties like children. A child on its mother's lap is occupied only with its games as if it had nothing else to do but to play with its mother. The soul should soar above the clouds, and, as no one can work during the darkness of the night, it is the time for repose. The light of reason can do nothing but deepen the darkness of faith : the radiance necessary to disperse it must proceed from the same source as itself. In this state God communicates Himself to the soul as its life, but He is no longer visible as its way, and its truth. The bride seeks the Bridegroom during this night ; she seeks

Him before her, and hurries forward; but He is behind her, and holding her with His hands. He is no longer object, or idea, but principle and source. For all the needs, difficulties, troubles, falls, overthrows, persecutions, and uncertainties of souls which have lost all confidence in themselves and their own action, there are secret and inspired resources in the divine action, marvellous and unknown. The more perplexing the circumstances the keener is the expectation of a satisfactory solution. The heart says "All goes well, it is God who carries on the work, there is nothing to fear." That very suspense and desolation are verses in the canticle of darkness. It is a joy that not a single syllable is left out, and it all ends in a "Gloria Patri"; therefore we pursue the way of our wanderings, and darkness itself is a light for our guidance; and doubts are our best assurance. The more puzzled Isaac was to find something to sacrifice, the more completely did Abraham place all in the hands of Providence, and trust entirely in God.

SECTION II.—*Diversity of Grace.*

The afflictions which the soul is made to endure are but loving artifices of God which will, one day, give it great joy.

Souls that walk in light sing the canticles of the light; those that walk in darkness sing the songs of the darkness. Both must be allowed to sing to the end the part allotted to them by God in the great Oratorio. Nothing must be added to the score, nothing left out; every drop of bitterness must be allowed to flow freely at whatever cost. It was thus with Jeremias and Ezechiel whose utterances were broken by tears and sobs, and who could find no consolation except in continuing their lamentations. Had the course of their grief been interrupted, we should have lost the most beautiful passages of Scripture. The Spirit that afflicts can also console; these diverse waters flow from the same source. When God appears angry the soul trembles; when He threatens it is terrified. The divine operation must be allowed to develop, for, with the evil it carries a remedy; so continue to weep and to tremble; let restlessness and agony invade your souls, make no effort to free yourselves from these divine terrors, these heavenly troubles, but open your hearts to receive these little streams from that immense sea of sorrows which God bore in His most holy soul. Sow in sorrow for as long as grace requires, and that same grace will gradually dry your tears. Darkness will disappear before the radiance of the sun, springtime will come with its flowers, and the result of your abandonment will be seen in the admirable diversity of the divine action. Indeed it is quite useless for man to trouble himself; all that takes place in him is like a dream. One cloud chases another like imaginations in the brain of the sleeper, some sorrowful, others consoling. The soul is the playground of these phantoms which follow each other with great rapidity, and on awaking it feels that, in all this, there is nothing to detain it. When these impressions have passed away it takes no notice of the joys or sorrows of dreams.

O Lord! it can be truly said that You carry Your children in Your arms during this long night of faith, and that You are pleased to allow an infinite variety of thoughts to pass through their minds; thoughts holy and mysterious. In the state in which these dreams of the night place them, they indeed experience the utmost torment of fear, anguish, and weariness, but on the bright day of eternal glory these will give place to a true and solid joy.

It is at the moment of, and just after the awakening that holy souls, returning to themselves, and with full right to judge, can never tire of admiring and praising the tact, the inventions and refinements of loving deception practised by the divine Spouse. They understand how impenetrable are His ways, how impossible it is to guess His enigmas, to find out His disguises, or to receive consolation when it is His will to spread terror and alarm.

At this awakening those who, like Jeremias and David, have been inconsolable in their grief, will see that in their desolation they have been a subject of joy to the angels, and of glory to God. The bride sleeps through the bustle of industries, and of human actions, and in spite of the sneers of sceptics. In her sleep she will sigh and tremble; in her dreams she will pursue and seek her Spouse, who disguises Himself to deceive her.

Let her dream; her fears are only born of the night, and of sleep. When the Spouse has exercised her beloved soul, and shown forth in it what can only be expressed by Him, He will develop the result of these dreams and will awaken it at the right time.

Joseph caused Benjamin to weep, and his servants kept his secret from this beloved brother. Joseph deceived him, and not all his penetration and wit could fathom this deception. Benjamin and his brothers were plunged in unspeakable sorrow, but Joseph was only playing a trick on them, although the poor brothers could see nothing but an evil without any remedy. When he reveals himself and puts everything right they admire his wisdom in making them think that all is lost, and to cause them to despair about that which turns out to be a subject of the greatest joy they have ever experienced.

Section III.—*The Generosity of God.*

The more God seems to despoil the soul that is in the state of abandonment, the more generous are His gifts.

Let us continue to advance in the knowledge of the divine action and of its loving deceptions. That which it withdraws from the perception, it bestows incognito, as it were, on the goodwill. It never allows it to want for anything. It is as if someone who had maintained a friend by bounties bestowed personally upon him, should suddenly, for the welfare of this same friend, pretend that he could no longer oblige him, yet continues to assist him without making himself known. The friend, not suspecting any stratagem in this mystery of love, feels hurt, and entertains all sorts of ideas and criticisms on the conduct of his benefactor.

When, however, the mystery begins to be revealed, God knows what different feelings arise in the soul; joy, tenderness, gratitude, love, confusion and admiration; followed by an increase of zeal for, and attachment to the benefactor. And this trial will be the means of strengthening the soul, and accustoming it to similar surprises.

The application is easy. With God, the more one seems to lose the more one gains. The more He strikes off of what is natural, the more He gives of what is supernatural. He is loved at first for His gifts, but when these are no longer perceptible He is at last loved for Himself. It is by the apparent withdrawal of these sensible gifts that He prepares the way for that great gift which is the most precious and the most extensive of all, since it embraces all others. Souls which have once for all submitted themselves to the divine action, ought to interpret everything favourably. Yes, everything! even the loss of the most excellent directors, and the want of confidence they cannot help feeling in those who offer themselves for that post.

In truth those guides who, of their own accord, run after souls, deserve to be distrusted. Those who are truly inspired by the spirit of God do not, as a rule, show so much eagerness and self-sufficiency. They do not come forward until they are appealed to, and even then they proceed with caution. May the soul that has given itself entirely to God pass without fear through all these trials without losing its balance. Provided it is faithful to the divine action, this all-powerful action can produce marvels in it in spite of every obstacle.

God and the soul work in common, and the success of the work depends entirely on the divine Workman, and can only be spoilt if the soul prove unfaithful. When the soul is well, all is well, because what is from God, that is to say, His part and His action are, as it were, the counterpoise of the fidelity of the soul. It is the best part of the work, which is done something like beautiful tapestry, stitch by stitch from the wrong side. The worker employed on it sees only the stitch he is making, and the needle with which he makes it, while all the stitches combined form magnificent figures which do not show until, every part being complete, the right side is turned outwards. All the beauty and perfection of the work remain in obscurity during its progress. It is the same with the soul that has abandoned itself to God; it has eyes only for Him and for its duty. The performance of this duty is, at each moment, but an imperceptible stitch added to the work, and yet with these stitches God performs wonders of which He sometimes allows a glimpse to be seen, but which will not be visible in their entirety till revealed on the great day of eternity. How full of goodness and wisdom is the guidance of God! He has so entirely kept for His own grace, and His own action, all that is admirable, great, exalted and sublime; and so completely left to our souls, with the aid of grace, all that is little, light and easy, that there is no one in the world who cannot easily reach a most eminent degree of perfection in accomplishing lovingly the most ordinary and obscure duties.

SECTION IV.—*The Most Ordinary Things are Channels of Grace.*

In the state of abandonment God guides the soul more safely the more completely He seems to blind it.

It is most especially with regard to souls that abandon themselves entirely to God that the words of St. John are applicable : "You have no need that any man teach you, as His unction teacheth you of all things" (1 Eph., St. John, ii, 20). To know what God demands of them they need only probe their own hearts, and listen to the inspirations of this unction, which interpret the will of God according to circumstances.

The divine action, concealed though it is, reveals its designs, not through ideas, but intuitively. It shows them to the soul either necessarily, by not permitting any other thing to be chosen but what is actually present, or else by a sudden impulse, a sort of supernatural feeling that impels the soul to act without premeditation; or, in fine, by some kind of inclination or aversion which, while leaving it complete liberty, yet none the less leads it to take or refuse what is presented to it. If one were to judge by appearances, it seems as if it would be a great want of virtue to be swayed and influenced in this manner; and if one were to judge by ordinary rules, there appears a want of regulation and method in such conduct; but in reality it is the highest degree of virtue, and only after having practised it for a long time does one succeed. The virtue in this state is pure virtue; it is, in fact, perfection itself. One is like a musician who combines a perfect knowledge of music with technical skill: he would be so full of his art that, without thinking, all that he performed within its compass would be perfect; and if his compositions were examined afterwards, they would be found in perfect conformity with prescribed rules. One would then become convinced that he would never succeed better than when, free from the rules that keep genius in fetters when too scrupulously followed, he acted without constraint; and that his impromptus would be admired as chef d'œuvres by all connoisseurs. Thus the soul, trained for a long time in the science and practice of perfection under the influence of reasonings and methods of which it made use to assist grace, forms for itself a habit of acting in all things by the instincts implanted by God. It then knows that it can do nothing better than what first presents itself, without all those arguments of which it had need formerly. The only thing to be done is to act at random when unable to trust in anything but the workings of grace which cannot mislead it. The effects of grace, visible to watchful eyes, and intelligent minds, are nothing short of marvellous.

Without method, yet most exact; without rule, yet most orderly; without reflexion, yet most profound; without skill, yet thoroughly well constructed; without effort, yet everything accomplished; and without foresight, yet nothing better suited to unexpected events. Spiritual reading with the divine action, often contains a meaning that the author never thought of. God makes use of the words and actions of others to infuse truths which might otherwise have remained hidden. If He wishes to impart light in this way, it is for the submissive soul to avail itself of this light. Every expedient of the divine action has an efficacy which always surpasses its apparent and natural virtue.

It is the nature of abandonment always to lead a mysterious life, and to receive great and miraculous gifts from God by means of the most ordinary things, things that may be natural, accidental, or that seem to happen by chance, and in which there seems no other agency than the ordinary course of the ways of the world, or of the elements. In this way the simplest sermons, the most commonplace conversations, and the least high-toned books, become to these souls, by the virtue of God's will, sources of knowledge and wisdom. This is why they carefully gather up the crumbs that sceptics trample underfoot. Everything is precious in their eyes, everything enriches them. They are inexpressibly indifferent towards all things, and yet neglect nothing, having a respect for, and making use of all things. As God is everywhere, the use made of things by His will is not so much the use of creatures, as the enjoyment of the divine action which transmits His gifts by different channels. They cannot sanctify of themselves, but only as instruments of the divine action, which has power to communicate His grace, and often does communicate it, to simple souls in ways and by means which seem opposed to the end intended. It enlightens through mud as well as through glass, and the instrument of which it makes use is always singular. To it everything is alike. Faith always believes that nothing is wanting to it, and never complains of the privation of means which might prove useful for its increase, because the Workman, who employs them efficaciously, supplies what is wanting by His action. The divine action is the whole virtue of the creature.

SECTION V.—*Nature and Grace the Instruments of God.*

The less capable the soul in the state of abandonment is of defending itself, the more powerfully does God defend it.

The one and infallible influence of the divine action is invariably applied to the submissive soul at an opportune moment, and this soul corresponds in everything to its interior direction. It is pleased with everything that has taken place, with everything that is happening, and with all that effects it, with the exception of sin. Sometimes the soul acts with full consciousness, sometimes unknowingly, being led only by obscure instincts to say, to do, or to leave certain things, without being able to give a reason for its action.

Often the occasion and the determining reason are only of the natural order; the soul, perceiving no sort of mystery therein, acts by pure chance, necessity, or convenience, and its act has no other aspect either in its own eyes, or those of others; while all the time the divine action, through the intellect, the wisdom, or the counsel of friends, makes use of the simplest things in its favour. It makes them its own, and opposes so persistently every effort prejudicial to them, that it becomes impossible that these should succeed.

To have to deal with a simple soul is, in a certain way, to have to deal with God. What can be done against the will of the Almighty and His inscrutable designs? God takes the cause of the simple soul in hand. It is unnecessary for it to study the intrigues of others, to trouble about their worries, or to scrutinize their conduct; its Spouse relieves it of all these anxieties, and it can repose in Him full of peace, and in security. The divine action frees and exempts the soul from all those low and noisy ways so necessary to human prudence. These suited Herod and the Pharisees, but the Magi had only to follow their star in peace. The child has but to rest in His Mother's arms. His enemies do more to advance His interests than to hinder His work. The greater efforts they exert to thwart, and to take Him unawares, the more freely and tranquilly does He act. He never humours them, nor basely truckles to them to make them turn aside their blows; their jealousies, suspicions, and persecutions are necessary to Him. Thus did Jesus Christ live in Judea, and thus does He live now in simple souls. In them He is generous, sweet, free, peaceful, fearless, needing no one, beholding all creatures in His Father's hands, and obliged to serve Him, some by their criminal passions, others by their holy actions; the former by their contradictions, the latter by their obedience and submission. The divine action balances all this in a wonderful manner, nothing is wanting nor is anything superfluous, but of good and evil there is only what is necessary. The will of God applies, at each moment, the proper means to the end in view, and the simple soul, instructed by faith, finds everything right, and desires neither more nor less than what it has. It ever blesses that divine hand which so well apportions the means, and turns every obstacle aside. It receives friends and enemies with the same patient courtesy with which Jesus treated every one, and as divine instruments. It has need of no one and yet needs all. The divine action renders all necessary, and all must be received from it, according to their quality and nature, and corresponded to with sweetness and humility; the simple treated simply, and the unpolished kindly. This is what St. Paul teaches, and what Jesus Christ practised most perfectly.

Only grace can impress this supernatural character, which is appropriate to, and adapts itself to each person. This is never learnt from books, but from a true prophetic spirit, and is the effect of a special inspiration, and a doctrine of the Holy Spirit. To understand it one must be in the highest state of abandonment, the most perfect freedom from all design, and from all interests, however holy. One must have in view the only serious business in the world, that of following submissively the divine action. To do this one must apply oneself to the fulfilling of the obligations of one's state; and allow the Holy Spirit to act interiorly without trying to understand His operations, but even being pleased to be kept in ignorance about them. Then one is safe, for all that happens in the world can work nothing but good for souls perfectly submissive to the will of God.

___

SECTION VI.—*Supernatural Prudence*.

The soul, in the state of abandonment, does not fear its enemies, but finds in them useful helps.

___

I fear more my own action and that of my friends than that of my enemies. There is no prudence so great as that which offers no resistance to enemies, and which opposes to them only a simple abandonment. This is to run before the wind, and as there is nothing else to be done, to keep quiet and peaceful. There is nothing that is more entirely opposed to worldly prudence than simplicity; it turns aside all schemes without comprehending them, without so much as a thought about them. The divine action makes the soul take such just measures as to surprise those who want to take it by surprise themselves. It profits by all their efforts, and is raised by the very things that are done to lower it. They are the galley slaves who bring the ship into port with hard rowing. All obstacles turn to the good of this soul, and by allowing its enemies a free hand, it obtains a continual service, so sufficing that all it has to fear is lest it should itself take part in a work of which God would be principal, and His enemies the agents, and in which it has nothing to do but to peacefully observe the work of God, and to follow with simplicity the attractions He gives it. The supernatural prudence of the Divine Spirit, the principle of these attractions, infallibly attains its end; and the precise circumstances of each event are so applied to the soul, without its perception, that everything opposed to them cannot fail to be destroyed.

___

SECTION VII.—*Conviction of Weakness*.

The soul in the state of abandonment can abstain from justifying itself by word or deed. The divine action justifies it.

___

This order of the divine will is the solid and firm rock on which the submissive soul reposes, sheltered from change and tempest. It is continually present under the veil of crosses, and of the most ordinary actions. Behind this veil the hand of God is hidden to sustain and to support those who abandon themselves entirely to Him. From the time that a soul becomes firmly established in abandonment, it will be protected from the opposition of talkers, for it need not ever say or do anything in self-defence. Since the work is of God, justification must never be sought elsewhere. Its effects and its consequences are justification enough. There is nothing but to let it develop "Dies diei eructat verbum"; "Day to day uttereth speech" (Ps. xviii, 3). When one is no longer guided by reflexion, words must no longer be used in self-defence. Our words can only express our thoughts; where no ideas are supposed to exist, words cannot be used. Of what use would they be? To give a satisfactory explanation of our conduct? But we cannot explain that of which we know nothing for it is hidden in the principle of our actions, and we have experienced nothing but an impression, and that in an ineffable manner. We must, therefore, let the results justify their principles.

All the links of this divine chain remain firm and solid, and the reason of that which precedes as cause is seen in that which follows as effect. It is no longer a life of dreams, a life of imaginations, a life of a multiplicity of words. The soul is no longer occupied with these things, nor nourished and maintained in this way; they are no longer of any avail, and afford no support.

The soul no longer sees where it is going, nor foresees where it will go; reflexions no longer help it to gain courage to endure fatigue, and to sustain the hardships of the way. All this is swept aside by an interior conviction of weakness. The road widens as it advances; it has started, and goes on without hesitation. Being perfectly simple and straightforward, it follows the path of God's commandments quietly, relying on God Himself whom it finds at every step, and God, whom it seeks above all things, takes upon Himself to manifest His presence in such a way as to avenge it on its unjust detractors.

SECTION VIII.—*Self-guidance a Mistake.*

God imparts life to the soul in the state of abandonment by means which seem more likely to destroy it.

There is a time when God would be the life of the soul, and Himself accomplish its perfection in secret and unknown ways. Then all its own ideas, lights, industries, examinations, and reasonings become sources of illusion. After many experiences of the sad consequences of self-guidance, the soul recognising its uselessness, and finding that God has hidden and confused all the issues, is forced to fly to Him to find life. Then, convinced of its nothingness and of the harmfulness of all that it derives from itself, it abandons itself to God to gain all from Him. It is then that God becomes the source of its life, not by means of ideas, lights, or reflexions, for all this is no longer anything to it but a source of illusion; but in reality, and by His grace, which is hidden under the strangest appearances.

The divine operation, unknown to the soul, communicates its virtue and substance by many circumstances that the soul believes will be its destruction. There is no cure for this ignorance, it must be allowed its course. God gives Himself therein, and with Himself, He gives all things in the obscurity of faith. The soul is but a blind subject, or, in other words, it is like a sick person who knows nothing of the properties of remedies and tastes only their bitterness.' He often imagines that what is given him will be his death; the pain and weakness which result seem to justify his fears; nevertheless it is under the semblance of death that his health is restored, and he takes the medicines on the word of the physician. In the same way the submissive soul is in no way pre-occupied about its infirmities, except as regards obvious maladies which by their nature compel it to rest, and to take suitable remedies. The languor and weakness of souls in the state of abandonment are only illusory appearances which they ought to defy with confidence. God sends them, or permits them in order to give opportunities for the exercise of faith and abandonment which are the true remedies. Without paying the least attention to them, these souls should generously pursue their way, following by their actions and sufferings the order of God, making use without hesitation of the body as though it were a horse on hire, which is intended to be driven until it is worn out. This is better than thinking of health so much as to harm the soul.

A courageous spirit does much to maintain a feeble body, and one year of a life spent in so noble and generous a manner is of more value than would be a century of care-taking and nervous fears. One ought to be able to show outwardly that one is in a state of grace and goodwill. What is there to be afraid of in fulfilling the divine will? The conduct of one who is upheld and sustained by it should show nothing exteriorly but what is heroic. The terrifying experiences that have to be encountered are really nothing. They are only sent that life may be adorned with more glorious victories. The divine will involves the soul in troubles of every kind, where human prudence can neither see nor imagine any outlet. It then feels all its weakness, and, finding out its shortcomings, is confounded. The divine will then asserts itself in all its power to those who give themselves to it without reserve. It succours them more marvellously than the writers of fiction, in the fertility of their imagination, unravel the intrigues and perils of their imaginary heros, and bring them to a happy end. With a much more admirable skill, and much more happily, does the divine will guide the soul through deadly perils and monsters, even through the fires of hell with their demons and sufferings. It raises souls to the heights of heaven, and makes them the subjects of histories both real and mystical, more beautiful, and more extraordinary than any invented by the vain imagination of man.

On then, my soul, through perils and monsters, guided and sustained by that mighty invisible hand of divine Providence. On, without fear, to the end, in peace and joy, and make all the incidents of life occasions of fresh victories. We march under His Standard, to fight and to conquer; "exivit vincens ut vinceret"; "He went forth conquering that he might conquer" (Apocal. vi, 2).

As many steps as we take under His command will be the triumphs we gain. The Holy Spirit of God writes in an open book this sacred history which is not ye tfinished, nor will be till the end of the world. This history contains an account of the guidance and designs of God with regard to men. It remains for us to figure in this history, and to continue the thread of it by the union of our actions and sufferings with His will. No! It is not to cause the loss of our souls that we have so much to do, and to suffer; but that we may furnish matter for that holy writing which is added to day by day.

SECTION IX.—*Divine Love, the Principle of All Good.*

To those who follow this path, divine love is all-sufficing.

While despoiling of all things those souls who give themselves entirely to Him, God gives them something in place of them. Instead of light, wisdom, life, and strength, He gives them His love. The divine love in these souls is like a supernatural instinct. In nature, each thing contains that which is suitable to its kind. Each flower has its special beauty, each animal its instinct, and each creature its perfection. Also in the different states of grace, each has a special grace. This is the recompense for everyone who accepts with good-will the state in which he is placed by Providence. A soul comes under the divine action from the moment that a habit of goodwill is formed within it, and this action influences it more or less according to its degree of abandonment. The whole art of abandonment is simply that of loving, and the divine action is nothing else than the action of divine love. How can it be that these two loves seeking each other should do otherwise than unite when they meet? How can the divine love refuse aught to a soul whose every desire it directs? And how can a soul that lives only for Him refuse Him anything? Love can refuse nothing that love desires, nor desire anything that love refuses. The divine action regards only the goodwill; the capability of the other faculties does not attract it, nor does the want of capability repel it. All that it requires is a heart that is good, pure, just, simple, submissive, filial, and respectful. It takes possession of such a heart, and of all its faculties, and so arranges everything for its benefit that it finds in all things its sanctification. That which destroys other souls would find in this soul an antidote of goodwill which would nullify its poison. Even at the edge of a precipice the divine action would draw it back, or even if it were allowed to remain there it would prevent it from falling; and if it fell, it would rescue it. After all, the faults of such a soul are only faults of frailty; love takes but little notice of them, and well knows how to turn them to advantage. It makes the soul understand by secret suggestions what it ought to say, or to do, according to circumstances. These suggestions it receives as rays of light from the divine understanding: "intellectus bonus omnibus facientibus eum"; "A good understanding to all that do it" (Ps. cx, 10), for this divine understanding accompanies such souls step by step, and prevents them taking those false steps which their simplicity encourages. If they make arrangements which would involve them in some promise prejudicial to them, divine Providence arranges some fortunate occurrence which rectifies everything. In vain are schemes formed against them repeatedly; divine Providence cuts all the knots, brings the authors to confusion, and so turns their heads as to make them fall into their own trap. Under its guidance those souls that they wish to take by surprise do certain things that seem very useless at the time, but that serve afterwards to deliver them from all the troubles into which their uprightness and the malice of their enemies would have plunged them. Oh! what good policy it is to have goodwill! What prudence there is in simplicity! What ability in its innocence and candour! What mysteries and secrets in its straightforwardness! Look at the youthful Tobias; he is but a lad, yet with what confidence he proceeds, having the archangel Raphael for his guide. Nothing frightens him, nothing is wanting to him. The very monsters he encounters furnish him with food and remedies; the one that rushes forward to devour him becomes itself his sustenance. By the order of Providence he has nothing to attend to but feasts and weddings, everything else is left to the management of the guiding spirit appointed to help him. These things are so well managed that never before have they been so successful, nor so blessed and prosperous. However, his mother weeps, and is in great distress at his supposed loss, but his father remains full of faith. The son, so bitterly mourned, returns to rejoice his family and to share their happiness.

Divine love then is, to those who give themselves up to it

without reserve, the principle of all good. To acquire this
inestimable treasure the only thing necessary is greatly to desire
it. Yes, God only asks for love, and if you seek this treasure,
this kingdom in which God reigns alone, you will find it. If
your heart is entirely devoted to God, it is itself, for that very
reason, the treasure and the kingdom that you seek and desire.
From the time that one desires God and His holy will, one enjoys
God and His will, and this enjoyment corresponds to the ardour
of the desire. To desire to love God is truly to love Him, and
because we love Him we wish to become instruments of His
action in order that His love may be exercised in, and by us.
The divine action does not correspond to the aims of a saintly
and simple soul, nor to the steps it takes, nor to the projects it
forms, nor to the manner in which it reflects, nor to the means it
chooses, nor to the purity of its intention. It often happens
that the soul can be deceived in all this, but its good intention
and uprightness can never deceive it. Provided that God
perceives in it a good intention, He can dispense with all the rest,
and He holds as done for Him what it will eventually do when
truer ideas second its goodwill.

Goodwill, therefore, has nothing to fear. If it fall, it can only
do so under the almighty hand which guides and sustains it in
all its wanderings. It is this divine hand which turns it again
to face the goal from which it has strayed ; which replaces it in
the right path when it has wandered. In it the soul finds resources for the deviations to which the blind faculties which
deceive it, render it subject. It is made to feel how much it
ought to despise them, and to rely on God alone, abandoning
itself absolutely to His infallible guidance. The failings into
which good souls fall are put an end to by abandonment. Never
can goodwill be taken unawares. That all things work for its
good is an article of faith.

Section X.—*We Must see God in all His Creatures.*

In the state of abandonment the soul finds more light and
strength, through submission to the divine action, than all those
possess who resist it through pride.

Of what use are the most sublime illuminations, the most
divine revelations, if one has no love for the will of God ? It was
because of this that Lucifer fell. The ruling of the divine action
revealed to him by God, in showing him the mystery of the
Incarnation, produced in him nothing but envy.

On the other hand a simple soul, enlightened only by faith,
can never tire of admiring, praising, and loving the order of

God; of finding it not only in holy creatures, but even in the most irregular confusion and disorder. One grain of pure faith will give .more light to a simple soul than Lucifer received in his highest intelligence. The devotion of the faithful soul to its obligations; its quiet submission to the intimate promptings of grace; its gentleness and humility towards everyone; are of more value than the most profound insight into mysteries. If one regarded only the divine action in all the pride and harshness of creatures, one would never treat them with anything but sweetness and respect. Their roughness would never disturb the divine order, whatever course it might take. One must only see in it the divine action, given and taken, as long as one is faithful in the practice of sweetness and humility. It is best not to observe their way of proceeding, but always to walk with firm steps in our own path. It is thus that by bending gently, cedars are broken, and rocks overthrown. Who amongst creatures can resist a faithful, gentle, and humble soul? These are the only arms to be taken if we wish to conquer all our enemies. Jesus Christ has placed them in our hands that we may defend ourselves; there is nothing to fear if we know how to use them.

We must not be cowardly, but generous. This is the only disposition suitable to the instruments of God.

All the works of God are sublime and marvellous; while one's own actions, when they war against God, cannot resist t he divine action in one who is united to it by sweetness and humili y.

Who is Lucifer? He is a pure spirit, and was the most enlightened of all pure spirits, but is now at war with God and with His rule. The mystery of sin is merely the result of this conflict, which manifests itself in every possible way. Lucifer, as much as in him lies, will leave no stone unturned to destroy what God has made and ordered. Wherever he enters, there is the work of God defaced. The more light, science, and capacity a person has, the more he is to be feared if he does not possess a foundation of piety, which consists in being satisfied with God and His will. It is by a well-regulated heart that one is united to the divine action; without this everything is purely natural, and generally in direct opposition to the divine order. God makes use only of the humble as His instruments. Always contradicted by the proud, He yet makes use of them, like slaves, for the accomplishment of His designs.

When I find a soul which does all for God alone, and in submission to His order, however wanting it may be in all things else, I say " This is a soul with a great aptitude for serving God." The holy Virgin and St. Joseph were like this. All else without these qualities makes me fear. I am afraid to see in it the action of Lucifer. I remain on my guard, and shut myself up in my foundation of simplicity, in opposition to all this outward glitter which, by itself, is nothing to me but a bit of broken glass.

SECTION XI.—*The Strength of Simplicity.*

The soul in the state of abandonment knows how to see God even in the proud who oppose His action. All creatures, good or evil, reveal Him to it.

The whole practice of the simple soul is in the accomplishment of the will of God. This it respects even in those unruly actions by which the proud attempt to depreciate it. The proud soul despises one in whose sight it is as nothing, who beholds only God in it, and in all its actions. Often it imagines that the modesty of the simple soul is a mark of appreciation for itself; when, all the time, it is only a sign of that loving fear of God and of His holy will as shown to it in the person of the proud. No, poor fool, the simple soul fears you not at all. You excite its compassion; it is answering God when you think it is speaking to you: it is with Him that it believes it has to do; it regards you only as one of His slaves, or rather as a mask with which He disguises Himself. Therefore the more you take a high tone, the lower you become in its estimation; and when you think to take it by surprise, it surprises you. Your wiles and violence are just favours from Heaven.

The proud soul cannot comprehend itself, but the simple soul, with the light of faith, can very clearly see through it.

The finding of the divine action in all that occurs at each, moment, in and around us, is true science, a continuous revelation of truth, and an unceasingly renewed intercourse with God. It is a rejoicing with the Spouse, not in secret, nor by stealth, in the cellar, or the vineyard, but openly, and in public, without any human respect. It is a fund of peace, of joy, of love, and of satisfaction with God who is seen, known, or rather, believed in, living and operating in the most perfect manner in everything that happens. It is the beginning of eternal happiness not yet perfectly realised and tasted, except in an incomplete and hidden manner.

The Holy Spirit, who arranges all the pieces on the board of life, will, by this fruitful and continual presence of His action, say at the hour of death, " fiat lux," " let there be light " (Gen. i, 14), and then will be seen the treasures which faith hides in this abyss of peace and contentment with God, and which will be found in those things that have been every moment done, or suffered for Him.

When God gives Himself thus, all that is common becomes
wonderful ; and it is on this account that nothing seems to be so,
because this way is, in itself, extraordinary. Consequently
it is unnecessary to make it full of strange and unsuitable marvels.
It is, in itself, a miracle, a revelation, a constant joy even with
the prevalence of minor faults. But it is a miracle which, while
rendering all common and sensible things wonderful, has nothing
in itself that is sensibly marvellous.

SECTION XII.—*The Triumph of Humility.*

To the souls which are faithful to Him, God promises a glorious
victory over the powers of the world and of hell.

If the divine action is hidden here below under the appearance
of weakness, it is in order to increase the merit of souls which are
faithful to it ; but its triumph is none the less certain.

The history of the world from the beginning is but the history
of the struggle between the powers of the world, and of hell,
against the souls which are humbly devoted to the divine action.
In this struggle all the advantage seems to be on the side of
pride, yet the victory always remains with humility. The image
of the world is always presented to our eyes as a statue of gold,
brass, iron, and clay. This mystery of iniquity, shown in a
dream to Nabuchodonosor, is nothing but a confused medley of
all the actions, interior and exterior, of the children of darkness.
This is also typified by the beast coming out of the pit to make
war, from the beginning of time, against the interior and spiritual
life of man. All that takes place in our days is the consequence
of this war. Monster follows monster out of the pit, which
swallows, and vomits them forth again amidst incessant clouds
of smoke. The combat between St. Michael and Lucifer, that
began in Heaven, still continues. The heart of this once magnificent angel, has become, through envy, an inexhaustible
abyss of every kind of evil. He made angel revolt against angel
in Heaven, and from the creation of the world his whole energy
is exerted to make more criminals among men to fill the ranks
of those who have been swallowed up in the pit. Lucifer is the
chief of those who refuse obedience to the Almighty. This
mystery of iniquity is the very inversion of the order of God ;
it is the order, or rather, the disorder of the devil.

This disorder is a mystery because, under a false appearance
of good, it hides irremediable and infinite evil. Every wicked
man, who, from the time of Cain, up to the present moment, has

declared war against God, has outwardly been great and powerful, making a great stir in the world, and being worshipped by all. But this outward semblance is a mystery. In reality they are beasts which have ascended from the pit one after another to overthrow the order of God. But this order, which is another mystery, has always opposed to them really great and powerful men who have dealt these monsters a mortal wound. As fast as hell vomits them forth, Heaven at the same time creates fresh heroes to combat them. Ancient history, sacred and profane, is but a record of this war. The order of God has ever remained victorious and those who have ranged themselves on the side of God have shared His triumph, and are happy for all eternity. Injustice has never been able to protect deserters. It can reward them only by death, an eternal death.

Those who practise iniquity imagine themselves invincible. O God! who can resist You? If a single soul has the whole world and all hell against it, it need have no fear if, by abandonment, it takes its stand on the side of God and His order.

The monstrous spectacle of wickedness armed with so much power; the head of gold, the body of silver, brass, and iron, is nothing more than the image of clay; a small stone cast at it will scatter it to the four winds of Heaven.

How wonderfully has the Holy Spirit illustrated the centuries of the world! So many startling revelations! so many renowned heroes following each other like so many brilliant stars! So many wonderful events!

All this is like the dream of Nabuchodonosor, forgotten on awaking, however terrible the impression it made at the time.

All these monsters only come into the world to exercise the courage of the children of God, and if these are well trained, God gives them the pleasure of slaying the monsters, and sends fresh athletes into the arena.

And this life is a spectacle to angels, causing continual joy in Heaven, work for saints on earth, and confusion to the devils in hell.

So all that is opposed to the order of God renders it only the more to be adored. All workers of iniquity are slaves of justice, and the divine action builds the heavenly Jerusalem on the ruins of Babylon.

SPIRITUAL COUNSELS OF
FR. DE CAUSSADE

I.—*Conformity to the Will of God.*

Written in 1731 to Sister Marie-Thérèse de Vomiénil, in the 9th year of her profession, and the 28th of her age.

For the attainment of perfect conformity to the will of God.

1st. At the beginning of each day, and of meditation, Mass, and Communion, declare to God that you desire to belong to Him entirely, and that you will devote yourself wholly to acquiring the spirit of prayer and of the interior life.

2nd. Make it your chief study to conform yourself to the will of God even in the smallest things, saying in the midst of the most annoying contradictions and with the most alarming prospects for the future : " My God, I desire with all my heart to do Your holy will, I submit in all things and absolutely to Your good pleasure for time and eternity ; and I wish to do this, Oh my God, for two reasons ; first : because You are my Sovereign Lord and it is but just that Your will should be accomplished ; secondly : because I am convinced by faith, and by experience that Your will is in all things as good and beneficent as it is just and adorable, while my own desires are always blind and corrupt ; blind, because I know not what I ought to desire or to avoid ; corrupt, because I nearly always long for what would do me harm. Therefore, from henceforth, I renounce my own will to follow Yours in all things ; dispose of me, Oh my God, according to Your good will and pleasure.

3rd. This continual practice of submission will preserve that interior peace which is the foundation of the spiritual life, and will prevent you from worrying about your faults and failings. You will put up with them instead, with a humble and quiet submission which is more likely to cure them than an uneasy distress, only calculated to weaken and discourage you.

4th. Think no more about the past but only of the present and future. Do not trouble about your confessions, but accuse yourself simply of those faults you can remember after seven or eight minutes examen. It is a good thing to add to the accusation a more serious sin of your past life. This will cause you to make a more fervent act of contrition and dispose you to receive more abundantly the grace of the Sacrament. You should not make too many efforts to get rid of the obstacles which make frequent confession disagreeable to you.

5th. To escape the distress caused by regret for the past or fear about the future, this is the rule to follow : leave the past to the infinite mercy of God, the future to His good Providence, give the present wholly to His love by being faithful to His grace.

6th. When God in His goodness sends you some disappointment, one of those trials that used to annoy you so much ; before all thank Him for it as for a great favour all the more useful for the great work of your perfection in that it completely overturns the work of the moment.

7th. Try, in spite of interior dislike, to show a kind face to troublesome people, or to those who come to chatter about their troubles ; leave at once prayer, reading, choir office, in fact anything, to go where Providence calls you ; and do what is asked of you quietly, peacefully, without hurry, and without vexation.

8th. Should you fail in any of these points, make immediately an act of interior humility—not that sort of humility full of uneasiness and irritation against which St. Francis of Sales said so much, but a humility that is gentle, peaceful, and sweet. This is a matter essential for overcoming your self-will, and to prevent you becoming a slave to your exterior or interior devotion.

9th. We must understand that we can never acquire true conformity to the will of God until we are perfectly resolved to serve Him according to His will and pleasure and not to please ourselves. In everything look to God, and you will find Him everywhere, but more especially where you have most completely renounced yourself. When you are thoroughly convinced that of yourself you are incapable of doing any good, you will give up making resolutions but will humbly confess to God : " My God, I acknowledge after many trials that all my resolutions are useless. Doubtless I have hitherto depended too much on myself, but You have abased me. You alone can do all things ; make me then, do such and such a thing, and give me, when necessary, the recollection, energy and strength of will that I require. Without this, I know from my former sad experiences, I shall never do anything."

10th. To this humble prayer add the practice of begging pardon at once or as soon as possible of all those who witnessed any of your little impetuosities or outbursts of temper. It is most important for you to practise these counsels for two reasons : first, because God desires to do everything in you Himself ; secondly, on account of a secret presumption, which, even in the midst of so many miseries, prevents you referring everything to God, until you have experienced a thousand times how absolutely incapable you are of performing any good. When you become thoroughly convinced of this truth you will exclaim almost without reflexion, when you act rightly, " Oh my God it is You who do this in me by Your grace." And when you do wrong : " This is just like me ! I see myself as I am." Then will God be glorified in all your actions, because He will be proved to be the sole author of all that is good. This is your path ; all the misery and humiliation you must take on yourself, and render to God the glory and thanks that are His due. All the glory to Him, but all the profit to you. You would be very foolish not to accept with gratitude a share so just and so advantageous.

II.—*Counsel for Outward Behaviour.*

Counsel for the outward behaviour of one called to the life of abandonment. Addressed to Sister Charlotte Elizabeth Bourcier de Monthureux.

When you wake raise your soul to God, realising His divine presence ; adore the Blessed Trinity, imitating the great St. Francis Xavier, " I adore You, God the Father, who created me, I adore You, God the Son, who redeemed me, I adore You, God the Holy Ghost, who have sanctified me, and continue to carry on the work of my sanctification. I consecrate this day entirely to Your love and to Your greater glory. I know not what this day will bring me either pleasant or troublesome, whether I shall be happy or sorrowful, shall enjoy consolation or undergo pain and grief, it shall be as You please ; I give myself into Your hands and submit myself to whatever You will."

Fix your attention on what strikes you at the beginning of the day and on that with which grace inspires you more particularly in the interior of your soul, keeping it before you quietly. Begin your prayer with it, then give yourself up completely to the Spirit of God and remain thus for as long as He pleases. Imitate the good woman who exclaimed, " My God, if You will not give me bread, at any rate give me patience."

Those who practise ordinary prayer in which the intellect is exercised should remember the subject of meditation prepared overnight, because if the mind is allowed to wander to all sorts of subjects, then the whole day will be out of order as a clock not set correctly at first will go wrong all day.

For the toilet, do all that is necessary, then think no more about it.

H

The way to hear holy Mass worthily is to represent to yourself the mystery of the Cross. Ascend Mount Calvary in spirit, and contemplate what takes place there as though you actually saw it. Admire first the justice of God who punishes His only Son for the sins of men of which He took on Himself the semblance and for which He had offered Himself as the atonement. Secondly, the greatness of God to whom such a reparation was due. Thirdly, the value of our souls reclaimed at such a price; fourthly the eternal happiness that Jesus Christ has merited for us and the eternal torments from which He has delivered us. Reflexions on these divine subjects should fill our souls with faith, hope, humility, compunction, gratitude and love. Those who cannot keep their minds steadfastly fixed on such high subjects should address themselves to the Blessed Virgin, who was present at this mystery, or to St. John, St. Mary Magdalen and the good Thief, and finally to our Lord Himself in token of their piety, and to give Him the honour due to Him on account of the excess of His immense and incomprehensible charity and mercy.

I have only two things to say on the subject of prayer. Make it with absolute compliance with the will of God, no matter whether it be successful, or you are troubled with dryness, distractions, or other obstacles. If it is easy and full of consolations, return thanks to God without dwelling on the pleasure it has caused you; if it has not succeeded submit to God, humbling yourself and go away contented and in peace even if it should have failed through your own fault; redoubling your confidence and resignation to His holy will. Persevere in this way and sooner or later God will give you grace to pray properly; but whatever trials you may have to endure never allow yourself to be discouraged. As to the Office, there are three ways of saying it, equally easy and solid. The first is to keep yourself in the presence of God and to say the Office with great recollection in union with Him, occasionally raising your mind and heart to Him. Those who can say it thus need not trouble to alter their method. The second way is to attend to the words in union with the mind of the Church, praying as she prays, sighing when she sighs, and deriving all the instruction from it; praising, adoring, thanking, according to the different meanings of the verses we are pronouncing. The third way is to reflect humbly that you are actually united to holy souls in praising God and in desiring to share their holy dispositions. You should prostrate yourself in spirit at their feet, believing that they are much more full of piety and fervour than yourself. These feelings are very pleasing to His divine Majesty, and we cannot be too deeply impressed with them. With regard to confession, be firmly convinced that you need not trouble about it, either on account of your miseries or of your sins. St. Francis of Sales says that after sorrow for sin there should be peace. This then is what you ought to aim at, and above all you should be full of great confidence in the infinite goodness of God, remembering that His mercy is greater than any of His works, that He glories in forgiving us, but cannot prove His generosity if we are wanting in confidence. He loves simplicity, candour, and uprightness, go to Him therefore with perfect confidence, in spite of all your weakness, misery and unfaithfulness. That will win His heart, and He will forgive everything to those who trust in His goodness and love.

Do not spend more than half-an-hour over your preparation. More than that would be waste of time, and would give the devil an opportunity to create trouble in your soul. This must be avoided more than anything, for peace of mind is a tree of life, the true root of the interior spirit, and the best preparation for the prayer of recollection and interior silence. The first quarter of an hour at the most can be occupied with the remembrance of your faults, all those that you forget after this examen will be as if non-existent, and you will be forgiven. The last quarter of an hour should be employed in exciting yourself to contrition, begging this grace from God, and endeavouring to obtain it quietly and without any effort of the mind, by the thought of the goodness of God and the great mercy He has shown you in withdrawing you from the world, where you would have been lost, and calling you to the religious life in which you can so easily save your soul ; or, by preserving you from dying in a state of sin ; or, by reclaiming you from a tepid, feeble and imperfect life, in which you ran the risk of being lost, even in the religious state.

After reflecting for some moments in this way you should think that contrition being purely spiritual is, by nature, not sensibly felt, and that sensible sorrow is so misleading that certain sinners, in spite of every sign, are refused absolution, because it is possible that a habit of sin—even of mortal sin to which the will consents, may subsist with it. The surest sign of true sorrow for which the greatest sinner will receive absolution is, to resolve by the grace of God never to commit these great sins again. Then say from the bottom of your heart : " Lord ! I hope You have given me the necessary contrition. I hereby ask Your pardon for all the sins I have committed; I detest them with all my heart because of the hatred You bear them. You see, my God, that I am truly sorry, not only for having committed them, but also because I am unable to feel all the sorrow I wish to have. You conceal this sorrow from me even in giving it, so that I may never be certain of having been pardoned, nor of being in a state of grace. It pleases You to keep me in this humble dependence in order to give occasion for faith and holy hope, the way by which You would conduct me. I am compelled to be satisfied with the remembrance of Your great mercy, and in it I will lose myself, and to it I will blindly abandon myself, fully and without reserve ; and I will do so, Oh my God ! with all my heart. Yes, Lord, I will rest willingly on You alone, accepting this state of uncertainty that is so terrible and in which all are kept, even the greatest saints and the souls most dear to You."

As regards the declaration of your sins ; tell those that you recollect simply and in as few words as possible, leaving the rest to the unbounded mercy of God without troubling about what you do not remember, or do not know. You can conclude by mentioning some greater sin of your past life. After that you may feel morally certain that you have received the grace of the Sacrament. The following is an easy way of practising frequent confession. To prevent more certainly all anxiety about the past and as a help for the future here is a counsel in a few words. Leave the past to the infinite mercy of God—the future to His sweet providence, and the present give up entirely to the love of God by our fidelity with the assistance of His grace, which will never fail you, except by your own fault.

While receiving absolution let this thought preoccupy you and, throwing yourself in spirit at the foot of the Cross, kiss the wounds in our Lord's sacred feet saying " Oh ! my God ! I ask but for one drop of that most precious and adorable Blood that You shed for my salvation. In Your goodness let it fall upon my sinful soul to cleanse it more and more from all its stains, and above all, from the grievous sins of my past life for which I very humbly ask pardon. I have a sure hope of obtaining it from that very great mercy You have so often shown to this miserable and vile creature." This done, I forbid you in the name of God, to think, voluntarily, any more either of the confession you have just made, of your sins, or of contrition in order to find out if you have been forgiven and are restored to grace.

This is a mystery known only to God, and one which He keeps to Himself ; and the devil makes use of it to disturb and trouble souls in order to make them waste time, and to deprive them of that sweet interior peace, which is the best disposition for communion, and without which they can derive little fruit from that heavenly feast. In such a state of anxiety and distress it is difficult to have any desire for this divine food ; it is even distasteful to us through our own fault, because, instead of rejecting and despising these foolish anxieties into which the evil one has thrown our souls we permit ourselves to be harassed and afflicted by them. Let them fall as a stone falls into the sea.

For Holy Communion these two points will suffice : before Communion let us act like Martha, and after like Mary,— that is to say we should prepare ourselves by fervent acts of virtue and of the good works adapted to our state, without uneasiness and without over-eagerness, and then reflect on Jesus Christ, on His infinite merits and love and remain united to Him in an ineffable peace, transcending all feeling.

Nature seeks self in everything, even in exercises of piety and virtue as well as in those actions prescribed by the necessities of this life. It was on this account that the saints sighed continually and were ceaselessly on their guard, looking upon themselves as their own greatest enemies. We should be particularly careful as regards those things for which we have an attachment and be ready to sacrifice anything that gives us pleasure to comply with the lawful demands of our neighbour, especially where the matter is one of obedience. The will of God should always prevail over our own desires however holy they seem to us.

III.—*Interior Direction.*

Method of interior direction, addressed to the same Sister.

1st. We attain to God by the annihilation of self. Let us abase ourselves till there is nothing of self to be perceived.

2nd. In the degree in which we banish all that is not God, we shall become filled with God, because where we no longer find self we shall find God. The greatest good we can do for our souls in this life is to fill them with God.

3rd. The practice of complete abnegation consists in having no other care but that of dying entirely to self to make room for God to live and work in us.

4th. The most excellent act of which we are capable, and one which in itself contains all other virtues, is to resign ourselves entirely to God by a total self-renunciation, and to lose self in the abyss of our own nothingness to find it no more save in God. This is the one thing necessary recommended by our Lord in the Gospel. Oh! the riches of nothingness! Why are you not known? The more completely a soul annihilates itself the more precious does it become in the sight of God. To lose yourself in your own nothingness is a sure way of finding God. Let us endeavour then to make the simple recollection of God, combined with a profound forgetfulness of ourselves and a loving and humble submission to His will become our sole task. This effort will keep far from us all that is evil and retain in us all that is useful for our salvation, and meritorious in the sight of God.

5th. Do not draw distinctions between the rest from labour, that is exterior, and that which is interior : it is all the same provided you submit willingly and keep interior peace—it is well to note this.

6th. In our intercourse with others let us be detached in a way that will show how far removed we are from all tenderness or feeling. It is inconceivable how small a thing will suffice to impede the soul, and for how long a time, often for a whole life-time a trifle is capable of preventing the wonderful progress that grace would have effected in our souls. God requires an empty space even in the most remote recesses of our nature in order to communicate Himself to our souls.

7th. It is in the most trying and annoying circumstances that you can practise the most perfect self-effacement and become confirmed in this matter by the loss of secondary things ; let us then cheerfully acquiesce in the loss of everything except the loss of God.

8th. Let no business matter, nor any occurrence whatever, have any value out of God, and let God be all in all to us.

9th. Let us never be eager about anything nor allow our hearts to be oppressed by anything whatever. Where there is neither interest nor affection, there is no eagerness, nor sadness; but a void that is ever peaceful and unchangeable. In this we shall be established when we have detached ourselves from all created things, and shall find ourselves where self-seeking ceases ; let us lose all to find all.

10th. When we have reduced ourselves to the Unity that is God, all that is not God is undesirable to us. If we but knew how to content ourselves with this supreme Unity we should never trouble ourselves about anything else. This truth thoroughly understood and well practised will enable us to cut off all super-fluous things, even those that seem good, holy, and necessary, but which, in the end, might do us harm instead of helping us to attain the object of all our aspirations—namely to be one with the Supreme Unity.

11th. Let our motto be that of blessed Giles of Assisi, " One to love, a single soul to a single God." Let us go further still and love our identity in this Unity, but let us forget all things else, and remember nothing but this Unity, this infinite Unity— God alone. This expression—unity—is very enlightening. It will make us cut off all multiplicity, all superfluity and will be very efficacious in inducing us to give our whole minds to God and to discover all that He desires from us. We shall find in it treasures of grace, of light, of innocence, of holiness and of happiness.

IV.—*Conduct after Faults.*

Concerning our conduct after having committed faults.

1st. Endure with humility before God the humiliation of your faults. After having been unfaithful to grace and after accidental failings remember always that you are nothing and have a holy contempt of yourself. This is the great advantage that God allows us to gain even from our faults.

2nd. Fear, especially if carried to excess after whatever fault you may have committed, proceeds from the devil. Instead of giving in to this dangerous illusion use every effort to repel it, and cast uneasiness away as you would cast a stone into the depths of the sea, and never dwell upon it voluntarily. However, should this feeling, by God's permission, be stronger than the will, then have recourse to the second remedy, which consists in allowing ourselves to be crucified in peace according as God permits and as the martyrs abandoned themselves to their tortures.

3rd. What is said about the fears that go with conspicuous faults applies equally to that feeling of uneasiness and distress which proceeds from constant little infidelities. This oppression of the heart is occasioned also by the devil. Despise and combat it as if it were a real temptation. Sometimes, however, God makes use of this anguish and excessive terror that certain souls suffer in order to purify them and make them die to themselves. If it is impossible to succeed in driving them away, the only remedy left is to endure this interior crucifixion peacefully in a spirit of absolute resignation to the divine will. This is the way to regain the peace and calm of a soul truly resigned to the will of God.

4th. The fears roused about the recitation of the Office are nothing but a mere temptation because actual attention is not necessary. In order that prayer may have all its merit it is sufficient to make it with virtual attention which is nothing more than an intention to pray well formed before beginning, and this, no distraction even though voluntary can recall. So you can say the Office quite well while at the same time enduring continual involuntary distractions, as the trouble caused by these distractions is the best proof that the wish to pray well is heartfelt; it is also a sign that the wish is genuine. Therefore this wish makes the prayer a good and true prayer. Although hidden from the soul on account of the trouble occasioned by these distractions the good intention, nevertheless, exists and is not hidden from the sight of God who gives us a double grace, first in hearing our prayers as He does all prayers rightly made, and then in concealing this from us in order that we may be mortified in everything, and on all occasions.

V.—*Temptations and Trials.*

On temptations and interior trials. Addressed to Sister Anne Marie-Thérèse de Rosen, confidante of the inmost thoughts of Madame de Lesen, through whom the latter communicated with Fr. de Caussade.

1st Principle. In the eyes of God violent temptations are great graces for those souls which by them suffer an interior martyrdom; they are the great battles in which great victories have made great saints.

2nd Principle. The keen pain and cruel torment endured by a soul attacked by temptations is a sure sign that it has not consented, at any rate, not with that full entire consent, that advertence and deliberation which constitute a mortal sin.

3rd Principle. During the darkness of these violent temptations the soul, fatigued and troubled as it must needs be, will commit many minor faults through weakness or negligence, surprise or thoughtlessness; but I maintain that in spite of these faults it merits more and is more pleasing to God and is truly better fitted for the reception of the Sacraments than ordinary persons, who, favoured with sensible devotion, have hardly any struggles to endure, nor any violence to do to themselves. The virtues of the former are much more solid having passed, and still passing, through such severe trials.

4th Principle. Whatever sins people who are tempted may have committed in the past, if for some years they have been firm and have given no voluntary consent, they will make the more progress in the ways of God the more humble they are rendered by these temptations, because humility is the foundation of all good.

5th Principle. Most people, not much advanced in the ways of God and of the interior life, set no value on any operations but those that are sweet and evident to the senses. It is certain, however, that those operations that are most humiliating, afflicting, and crucifying, are most calculated to purify the soul and to unite it intimately with God. Also, all masters in the spiritual life are agreed in recognising that more progress is made in patient endurance than in action.

6th Principle. As God converts, proves, and sanctifies seculars by temporal afflictions and adversities, so He usually converts, proves, purifies and sanctifies religious by spiritual trials and interior sufferings a thousand times more grievous ; such as dryness, weariness, loathing, sinkings of the heart, spiritual despondency, humiliating temptations, violent and continual, excessive fears of being in mortal sin, terrors about His judgments and fear of reprobation. If, as spiritual books, preachers, directors of souls and good Christians aver, incessant afflictions are necessary for people in the world, and that without them many would be lost ; why not say the same on interior crosses without which a multitude of Religious would never arrive at the perfection of their state ? Experience shows daily that the most ordinary way by which God conducts the religious whom He most loves is that of greater interior trials ; whereas, in regard to seculars who are dear to God, it is by the way of temporal adversity. Therefore we who preach patience, submission and a loving resignation in their troubles to seculars, ought in our own trials to apply the same rule to ourselves that we know so well how to give others. Do not interior crosses come also from God ? Are they less mortifying, and, therefore, less salutary ? Does God demand less submission from us, and is our patience less pleasing to Him ?

7th Principle. By the effect of His merciful wisdom, and to keep His elect in a state of dependence on His grace, in a more complete abandonment to His mercy, and in a state of greater humiliation, God hides from them nearly all the interior operations of His divine Spirit, the holy dispositions He accords them, the good desires He inspires, and the infused virtues with which He has enriched them. And for this purpose what are the means He employs ? Let us pause to admire His wisdom and goodness. He makes use of the continuance and violence of temptations, of the trouble they cause in the soul, and the fear of having yielded to them. He hides the great virtues these souls acquire and the great victories they gain by allowing them to suffer slight defeats ; and the ardent desire they have to make worthy communions by the fear of having made bad ones, their fervent love of God by their fear of being wanting in love for Him. Whereas they feel the greatest horror at the smallest faults He allows them to be saddened by the continual imperfections they imagine themselves to commit. He permits them to think all their good works badly done, and that they always give way to the first stirrings of all their passions, while, all the time they are gaining the victory.

Nevertheless, as God, in keeping them in this state of humiliation and abandonment, does not wish to deprive them of all consolation and confidence during their trials, He makes known their state to enlightened directors, and if these souls are simple and obedient they may be assured of never being deceived. From the foregoing principles we can easily derive light in the doubts which occasionally assail us as regards communion and the fulfilment of other duties.

First Rule. The fear of communicating should never deter us, especially if our confessor enjoins it. God does not usually allow him to be deceived. Even if that should happen the penitent cannot be deceived in submitting, nor commit sacrilege, because blind obedience given in good faith to a director can never lead us astray in the sight of God. Should these sufferings and temptations become redoubled after communion, instead of preventing the fruit of it, if endured peacefully and with humble resignation united to an abhorrence of evil, it does but increase it. This abhorrence is made sufficiently apparent by the pain and martyrdom these temptations cause, which those who really give way never experience. Books that treat of the effects of communion addressed to the generality of the faithful only speak of the ordinary effects, but there are many particular cases where quite contrary effects are experienced. Then communion produces a much more precious fruit, for, while the vehemence of the temptation increases with a lively sense of weakness, it serves to augment our merit and to develop in our hearts feelings of the most profound humility.

Second Rule. Violent efforts to prepare for Communion are only pleasing to God in principle, but the result is disappointing because the soul becomes troubled and harassed. The intensity of these efforts must be moderated; everything that has to do with God, or the things of God should be done sweetly, tranquilly, and without effort. The best preparation for Holy Communion in this sad state is to endure patiently and with resignation this interior martyrdom. Preserve at any cost the peace in which God dwells and in which He is pleased to work. It is not grace but self-love that makes you keep away from Communion in order to escape the tortures and agonies that the soul endures by God's permission, to destroy in it this same miserable self-love. Go then without fear and even with a kind of joy to bear these interior operations that are so purifying and so sanctifying. The most wonderful good effects will be experienced eventually; effects that God hides from the soul at the time for its good. Therefore bear yourself as a criminal in His presence, and as a victim of His merciful justice. This is the best attitude for a soul in this state, adopting any other it would never find peace. This apparent destitution and abandonment has but one aim, which is to increase self-distrust and to compel the soul to cast itself with greater confidence into the arms of God. It sees no other help and even that it cannot see. Faith and faith alone must suffice without any other support. The sensitive part of the soul can do nothing to affect the will, and God expects nothing from it but the free choice of the will which has complete mastery over its acts. The best disavowal of the temptation is the extreme horror of its attacks. No good can be attained by making a multitude of acts, these would only serve to trouble and fatigue the soul. It had best keep to the following act which comprises all that is required of it. " Lord, You are all-powerful and goodness itself, it is for You to defend me and to preserve me from all evil, that is beyond my power. I accept this suffering for love of You, only keep me from all sin." Afterwards let it remain in peace in the midst of the storm. It will find itself strengthened without knowing how by the hidden hand of God.

Third Rule. The fact of being incapable of sustained thought, or of producing acts in prayer need not sadden the soul ; for the best part of prayer and the essential part is the wish to make it well. The intention is everything in God's sight either for good or evil ; now this desire it has to the extreme of anxiety— therefore it is only too keen, and has to be moderated. The soul must be kept peaceful during prayer and end prayer in peace. Instead of making so many resolutions let it be content to say : " My God make me perform such and such a good action' avoid such and such a bad one, because I am unable of myself to do anything. I feel my weakness too much, and my past experience teaches me that without You I can do nothing, and that if You do not act in me by the power of Your grace nothing will be effected." For directing the intention the soul abandoned to God need not make many acts, neither is it obliged to express them in words. The best thing for it is to be content to feel and to know that it is acting for God in the simplicity of its heart. This is making good interior acts ; they are made simply by the impulsion of the heart without any outward expression, almost without thinking ; just as worldly people without avowing it have but one end in everything—which is the satisfaction of their sensuality, their avarice, or their pride ; God seeing their intention which is hidden in their own hearts will punish them for it. The chief principle of the spiritual life is to do everything, interior as well as exterior, peacefully, gently, sweetly, as St. Francis of Sales so often recommends. The moment we desire to form an act, it is already formed and held as accomplished, because God sees all our desires, even the first movements of the heart. Our desires, says Bossuet, are, with regard to God, what the voice is with regard to men, and a cry

from the depths of the heart, even unuttered, is of the same value
as a cry sent up to Heaven. For the rest, all the acts made
in a state of the greatest aridity are usually better and more
meritorious than those that are accompanied by sensible devotion. Forebodings about the future should not be indulged in
except with due submission and resignation to the holy will of
God, and this practice ought to have for aim, not so much the
making of formal acts as the keeping of our hearts in a certain
habitual state of readiness by which it seems to say to God every
moment and in every circumstance, "Fiat, fiat! Yes, I desire
and accept all, only preserve me from all sin. Yes, my heavenly
Father, always, yes." This "Yes," uttered with all the heart
contains the greatest acts, and expresses the greatest sacrifices.

Prayer.

Prayer of the Rev. Fr. de Caussade to obtain holy abandonment to the divine will.

Oh my God when will it please You to give me the grace
to remain habitually in this union of my will with Your adorable
will, in which, without uttering a word all is said, in which all is
accomplished by allowing You to act, in which one's only occupation is that of conforming more and more entirely to Your
good pleasure; in which, nevertheless, one is saved all trouble
since the care of all things is confided to You, and to repose in
You is the only desire of one's heart? Delightful state, which,
even in the absence of all sensible faith, affords the soul an
interior joy altogether spiritual. I desire to repeat without
ceasing by this habitual disposition of my heart, "Fiat," yes,
my God, yes, all that You please, may Your holy will be done
in all things. I renounce my own will which is very blind,
perverse, and corrupt in consequence of its wretched self-love,
the mortal enemy of Your grace, of Your pure love, of Your
glory, and of my own sanctification.

Prayer to be said in temptation :

Oh my God! preserve me by Your grace from all sin, but as
for the pain by which my self-love is put to death, and the
humiliations which crucify my pride, I accept them with all my
heart; not so much because they are the effects of your justice,
but as benefits of your great mercy. Have pity on me then,
dear Saviour, and help me.

Second Part

LETTERS ON THE PRACTICE OF ABANDONMENT TO DIVINE
PROVIDENCE.

FIRST BOOK.

ON THE ESTEEM FOR AND LOVE OF THIS VIRTUE.

LETTER I.—*Happiness and Peace of Abandonment.*
To Sister Elizabeth Bourcier de Monthureux.
The happiness and peace of a soul entirely abandoned to God.
—Perpignan, 1732.

Madame and very dear Sister. You do well to give yourself
up entirely and almost solely to the excellent practice of an
absolute abandonment to the will of God. In this lies for you
all perfection, this is the straight path leading most quickly and
surely to a profound and unchangeable peace; it is also a secure
safeguard to preserve this peace in the depths of the soul even
in the midst of the most violent storms. Far from doing it
harm, these storms will serve infallibly, not only to increase
its merits, but also to strengthen more and more this union of
the created will, with the divine will, and it is this which renders
the peace of the soul unchangeable. Oh, what happiness! what
grace! what a certainty as to the life to come, and what unalterable peace does she possess who belongs to God alone, who has
no being out of God; who has no other support, no other help,
no other hope but God alone.

What a beautiful letter one of your Sisters has written to me
on this subject! She says that for a whole month this one
thought consoled, sustained and encouraged her so strongly
that instead of reluctance to practise this virtue, she felt it a
source of peace, and of an inexplicable joy. It seemed to her
that God took the place of director, of friend, and willed to be
all things to her Himself. The more we become accustomed to
these thoughts, the more settled will be our peace; and the fixed
determination to seek God only, and to unite our will to His,
is, in the best sense of the word, that " goodwill " to which peace
has been promised.

How can created things trouble a soul which neither desires
nor fears them? Let us endeavour to arrive at this state and
then our peace will be firmly established. Let us imitate the
holy Archbishop of Cambray who said of himself, " I endure all
until the worst comes to the worst, and then, finally, I find
peace in complete self-renunciation."

LETTER II.—*A Short Way to Perfection.*

This abandonment is the shortest way to arrive at perfect love and perfection.

———

Your letter, my dear Sister, put me in mind of the Gospel, where we see a young man approaching our Lord to ask Him the way to eternal life. Our good Master replied that he should keep the commandments, and when the young man answered that he had kept them faithfully from his youth, our Lord said, " If you would be perfect, go, sell all that you have and give to the poor, and come, follow Me." Your request is exactly the same as that of the young man. You want me to show you the shortest and surest way to attain perfection which is the fulness of life eternal.

If I did not know you as I do I should answer that the first thing to do is to keep your rule, because the rule is to every Religious the only sure road to perfection. But I am aware that you have kept it with scrupulous fidelity for a long time : therefore, what you wish to learn at present is by what particular practice a Religious who faithfully fulfils all her duties can arrive at a high degree of sanctity. To this question, my dear Sister, my reply will be exactly similar to that of our good Master. If you would be perfect, divest yourself of your own views, of all high notions of yourself, of studied elegance, of all reflexion of your own conduct ; in fine, of all that you can call your own, and give yourself up without reserve and for ever to the guidance and good pleasure of God. Abandonment, yes, entire, blind, absolute abandonment ; this, for souls circumstanced as you are is the height and the whole of perfection, because perfection consists in perfect love, and because for you the practice of abandonment is another word for the practice of pure love.

It is true that love, even the purest, does not exclude in the soul the desire of its own salvation and perfection ; but it is equally incontestable that the nearer the soul approaches the perfect purity of divine love the more its thoughts and reflexions are turned away from itself and fixed on the infinite goodness of God. This divine goodness does not compel us to repudiate the happiness it destines for us, but it has every right, doubtless, to be loved for itself alone without any reflexion on our own interests. This love which includes the love of ourselves but is independent of it, is what theologians call pure love, and all agree in recognising that the soul is so much the more perfect according to the measure in which it habitually acts under the influence of this love, and the extent to which it divests itself of all self-seeking, at any rate unless its own interests are subordinated to the interests of God. Therefore total renunciation without reserve or limit has no thought of self-interest—it thinks but of God, of His good pleasure, of His wishes, of His glory; it neither knows, nor desires to know aught else. Far from making its own interests a reason for its love, the soul, truly detached, generously accepts and embraces all that tends to annihilate them; darkness, uncertainty, weakness, humiliations! all these things give it pleasure directly it perceives that it so pleases the Beloved, because the pleasure and satisfaction of its Beloved form all its own pleasure and satisfaction. It neither has a will, nor a desire, nor a life of its own but is completely lost, engulfed, and, as it were, annihilated in the depth of the dark abyss of the will of Him whom it loves.

I could tell you of souls known to me, which, having crossed this terrible pass of total abandonment, and thrown themselves into the deep abyss of the incomprehensible will of God, could not refrain from crying out in a transport of joy and holy confidence, "Oh! will of my God! how infinitely holy, just, and adorable it is, and still more lovable and beneficent. If it be entirely accomplished in me, I shall infallibly find true satisfaction in this life and eternal happiness in the next. Infinite mercy could not permit anything which did not tend to the greater good of His poor creatures. These only can be lost by the perversion of their own will, and by preventing the accomplishment of those designs which are always holy and most merciful. Give me then, oh my God, the grace to destroy by complete detachment this foolish resistance, and henceforth be assured that Your holy will shall be done in me; while I shall be equally assured of salvation and perfection."

LETTER III.—*Peace in Turmoil.*

To Sister Marie Thérèse de Vioménil. To be applied to herself.
Profound peace can be enjoyed in this abandonment even amidst the bustle of business matters.—Perpignan, 1740.

What I have always feared has come to pass. I have no power to refuse a charge that is contrary to all my predilections and for which I do not believe myself to have any aptitude. In vain have I groaned, prayed, implored, and offered to remain all my life in the vicariate of Toulouse: I have been compelled to make the sacrifice—one of the greatest of my whole life. But now I see plainly the hand of Providence. The sacrifice having been made and reiterated a hundred times God has taken from me all my former repugnance, so that I left the mother-house, which you know how much I loved, with a peace and liberty of spirit which astonished even myself. More still! When I arrived at Perpignan I found a large amount of business to attend to, none of which I understood; and many people to see, and to deal with; the Bishop, the steward, the king's lieutenant, the Parliament, the garrison staff. You know what horror I have always entertained for visits of any sort, and above all for those of grand people. Well! none of these have given me any alarm; in God I hope to find a remedy for everything, and I feel a confidence in divine Providence which enables me to surmount all difficulties. Besides this I enjoy peace and tranquillity in the midst of a thousand cares and anxieties, such as I should have imagined ought naturally to overwhelm me. It is true that what most contributes to produce this great peace is, that God has rendered my soul impervious to fear, and I desire nothing for this short and miserable life. Therefore, when I have done all in my power or that I felt before God that I ought to do, I leave the rest to Him, abandoning everything entirely and with my whole heart to divine Providence, blessing Him beforehand for all things and wishing in all, and above all, that His holy will may be done because I am convinced by faith and by numerous personal experiences that all comes from God, and that He is so powerful and such a good father, that He will cause everything to prosper for the advantage of His dear children. Has He not proved that He loves us more than life itself since He has sacrificed His life for love of us? Therefore, as He has done so much for love of us, are we not convinced that He will not forget us? I entreat you, then, not to worry about me and my affairs. Do the same that I have constrained myself to do. Directly I have taken measures before God and according to His will I leave all the rest to Him, and look to Him for success. I wait for this success with confidence, but also in peace; and whatever takes place I accept, not for the satisfaction of my impatient desires, but keeping pace with divine Providence, who rules and arranges all for our greater good, although generally we do not understand any of His ways. And how can we dare to judge Him, poor ignorant creatures as we are, and blind as the moles that burrow underground.

Let us accept all from the hand of our good Father and He will keep us in peace in the midst of the greatest disasters of this world, which pass away like shadows. In proportion to our abandonment and confidence in God will our lives be holy and tranquil. Also where this abandonment is neglected there can be no virtue, nor any perfect rest.

You were wrong in being surprised that I was not so at the views and plans of N., for, besides that nothing surprises me in this life, you ought to know my way of always looking at the best side of things, and setting everything in a favourable light as St. Francis of Sales advises. This fortunate habit protects me from danger, and somehow makes it impossible for me to think badly, to judge harshly, or to speak uncharitably of anyone, whoever he may be.

I strongly advise you to adopt it; it will greatly contribute to the preservation of the peace of your soul, and the purity of your conscience. Believe me, and sacrifice all human feelings, consoling yourself for all by abnegation and confidence in God alone, Who alone can fill the place of all else.

LETTER IV.—*Liberty of Spirit*.

My dear Sister,

I am touched at your wish to share in my trials, but I am happy in being able to reassure you. It is true that, at first, I felt a keen pain at finding myself loaded with a multitude of business affairs and other cares quite contrary to my attraction for silence and solitude; but notice how divine Providence has managed about it. God has given me the grace not to attach myself to any of these affairs, therefore my spirit is always at liberty. I recommend the success of them to His fatherly care, and this is why nothing distresses me. Things often go perfectly, and then I return thanks to God for it, but sometimes everything goes wrong and I bless Him for that equally and offer it to Him as a sacrifice. Once this sacrifice is made God puts everything right. Already this good Master has, more than once, given me these pleasant surprises. As regards having time to myself, I have more here than elsewhere. Visits are rare now, because I only go where duty obliges me, or necessity calls me. The Fathers themselves knowing my tastes, soon left me alone, and as they are aware that I do not act in this way out of pride or misanthropy, they do not take exception to my conduct, and indeed many are edified by it. Nevertheless I am not quite so dead as you seem to think, but God has given me grace not to care how discontented people are with me for following my own bent. It is He alone whom we ought to have any great interest in pleasing; as long as He is satisfied that is enough for us all, other things are a mere nothing. In a short time we shall appear before this great and sovereign Master, this infinite Being. Alas! of what avail will it be to us then for eternity to have done anything except for Him and inspired by His grace, and His holy Spirit? If one became more familiarised with those simple truths, what repose would not our hearts and souls enjoy during this present life? From how many idle fears, foolish desires and useless anxieties should we not be delivered; not only concerning

I

this life, but also the next. I assure you that since my return
to France I begin to look forward more than ever with great
peace and tranquillity to the end of this sad life. How could
I experience aught but joy at seeing the end of my exile
approaching ?

LETTER V.—*Recourse to Providence.*

To the same Sister.—Perpignan, 1741.

I am constantly experiencing here the action of divine Providence, for no sooner do I make a sacrifice of everything to Him
than He rectifies and makes it all turn out for the best. When I
find myself at the last resource I place all my needs in the hands
of that good Providence from whom I hope all things. I have
recourse to Him always. I thank Him without ceasing for all,
accepting all from His divine hand. Never does He fail those
who put their whole trust in His protection. But how do people
usually act ? They substitute themselves, blind and powerless
as they are, for that divine Providence infinitely wise and infinitely good. They build on their own efforts and thus withdrawing themselves from the ruling of divine love they deprive
themselves of the helps they would have received had they kept
within its shelter. What folly ! How can we doubt that God
understands our requirements better than we do ourselves,
and that His arrangements in our regard are most advantageous
to us although we do not comprehend them ? We might make
use of the small amount of sense we possess to decide that we will
allow ourselves to be guided by that sweet Providence even
though we cannot fathom the secret activities it employs, nor
the particular ends it desires to attain. Should you remark
that if it is sufficient for us passively to submit to be led then
what about the proverb, " God helps those who help themselves " ?
I did not say that you were to do nothing—without doubt it is
necessary to help ourselves ; to wait with folded arms for everything to drop from Heaven is according to natural inclination,
but would be an absurd and culpable quietism applied to supernatural graces. Therefore while co-operating with God, and
leaning on Him, you must never leave off working yourself. To
act in this way is to act with certainty and consequently with
calmness. When, in all our actions we look upon ourselves as
instruments in the hands of God to work out His hallowed
designs, we shall act quietly, without anxiety, without hurry,
without uneasiness about the future, without troubling about
the past, giving ourselves up to the fatherly providence of God
and relying more on Him than on all possible human means.

In this way we shall always be at peace, and God will infallibly turn everything to our good, whether temporal or eternal.

LETTER VI.—*Alone with God.*

To the same Sister. Abandonment ameliorates the wearisomeness of solitude.

My dear Sister,

You are giving yourself unnecessary trouble about me. You have persuaded yourself that I look upon the isolation in which I live as a misfortune, whereas this is far from being the case. Every day I bless God for this happy stroke of His providence. I learn by it to die to all things in order to live to God alone. I was not so shut away at ——. There, many events both within and without kept me up, and made me feel alive ; now, there is nothing of that kind. I am in a veritable desert alone with God. Oh ! how delightful it is ! Great interior desolation is joined to this exterior solitude. However painful to nature such a state may be, I bless God for it because I have no doubt that it is good for me. It is a universal death to all feeling even about spiritual matters, a sort of annihilation through which I must pass in order to rise again with Jesus Christ to a new life, a life all in God, a life stripped of everything, even of consolation, because in that the senses take part. God wishes to leave me destitute of all outward things, and dead to all to live only to Him. May His holy will be done in all things, and for ever ! This is the strong pillar to which we must remain firmly fastened, this is the solid immovable foundation of all our perfection. You see, my good Sister, how little I require your compassion, since the subject on which you pity me most is precisely the subject of my joy. I must own, however, that the extreme solitude in which I found myself here so suddenly did not at first appear at all pleasant to me except in the superior part of my soul, but very soon my whole soul participated in it. Once more have I learnt by experience that we cannot do better than to follow step by step the course appointed by divine Providence. That is my great attraction, and more than ever am I resolved to devote myself to it blindly, without reservations and in all things, such as places, employments, seasons, in fine for everything. For a long time I have contented myself with asking God for one single grace, which is that I may have no other desire than to please Him, and no other fear than to offend Him. If He gives me this grace I shall be rich indeed both for time and eternity. I wish for you as for myself, only this. What can one fear who abandons oneself entirely to God? Besides the peace of mind it brings we shall find our perfection therein. If greater merit is gained in sacrifice what can be more meritorious than the entire sacrifice of our own will even in those things that seem to be most reasonable and holy, to the fulfilment of the will of God alone? Let us then have no other employment, no other ambition but that of uniting our will to the most merciful will of God, and let us be well assured that this will be our salvation even when we imagine that all is lost.

LETTER VII.—*A Holy Community.*

The happiness experienced by a Community of Poor Clares in practising abandonment to God.

My dear Sister,

I have made a discovery here that has given me more satisfaction than anything else could have done. In this town of Albi there is a convent of Poor Clares of the Great Reform, entirely separated from the world, who take no dowry and live on daily alms. The Superior is the most saintly person I have ever encountered in my life. I felt beforehand a great interior drawing to have a share in their holy intercourse, and nearly all of them have told me that they felt the same about me. I believe that God intends to bestow some great graces on me through their holy prayers. They lead a very interior life and practise abandonment to God with a remarkable perfection. When I assured them that on every occasion that presented itself I would try to procure alms for them, they seemed to be quite scandalised and begged me to think only of their spiritual needs and to make them more detached and more holy by my instructions and prayers. You cannot imagine anything more wonderful than their union, candour, and simplicity. Impressed by their great austerities I asked them one day if such a hard life did not affect their health and shorten their lives. They replied that there were hardly ever any invalids amongst them, and that very few died young, most of them living to be over eighty. They added that fasting and mortification contributed to improve their health and to prolong life, which good cheer usually tended to shorten. I have never beheld such gaiety and holy joy anywhere else as among these good nuns. To please them I had to talk continually on spiritual subjects as they could not tolerate gossip and worldly news, but said " of what use is all that to us "? I assure you, you would be edified and very glad on my account of this fortunate discovery, for, although I have often visited this place before, I knew the Community only by name, and looked on the nuns as dead to all; buried and quite out of sight.

What a favour and consolation for me! I might add it is fitting also to praise and magnify God for the wonders He has worked in these souls.

LETTER VIII.—*Our Dependence on God.*

To Sister Marie-Anne-Thérèse de Rosen (1724).

Concerning motives for abandonment on account of the goodness and greatness of the divine Majesty.

My dear Sister,

Do not ask me for new ways of acquiring the friendship of God, and of making rapid progress in virtue. I know only one way which I have more than once explained to you, and of which my daily experience demonstrates more and more clearly the infallible efficacy. This secret is, abandonment to divine Providence. Bear with me for calling your attention to it once again, and do not grow weary, either, of learning what I do not weary of teaching you. I should like to cry out everywhere, " Abandonment! abandonment!" and again " Abandonment!" unbounded and unreserved; and for two good reasons.

1st. Because the greatness of God and His sovereign dominion over all, require that all creatures should bow before Him, that all should be cast down, and as it were annihilated before His supreme Majesty. There is no comparison between His infinite greatness and our nothingness. It is above all things, comprehends all things, absorbs all things in its immensity. Or, rather, it is all things since all things that have a separate exist-ence from the Divinity have received their being from Him in creation and still continue to receive it in their preservation which is creation renewed unceasingly. Thus the existence we have received from God remains, as it were, in the bosom of the Divinity and never leaves its service, but remains plunged and engulfed therein. God, then, is the author of all being, nothing is, nor lives, nor subsists, nor moves, but by Him, and in Him, He is Who is, by Whom and in Whom all exists, and Who is in all things.

Things, compared with nothingness, seem to have an existence, but, compared with God, they seem nothing; they only possess being and substance by the gift of God; while He alone exists of Himself, and owes nothing to any other than Himself. There-fore as everything belongs to Him, necessarily everything will return to Him that His supreme dominion may be glorified by all His creatures. Those creatures that have not the gift of

reason glorify Him according to their state in following with
complete exactness and perfect obedience the laws of their
nature; but He has a right to expect from His reasonable
creatures a glory far more worthy of Him; which results from
their voluntary abandonment. And what more just and noble
use could any reasonable creature make of its liberty than in
rendering to God all it has received from Him, and in offering
Him in advance all that may be added to it in the future?
Understand me thoroughly; the homage that God expects from
us He alone can give us power to render Him in giving us the
thought, the desire, and the will. Also if He gives us this grace,
and if we profit by it, far from taking the credit to ourselves we
ought to thank Him for it as the crown of all His other benefits.
The impulsion which prompts us to offer up this last thanksgiving is yet another grace, as well as the thought that projected
the act. Thus, each of our moments, each of our actions, in
increasing our debt, forms new ties and makes us depend more
entirely on the divine goodness. At this thought, our spirit,
our heart, our soul remain as though engulfed, lost, annihilated
in the profound abyss of this sovereign dominion.

Our merits, regarded in this light, far from inspiring us with
pride will pierce us with the idea of our own utter dependence,
which, as we see more clearly we shall understand better; and
we shall finish by arriving at the complete annihilation of our
entire being before God. Thus alone shall we be true, and shall
be before God in our proper state—that of nothingness. Thus,
also, shall we practise perfect abandonment. To keep oneself
always in this interior disposition is what Holy Scripture calls
" walking in justice—in truth," outside this state there is nothing
but falsehood and injustice towards God. Injustice because we
deprive Him of the glory that belongs to Him; falsehood because
we flatter ourselves in appropriating what can never belong to us.

2nd. The second motive to induce us to abandon ourselves
without reserve is, that, unless God receives from His creatures
the homage due to His infinite Majesty He cannot give free vent
to His infinite goodness. All that His creatures bring to Him
by a total renunciation He wills to return to them by a gratuitous
gift of His mercy; or rather, He repays infinitely more than they
have given Him, because in return for the gift of their limited
being He bestows on them His infinite riches. Therefore at the
bottom of this abyss of renunciation where we should expect
to find nothingness we find infinitude. What an exchange of the
divine liberality! What ingenuity of divine wisdom! What a
contrivance and surprise of the divine goodness!

LETTER IX.—*The Goodness of God.*

To Sister Marie-Thérèse de Vioménil.

Another fresh motive for abandoning ourselves to God.   His fatherly providence.

———

I do not understand your uneasiness, my dear Sister, nor why you take pleasure in tormenting yourself as you do about the future, when your faith teaches you that the future is in the hands of an infinitely good Father Who loves you more than you love yourself, and who understands what is necessary for you much better than you.   Have you forgotten that everything that happens is ordained by divine Providence ?   And if we recognise this truth how is it that we are not humbly submissive in every event both great and small to all that God wills or permits ?   Oh ! how blind we are when we desire anything other than what God wills !   He alone knows the dangers that threaten us in the future, and the helps we shall require.   I am strongly persuaded that we should all be lost if God were to grant us all that we asked for, and this is why, says St. Augustine, God out of compassion for our blindness, does not always hear our prayers, and often gives us the exact contrary to what we asked Him, as being in truth better for us.   Truly it seems to me that in this world nearly all of us are like people who in madness, or delirium, ask for exactly what will cause their death, and to whom it is refused out of charity, or in pity.   Oh my God ! if this truth were but understood, with what blind abandonment would we not submit to all the decrees of Your divine Providence !   What peace and tranquillity of heart should we enjoy about all things and in all things, not only as to outward events but also about the interior state of our souls.   Even if the painful vicissitudes through which God makes us pass should be in punishment for our unfaithfulness, we ought to say to ourselves, " God wills it by permitting it," and humbly submit.   We must then detest the offence and accept the painful and humiliating consequences, as St. Francis of Sales so often recommends.   Would that this principle, thoroughly grasped, could put an end to the troubles and anxieties that are so useless and so destructive of our peace of mind and spiritual progress.   Shall I never be able even with the help of grace to introduce into your soul this great principle of faith, so sweet, so consoling, so tranquillising ? " Oh my God ! " we ought to repeat, " may Your will be accomplished in me and never my own.   May Yours be accomplished because it is infinitely just and also infinitely advantageous to me.   I acknowledge that You can will nothing that is not for the greatest benefit to Your creatures as long as they are sub-

missive to Your commands.   May my wishes never be granted
if they do not agree perfectly with Yours, because in that case
they would be disastrous to me.   And if ever, my God, it happens
that either through ignorance or passion I should persist in
desiring things contrary to Your will, may I always be refused
or punished, as the effect, not of Your justice, but of Your
compassion and great mercy."

"Whatever happens," said St. Francis of Sales, "I shall always
side with divine Providence, even if human wisdom tears her
hair out with spite."   If you were more enlightened you would
judge very differently from the ordinary run of human beings;
then, too, what a source of peace and strength this way of looking
at things would prove to you.   How happy are saints! and
how peacefully they live! and how blind and stupid we are in
not accustoming ourselves to think and act as they do, but to
prefer living shut up in thick darkness which makes us wretched
as well as blind and guilty.   Let us then make it our study,
aim, and purpose to conform ourselves in all things to the holy
will of God, in spite of interior rebellion.   Even about this
rebellion we must acquiesce in the will of God, for it compels
us to remain always before Him in a state of sacrifice as to all
things; in an interior silence of respect, adoration, self-effacement, submission, love, and an entire abandonment full of
confidence to His divine will.

LETTER X.—*Continued Troubles.*

To the same Sister.

My dear Sister,

I am sorry that your troubles continue, but I should be much
more sorry if you refused to profit by them, at least in the way
of making a virtue of necessity.   Remember our great
principles:

1st.   That there is nothing so small, or so apparently indifferent which God does not ordain or permit, even to the fall
of a leaf.

2nd.   That God is sufficiently wise, and good and powerful and
merciful to turn even the most, apparently, disastrous events
to the advantage and profit of those who humbly adore and
accept His will in all that He permits.   Is there anything more
consoling in religion than these two principles?   When we know
too that our natural dislikes and rebellions, far from preventing
the merit of submission, do but increase it as long as this sub-

mission is sincere in the higher part of the soul ; when we know further that these fits of impatience and vexation which are only half voluntary, are the effect of frailty, and do not destroy our submission, but only slightly diminish its merit.

These imperfections are often useful to us by rendering us more humble, and preventing us from losing all our merit through a vain self-complacency. Do you recollect this wise saying of Fénélon ? " It is a great grace of God to be willing to suffer, not in a grand and heroic way, but quite humbly, and in small things because in this way we gain patience and become little and humble at the same time."

As for the grievous trials of which you speak, add them to your cross as an extra weight that divine Providence allows you to carry, and instead of one " Fiat," say two, then remain in peace in the superior part of your soul whatever storms and tempests rage in the inferior part. The latter resembles the base of a high mountain where bad weather is usually encountered, however fine and clear the sky is at the summit. Try then to keep yourself always on the summit in those serene heights above the thunderstorms and every disaster.

It seems to me that your thoughts dwell too much on creatures. As for me, thank God I see only Him in all things. Everything helps me to Him. Since it is He that has placed us where we are, dependent on those who afflict us, it is, therefore, on Him alone that we must depend. It is He alone, I am certain, who inspires or allows the actions of men. I will accept nothing that does not come to me from Him, will owe no obligation to any one but Him, will thank no one but Him alone. If you call to mind how little men contribute to the existing state of things you will see that it is divine Providence who manages everything in a manner singularly adapted for the welfare of those who submit to Him, and who disposes everything for their best advantage. God can produce occurrences, and arrange necessary circumstances as seems good to Him, may He be blessed for all, in all, and for ever.

I am aware that my direction is considered rather too simple, but what does that matter ? This holy simplicity hated by the world is, to me, so delightful that I never dream of correcting it. Everyone to his taste. I respect those who are wise and prudent, but content myself with remaining one of those poor, simple and little people of whom Jesus Christ speaks, and after His example St. Francis of Sales. Let us be sure that God arranges all for the best. Our fears, our activities, our urgencies make us imagine inconveniences where in reality they do not exist. Let us follow step by step the ways of divine Providence, and when we realize what is required of us let us desire that and nothing else. God knows much better than we do ourselves what is most suitable for us, His poor creatures. Our misfortunes and sufferings often result from the accomplishment of our own desires. Let us leave all to God and then all will go well. Abandon to Him everything in general : that is the best way, indeed the only way of providing infallibly and surely for all our real interests. I say " real " because there are false interests that lead to our ruin. The abandonment to divine Providence which I practise and counsel others to adopt is not so heroic nor so difficult as you seem to imagine. It is the centre of a solid peace, and in it I find an unchangeable repose, proof against the most trying events. Oh! how well repaid we are for the small and miserable sacrifices we make for God! And then, once made, there are no more to make, because we no longer have any other desires. We cannot entertain even a wish for ourselves apart from the will of our sovereign Master, nor without His permission. What a happy state both for this life and the next!

LETTER XI.—*Good Wishes.*

To the Sisters of the Visitation at Nancy (1732).

Mutual good wishes between souls who seek nothing but God alone.

My very dear Sisters,

Your good wishes for me are quite heavenly ; they are evidently dictated by the heart, but what a heart! One that is entirely spiritual and interior, which sets no value on anything but what is divine, and has no interests but those for eternity.

Profiting by such an example I return you a thousand good wishes of the same sort, and in the same spirit as yours, and particularly that God will be pleased to preserve and increase more and more : 1st. The love of solitude and silence which forms the spirit of recollection so necessary for the interior life ; 2nd. The spirit of peace and charity, of union, and of detachment and interior abnegation which preserves that sweet and tranquil peace in the soul, which is the true happiness of this present life and the foundation of the interior life ; 3rd. An attraction for the practice of the presence of God, and for heartfelt prayer, for these are the mainsprings of the spiritual life ; 4th. The sincere will to be all for God which incessantly renews the spirit of fervour ; 5th. An entire and perfect union of our wills with the will of God, which will make us contented with our spiritual poverty because God wills it. Thus we sacrifice our self-love however deep-rooted and hidden it may be.

These rules are indispensably necessary for certain souls who, although indifferent to all other things, yet afflict themselves about their interior miseries. In' the practice of them they will find peace. In this way all that is wanting to us will be supplied, all our miseries will be remedied, and our poverty enriched. For there can be no greater treasure in our souls than conformity to the will of God, submitting our own wills to His, even if it should be at the expense of those interests which are most dear to us and which we regard as most desirable. Since we ought to desire virtues only to please God, will it not be to wish to have them all in wishing to conform to the divine good pleasure, and with so generous and so perfect a conformity extending to all things with the sole exception of an offence against God?

I congratulate you with all my heart on the joy you feel in celebrating the anniversary of the foundation of your house, but most of all on the fact that your house was founded in the poverty of the Crib and in confidence in divine Providence. The virtues of your saintly first Sisters were built on this rich foundation and have helped to construct the edifice. Your virtues will, I hope, maintain it and bring it to perfection for the honour and glory of its divine Master who is its sole proprietor.

SECOND BOOK.

ON THE EXERCISE OF THE VIRTUE OF ABANDONMENT.

LETTER I.—*Some General Principles.*

To Sister Marie-Antoinette de Mahuet (1731).

On the principles and practice of abandonment.

My dear Sister,

Our Lord has given me something better for you than that which you desired, something that it did not occur to you to ask for. It is a summary of some general principles to guide your conduct in life, with an explanation of the easiest way of putting them into practice.

1st Principle. The mainspring of the spiritual life is a good will, that is to say, a sincere desire to belong to God entirely and without reserve ; consequently it is not possible to renew too frequently this holy desire in order to strengthen it, and to make it more lasting and efficacious.

2nd Principle. The firm resolution to belong to God should produce in you a determination to think only of Him, and this can be practised in two ways, first by accustoming yourself never voluntarily to entertain thoughts, or to reflect on subjects which do not concern God directly or indirectly as do the duties of your state in general, or in particular. The best way of dealing with idle thoughts is not to combat and still less to be anxious and troubled about them, but just to let them drop, like a stone into the sea. Gradually the habit of acting thus will become easy. The second way to think only of God is to forget every-thing else, and one arrives at this state by dint of dropping all idle thoughts, so that it often happens that for some time one may pass whole days without, apparently, thinking of anything, as though one had become quite stupid. It often happens that God even places certain souls in this state, which is called the emptiness of the spirit and of the understanding, or the state of nothingness. This annihilation of one's own spirit wonderfully prepares the soul for the reception of that of Jesus Christ. This is the mystical death to the workings of one's own activity, and renders the soul capable of undergoing the divine operation. This great emptiness of the spirit frequently produces another void even more painful—that of the will ; so that one has seemingly, no feeling, either for the things of this world, or even for God, being equally callous to all. It is often God Himself who effects this second void in the souls of certain people. One must not, then, try to get rid of this state, since it is a preparation for the reception of God's most precious operations, and is the second mystical death intended to precede a happy resurrection to a new life. This two-fold void must therefore be valued and retained. It is a double annihilation very difficult for pride and self-love to endure, and must be borne with the holy joy of an interior spirit.

3rd Principle. We must confine our whole attention to fulfilling as perfectly as possible the holy will of God to its full extent, abandoning everything else to Him, such as, the care of all our temporal and also our spiritual interests, as, our advancement in virtue. The practice of this double abandonment is, first—every time we feel in our hearts a desire, or a fear, or have ideas and form projects regarding our own interests or those of our parents and friends, to say to God, " Lord, I sacrifice all this ; I give up all my miserable interests to You. May all that You please, all that You wish, happen. However, as there may be occasions when it is reasonably necessary to think and to act, I beg You to give me the thought at the right time, and thus I shall do nothing but follow what You deign to inspire, and I accept in advance either good or adverse results." Having made this interior act we should let all our fears and desires drop like a stone, without troubling ourselves any more about them, being assured that God will give us, in His own good time, the thought and impulse to act according to His holy will and divine intention.

As for the practice of the second kind of abandonment which is that of progress in perfection, it is a most difficult subject very badly set forth by spiritual writers, and one about which most mistakes are made, mistakes that produce nothing but trouble, and retard our progress in the ways of God. Here is a very simple method given by Jesus Christ to St. Teresa when He appeared to her : " Daughter," He said to her, " never think of anything but how to please Me, to love Me, and to do My will, and I, on My side, will attend to all your affairs, both temporal and spiritual." To thoroughly grasp this lofty precept look upon yourself as one who has entered the service of a king, like Solomon for example, the greatest, wisest and best of kings. However little nobility of feeling, refinement of heart, good sense or ability such a person might possess, he would doubtless address his master in these terms, " Lord, since I know that You are a Prince, as good as You are powerful, as liberal as You are magnificent, I give myself to You without reserve ; I will serve You without knowing how much You will pay me by the day or the year, nor even at the end of my time. I promise to think

only of Your interests, and mine I leave to Your discretion, or
rather, to Your goodness and generosity." Often apply this very
imperfect and mean comparison to the great Master we serve
and be assured that if the great King would not endure to see
himself surpassed in liberality by one of his servants neither will
the all-powerful and infinitely good God allow Himself to be
outdone by His miserable creatures. The practice of this
principle and the consequences to be deduced from it are :

1st. An intense desire takes possession of me to acquire the
gifts of prayer, humility, sweetness, and the love of God. To
this I answer, " Do not let me think so much of my own interests ;
my business is to occupy myself simply and quietly with God,
to accomplish His will in all that He requires at present. That
is my task, all the rest I leave to God ; my progress is His business, as mine is to busy myself for Him and to obey His orders."

2nd. It occurs to me that I am still very imperfect, full
of faults and defects, infidelities and weakness ; when shall
I be freed from these miseries ? " By God's grace I have no
affection for my faults, I am determined to combat them, but
I shall only be freed from them when God pleases ; that is
His business ; mine is to hate these faults, and to make a point
of combating them with patience, sorrow and humility till it
shall please God to render me victorious."

3rd. I begin to think that I am so blind that I cannot see
my faults, even when I have to weep for them before God and
to confess them. I reply without hesitation, " But I wish to
know my sins, I no longer live in a state of voluntary dissipation,
I quietly employ a little time in self-examination." This is
all that God requires, " He will give me more light and knowledge
when He considers it necessary ; that is His business. I have
placed the affair of my spiritual progress entirely in His hands,
it is therefore sufficient for the present to accuse myself of the
daily faults that God reveals to me, and some sin of my past
life."

4th. It strikes me : Have I ever made a good confession ?
Has God forgiven me ? Am I in a state of grace, or not ?
What progress have I made in prayer and in the ways of God ?
I at once answer : " God has willed to hide all this from me to
make me abandon myself blindly to His mercy ; I submit,
and adore His judgments. I wish to know only that which He
desires me to know, and to walk in darkness if such is His will ;
it is His business to know my state, mine to occupy myself
about Him alone, to serve Him and to love Him as much and
as well as I can ; He will take care of all the rest, I depend upon
Him."

5th. But for a long time past I have asked Him for certain graces ; to obtain them I have begged the intercession of those powerful advocates the ever-blessed Virgin, Saint Joseph, the Holy Apostles and all the Saints in heaven, and it seems as if nothing will move Him : " He is the Master, may His will be accomplished in all things ; I desire neither graces, not merits, nor perfections beyond those it pleases Him to give me, His will is enough for me and shall always be the rule of my desires."

LETTER II.—*The Three Degrees of Virtue.*

To Sister Marie-Thérèse de Vioménil (1731).

A general plan of the spiritual combat.

" God has left man in the hands of his own counsel ; life or death, good or evil are before him, what he chooses will be given to him." By these words holy Scripture makes us understand that man is a free agent, and that his salvation depends on the good use he makes of his liberty. It is true that since the fall of man his will has become weakened towards good, and turned towards evil, but with the help of grace which never fails him, it is always in his power to strengthen his will towards good, although naturally so weak ; and to fortify it against evil towards which it is, unhappily, so much inclined.

There are three degrees of virtue which the liberty of our enfeebled will can practise only with great pain, and much difficulty. 1st. That virtue essential for salvation, the neglect of which constitutes a mortal sin. 2nd. That virtue enjoined by a less stringent precept the omission of which is a venial sin. 3rd. That perfect virtue that we cannot neglect without a diminution of merit.

All these inclinations which weaken in us the resolution to fulfil our essential obligations, such as, hate, revenge, anger, inordinate attachments, avarice, envy, etc., are so many sources of spiritual ruin. The same can be said, proportionately, of those inclinations which incite us to commit venial sin, or voluntary imperfections, because whoever neglects small faults will fall little by little into grave ones, says the Holy Spirit ; and to be lax in the pursuit of perfection in but one point will prevent the acquisition of it for ever. Therefore, every victory by which our will is strengthened in the practice of virtue is a sign of predestination and of salvation. Our principal aim, then, ought to be to fortify continually our will towards virtue, and to overcome our inclination towards evil. We have three means to assure and hasten the success of this undertaking.

The first is to make great sacrifices to God by overcoming all repugnance in that which costs us the most. The second is to make all those daily little sacrifices for which occasions are frequent and continual, and this with a constant generous and universal fidelity.

The third means and the greatest is prayer, but prayer that is humble, simple, and inspired by the Holy Spirit; because it is He, as St. Paul says, who teaches us to pray and who prays in us "with unspeakable groanings." The Publican is an excellent model of prayer: he prayed silently, with deep and humble compunction. The greatest sinners and the most imperfect can pray like him and thus from the depths of their misery will rise by degrees, if they remain faithful, to the highest sanctity.

LETTER III.—*The First Work of God in the Soul.*

To Madame de Lesen (1731).

On the first work of God in the soul.

I am not at all surprised at the effect of the first meditation on the great truths, and I thank our Lord for it, and congratulate you. You required these keen feelings, and I believe they are likely to last until they produce in you the spirit of compunction and of humility which should form the foundation of your spiritual structure, and the beginning of your spiritual infancy. The agitation which accompanied these feelings was too great, but if I am not mistaken, it was involuntary and perhaps necessary as an effect of divine justice. The same feelings when they recur will be quieter and more tranquil. I was aware before receiving your letter that God had given you great graces, and I guessed that you had not properly corresponded with them, and this I realise now better than before.

1st. Your soul is like a huge hall, quite bare, or at least very badly furnished.

2nd. It will never be a fit dwelling for our sovereign Lord if He Himself does not give and arrange the valuable furniture suitable for such a guest.

3rd. He will never make His arrangements nor bestow His gifts on your soul except in the silence of prayer. You have, therefore, only to keep the hall swept and clean with the help of grace, then let Him who takes care of the beautiful furniture with which it ought to be decorated, arrange it according to His own taste.

Do not meddle then without necessity in a work which your interference would spoil. Let it alone, and imagine yourself

a canvas on which a great master is about to paint a picture, and
arm yourself with courage because I foresee that it will take a
considerable time to pound and mix the colours, and then to lay
them on, arrange them and vary the tints.   You must keep the
canvas prepared and get it stretched and nailed to the frame ;
this is humiliation next to annihilation of self and an act of
resignation and total abandonment inasmuch as you lose your
own will in the will of God.

LETTER IV.—*Practice of Abandonment.*

To Sister Marie-Henriette de Bousmard, on the general
practice of abandonment.

You are quite right, my dear daughter, to say what you do
and it was the favourite maxim of St. J. F. de Chantal, "Not
so much talk, so much science, nor so many writings, but more
good practice."   In fact with regard to those souls who have
acquired the habit of avoiding all deliberate faults, and of
fulfilling faithfully all the duties of their state, all perfection
is contained in the exercise of a continual resignation to the
will of God in all things, of a complete abandonment to all the
arrangements of divine Providence whether exterior or interior,
at present or in the future.   A single "fiat," or, as St. Francis
of Sales said, "Yes, my heavenly Father, yes, always yes,"
said and reiterated by the habitual disposition of the heart
without even the necessity of pronouncing it interiorly, is the
short and straight path to the highest perfection, because it
is a continual union with the holy and adorable will of God.

To arrive so far it is not necessary to make a great deal of
fuss, only two things are necessary : 1st, To be profoundly persuaded that nothing takes place in this world either spiritually
or physically, that God does not will, or at least, permit ; therefore we ought no less to submit to the permissions of God in
things that do not depend upon us, than to His absolute will.
2nd, Believe firmly that everything that God wills or permits
will, according to the purpose of an all-powerful and paternal
Providence, turn always to the advantage of those who practise
this submission.   Resting on this two-fold assurance let us
remain firm and immovable in our adhesion to all that God
pleases to ordain in our regard.   Let us acquiesce in advance
in a spirit of humility, love and sacrifice, to all the imaginable
decrees of His providence, let us assure Him that we shall be
satisfied with all that contents Him.   It is not always possible
for us, doubtless, to feel this satisfaction in the inferior part of
our soul, but we will, at least, keep it in the higher part of the
spirit, in that highest point of the will, as St. Francis of Sales
puts it ; it will then be all the more meritorious.

K

LETTER V.—*Means of Acquiring this Practice.*
On the means of acquiring abandonment.

———

You speak truly, my dear Sister, and it is indeed the Spirit of God who inspired your remark ; one of the greatest obstacles to the reign of the divine Spirit in our hearts is our own miserable nature which recoils from the sort of captivity and death with which the holy abandonment enables us to purchase a share in the liberty and life of God.

But this same Spirit who has made you so well understand the evil, will assist you to apply a remedy for it. In a few words this is what you ought to do to arrive at pure love, and total abandonment. 1st, You must desire it ardently, and energetically will to acquire it, no matter at what cost. 2nd, Believe firmly and often say to God that it is absolutely impossible for you, left to yourself, to acquire such perfect dispositions, but that grace will make everything easy, that you hope for this grace through His mercy, and ask for it by and through Jesus Christ.

3rd, Humble yourself quietly and peacefully for as long as you are kept back from this holy captivity; do not be discouraged, but, on the contrary, protest to God that you are awaiting with confidence the moment when it shall please Him to grant you this decisive grace which will make you die to yourself to live a new life in Him, a life hidden with Jesus Christ our Saviour.

4th, If you are submissive to the inspirations of the Spirit of God you will beware of making your progress depend on the vividness and sensible sweetness of interior impressions. This divine Spirit on the contrary will make you set more value on operations that are almost imperceptible, because the more subtle and profound they are and the more withdrawn from the senses, the more divine they become. Then it is that you become more entirely for God, because you will tend to Him with your whole being and with all your powers, uniting yourself to Him without particularising anything, as every being seeks its centre. Be persuaded besides that you still have a great way to go. You will have to work and to grow for a long time, but concerning this as about all other things you ought to say " Oh my God, Your holy and most amiable will shall always be the exact measure of my desires however holy, just, or apparently perfect they may be. I desire neither grace nor sanctity but at the time appointed and in the precise degree You will, nothing more, nothing less. If all the Saints and holy Angels prostrated themselves before Your throne to ask You for a single degree more of grace or of glory than You have destined for me I should refuse it, because I prefer to remain exactly and simply, Oh my God, in the position You have been pleased to ordain for me." I implore you, and this is my last word, never to have, in any of your actions, any other motive than the pure love of God and His greater glory. At the same time you need not exclude motives of hope, and of fear, and whenever the Holy Spirit inspires you with these do not hesitate to entertain them, but pure love should reign in your heart above every other sentiment. You should desire, and very ardently, your salvation and perfection ; but, even in this desire have the glory of God at heart much more than your own happiness. Nothing is more likely than this habit of mind to enable you to make great strides in virtue, and great merit. The smallest actions inspired by this love are, beyond comparison, of more value than the greatest performed with other good motives. But do not forget that you will make the more certain progress the more pure love induces you to renounce yourself even in the smallest things. If it did not lead to this it would not be pure love.

Be carefully on your guard against the snares that the enemy will lay in your path to make you forsake your good intentions. Do not seek for, nor expect from creatures anything but forgetfulness and contempt, and may the joy of resembling Jesus Christ your divine Example make this contempt dearer to you than all the glory of the world. Let no occasion escape, however slight it may be, of perfecting in you this divine likeness, and after having faithfully profited by these slight trials humble yourself for not being judged worthy of greater ones.

LETTER VI.—*Rules for General Direction.*

To Sister Marie-Thérèse de Vioménil.

General direction.

My dear Sister,

1st. Do not burden yourself with vocal prayers besides those that are of obligation, but apply yourself especially to acquiring interior perfection and to mental prayer.

2nd. It is very useful to try and prevent faults by acts of penance, but it would be better still to endeavour to expiate them after having committed them, than to multiply your penances in advance without real necessity.

3rd. Moderate and supernaturalise your affection for those who are dear to you.

4th. In order to excite yourself to fervour profit by the good examples and conservations of spiritual persons; but do not ever show contempt for, nor give way voluntarily to any dislike of others.

5th. Do not be so much vexed with yourself for being so often at war with your miserable nature; heaven is worth all these combats. Perhaps they will soon end, and you will speedily gain a complete victory. After all, they pass away and our rest will be eternal. Remain then in peace and let your humility be always united to confidence.

6th. Profit by bodily infirmities to strengthen your soul by the spirit of resignation to the will of God, and of union with Jesus Christ.

7th. Be careful to die to yourself; to renounce your natural inclinations; to stifle on every occasion human passions and tenderness. This kind of mortification is most essential; it does not injure the health, and is more efficacious than corporal austerities in multiplying merits, and in realising the designs of God, Who desires you to belong to Him entirely and without reserve.

8th. Labour to profit faithfully but peacefully by all the different states through which it pleases our Lord that you should pass for His glory, and your own perfection.

9th. It is necessary that zeal for one's own advancement and for that of others under one's care should be earnest and energetic, but never restless, nor accompanied with anxiety and distrust.

10th. Apply yourself to becoming more and more interior and aspire to all the perfection of your holy state by a perfect regularity. Humble yourself unceasingly before God so that He may render you victorious over yourself. You have need of a very powerful assistance to overcome your sensitiveness, and to destroy the fastidiousness natural to you, before you die, because these defects are the result of your character and temperament. True, this consideration somewhat excuses the faults, and excites the good God to compassion for His poor spouse, but nevertheless you must continue to fight so that even if your miserable pride and self-love are not absolutely destroyed before your last hour, death will, at any rate, find you at war with them, and trying to destroy them. Your principal weapons should be divine love, an infinite gratitude for God's grace, complete confidence in Him and a profound contempt for yourself, but without discouragement, and in peace.

You will derive ever-increasing strength in Holy Communion, in prayer, in humility, sweetness, patience, obedience, mortification, and above all in interior abnegation.

11th. Illness and infirmities accepted in submission to the will of God with humble thanksgiving, and in union with Jesus Christ, are very useful to expiate the past and to weaken the old Adam ; they help also to make us die spiritually to all things before having to die naturally, which death in ending our transient ills will make us enter, let us hope, into the enjoyment of eternal happiness. As this kind of penance is sent to us by God Himself, and as we are thus unable to mortify ourselves exteriorly, we must make up for it by interior mortification, applying ourselves more earnestly to the destruction of self-love, pride, fastidiousness, and criticism of others, all of which are its bad fruits. Finally endeavour to become humble and simple as a little child for the love of our Lord, in imitation of Him, and in a spirit of peace and recollection. If God finds this humility in us He will prosper His work in us Himself. Persevere in being faithful to grace for the greater glory of God and for the pure love of Him. All consists in loving well, and with all your heart and in all your employments, this God of all goodness.

12th. According to our advance in the course of our earthly pilgrimage let us endeavour to increase in solid fervour, the perfection of our holy state, and the particular designs of God in our regard. When He grants us attractions and sensible devotion let us profit by them to attach ourselves more firmly to Him above all His gifts. But in times of dryness let us go on always in the same way, reminding ourselves of our poverty and also thinking that, perhaps, God wishes to prove our love for Him by these salutary trials.

13th. Let us be really humble, occupied in correcting our own faults, without reflecting on those of others. Let us see Jesus Christ in all our neighbours, and then we shall have no difficulty in excusing them as well as helping them and taking care of them. His example ought to be sufficient ; look at His patience with His disciples who were so rough and ignorant. Let us turn all our energies to glorifying God in ourselves and in those who think well of us. Let us live hidden in Jesus Christ and dead to all created things and to ourselves ; without this, Jesus Christ will not deign to dwell in us, at any rate, not in the way He aims at, which is in absorbing all our human life in His divine life. Besides we must bear with ourselves also out of charity as we put up with others, humbling ourselves and punishing ourselves for our faults as soon as possible. While praying for ourselves, let us also pray for sinners who are our brethren.

LETTER VII.—*Rules for Direction.*

To Sister Marie-Thérèse de Vioménil (1731), on the same subject. Rules, etc.

———

My dear Sister and very dear daughter in our Lord, may the peace of Jesus Christ be always with you.

1st. I thank God for all the good thoughts with which He inspires you. As long as you keep this good intention of belonging to God without reserve, resigning yourself entirely to His good pleasure, and fearing neither dryness, darkness, temptation, nor destitution, all will turn to your spiritual profit.

2nd. The fear of being mistaken about being at peace in the midst of interior troubles is very useless. What you unwittingly disclose to me proves that this peace is very real; it is the foundation of all else and a great grace which you must preserve at all costs. All the attacks and stratagems of the devil are aimed to make you lose it, or to diminish or disturb it ; but keep firm in faith and confidence through abandonment. Take care not to pledge yourself by vow to anything whatever.

3rd. To be completely severed from creatures in the intention and the affections is a great favour which infallibly leads to pure love and divine union.

4th. The secret presentiment of approaching death may come either from God or from the devil. If it detaches you more completely from all things, without disturbing you or creating discouragement and distrust, it comes from God; if not, it must be rejected, because all that comes from God has a good effect, and it is entirely from the effects that the spirit it proceeds from is discerned. All the repugnance that you feel is intended to detach you more completely from all human support, so that you may have none but God alone ; your interior practices about this are very good. But I am surprised that you have not yet learnt that when God permits this darkness all feeling for good disappears like the sun during the night. All that can be done then is to remain firm and peaceful, waiting for the return of the sun and the dawn of day when all will be as usual. I give you permisson to write one, two, three, or four letters during the year, and whenever, after imploring the help of God, you deem it necessary, and if I should think the same, I shall be very particular to reply to you.

———

LETTER VIII.—*Advice on Prayer.*

To Sister Marie-Anne-Thérèse de Rosen. Excellent advice on prayer, to souls called to a life of abandonment.

1st. Apply yourself to prayer by a simple glance at the subject, that is to say by a single apprehension of its object, by faith without any reasoning.

2nd. I advise you to pause longer on that which is most likely to humiliate you, and to destroy self-love. The more distressed you feel, and penetrated with a sense of your misery, the more disposed you will be to receive the gifts of God.

3rd. Do not be uneasy about distractions, but when you perceive them, collect your mind and, above all, your heart by an act of faith in the presence of God, and in a holy repose. If that does not succeed you can only resign yourself. The state of distraction is often a cross more meritorious than the prayer itself, for it unites our will with the will of God Who is all our good.

4th. The result of the prayer will prove its efficacy. Solid faith is incomparably better than faith that is sensibly felt, under its guidance the soul makes more rapid progress, and proceeds with greater certainty.

5th. Hear Holy Mass with great recollection, and give yourself up to a boundless confidence in the divine goodness, while relying on the merits of the divine victim, Jesus Christ.

6th. The way of dryness and aridity is greatly preferable to that of consolations, although it is painful. It is only in this way that solid virtue can be acquired; in the other way, the most apparently, perfect dispositions are subject to failure at the slightest breath of aridity or of temptation. God usually sends trials to those souls who have enjoyed for some time spiritual sweetness and consolation.

7th. When it pleases the divine goodness to make a soul advance in the way of pure love, fear makes no impression on it. As fear is the forerunner of love, perfect love casts out fear, as St. Augustine says, following St. John. Those who are charged with the guidance of such a soul should carry out the designs of God by conducting it in the ways of love and confidence. If the occasion arises where fear is necessary for the avoidance of evil, God will certainly bestow it. Let this soul continue then to love without troubling about other things, and above all let it avoid all anxiety and perplexity, for this temptation is more to be feared than any other by those who follow this way. One must then always recommend them to keep, at all costs, interior peace, and to reject as an envoy of hell everything which tends to disturb, or diminish it. For the rest, know that the most perfect, is that which is the most simple, and the most simple, is that which contains the least of our own, the fewest ideas, imaginations and reasonings ; in which one single feeling continues longer than the rest. The longer the feelings inspired by grace continue in the soul, the more will it become impressed with them, and the more easily will it act under their influence. That of divine love which contains in an eminent degree all other virtues should form its ordinary food : when it masters all the affections of the soul it will effect in it an enthusiasm and a sort of enchantment which will make it run in the ways of holiness.

LETTER IX.—*Danger of Delusion Explained.*

To Sister Marie-Anne-Thérèse de Rosen (1731), on the same subject. The danger of delusion in the prayer of recollection.

My dear Sister,

Always listen to that great interior Director, who alone can give light and strength to us in our necessities. Do not use books when He speaks interiorly. Let your main point be a holy repose in the divine presence ; never leave it, do not break the sacred silence unless God gives you an attraction for some holy and useful colloquy, after which re-enter your fort and sanctuary which is no other than recollection and interior silence in the presence and the sight of your Beloved. In Him alone, and in this simple and sweet repose in God will you find all light., courage, strength, sweetness, patience, humility, resignation, peace and rest for your soul. I wish you all this to the highest perfection. Do not be afraid of darkness and dryness in prayer ; when one knows how to unite one's will to the holy will of God, accepting all that He wills, one is safe and has everything. This is, according to St. Teresa, the most perfect prayer and the most perfect love. You did very wisely in explaining to the Rev. Fr. —— the subject about which you write to me. I have so much respect for his views that I should consider myself mistaken, if mine were opposed to his. I have always thought, with him, that no one ought to meddle with the prayer of recollection unless he be called to it, and also that this grace cannot be merited by good works, nor can anyone succeed in it by any effort of his own. I have only added, with Fr. Surin and other authors, that one can, indirectly and beforehand, dispose oneself to receive this great gift of heaven by removing obstacles, first by a great purity of conscience, secondly by purity of heart,

thirdly of spirit, and fourthly of intention which will carry a
soul very far on the road to it ; and that having so far disposed
oneself, one ought by short and frequent pauses, as if waiting
to listen, give free course to the interior spirit.

Will you read this to the Rev. Fr., or send him this little
paper if you are not able soon to see him to speak to ? Tell him
when you see him, I beg of you, that I consider him bound in
conscience to disabuse in my name all those persons whom he
considers to have been misled, and that I depend upon him in
this matter as I do not know whom it concerns.

But in order to proceed with all due discretion and the prudence
necessary, I beg him first to be good enough to consider these
two points. 1st, That he ought to certify himself of the fact
by gaining some knowledge of the interior state of the persons
in question, because only to hear about it at second hand does
not throw much light on a secret and altogether interior subject.
But it may be said that these persons are known to be very
imperfect and have been seen to commit many faults at which
others have taken scandal. My reply to this is the second
point. Experience in direction teaches us that beneath very
imperfect appearances God often hides great interior virtues
known only to Himself. Therefore I do not believe that these
persons can be accused of being misled and mistaken in their
manner of prayer, especially as it often happens that their faults
and imperfections are grossly exaggerated by a want of charity
or by still worse motives. I remember now that St. Teresa
said, speaking of herself, that this method of prayer was a subject
of suspicion in her ; and that what made it seem a mistake and
delusion of the devil was that the most enlightened persons
whom she consulted could not reconcile in their minds such a
gift of prayer with her conduct at that time ; that is to say,
with her eagerness to go to the parlour, to know, to see, and to
be seen, to chatter with relations and worldly acquaintance,
thus losing a great deal of time and neglecting her soul ; for she
herself tells us that this was, then, her state : " And this," she
adds, " is why all who knew me considered my prayer to be
nothing but delusion." With regard to this I have come across
directors who have had experience about it, and they said
that God sometimes gives this prayer, 1st, To great sinners
at the beginning of their conversion, in order that this work of
their conversion should be more speedily and completely effected.
2nd, To very imperfect souls to enable them to correct their
failings more easily and promptly. But what is added, and
what I believe to be very true and correct is, that it is extremely
rare to find this gift retained at the same time as faults, and
considerable imperfections, especially if these be habitual,

frequent, and recognised, without any efforts being made to correct them.

LETTER X.—*Delusions in Prayer.*

On the same subject.

This is my reply about the person in question. It seems to me that her prayer of recollection is more from the mind than from the heart. It is the opposite of what it should be, for in order that prayer be fruitful the heart should have a greater share in it than the intellect, in fact it is entirely a prayer of love ; the soul resting in God loves Him without the knowledge of that which it loves, nor how this love is produced in it. But the reality of it is manifested by a certain warmth it feels in the heart, by an irresistible attraction to this divine centre, which it seeks without seeing distinctly what it pursues, and to which it yields, and from which nothing can distract it. From this arises the great facility of this prayer which is a sweet rest for the heart, and continues without effort for as long as it is desired. Therefore, if the person of whom you speak experiences as a preliminary, a great exertion of the mind, it is a sign that her recollection is not yet what it should be. The remedy for this seems to me to be, 1st, When carried away by this great recollection to concentrate the attention on the movements and affections of the heart, as if to retain and enjoy this delightful repose ; there is such a charm about this feeling of sweetness and joy that it engrosses the whole attention of the soul, which thus understands better that it loves ; while the mind without effort, and almost without voluntary application, finds itself captivated by this feeling which is, as it were, the food of the heart. 2nd, If, notwithstanding all efforts to the contrary, the intensity of thought continues, forbid this person to spend more than two hours, at most, in prayer ; and during her reading, and at other times, tell her not to purposely try to get recollection, but only to give herself up to it when God impels her, remembering always to fix her attention interiorly on the affections of her heart, to enjoy in them, at leisure, this sweetness, delightful repose and interior peace. 3rd, Tell her always to employ a little time to examine how her prayer was made ; at its beginning, in its progress and at its conclusion ; that is to say, firstly, what form did the recollection take ? secondly, if it produced in her distinct thoughts and feeling, or, if this sweet sleep was too profound to enable her to remember anything ? thirdly, how she felt when this state ceased ; for example did it leave her in a state of great recollection, with a great desire to act rightly, to attach herself entirely to God, and to please her divine Master only ?   Let us be thoroughly persuaded that we can find God everywhere without the least effort ; because He is truly present to those who seek Him with all their hearts, although they may not be always aware of His presence.

Therefore whenever you are no longer occupied with created things so that you have ceased to think any more about them, know that your soul is then occupied by God, and in God without your knowledge.   And this is the reason : God, being that hidden and invisible object to which tend all the desires of a right heart ; from the moment it turns its desires away from creatures, they then find their natural centre, which is God ; and by continually dwelling in this centre they gradually increase until they become very distinctly felt and produce strong outbursts of love.   Therefore the true presence of God is, to speak plainly, but a kind of forgetfulness of creatures with an interior desire to find God.   You thus perceive in what consists the divine interior and exterior silence, so precious, so desirable, and so advantageous ; true earthly paradise in which souls who love God already enjoy a foretaste of heavenly happiness.

LETTER XI.—*The Impressions of the Holy Spirit.*

To Mother Louise-Françoise de Rosen (1735), on the practice of abandonment in the different states of the soul.

My dear Sister,

Peace in our Saviour Jesus Christ. When we are attentive and docile to the interior spirit, it guides us so surely that we very rarely make false steps. I commend, however, the wise precaution of occasionally explaining oneself to the priests of Jesus Christ in a spirit of self-distrust. God has so greatly blessed this humility in you that I was almost inclined to write only, " All is well, go on as you are doing." However, for your consolation I will add what God may inspire after a re-perusal of your letter. I admire what you say—" I do not care to speak, nor to write, nor to read much." This alone indicates a spirit usually well occupied interiorly ; and a good spiritual writer has said of such a one that without working it is well occupied. Another calls this happy disposition, holy leisure, a holy idleness, in which although apparently doing nothing, everything is done, in saying nothing, all is said.

1st. I find nothing but what is good in the three dispositions you experience alternately; firstly of faith, secondly of tastes and feelings, thirdly of subversion and suffering; but their value differs. The first is the most simple, the most certain, and is less favourable to the growth of self-love; the second is more pleasant and requires a great detachment from all taste and feeling even from that which is divine, so as to attach yourself solely and purely to God, as Fénélon expresses it. The third is painful, and often very crucifying, but then it is also the best, because all that mortifies the interior purifies it, and consequently disposes it for a more intimate union with the God of all purity, and of all sanctity.

2nd. Thanks to the goodness of God you behave very well in all these states, and have only to go on in the same way; but you explain yourself in a manner that might be misunderstood by those who have no experience of this state of prayer. You say that you do nothing; yet you must all the time be at work, otherwise your state would be one of mere laziness; but your soul acts so quietly that you do not perceive your own interior acts of assent and adhesion to the impressions of the Holy Spirit. The stronger these impressions are, the less is it necessary to act; you must only follow your attraction and allow yourself to be led quite calmly, as you so well express it.

3rd. Your way of acting in times of trouble and distress, gives me great pleasure. To be submissive, to abandon yourself entirely without reserve, to be content with being discontented for as long as God wills or permits will make you advance more in one day than you would in a hundred spent in sweetness and consolation. It is a good, beautiful and solid practice. Teach it to all, and especially to poor Sister N. Properly speaking she only requires this one point—and this constantly practised by her will sanctify her, and sweeten all her spiritual trials: with this single practice she will become a different being, as if she had been remodelled and transformed.

4th. Your total abandonment to God, constant and universal as it is, and practised in a spirit of confidence and of union with Jesus Christ doing always the will of His Father, is, of all practices the most divine and the most certain to succeed: try to instil it into everyone, especially the good Sister of whom I have just spoken.

5th. The grace and light which enable you to combat and to stifle the feelings of nature on every occasion of which you have told me, deserve to be especially retained. Care and fidelity in corresponding fully with these graces even on the smallest occasions will serve to increase them; but never expect to be free from feeling the first movements, they will help to keep

alive interior humility which is the foundation and guardian
of every virtue.

6th.   As to your ordinary faults you must know that directly
our imperfections are really displeasing to us, and that we are
sincerely resolved to combat them without exception, from that
moment there is no longer any affection for them in the heart;
and consequently no obstacle to our union with God.   Therefore
what we ought to work at with all our strength is, to diminish
the number of these faults and imperfections. If, however, we
fall again through frailty, surprise, or otherwise, we should at
once courageously rise again and return to God with the same
confidence as if nothing had happened, and having humbled
ourselves in His presence, beg His forgiveness without feelings
of vexation, anxiety, or agitation. Humility will supply for
the want of fidelity, and often makes good our faults with advantage to ourselves.   Finally should there be, with regard to your
neighbour, any little reparation to be made, never omit the
opportunity of generously overcoming pride and human respect
by making it.

7th.   When you experience, involuntarily, the first irregular
movements of any passion, give yourself time, before they are
stifled by the help of grace, to thoroughly recognise to what
lengths pride and passion would have carried you without such
help. In this way you will acquire by personal experience a
complete knowledge of that deep abyss of perversity into which
you, like so many others, would fall if God did not uphold you
It is by this practical knowledge, these oft-repeated feelings, and
frequent personal experiences, that all the saints learnt that
profound and heartfelt humility, self-contempt and holy hatred
of themselves of which we find so many proofs in the history of
their lives and which formed the most solid foundation of their
perfection.

8th.   With regard to your trials and temptations, I understand
from all that you tell me, that the Holy Spirit has so well regulated your thoughts, feelings and conduct in these matters,
both exteriorly and interiorly, that I have nothing further to
add. In the marks of esteem and friendship that are shown
to you without your own seeking, if they cause you annoyance
instead of pleasure, then the pain and trouble will prove their
own antidote.   There could not be anything but great merit
in suffering patiently in conformity to God's will and the arrangements of His providence and following the example of Jesus
Christ, suspicions, rash judgments, envy, jealousy, etc., without
attempting to clear yourself, except in so far as the edification
of your neighbour enjoins. When you are exposed to all sorts
of criticism and unjust accusations go on in your own way without

making any change in your conduct, according to the pleasure
of divine providence and keeping pace with His plans; this
is truly to live by faith alone with God in the midst of the bustle
and confusion of creatures. In such a condition exterior things
can never penetrate to the interior, and neither flattery nor
contempt can disturb the peace that you enjoy. This is to
live a truly interior life. As long as this state of independence
has not been acquired, virtues that have a most attractive
appearance are not really solid, but very superficial, and liable
to be overthrown by the faintest breath of inconstancy or contradiction.

9th. Be well on your guard against all these illusions which
aim at making you follow your own ideas, and prefer yourself
to others. The spirit of self-sufficiency and criticism of one's
neighbour seems to many persons a mere trifle; but it is nevertheless undeniable that this spirit is much opposed to religious
simplicity, and that it hinders a great many souls from attempting
an interior life. It is not possible, in fact, to begin this life
without the help of the Holy Spirit, who only communicates
Himself to the humble, the simple, and those who are little in
their own eyes.

10th. Your way of resisting all sorts of temptation; profound,
gentle, simple, and almost imperceptible as it is, is a pure grace
from God: keep to it; that simple look at God is worth infinitely
more than any other sort of act. The peaceful doubts you
experience after the temptation has ceased are caused by a chaste
fear which you must never lay aside; as for anxious doubts
born of self-love, they must be despised and driven away.
With regard to the rest, there is nothing easier to recognise,
and discover, than the deceits and illusions incident to the prayer
of faith, and of simple recollection; and that by the infallible
rule of Jesus Christ; the tree is known by its fruits. Therefore
all prayer that produces reformation of the heart, amendment
of life, the avoidance of vice, the practice of the evangelical
virtues and the duties of one's state, is a good prayer. Also
all prayer which does not produce these fruits, or which produces
their opposite, is a false prayer and produces the fruit of a bad
tree, even were it accompanied by raptures, ecstasies and miracles.
The paths that lead us to God are those of faith, charity and
humility, therefore all that makes us walk in these paths is
useful to us, and whatever leads us away from them is dangerous
and hurtful. This is the safest and most infallible rule to prevent
and reform all that is evil, all that is illusory, and it is within
everyone's power.

I greet, very cordially, your good Sister. Please tell her
from me to allow herself to be always guided by the interior

spirit, and thus to be ready, as she is, to abandon herself completely into the hands of God, equally content when He gives, or when He takes away, and with that apparent nothing that He leaves her ; as it pleases Him.   In this is all perfection and the true progress of a faithful soul.   How pleasing you must be to God in recommending so unceasingly to His spouses this holy abandonment which alone can unite them entirely to Him.

LETTER XII.—*Peace and Submission.*

On the practice of abandonment and the peace of the soul.

My very dear Sister,

May the peace of Jesus Christ be always with us, and in us, since God does not act freely except in peaceful hearts.   I rejoice, and congratulate you on the peace that our Lord gives you in the practice of an entire conformity of your will to the designs of His good providence.   This peace, as you know, is the foundation of the interior life for many reasons, but principally because it is the health and strength of the soul ; as trouble produces languor and weakness, acting on the soul in the same way that fever acts on the body.   In the second place, because agitation and anxiety in the soul are an obstacle to the hearing of the gentle voice and soft breathing of the Holy Spirit.   To keep yourself in this peace which will, I hope, continually increase, there is no better way than always to practise total abandonment, and that absolute resignation of which I have already spoken to you.   You will, without doubt, succeed, if you never lose sight of the great and consoling truth that nothing happens in this world but by the command of God, or, at least, with His divine permission ; and that, whatever He wills, or permits turns infallibly to the advantage of those who are submissive and resigned.   Even that which most disturbs our spiritual plans changes into something better for us.   Keep firmly by this great principle and the most violent tempests will not be able to trouble the depth of your soul, even though they may ruffle the surface by disquieting the feelings.

When, in prayer, you experience certain inclinations and a sweet repose of soul adn heart in God, receive these gifts with humility and gratitude, but without attaching yourself to them. If you liked these consolations for themselves you would compel God to deprive you of them, for, when He calls us to pray it is not to flatter our self-love, or to cause us to feel complacency in ourselves, but to dispose us to do His holy will, and to teach us to conform ourselves always more perfectly and in all things to it. When distractions and dryness follow consolations, you know how you ought to bear them, I mean, in peace, submission, and abandonment for as long as it pleases God to permit them to continue. You know, also, that the only hurtful distractions are those that are voluntary, therefore, all those that are displeasing do not prevent the prayer of the heart, and the desire. Do not ever force yourself to fight against these obstinate distractions, it is better and safer to let them alone, as one takes no notice of the various follies and extravagancies that, in spite of ourselves, pass through the mind and imagination. What has happened to you before will happen again ; God will cause you to experience after prayer what He has refused you at the time in order to make you understand that it is the effect of His grace alone and not of any effort or industry of yours. Nothing serves better to keep us in dependence on grace, and in a state of abjection in our own eyes : and this produces humility of heart and mind. During the day try to keep yourself united to God, either by frequent aspirations towards Him, or by the simple glance of pure faith ; or better still, by a certain calm in the depths of your soul and of your whole being in God, accompanied by a complete detachment from all the exterior objects of this world. God Himself will show you which of these three ways will best suit you to unite yourself to Him, by the attraction to it, the taste for it, and the facility in the practice of it which He will give you, for this union is in proportion to the degree of grace to which the soul is raised. Each of these states has its special attraction ; one must learn to know one's own, and then follow it with simplicity and fidelity, but without anxiety, uneasiness, or haste ; always sweetly and peacefully as St. Francis of Sales says.

LETTER XIII.—*Peace and Confidence.*

On the same subject.

What you tell me about the peace and tranquillity you experience has given me great pleasure. You must remember all your life that one of the principal reasons why certain souls do not advance is, because the devil continually throws them into a state of uneasiness, perplexity, and anxiety which makes them incapable of applying themselves seriously, quietly, and with constancy to the practice of virtue. The great principle of the interior life is the peace of the soul, and it must be preserved with such care that the moment it is attacked all else must be put aside and every effort made to try and regain this holy peace, just as, in an outbreak of fire everything else is neglected to hasten to extinguish the flames. Read, from time to time, the treatise on the peace of the soul which is to be found at the end of the little book called "The Spiritual Combat," and which the ancient fathers very truly called "the road to Paradise," to make us understand that the high road to Heaven is this happy peace of the soul. The reason of this is that peace and tranquillity of mind alone give great strength to the soul, to enable it to do all that God wishes, while, on the other hand, anxiety and uneasiness make the soul feeble and languid, and as though sick. Then one feels neither taste for, nor attraction to virtue, but, on the contrary, disgust and discouragement of which the devil does not fail to take advantage. For this reason he uses all his cunning to deprive us of peace, and under a thousand specious pretexts, at one time about self-examination, or sorrow for sin, at another about the way we continually neglect grace, or that by our own fault we make no progress; that God will, at last, forsake us, and a hundred other devices from which very few people can defend themselves. This is why masters of the spiritual life lay down this great principle to distinguish the true inspirations of God from those that emanate from the devil; that the former are always sweet and peaceful inducing to confidence and humility, while the latter are intense, restless, and violent, leading to discouragement and mistrust, or else to presumption and self-will. We must, therefore, constantly reject all that does not show signs of peace, submission, sweetness and confidence, all of which bear, as it were, the impression of the seal of God; this point is a very important one for the whole of our life. You ask me for some rules by which to regulate the thoughts of the mind during the day—to which I answer:

1st. That it is better to approach God and virtue by the affections of the heart than by the thoughts of the mind, and it is an important counsel to nourish the heart and make the mind fast; that is to say, to desire God, sigh after God, long for the holy love of God, for an intimate union with God, without amusing yourself with so many thoughts and reflexions. Therefore it is more useful to occupy yourself with the affair of belonging to God without reserve; with the desire to lead an interior life, with a profound humility, fervour, the gift of prayer, the love of God, the true spirit of Jesus Christ, and with the practice of those virtues which He taught by word and His divine example, than to make a thousand useless reflexions about them. If you do not feel any of these desires the mere wish to have them, the mere raising of the heart is sufficient to keep your soul recollected and united to God. Therefore, once more, the mere raising of the heart to God, or towards certain virtues in order to please God, will do more to help you on than all your reflexions

L

and grand reasonings. This is called being led to God by inclination, attraction and affection; and this way is gentler,
surer, and more efficacious than all those beautiful lights, unless,
indeed, God infuses them by His grace and special favour;
and even then, unless these lights are united to a certain taste
and an interior attraction which touches and charms the heart,
we usually make no progress.

2nd. God often permits souls to suffer from that emptiness
of the mind of which I have spoken before, and in such cases it
would be useless to wish to have distinct thoughts since God
has deprived us of them. It would even be hurtful to make
efforts to think or to reflect much; from which I conclude that,
in any state, it is better to remain before God peacefully, acquiescing heartily in His will as to what He gives or takes away
without doing more than retaining in the depths of the soul a
sincere desire to belong entirely to God; to love Him ardently
and to be ultimately united to Him, or else, as I have explained,
to wish to have these desires.

3rd. As God gives lights and thoughts when He pleases,
either in prayer, or at other times; if you find that these lights
and thoughts come quietly and gently, you can dwell upon them
for as long a time as you feel any attraction or repose, content
to let them go whenever God pleases, without making any effort
to retain them; otherwise it would seem as if they were your
own, and would act against that perpetual dependence in which
God wills to keep those souls which He calls to the interior life.
And it is especially to keep them in this continual dependence
that, sometimes, God does nothing but give and take away in
turns, almost unceasingly; and this produces in those souls
perpetual changes. It is through these different changes and
constant vicissitudes that God Himself exercises these souls
in a perfect submission of mind and heart in which consists true
perfection. The conduct of God in the interior of the souls He
loves and wishes to raise to a perfect and solid virtue somewhat
resembles that of a wise and firm mother who, to overcome the
obstinacy and self-will of her child, and to make him perfectly
submissive and obedient, gives, and takes away again what he
likes best, and continues to do so until she has overcome his
rebellious spirit. Oh! if we could only understand the loving
conduct of God, what peace would be ours, and what submission
we should practise in the midst of these spiritual vicissitudes
and changes of the interior state. From this I draw the conclusion which I have often explained to you before that, in
certain circumstances, the most efficacious way of making
spiritual progress is the simple one of acquiescing in the will of
God. "I agree to all, Lord, I wish what You wish, I resign

myself entirely to Your will." This is called desiring nothing and being prepared for everything; nothing for oneself, and everything by resignation : it is called walking before God in the greatest simplicity. This method, in a certain sense, has nothing disturbing about it, because this simple adhesion of our will to the will of God comes almost spontaneously as a drawing and attraction, and finally as a sweet habit.

You are surprised that having heartily made certain sacrifices for God, temptations about them should return, most violently, so as to cause you anxiety. It is necessary that this should happen, to prevent self-complacency and self-love which would spoil all. Be satisfied, then,t hat God has inclined you in the first place by His grace to make these sacrifices for Him, and firmly resist the temptations to retract them. God intends through them to keep you humble ; the mind is naturally so inclined to vaunt itself and to be puffed up about everything and to appropriate to itself all that is good and virtuous by self-complacency, that without the help of these oft-repeated trials of our misery and feebleness we should flatter ourselves to have had a great share in the victory, and should thus lose all the fruit we might have gained. In withdrawing from the truth of our own nothingness we go on in vanity and lies which are so opposed to God who is essential truth.

Thus it is that the actual and almost unintermittent exper-ience of our own weakness becomes the protection of those virtues that faith makes us practise. From this it happens that according to the progress we make God gives us correspond-ing light, and a more lively realisation of our misery and poverty, to retain in us the treasures of grace and virtue of which our enemies would deprive us if God did not bury them in an abyss of misery well-known to ourselves, and keenly apprehended by us. This will enable you to understand how it happens that the most saintly persons are always the most humble, and have the poorest opinion of themselves. It is because, by our great inclination to vanity we compel God to hide from our own eyes the small amount of good that we do by the help of His grace, and all our spiritual progress and the virtues He bestows upon us without our knowledge. This is a very touching proof, not only of our own misery, but also of the wisdom and goodness of our God, who is reduced, so to speak, to hiding from us His greatest benefits for fear that we should love them and appro-priate them by vanity and scarcely perceptible self-satisfaction. From this great rule it follows that our wretchedness, thoroughly well recognised and experienced, is worth more to us than an angelic virtue the merit of which we unjustly attribute to our-selves. This rule, deeply engraved in the soul, keeps it always in peace in the midst of a lively realisation of its misery, since it regards these feelings as very great graces from God, as indeed they are.

LETTER XIV.—*Singular Favours of God.*

To Sister Anne-Marguerite Boudet de la Bellière (1734). On the practice of abandonment during consolations.

My dear Sister,

What you tell me about the extraordinary circumstances attending your vocation is more useful than you imagine, because a director who recognises a call of Providence in a vocation has the right to conclude that God has special designs on the soul so singularly chosen, and that He desires to find in it a devotion proportioned to the predilection He has shown it. I thank God for the first grace, and still more for the second which consists in making you know and appreciate this singular favour. I conclude from these favours that you are of the fortunate number of those from whom God expects a particular fidelity, and who would run a great risk if they failed to correspond to the loving kindness of their heavenly Spouse, or if they wounded the divine jealousy of His love. It is true that in the interior life you must be prepared for continual vicissitudes. This is the law to which all the transitory things of this life are subjected by God, and this law is so universal that to remain always in the same state must be looked upon with suspicion. What must you do now, then, that God is overwhelming you with lights and caresses?

1st. You must wait, and prepare yourself for the distressing absences of your Spouse : also in His absence you must look forward to His return, and sustain yourself with the hope of it.

2nd. You must not give yourself up too completely to these affections and consolations for fear of becoming attached to them. You should use the same moderation and the same sobriety with regard to them as a mortified person does with regard to the dishes at a feast.

3rd. Your present method of prayer is more a gift of grace than your own. Therefore let grace act, and remain in a position of humble docility, keeping with calmness and simplicity your interior glance fixed lovingly on God, and on your own nothingness. God will then effect great things in your soul without your knowledge either as to what they are, or how He works. Be careful not to give way to curiosity ; be content to know and to feel that it is a divine operation, trust Him who works in you and abandon yourself entirely to Him so that He may form and fashion you interiorly as best pleases Him. Is it not enough that you should be to His liking and taste ?

4th. During these happy moments have no other fear than that of becoming more attached to these gifts and graces than to the Giver and Benefactor. Do not value nor enjoy these graces and favours except in as far, as they serve to inflame your soul with divine love, and are useful to help you in acquiring those solid virtues which please your heavenly Lover: self-abnegation, humility, mortification, patience, sweetness, obedience, charity, and gentle forbearance with your neighbour. Know that the devil is not the author of favours such as these, and that he can never deceive you if you only make use of these tastes and attractions for the acquisition of those solid virtues which faith and the Gospel teach and prescribe for us. Let God act; do not by your natural activity place obstacles in the way of His holy operations, and be faithful to Him in the smallest things for fear of exciting or provoking His divine jealousy.

5th. The most simple thoughts, and those that lead more directly to a filial confidence are the best in prayer. How pleasing to God are those prayers that are, at the same time, simple, familiar, and respectful, and how irresistible they are to Him. I wish you, with all my heart, a continuation of this simple and humble gift of prayer which is the greatest treasure of the spiritual life.

6th. You say that you cannot understand how the strong antipathy that you formerly entertained for your present state of life should have given place to such a perfect love of it. It is, my dear Sister, because, by different interior operations, you soul has, so to say, been re-modelled, somewhat in the way that an old metal or silver pot is re-cast to make an entirely new one, shining and bright. There will be many other remouldings in your soul if you become quite detached from consolations, faithful to grace, and completely resigned to God's good pleasure in aridity, trouble and desolation.

7th. I feel, as you do, that it is God's will that, little by little, you should die to all things, in order to live only in Him, for Him, and by Him; that is to say, to have neither thoughts, desires, plans, views, ambitions, affections, joys, fears, hope, nor love but for Him. But before arriving at this entire detachment, which is what is called a mystical death, you will have to endure cruel agonies. From henceforth you must prepare yourself for this, as, in bygone times, the virgins and the rest of the faithful prepared themselves for martyrdom, because this is in reality a true martyrdom beginning in love, and tending to the consummation of love. But be of good courage; God will uphold you and will give you now and then, breathing-space for the enjoyment of heavenly graces and of a delightful sweetness with which He will fill your soul as with a heavenly manna to nourish and fortify it during its sojourn in the desert of this world.

8th. What a fortunate attraction it is which unceasingly recalls you interiorly! What a holy dwelling, and blessed retreat has the heavenly Spouse made for Himself in your soul, where He makes Himself known to you and speaks to your heart in the most profound and loving silence, without sound of words, or confusion of fugitive thoughts! This should be your permanent dwelling and when you perceive yourself on the point of quitting it, try very gently to return, and to re-enter this divine trysting-place. It is in this that it is most necessary for you to be faithful.

9th. As concerns your extreme weakness and misery during times of aridity, and in the absence of the heavenly Bridegroom, you need not be in the least surprised at it and still less excessively afflicted or troubled. All good souls suffer in the same way, and God acts thus to remind us, by a hundred personal experiences, that we are nothing without Him, so that we shall attribute to Him alone all the glory of the little good that we perform by the help of His grace, and appropriate nothing to ourselves but evil.

10th. During this time that immediately follows the entrance of a soul into the state of recollection, you would hardly believe how necessary it is, not only to deny itself every useless pleasure and natural satisfaction, but also conversations, even pious ones, that are too long. It is often a device of the devil to feed pride, self-love, and foolish self-esteem, and to draw us gradually away till we forget God even in speaking about Him and about our own souls. We escape this danger when by continual efforts we have acquired a habit of living an interior life, and become accustomed to let the heart speak, rather than the intellect.

11th. Preserve most jealously a great taste for silence and solitude : the desire of it is enough for the present, and later, the time will come to put it into practice.

12th. It is certain, also, that familiar correspondence by letter, even in the most harmless way, is an obstacle to perfection, especially in youth. One of your former directors has already given you this advice and you did well in obeying him. This little sacrifice was very pleasing to God, and will have obtained for you the grace to make a second which I judge necessary. I see that it is incumbent on you to make continual progress in the way of detachment, and also that the special graces bestowed on you by God give Him the right to expect a corresponding fidelity on your part. After weighing the matter well in the sight of God, and in the interests of your soul this is what I think; I wish you to tell the person quite simply, that your director, whose advice you wish to follow, tells you that this letter-writing, though of the most innocen tdescription, must be given up, as a little sacrifice which he desires and exacts, although he knows quite well that there is no danger either on your side or the other, as you have declared that the correspondence is with an upright man, a good Religious who is a relative : and that in spite of knowing all this the director is firm, and will maintain his prohibition, under the penalty of refusing any longer to undertake the care of your soul and that you neither wish nor dare to disobey him.   I believe that this declaration, made with quiet energy, will suffice to give your soul its full liberty.

13th.   I thoroughly understand the miserable self-love of which you speak, and its natural result in the instinctive and indeliberate seeking after your own ease and comfort.   This self-love is so deeply rooted in us, that only its opposite, divine love, can cause its death.   It is enough, at present, to grieve about it, and to humble yourself before God.   The prayer He gives you is a sacred fire which will insensibly consume all these evil inclinations, as fire consumes straw ; so, have confidence in God, and wait patiently till this wretched straw is completely consumed.

LETTER XV.—*Heartfelt Prayer.*

To Mother Louise-Françoise de Rosen on the same subject.

My dear Sister,

I see no cause for anxiety in the state of your soul as you describe it in your letter.

1st.   The feelings of gratitude, of joy, and of self-effacement which keep you in union with God for entire days without any relaxation are the effects of one of those operations which you have already experienced.   You have but to accept this gift with humble gratitude, and I can only congratulate you on the grace God has bestowed on you.

2nd.   There is a language of the heart which only God can understand, and which is expressed by desires and other interior movements, as men converse with the voice and articulate words.   This is called heartfelt prayer altogether interior and spiritual.   In this the Holy Spirit, in the inmost sanctuary of the soul, listens, speaks, instructs, silences, turns and forms it according to His pleasure.   It is the work of the divine Spirit on the created spirit of which the soul hardly understands anything, apparently, and yet, nevertheless, is completely revived by the impressions made upon it. In this also, it only remains to receive in all simplicity the gift of God, and since it pleases Him to communicate Himself to the soul in secret, and as it were, " incognito," it should carefully abstain from opposing His designs by eager investigations or indiscreet curiosity.

3rd. Your thoughts and feelings about the happiness of the saints are founded on truth, for it is of faith that the essence of that sovereign happiness is but the ebbing and flowing of the very happiness of God. A small share of this happiness He imparts to certain souls here on earth, to attract them to Himself, and to inspire them with a distaste for all else; so transitory impressions have their good effect, for which reason we are permitted to desire, and to enjoy them with interior moderation and sobriety.

4th. The comparison of the stone which has to be cut with blows of the hammer on the chisel, and afterwards to be polished, is very just. You have only to allow yourself to be shaped and modelled, and to be careful not to destroy the form and shape given by the divine Workman, by thoughts and actions that obviate His industry.

LETTER XVI.—*The Operations of Grace.*

To Sister Marie-Anne-Thérèse de Rosen (1734). The operations of grace.

———

My dear Sister,

I have read your letter with much consolation and spiritual joy. I bless God from my heart for having been pleased to glorify Himself in your weakness and poverty. We celebrate to-day the feast of St. Agatha, and in her collect we pray that as He has chosen the weaker sex to show forth His mighty power, so we might by her intercession be brought nearer to Him. I have applied this thought to you.

1st. Your great attraction towards simplicity is a grace that can have no other effect than to unite you more closely with God, for simplicity tends to unity, and this can be obtained, first, by a simple and loving interior looking to God in pure faith, whether this interior looking is perceptible by its sweetness, as at present, or becomes almost unknown to the senses by being in the depths of the soul, or in the apex, or point of the spirit. Secondly, by keeping guard over all your interior senses in a profound silence. Thirdly, by only making repeated acts and reflections according as God gives you the thought, attraction, and impulsion.

2nd. This indistinct knowledge, or rather, this strong impression that you have of the immensity of God is the work of grace, which produces, and leaves in the depth of the soul very salutary effects that no one has ever been able to explain, and on which it is best not to reason nor even to dwell unless God, Himself, impels us. Do not interfere with this impression, nor distress yourself when it pleases God to take it away. The soul will thus be prevented from becoming more attached to the gifts of God than to God Himself, and from ruining all the operations of grace by attributing the good effects they produce to itself.

3rd. The holy Scripture says that God dwells in inaccessible darkness to the spirit of man, but when He introduces a soul into that darkness it becomes luminous to it. Then can it see all without seeing anything, it can hear all without hearing, and gain knowledge without knowing anything. This is called wise ignorance, or, as St. Denis explains it, the darkness of the light of faith. All that is necessary to know about it is that it is an operation of grace; allow yourself to be immersed in it with joy, let yourself be engulfed and lost in it as much as God pleases.

4th. This attraction to and taste for mental prayer, and this profound peace and silence full of admiration and love are marked effects of the prayer of recollection. But to remain in a kind of inactivity, like an empty space, or a mere instrument waiting for the master-hand of the worker, is another operation of grace. In this state you have only to follow the guidance of the Holy Spirit. Wait patiently in silence and resignation, as the holy king, David, said, " Like a servant waits with her eyes fixed on her mistress to forestall and accomplish her commands at the least sign from her "; if nothing is said, still wait in the same interior spirit of submission and abandonment. Should grace inspire particular and formal acts, perform them quietly, following step by step the impulse given for that purpose, and stop directly it ceases, to resume once more the same silent attention.

5th. This spirit of total abandonment, with the fervent and reiterated petition to accomplish all that God wills, frequently prognosticates a transition to an interior state of trial extremely hard and crucifying . All that can be done is to prepare yourself generally, before God, by a complete self-distrust and a great confidence in Him ; and by a general abandonment to all without particularising anything unless God makes it clear to you. On this subject I say to you that if for want of tyrants there are no longer martyrs for the faith to the shedding of blood ; Jesus Christ will continue to have martyrs of grace. The torments of the body give place with advantage to the different interior sufferings which souls have to endure to purify them more and

more and to render them better fitted for a more strict and
intimate union with the God of all purity and holiness. The
feeling of confusion and of interior annihilation is caused by the
action of the Spirit of God; all the graces He gives us should
always bear the sign-manual of humility, and all that has not
this sign must be regarded with suspicion, and likewise everything that has the slightest shadow of pride, presumption, or
vain self-satisfaction.

6th. Having once experienced the sweetness, efficacy, and
purity of the divine operations, I am not surprised at the sort of
horror you entertain for your own efforts which are nearly always
hurried, wild, uneasy, and followed by a thousand fruitless self-
examinations. It is not a bad thing to remain inactive when you
do not think yourself to be actuated by the Spirit of God; as
long as one of these two conditions can be found in this state—
that this inaction does not last long, or else that it is a peaceful
waiting which is not idleness, since there is in it that interior and
loving attention to God, with faith, desire, and hope of His holy
operation, which are so many acts, and so many movements
of the mind and heart, forming the essence of true interior prayer.

You must not scrutinise spiritual things so much, but follow
God with simplicity, as St. Francis of Sales says : " To do otherwise is to oppose the holy simplicity that pertains to candid and
innocent souls."

All that is caused by, or proceeds from the love of God, says
your saintly Father, is sweet and gentle, like this very holy
love itself; and the signs of a self-seeking nature are the confusion, haste, and anxiety of a self-love that is perpetually eager,
anxious, and impetuous.

7th. I understand that your attraction has always been the
knowledge and love of God in, and through Jesus Christ. The
simple perception, or consideration of these mysteries, accompanied by holy affections, is already a very good method of
prayer. When all the contemplation of the mind, and the
affections of the heart are gathered into one point, for instance—
the Deity, the prayer is much simplified, is better and more
divine; but you must not imagine that this method will always
continue : usually it is not a permanent state, but a fugitive
grace. When it has passed, you must return to the simple
contemplation of the mystery with some affections of the heart,
gentle, peaceful, without effort or too much examination.

8th. Be careful, during the time of prayer, not to reflect
on yourself, or your method of prayer, because to examine
closely in this way, one often leaves off looking at God to look at
oneself, to reflect and, as it were, to turn back on oneself simply
out of self-love which, not having been entirely given up, falls

back naturally on itself. When divine repose begins, do not think of its sweetness but only of God in whose heart your soul should rather seek charity and the infusion of those virtues which fill the soul during that happy sleep, than its own repose. For the rest you could not hear Mass nor recite the Office in a more worthy manner than with these interior dispositions, but you must prepare to be weaned from the milk of spiritual infancy. and to eat the bread of the strong. May God be praised for this beforehand.

9th. Certainly the more annihilated and empty of created things a soul becomes the greater will be its capacity for divine love, and the more abundantly will this love be infused into it. Then the soul drinks long draughts of love with a delicious satiety, and an insatiable thirst. One must then be content to drink at the source, and not make unseasonable commotion. Formal acts of charity would be greatly out of place when one feels that the heart is entirely submerged in charity. God wills that by dint of plunging and replunging your soul in this ocean of charity your heart may become inebriated with this holy love, and set on fire with these pure and divine flames. To attain this you must think of two things only—first to detach your mind and heart more and more from all created things, secondly to allow God to act, for He alone produces these effects in your soul. Still you can, and ought, to desire and to ask for a greater love of God, when you feel inclined, and impelled to do so ; but this you will do almost without thinking and without being able to help yourself.

10th. God carries out His work with any tools He pleases, and sometimes effects wonderful things with very weak instruments. Therefore do not deny yourself to those souls whom He has inspired to appeal to you : say quite simply what you think and give them what God has given you for their benefit, and rest assured that He will give His blessing to your simplicity, and to the humility of these good souls. When God sends someone to us in whatever way it may be, it is not meddling to help others, but the best way of showing our love and gratitude to Him. Even when they seem to repel you, stand your ground, and endure all for the glory of your great Master.

LETTER XVII.—*Attraction to the Interior Life.*

To Mother Marie-Anne-Sophie de Rottembourg (1738).
On docility to the interior impressions of the Holy Spirit : and
peaceful waiting.

Reverend Mother,

All that you tell me about the interior attraction of many of
your daughters to holy recollection, and the measures you take
to turn aside the obstacles, specious and well-disguised as they
are, by which the devil tries to prevent them, can only come
from the Holy Spirit. I have nothing further to remark about
it. Follow quietly and step by step, the light that God gives
you. What a consolation and joy for me it is to learn that all
those good sisters whom I know best, and am most interested in,
are just those that are most attracted to and have the greatest
desire for the interior life. I beg you to congratulate them from
me for this gift of God, and to greet them all, particularly your
dear Sister Marie-Anne-Thérèse de Vioménil. How delighted I
am to hear that she is persevering in this work. The seven you
mention, with whom you have formed a holy league for the
renewal of an interior spirit in your community, will gradually
make proselytes, and before long will win over the whole house.
As to yourself, profit by your experiences and never forsake
the plain path of pure faith which God has made you enter upon
for any reason whatever. Do not forget that in this path the
operations of God are almost imperceptible. The work of grace
is accomplished in the innermost recess of the spirit, that which
is the furthest from the senses, and from all that can be felt.
To confirm you in this way you must remember first that this
is what Jesus Christ meant when He said that we must worship
the Father in spirit and in truth ; secondly, that what is evident
to the senses is, so to say, only a mark of grace ; as Fr. Louis
Lallement says ; thirdly, that Mother de Chantal has very justly
said that the more simple, deep and imperceptible are the
workings of God, the more spiritual, solid, pure and perfect they
are. That spirit of peace in yourself and in the others is one of
the greatest gifts of God. Follow this spirit and all that it
inspires ; it will work wonders in yourself and in your neighbour.
When we have learnt to remain in interior peace, God will teach
others by our example without the sound of words to be peace-
able and obedient, so that directors will only have to say to us,
" Listen attentively to the voice of the Spirit of God," or,
better still, " Be faithful in following the interior impressions
of His grace." This is what St. John said to the first Christians,
" You have no need that any man teach you, but as His unction
teacheth you all things, and is truth, and is no lie. And as it

has taught you, abide in Him." Follow faithfully and obediently, when you feel it, this divine unction; wait for it peacefully and with confidence when its impression becomes indistinct; this is the best way of making rapid progress in the way of perfection without danger of going astray. Why do we always wish to substitute our own action for that of the divine Worker who labours in us without ceasing to make us perfect? How much more progress should we not make if we took more care not to interfere with His action, but to abandon ourselves to Him, and to wait for Him? The Holy Scriptures frequently recommend us to " wait on the Lord " and there is hardly any means better calculated to make us holy. There is nothing to which souls already sufficiently exercised in the active life and the fulfilment of the precepts should more earnestly apply themselves, than to these peaceful waitings. It is the way to acquire the spirit of prayer, of holy recollection, and of a most intimate union with God. Our God is infinitely liberal, and His hands are always full of graces which He only desires to pour out on us. To receive abundantly of these graces all that is necessary is, to prepare our hearts and to remain always in readiness. But the dryness and weariness of this waiting tire those souls that are impatient and impetuous, and dishearten those who think only of their own interests instead of allowing themselves to be led by the pure love of God which consists in conforming our will always with His. There is no treasure in the world to be compared to this. But people are always rushing after all sorts of chimerical perfections and lose sight of the only true perfection, which is the fulfilment of the divine will; this infinitely wise and sweet will, which, if we allow it to guide us, will show us close at hand and at every moment what we are so laboriously and uselessly hunting for elsewhere.

LETTER XVIII.—*Desires to be Moderated.*

To Sister Marie-Anne-Thérèse de Vioménil. Advising her to moderate her desires and fears.

Salutary fear causes neither disturbance, uneasiness, nor discouragement. If fear produce contrary effects you must drive it away, and not allow it to take possession of you, as in this case it comes either from the devil, or your own self-love. We must always remain in the presence of God, waiting His pleasure even about our most lawful desires, and the projects that seem most saintly; and must be always submissive and resigned to His holy will. Why? Firstly, because the desires of God should be the only rule of all our desires. The most certain way of arriving at perfection is to submit, and to persevere in adhering to all the interior and exterior circumstances in which we find ourselves by the permission of that divine Providence who rules everything, and disposes everything, even to the fall of a leaf from the tree, or a hair from our heads. Secondly, because the giving up of our own will is a necessary and important condition of our sanctification.

Nothing is so calculated to make us acquire this abnegation than the delays we meet with in the execution of our good purposes. It is on this account that God often delays their accomplishment for entire years. Then, indeed, do we require faith, abandonment and confidence. But what makes this trial all the more bitter is that sometimes we do not feel that we have any of these virtues, because we are deprived of the power of making formal acts. What is to be done in this case ? We must sustain ourselves by the simple light of bare faith, and by frequent recourse to God interiorly to implore His divine assistance, humbly confessing our impotence and misery. In this way we shall take part in the designs of God who seems occasionally to leave us to our own devices, to make us understand how little we can do when left to ourselves. What a great favour ! and what an important virtue we shall have acquired in learning by repeated personal experiences the depths of our weakness, misery and poverty, and the continual need we have of the sustaining power of God to raise, enlighten and animate us by the interior influence of His grace.

The deep impression that God has given you of a keen desire to divest yourself of your own will to follow His is a most precious grace ; to guard and increase it you must, with all your heart and soul, make every effort, as often and for as long a time as you can, especially at prayer. I could wish that you were able to spend your whole life in this exercise alone, in great interior silence allowing the Holy Spirit to work in you by His grace ; but all without violence or effort ; gently, tranquilly, peacefully, because God only dwells in peaceful souls in which He takes His delight.

***

Letter XIX.—*To Aim at Simplicity.*

To Sister Marie-Anne-Thérèse de Rosen. To aim at Simplicity.

***

My dear Sister,

Only a few days ago I answered at some length your last letter but one. If you find that, through me, God does not do much for you, you ought to conclude that my help is not necessary for you, or else that He will Himself provide for your necessities. How well He can do without us when He chooses ! One single word uttered by Him to the ear of the soul is more instructive than all the discourses of men. The least little breath of grace wafts our ship more speedily on its course, and makes it arrive more surely and speedily into harbour than all our oars, sails, and sculls. I am delighted to hear that you are beginning to learn this, or rather that you daily have fresh and more touching proofs of it. Keep in this state : the interior silence of respect and submission alone, kept humbly in the presence of God if He does not command us to act, will sanctify our energies, soften our anxieties, and pacify our troubles, and that in one moment. Remain in this state of unity and simplicity ; multiplicity throws the mind into trouble and confusion, scatters and disorders our powers without our being able to perceive it. Many desires trouble the soul, says the Holy Spirit. Here is a practice which I advise you to follow in order to reduce all your desires to a single one ; take this truth well to heart. " I have been created and put into this world to serve God, to love Him, and to please Him ; that is my task here ; what does He wish to do with me in this world and the next ? to what degree of glory will He raise me ? That is for Him to determine ; it is His business, it is, so to say, His task ; each to his own business, the doing of that is the only thing to think of. Please God I will think of mine as willingly as God thinks of His." I remain in Him and through Him—my dear Sister. Yours, etc.

LETTER XX.—*Holy Simplicity*.

To Sister Anne-Marguerite Boudet de la Bellière. On the same subject.

My dear Sister,

The way in which you take your little trials is infinitely pleasing to God, and I do not fear to give you this assurance, because in so generously renouncing, as you do, all interior sweetness and consolation for the love of Him, you merit to receive them more abundantly when the time arrives. The little, you tell me, that you have remembered of what I told you, is the essential part, and that ought to suffice. God sees the heart, and that is all that He wants. Perfection does not consist in a multiplicity of acts even though interior ; on the contrary the more we advance the more is God pleased to make it out of our power to produce many acts, but invites us to remain in His presence in a state of silence and humble recollection. Follow this attraction of grace. Be content to renew from time to time a simple act of faith and of charity, accompanied by total resignation and filial confidence. In all the different changes both interior and exterior, say always from the depths of your heart, " My God, I wish what you wish, I refuse nothing from Your fatherly hand, I accept all, and submit to all." In this simple act, continued, or rather habitual, consists our whole perfection. Also in this the heart and soul are kept in peace at their centre even when agitated on the surface by different trials and emotions that war against it. The better you understand how to maintain this holy interior simplicity the greater will be your progress, or to speak more correctly, the more God will help you to advance.

Do not, however, expect to be able to measure the progress you make ; that is impossible for this reason, that your progress depends more on the work of God in your soul than on your own acts, and that this work being purely spiritual, on that account is hardly perceptible.

However, I give you some signs by which you may recognise in future the results of the divine action in your change of heart.

1st. A holy indifference which resembles a sort of insensibility to all things of this world.

2nd. A fund of peace from which it follows that you will not trouble yourself about anything, even about your faults and imperfections, and far less about those of your neighbour.

3rd. A certain attraction towards God and the things of God ; a sort of hunger and thirst after justice, that is to say, after virtue, piety, and all perfection. This hunger, which is very keen, is, nevertheless, exempt from eagerness and trouble, and leads you to will always what God wills, and nothing more ; to bless Him in spiritual poverty as much as in abundance.

Remember always this great saying of Jesus Christ : " If you do not become like little children you shall not enter into the Kingdom of Heaven." Be on your guard never to infringe, in the slightest degree, this holy simplicity, so little known, so little esteemed, yet so precious in the sight of God. Be always more and more upright and simple in your thoughts, words, opinions, actions, and behaviour. There are people who want to be just the contrary, and who pretend to be, out of vanity. How very far are these people from the Kingdom of God, since they have not even the foundation of it, which is humility. Whenever you go to pray, or leave it with a quiet, recollected, and well-disposed mind, you will always derive some fruit from it one way or another, and all the more when you believe that God is farthest from you, for then He will be nearest. Do not make a number of acts during prayer, but make a few very quietly, with the greatest repose of mind and heart, and in the greatest tranquillity

possible.   During the day do not force yourself to make so many
different acts, and still less to feel fervour and devotion in making
them;   keep yourself firmly, humbly, and patiently in peace,
tranquil and quite resigned in this emptiness of the mind and of
the will.   It is this emptiness of the spirit which conduces to
pure love, and union with God.

LETTER XXI.—*Different Attractions of Grace.*
To Mother Thérèse Françoise de Rosen.   On the different
attractions of grace.

My dear Sister,
    The tendencies, on the subject of which you consult me, are
not rare among souls who, like you, have been called by God to
unite themselves with Him by a loving abandonment.   Sometimes, you say, you feel yourself drawn to adore the divine Majesty
with humility mixed with love, and by very distinct acts which
arise of their own accord apparently, and are very delightful,
filling the soul with a great contentment.   At other times you
are inclined to remain in complete repose with a clear apprehension of the presence of God, and without the power of forming
distinct acts, unless with violent efforts, even during holy Mass,
and then you feel obliged to take a book, and to do violence to
yourself to escape from this apparent inaction which occasions
you uneasiness : this is as near as possible to the two states, the
principal traits of which you have depicted in your letter, and
on the subject of which you desire my counsel.   This is what I
think about it.   In the first place it is certain that each of these
two states is a gift of God, but the second seems to be the best ;
first because it is more simple, more profound, more spiritual,
and further removed from the senses, consequently more worthy
of God Who is a pure spirit, and Whom we must worship in spirit
and in truth ; secondly, because it is an exercise of pure faith,
which is less satisfying to the soul, less reassuring, and consequently, in which there is more of sacrifice and of perfect abandonment to God.   Thirdly, because in this state it is the Holy Spirit
that acts with the approval and consent of the soul, while in the
first state, it is the soul that acts with the grace of God and this
is more like ordinary affective prayer.   Well ! you must understand that those operations in which God has the greatest share,
and the creature the least, must be the most perfect.   From this
it follows that in this second state there is no serious danger of
wasting time nor consequently any reason to fear that you do not
fulfil the precept to hear Mass.   You may adhere to this decision
without the slightest scruple.   And if, further, you wish to have

my advice as to how to behave with regard to these two states when you experience them, I will give it to you. First, whenever the second attraction is strongly experienced, and absorbs you, in some measure, in spite of yourself, you ought to allow yourself to be gently drawn on, otherwise you would be resisting the inspiration and secret operations of the Holy Spirit within you, and thus would be acting according to your own ideas, out of self-love and in order to become satisfied and reassured. Now you must seek, in all things, not your own satisfaction however spiritual it may be, but the perfect satisfaction of God.

If this attraction should not be very strong nor very urgent, you ought, nevertheless, to second it by keeping yourself in a profound silence to give more opportunity for the inmost operations of the Holy Spirit. This, at any rate, is the advice I give you for long hours of prayer; because, when you have only a short time for prayer, as in short visits to the Blessed Sacrament morning and evening, it would be more useful to cultivate the first attraction you mentioned. You could then make formal acts of adoration and love of God. But I will remind you of the counsel St. Francis of Sales gave to a person who followed the same method : I should wish these particular acts to be made without much feeling or effort, so that they may flow and be distilled from the highest point of the mind, as the same saint expresses it; because it is a received opinion that the more simple and above the senses these operations are, so much the more profoundly spiritual, and, consequently, perfect do they become. To pray according to your first method is to pray by formal, successive and perceptible acts; to pray according to the second method is to pray by implicit acts, experienced, but in no way expressed nor perceptible except confusedly. Or, in other words it is to pray by a simple but actual inclination of the heart; now this simple and real inclination of the heart contains all, and says all to God without, however, express words. The different names that are given to this method of prayer will make you understand it perfectly; it is called a loving waiting on God, a simple looking, or pure faith and simplicity tending to God; the prayer of surrender and abandonment to God, arising from the love of God, and producing an ever increasing love of God. By these examples you will see that this method is of more value than the other; you must, therefore, make it your principal exercise, without, however, neglecting the first at certain times as I told you above. Yours in our Lord.

LETTER XXII.—*Fidelity to the Call of God.*

To a Postulant.   On abandonment in the trials to which vocation is subject.

———

All that you have told me, and written to me, makes me convinced that God calls you to religion, and, in particular, to the Order of the Visitation.   Your interior attraction to this Order, and the reasons you allege for it do not leave a doubt of this double vocation; for, as there is one for religion in general, there is also one for this or that community in particular.   It only remains for you to be faithful to the call of God and thus to make sure your predestination.

Now, this fidelity requires three things of you; first you must endeavour to preserve in your heart in spite of every obstacle both exterior and interior, this attraction towards God with the sincere desire to follow it when He Who has given it to you will Himself provide the means by which you will be able to concentrate yourself to His service in reality, as you have already done beforehand in your mind and heart.   Your second duty is to hope against hope as Abraham did; that is, to believe firmly that, as God is all-powerful and that nothing in the world can resist Him, He will know how to overcome all the obstacles and oppositions of men in His own time.   All minds and hearts are in His hands and He can turn them as He will without effort. It was by His simple " Fiat " that He created all things out of nothing.   Therefore, when the time arrives, He has but to say " Fiat " and all the obstacles to your vocation will be removed. At present He allows these obstacles to try your patience, your faith in Him, and your firm reliance on His powerful succour. Therefore, do not be alarmed, but continue to trust firmly in God. Do not trouble yourself nor torment yourself at all, but submit to God generously; accept all the trials He sends you, saying to Him without ceasing, " Lord may all that You will be accomplished in me, at the time, and in the way that pleases you; I accept all and sacrifice my own interests, my wishes, and all the desires of my heart to have none other than to obey and please You in all things."   Your third duty is a great fidelity to all your exercises of piety; prayers, readings, meditations, masses, confessions, Communions, examens, and interior recollection ; frequent raising of the heart to God without ever giving up in the slightest degree any of these practices, either through grief, trouble, disgust, weariness, dryness, or for any other reason whatever.   These trials are necessary to detach you from everything and to keep you united to God Who alone should be your light, your support, your consolation and your strength.   Apparently it is to make you practise this abandonment better that God has permitted you to be forbidden to enter the Visitation, so that, receiving no consolation except from Him directly, you should attach yourself purely and solely to Him and thus gain great merit.

You must, therefore, obey His orders in obeying those who have the right from Him to command you. If the command should prejudice the welfare of your soul God will not allow it to persist. He can easily put aside the obstacle when it is necessary, therefore rest quietly and without the slightest anxiety in the arms of His merciful providence as a little child rests on the breast of its mother.

LETTER XXIII.—*The Value of Good Desires.*
To the same person.   On the value of good desires.

The increase of the desire to consecrate yourself to God is an additional grace of His mercy. To suffer all the pain of being unable to accomplish these ardent desires is, insomuch as you bear it with resignation, to correspond well with this grace, and to merit its continuance. The interior effort to maintain yourself in this state of resignation is a sort of martyrdom that will, sooner or later, be rewarded. God will carry out the pious design with which He has inspired you, the delay is intended to try your fidelity. If, in the meantime, you are getting on in years, you need not consider that, because you already possess the best part of what you wish for, which is, the strong desire to consecrate yourself to God. This desire is, in the sight of God, the best part of the sacrifice, or, to speak correctly, it is the entire sacrifice since you have already given yourself to Him in heart and soul, and are now sacrificing your most earnest desires in awaiting patiently the time chosen by His providence. Possibly this last sacrifice is of more value than the first, since by it you renounce more entirely your own will. Therefore be at peace and quite tranquil in the presence of Him who sees to the bottom of our hearts and who takes all your good desires for performance. He has no need of anything that you could give Him; but He loves a heart that is ready and willing to sacrifice all. The fear of death and of the judgments of God is a good thing as long as it does not go so far as to cause you trouble and anxiety; then it would be an illusion of the devil. For, what is it that makes you afraid? Is it because you have not yet done what you have not been able to do? Does God require what is impossible? Is it, as you add, because you have, as yet, done nothing for heaven? Be careful again in this; it is a delicate subject for it seems as if you wanted to acquire merit for your own assurance. This is not real confidence which can only be founded on the mercy of God, and the infinite merits of Jesus Christ.   Any other confidence would be vain and presumptuous, since it would rest on your own nothingness, and I know not what wretched works which have no value in the sight of God.   Without depending in any way on ourselves let us try and accomplish, with the help of God's grace, all that He demands of us, and hope only in His goodness and in the merits of Jesus Christ, His Son.

You are right in saying that more grace is required to save us in the world than in religion.   From this I form the opinion that, evidently, a much more distinct vocation is necessary for those who have to remain in the world, than for the religious state ; but, at the same time there are particular graces given to those who, against their will, have to remain in the world. God is then, as it were, obliged to take care of them.   Therefore fear nothing, you are already a Religious in heart and soul. Try to subject your mind, feelings, and actions to the spirit of the rules of this holy state, by a humble resignation and a perfect confidence in the fatherly goodness and power of that heavenly Spouse whom you have chosen.   He, also, regards you as His beloved Spouse.

LETTER XXIV.—*The Call of God a Sign of Predestination.*
To the same person.

You are quite right to consider the design with which God has inspired you as one of the greatest graces.   It is the surest sign of the predestination of a soul by God when He calls it to His divine service.   On this, not only its eternal salvation depends, but even temporal happiness, since experience proves that peace and true contentment in this world can only be found in the service of God.   Besides, the depravity of the times is so great, that it is very difficult to serve God perfectly out of religion.   It costs so much to serve God in the world, that people often lose courage and give up their good intentions. You must, therefore, thank our Lord without ceasing for the gratuitous grace He has given you, in preference to so many others who are lost in the world while leading in it a life full of sorrow and disappointment.   In the second place you must trust in the goodness of God, and firmly hope that the design with which He has inspired you, He will bring to a successful conclusion.   It is often for our greater advantage that He defers the accomplishment of our most holy desires.   His providence can by hidden, but infallible means, cause things to succeed in spite of every obstacle, even when success seems absolutely impossible. God often allows His work to be thwarted in order to make the exercise of His power more striking, and to show us that He is absolute master of all, and that, as without Him we can do nothing, so with His assistance we shall be able to accomplish what appears impossible in our eyes. In the third place you must resign yourself entirely to whatever is the will of God, telling Him frequently that you wish to depend on Him for everything, and that you will have no other will but His. In this way when anything happens to cross your, apparently, most just desires you must, before all, make the sacrifice of them, and then remain in peace, for nothing is so opposed to the Spirit of God and to the marks of His grace, than interior distress, produced by a too great eagerness for even the best and holiest things. Moderate this indiscreet zeal, this too impetuous impulsiveness, and direct all your efforts to the fulfilment of the holy will of God in all things, renouncing your own will however holy and reasonable it may appear to you. There is, truly, no solid. virtue nor true sanctity apart from an entire resignation to, and acquiescence in the will of God. If you feel an occasional repugnance to submit yourself to what God ordains, you should go to Him at once interiorly by prayer, and implore Him to subject your will to His in all things, and to give you strength to overcome your repugnance and your self-love which desires its own satisfaction in even the holiest things. Nevertheless, as it is God's rule that we should do all in our power to cause the good desires with which He has inspired us to succeed, this is what you ought to do.

1st. Frequent the Sacraments as often and as well as you can.

2nd. Live in a great purity of conscience by avoiding the slightest fault that might keep God at a distance from you.

3rd. Every day, at your convenience, spend some time in spiritual reading which will take the place of meditation when you are unable to make it.

4th. During the course of the day raise your mind and heart to God as often as possible, especially when you experience pain, weariness, disappointment, or any repugnance. Offer them to Him as a continual sacrifice. In this way you will obtain constant fresh graces and heavenly inspirations, to which it is of infinite importance that you should be faithful, because it is particularly to this fidelity that God usually imparts His greatest gifts, and above all, that of perseverance.

LETTER XXV.—*God Only Desires What We are Able to Give.*
To the same person.

_____

The sort of martyrdom you are suffering will, if you endure it
with patience and perfect resignation, be very pleasing to God,
for all perfection consists in conforming your will entirely to the
will of God in all things ; that is to say, that you must never
will anything else but what God wills. Now, it is of faith that
God wills everything that happens to us, except sin, because
with the exception of sin nothing happens in this world but by the
hidden dispensations of Providence. This taken for granted, I
cannot understand why you should suffer so much at the post-
ponement of your sacrifice, since it is God who puts obstacles
to it, and thus shows you that He only requires of you the desire
to make it until such time as He, Himself, gives you the means
and power to do so. But beware lest, since we always try to
gratify our own will in all things, this inability should wound
your self-love, make you lose interior peace, and cause all sorts
of troubles. It is a sure sign that we are seeking rather to indulge
our own self-love than to please God when we prefer our own will
to His. For if we only desired to do this holy will we should
always be content and tranquil with this thought, God only
requires of me what I am able to give Him, and that is, the desire
to consummate my sacrifice ; and, according to His will this
desire should be quiet, peaceful, and submissive to all the designs
of His divine providence : but suppose I should never be able
to accomplish my holy desires ? Very well! that would
prove to me that God does not require it, and I should be satisfied
to do His holy will ; because it would then be obvious that God
did not wish for the sacrifice itself, but only that I should be
willing to make it.

It was thus that God acted with regard to Abraham, whose
generous readiness to sacrifice his son Isaac He rewarded as
though the sacrifice had been consummated. It has been the
same with many of the saints who had a very strong desire for
martyrdom without being able to carry it out. God, not permitting nor desiring the actual sacrifice, is satisfied with the
sacrifice of desire, which, in His sight, is the same thing.

But, suppose that in consequence of this I am obliged to live
in the world, what will become of me ? These are vain fears
put into your mind by the devil to make you lose the peace of
your soul. You must abandon yourself entirely to God, and put
your whole trust in Him. He is powerful enough to make you
stand firm in the world, and good enough to sustain you when it
is by the arrangements·of His providence that you live in it.

You could not do better, therefore, than to practise recollection and abnegation in renouncing your own will in everything, but particularly in your too eager desires, however holy they may be ; for this excessive vehemence, and these restless struggles show much imperfection and self-love. These defects are still more clearly shown in the vexation and distress to which you give way after falling into certain faults ; for these feelings are never produced by the love of God, which, on the contrary, conduces to peace ; but by a discontented self-love, and a secret pride stung by the sight of your own imperfections. A soul that is truly humble, instead of entertaining these useless and dangerous feelings, will, after a fall, humble itself gently and tranquilly before God without any uneasiness on account of it. It will feel sorry without anxiety and beg forgiveness without disturbance, and even thank Him for preventing it falling into greater sins.

LETTER XXVI.—*On Abandonment as to Employments and Undertakings.*

To Sister Marie-Thérèse de Vioménil.

My dear Sister,

If you could but understand, once for all, that everything that God wills must succeed, because He knows how to make even difficulties and the opposition of men conduce to the fulfilment of His designs. Believe me, if it be for your greater advantage, in vain will men try to prevent its success ; but if, on the contrary, it will not be advantageous to you, what better can God do than to prevent it ? Now God alone can look into the future and see all its consequences ; as for us, we are poor blind creatures, who have to fear all sorts of danger even in the events that appear to have the best promise of success. What better could we do than to place the whole matter in God's care ? Could our future be more secure than in the all-powerful hand of that adorable Master, of that good and loving Father ? who loves us more than we love ourselves ? Where could we find a safer refuge than in the arms of divine Providence ? This is the blissful centre in which our hearts should find their repose. Withdrawn from this there is no solid peace, nor comfort, nothing but discomfort, anxiety, and bitterness of heart, miseries in the present life, and danger to eternal salvation.

LETTER XXVII.—*Acceptance of Duties.*

To Mother Marie-Anne-Sophie de Rottembourg (1738). On abandonment in the acceptance of duties.

May the peace of Jesus Christ reign always in your heart, and may the most holy will of God be ever accomplished in, and by you. I already knew of your election, Rev. Mother, and rejoiced at it at once in God, because I did not doubt that it would be pleasing to all the community and for their spiritual profit.

As long as you retain your present dispositions your office, however calculated it may seem to relax your spirit, will not be at all injurious to you, for I remember to have read that our duties and employments do not hurt us so much as the eagerness, anxiety and trouble that arise from the activity of our nature, and the desire to succeed in everything before the world.

The celebrated M. de Renti said that it made no difference to him, nor did he experience any difficulty in keeping recollected whether he was at prayer in his oratory, or working, or in any occupation done for the love of God, or the good of his neighbour. We should be able to say the same, if we were as detached as he and as free from all self-seeking.

You do not do well, therefore, in so strenuously opposing the office that Providence had allotted to you. God forgive you, but do not go on with it. To desire nothing, and to refuse nothing, was the maxim of St. Francis of Sales. I advise you to make it yours. Any fresh proof that you are likely to receive of the visible succour of heaven, will render you without excuse if you do not ground yourself in an unreserved abandonment, and an unlimited confidence. Sister N. has committed the same kind of fault, but she is less excusable, as she would not yield to the entreaties that were made to her. Please tell her how little edified I was at her conduct. The hope of being better able to preserve recollection has made her lose the occasion for practising a host of virtues. If she had had the simplicity to submit, she would have practised at the same time the virtues of obedience, charity and zeal. I do not speak of abnegation which she would also have practised so excellently in overcoming her antipathy, and in giving her services so generously to the community in the duty that was offered her. Even the want of capacity that she believed she recognised in herself should have been a greater incentive to its acceptance, for the harm which might have resulted to the community through her incapacity, was no business of hers, as she did not try in any way to obtain this office, and therefore it could have had no other result for her than merit. To how many little acts of humility, patience, and endurance of inconveniences, and constraint; how much vigilance, and charity would not this incapacity have given occasion for? But she had not the courage to face these sacrifices, and has given in to her self-love while she imagined she was following the dictates of humility. At least let her humble herself profoundly before God, let her learn to become very little in her own eyes, and omit nothing that could repair the disedification she has given her Sisters.

LETTER XXVIII.—*To Will Only What God Wills.*

Everything that tends to lessen the strength of our passions or to hold them in check is a singular grace of God. Give yourself up, therefore, to the attraction which this holy repose has for you, and allow no free entrance either in your mind or heart to anything like desire, fear, hope, sadness, joy, or voluntary despondency, so that, in this way, the peace of God will dwell within you, and the less sensible it is the more is it to be prized as it can come only from God. When one does not interfere in anything that does not concern one, a delightful solitude can be found everywhere; however, those difficulties and importunities with which divine Providence allows us to be afflicted are preferable to this solitude. It is true that the former condition is pleasanter, and more consoling, but the latter being more painful, is also more meritorious when it is arranged by God without our own choice. From this I conclude that there are many ways that lead to God but that each person should follow her own without envying that of her neighbour. Not to will to be otherwise than God wills—in this is contained all present happiness with the hope of eternal joy. Let us always distrust our eagerness, especially for good works; let us put up patiently with what God puts up with, and after having done all that, in reason, we could do, or thought we ought to do according to the light God gave us, let us remain quiet and peaceful, abandoning ourselves in all things to His adorable will.

LETTER XXIX.—*To Leave All to God.*

To the same person. Only God knows what is expedient for us.

My dear Sister,

You say you wish to know the time of my return. To tell you the truth I do not know myself, and do not wish to know; I give and abandon myself entirely to divine Providence in everything, and for everything from day to day. Do the same as far as you can, nothing could be better.

Oh! my dear Sister, how much I desire you to taste the sweetness of this hidden manna, which to the true Israelite has the flavour of the most delicious food. Let us desire only God, and God will satisfy all our desires. Let us blindly abandon ourselves to His holy will in all things, and by doing so we shall be delivered from all our cares. We shall then find, that, to advance in the ways of salvation and perfection there is, after all, very little to do, and that it suffices without so much examination about the past, and reflexion as to the future, to place our confidence in God at the present moment, and to regard Him as our good Father who is leading us by the hand.

God forbid, then, that I should make any attempt whatever to throw light on the complete ignorance in which I am as to my destination. I much prefer to remain in this ignorance, abandoned to God, with no cares nor anxieties, like a little child reposing on the breast of a good and loving mother; willing only what God wills, and desiring nothing contrary to His wishes. In this happy state of abandonment I find peace and a complete rest for the heart and mind, and this protects me from a thousand useless thoughts and from all uneasy desires and anxieties about the future. God has made me pass through many places, conditions and duties, and in all of them were mingled so much that was good and also so many hardships that, had I to pass through them again, I should not be able of myself to make a choice. Only God knows what is expedient for us, He loves us more than we love ourselves; what better can we do then, than to leave all to His will to choose for us? If we could but realise that the only great and important affair in this world is that of our eternal salvation. Provided we succeed in this, all will be well, and we need trouble about nothing else. Besides, if I sought my own pleasure I do not see where I could find any better than to be like a bird on a branch, without any certainty about my stay. This uncertainty leads to a more complete abandonment, and this again forms my peace. It delivers me from the care of guiding myself and gives me the assurance of arriving safely at my journey's end supported by God, and following the steps of His divine Providence. From whom else could I receive such a consoling assurance? There is no one capable of giving it to me however perfect his friendship.

LETTER XXX.—*Resignation in Sickness.*

To the same person.   On abandonment in sickness.

Your incurable complaints would affect me with a very great compassion did I not know that they form a great treasure for you in eternity.   It is a sort of martyrdom, a kind of purgatory, and an inexhaustible source of every species of sacrifice, and of acts of continued resignation.   I assure you that all this, borne as you are doing it, without complaint, or murmuring, is very likely to sanctify you.   Even if you only practised the patience of ordinary good Christians you would gain a great deal of merit; but, from what you say I gather that you are doing more than this, and the involuntary rebellion of nature and occasional little signs of impatience which escape you in spite of yourself will not impede your union with God which remains in the centre of your heart.   Your life may well be called a hard and laborious one, a life of pain and trial, it will, therefore, be your purgatory in this world and deliver you from that of the next or at any rate shorten it considerably.   This is why I do not dare to ask God to deliver you from a trouble that must soon end, and for which you will have to thank Him for all eternity as a special sign of His mercy.   The only request I could make Him for you is an increase of His love, and the virtues of submission, patience, and resignation which will greatly add to the merit of your sufferings.   To feel no fear at the thought of death is a grace from God.   As for your sufferings and the outward annoyances you have to endure, bear them as you do your physical ills.   God does not require more; just a daily " fiat " applied to all your exterior sufferings ought to work your salvation as well as your perfection.   All that books or directors can say may be reduced to this one word, " Fiat, fiat," at all times and for everything, but especially in the penitential and crucified life to which it has pleased Providence to reduce you. Tobias in his blindness, Job on his dung-hill, and so many other saints prostrate on beds of suffering did no more than this. It is true that they did it more perfectly, and with greater love. Let us try to imitate their virtues as we share their trials, and one day we shall assuredly share their glory.

LETTER XXXI.—*Conduct in Sickness.*

To Sister Marie-Antoinette de Mahuet (1735).

Although your illness is not serious I am sure you act like those generous souls, who, in their least discomforts go on till the worst comes to the worst, in order to have occasion to make greater sacrifices for God. But, it is usually said, in order to offer the sacrifice of one's life to God ought one not to feel better prepared for death! and I am so unprepared! To these fears I urge you to reply in the following manner. Whether ready and prepared to die or not, I am always ready, always disposed to do the will of God. Your blessed Father St. Francis of Sales said a very remarkable and consoling thing on this subject that would suit all sorts of people : " I believe," said he, " that God would not condemn the greatest sinner on earth, however great his crimes, who at his last moments made a generous offering of his life, abandoning himself entirely to His divine will and loving Providence." And I truly believe it, since such an act is one of perfect love capable of blotting out all sin even without confession, like baptism and martyrdom. Often let us make these acts of love, then, by placing in the hands of God all that He has lent us, because He could not give us anything absolutely. And since, according to the words of Jesus Christ we must become little children again, let us imitate those little ones whose father, to try their dispositions, makes them return some of the playthings and sweets he has given them. They would be very silly and very selfish if they did not at once say, " Dear father, take what you like, you can have them all." After all, what do these poor children give, and to whom does it really belong ? All the same the father's heart is touched by these little signs of a good disposition. " Oh you good children, you dear children ! " and he kisses them and is always more generous towards them in future. This is how our good God will act towards us, whenever He gives us occasion to offer Him some sacrifice.

LETTER XXXII.—*Patience with the Faults of Others.*

To Sister Marie-Thérèse de Vioménil. On bearing with your neighbour and yourself.

My dear Sister,

It is a great grace to see others behaving badly without feeling bitterness, indignation, impatience, or even disturbance. If, for good reasons, you speak about it, watch over your heart and your tongue, so that nothing may escape you that would not be approved by God : and have good motives for whatever you say. Humble yourself quietly and lament in peace those faults that may have crept in during such talks. Often ask God to give you great charity and circumspection, and then remain tranquil. Keep yourself in the holy desire to belong entirely to God ; pray with faith, confidence and resignation, and above all humble yourself profoundly before His divine Majesty. It is for Him to finish the work He has begun in you ; no one else would be able to succeed in it, but know that there are many sacrifices to be made before God can take possession of our hearts by the ineffable delights of His pure love. Let us sigh for this happiness, and let us never weary of begging for it ; let us purchase it by generous sacrifices, we shall never be able to pay too much for it. As our hearts cannot exist without love, shall we not go to the Heart of our God to derive from it the sustenance that alone can appease our hunger ? May this divine love come then, and take possession of our hearts, may it sustain them, set them on fire and transform them into itself. Let us abandon ourselves without reserve to God and not interfere with His loving providence but think only of keeping straight in the road that God has marked out for us from all eternity, and in which we find ourselves at the present moment. One can dispute unendingly about predestination, and such arguments can only serve to make salvation seem more difficult ; what is, however, undeniable is that there is no better expedient to insure predestination than the actual and continual accomplishment of the will of God.

LETTER XXXIII.—*Patience with Oneself.*

To the same person. On bearing with herself.

My dear Sister,
We must submit to God in all things and about all things ; as to the state and condition in which He has placed us, the good or evil circumstances that He has allotted us, and even as to the character, mind, nature, temperament, and inclinations with which He has endowed us. Practise yourself, therefore, in being patient with regard to yourself and in this perfect submission to the divine will. When you have acquired this you will enjoy great peace, and not distress yourself about anything, nor get out of humour with yourself, but put up with yourself with the same gentleness which you should use towards your neighbour. This is a more important matter than you would imagine, and just at present is most essential to your sanctification. Keep

it, therefore, always before your eyes, and make frequent acts of submission to the holy will of God, of charity, of endurance, and of gentleness towards yourself even more than towards your neighbour. You will never attain to this without great efforts.

A soul to whom God makes known its defects is much more burdensome to itself than its neighbour ever could be to it, because the latter, however near to us, is not always with us ; at any rate is not within us, whereas we carry ourselves about with us, and cannot leave ourselves for a single moment, nor completely cease to behold ourselves, to feel ourselves, and to carry about with us everywhere our imperfections, and our faults. But see wherein the infinite goodness of our God shines forth ; for the sorrow and shame that our faults cause us are their own remedy, provided that this shame never turns into defiance, and that the sorrow is inspired by the love of God, and not by self-love. Sorrow born of self-love is full of vexation and bitterness ; far from healing the wounds of our soul, it only serves to poison them. On the other hand, sorrow produced by the love of God is calm and full of resignation ; while detecting the fault it delights in the humiliation which follows, and from this it results that much merit is gained, and thus even from losses we make profit. Cease then from tormenting yourself on account of your defects and of the imperfection of your works. Offer to God the sorrow they occasion you, and allow His divine Providence to make good these slight infidelities by many little crosses and sufferings of all kinds. Arm yourself only with patience, raise yourself again as soon as possible and deplore your falls with a sweet, tranquil humility. God wishes you to act thus, and by this indefatigable patience you will render Him more glory and will make more progress than the most violent efforts would have enabled you to do.

LETTER XXXIV.—*Preparation for the Sacraments.*

To the same person. On preparation for the Sacraments, prayer, reading and conduct.

Believe me, my dear Sister, that peace of mind, confidence, and abandonment to God, with the desire of being united to Jesus Christ are the best preparation for the Sacraments. But the devil tries to deceive people, and leaves nothing undone to disturb the interior peace of the soul, for he well knows that once this divine peace is firmly established in the heart, all will be easy to us, and we shall fly, as it were, in the ways of perfection. Do not let us be deluded, then, by any pretexts of which he may make use, however specious they may be, and let us go to God humbly with the simplicity and confidence that St. Francis of Sales advises, in the uprightness of a heart that sincerely seeks Him. As to prayer you well know what I have so much recommended to you ; do not allow yourself to be discouraged, nor vexed at your distractions. Manage, however, that your interior turning to God and the raising of your heart to Him during the day may become so frequent that that alone, in case of need, will take the place of prayer, without, however, leaving off making it as well as you can. Apply yourself especially to reading the letters of St. Francis of Sales, you will find them so well suited to your present state and condition that you could read them as though the saint had written them to yourself from heaven, and as though the Holy Spirit had dictated them to him for you.

You wish to know what it is that I ask of God for you in particular. It is this, and for such easy things that their very facility will charm you.

1st. The moderation of your exterior conduct, which will be a wonderful help to you in gradually overcoming your passions ; in other words, to speak gently, to act quietly, without any vehemence or impetuosity just as though you were of a phlegmatic temperament.

2nd. Interior gentleness towards yourself and others, at least of the kind that nothing contrary to this virtue may show in your exterior conduct ; or that, if for a moment you should forget yourself you will not fail to make reparation and to rise without delay.

3rd. An entire abandonment to divine Providence as to the success of everything, without excepting your own advancement in virtue ; not wishing to be better than God wishes you to be, and saying always, " I wish only what God wills."

4th. A peace of heart that nothing can disturb, not even your own faults and sins, and which will make you return to God with a peaceful and quiet humility, as though you had not had the misfortune to offend His divine Majesty or that you were assured of pardon. Follow this advice with simplicity, and you will see how God will help you.

LETTER XXXV.—*Conduct in a Time of Rest.*

To a secular. On conduct during a time passed in the country.

This is what you should do during the time you spend in the country. If you faithfully follow my counsels, they will sanctify this time of rest and make it bear fruit.

1st.   Approach the Sacraments as often as you are allowed to do so.

2nd.   Offer to God each morning the recreations of the day and with them the different pains both exterior and interior with which He is pleased in His goodness to season them, and say from time to time : " Blessed be God in all things and for all things ; Lord may Your holy will be done."

3rd.   As you are less busy than others, employ more of your time in reading good books, and in order to make this more efficacious, set about it in this way.   Begin by placing yourself in the presence of God, and by begging His help.   Read quietly, slowly, word for word to enter into the subject more with the heart than the mind.   At the end of each paragraph that contains a complete meaning, stop for the time it would take you to recite a " Pater," or even a little longer, to assimilate what you have read, or to rest and remain peacefully before God. Should this peace and rest last for a longer time it will be all the better ; but when you find that your mind wanders resume your reading, and continue thus, frequently renewing these same pauses.

4th.   Nothing need prevent you continuing the same method, if you find it useful to your soul, during the time you have fixed for meditation.

5th.   In the course of the day, occupy yourself about things that are necessary, and that obedience requires of you, and which divine Providence has marked out for you.

6th.   Be careful to drop vain and useless thoughts directly you are conscious of them, but quietly, without effort or violence.

7th.   Above all drop all anxious thoughts, abandoning to divine Providence all that might become a subject of preoccupation for you.

8th.   In raising your heart to God, often say to Him, " Lord deliver me from so many reflexions which, however good in appearance, might keep me in my own way, and in a dangerous confidence in myself.   Substitute Your divine Spirit for mine, transform and remodel all the powers of my soul by this holy Spirit and by His holy operations."   At other times say, " When will it please you, oh my God, to teach me the great secret of understanding how to keep myself in interior peace and silence, to allow of Your effecting in my soul all the changes You know to be necessary ?   Lord, this I desire with all my heart, and ask it of You with the greatest earnestness through Jesus Christ Your Son, in order that You may be able to establish gradually within me the reign of Your ineffable peace, of Your grace and of Your divine love.   And since for this You require the co-

N

operation of Your poor unworthy creature, I will prepare myself with the help of Your grace, by being faithful to all the little practices that have been recommended to me ; I hope that You will bless and second this blind submission, and I offer You beforehand all the pains of my mind, and rebellions of heart which You may permit in order to try me ; I resign myself to them and from henceforth offer them to You in sacrifice."

LETTER XXXVI.—*On Life and Death.*

To Sister M. Antionette de Mahuet (1742). On life and death, consolations and trials.

Here I am again at Albi, in a very agreeable climate, and among sociable people in whom the only fault I find is that of being too kind to me who always prefer solitude. The frequent invitations I receive are, to me, a veritable cross, and God will without doubt send me many others to temper the pleasure I feel in finding myself for the fourth time in a country that I have always loved so much. Blessed be God for all. He sows crosses everywhere ! but I have already made a sacrifice of all, have accepted and offered in advance all the afflictions He is pleased to send me. This intention made beforehand renders trials much easier to bear when they come and makes them seem much lighter than imagination depicted them. Therefore I am overjoyed to find myself where God wishes me to be by the arrangements of His loving providence which always leads me as though by the hand. This paternal solicitude of which I am continually the object, redoubles my confidence. Although I am always in perfect health I feel that the years, so rapidly passing, will soon bring me to that eternal goal to which we are all hastening. True ! this thought is bitter to nature but by dint of considering it as salutary it becomes almost agreeable as a disgusting remedy gradually ceases to appear so when its good effects have been experienced. One of my friends said the other day that in getting old it seemed to him that time passed with increasing rapidity, and that weeks seemed to him as short as days used to be, months like weeks, and years like months. As for that, what do a few years more or less signify to us who have to live and continue as long as God Himself? Those who have gone before us twenty or thirty years ago or even a century, or those who will follow us twenty or thirty years hence will neither be behindhand not before others in that vast eternity, but it will seem to all of us as though we began it together. Oh ! what power does not this thought contain to soften the rigours of our short and miserable life which, patiently endured, will be to our advantage. A longer or a shorter life, a little more, or a little less pain, what is it in comparison with the eternal life that awaits us? for which we are making rapidly, incessantly, and which is almost in sight, for me especially who am as it were on the brink, and on the point of embarking. It is therefore time, I ought to say with St. Francis of Sales and Fr. Surin, to prepare my small equipment for eternity. Now the best equipment is that which appeared for us in the crosses which we bear lovingly, and the great sacrifices we make for God in doing His holy will. Nothing will console us more at the hour of death than our humble submission to the different arrangements of divine Providence in spite of the subtle imaginations of self-love often hidden under the most spiritual disguise and the most specious pretexts.

Do not be surprised then, my dear Sister, at being placed by God in this necessity of practising abandonment. The vicissitudes of good and evil, of illness and cure through which He makes you pass are well calculated to keep you in a state of continual dependence upon Him and to impel you to make acts of confidence of the most meritorious kind. To make a holy use of sufferings mitigates them considerably, and renders them extremely profitable. To bear them well is to make a great sacrifice comparable to that of those generous Christians who formerly confessed their faith at the stake; because the sufferings of life and the sorrows attached to the different states make martyrs of Providence, as the tortures inflicted by tyrants made martyrs of faith and of religion. I find, too, that the comparison of which you make use is very just. Yes, our life is like the journey of the Israelites across the desert amidst a thousand trials and followed by the too just judgments of God. Let us imitate the faithful Jews in recognising the divine equity in the chastisements He inflicts on us, and in regarding all our afflictions both visible and hidden as the work of God and not that of man's injustice. God, says St. Augustine, would not allow any evil to happen, if He were not sufficiently powerful and good to turn it all to the greater good of His elect. Let us make use of our present evils, to escape those that are eternal, and to merit the rewards promised to faith and patience. The time will come, and it is at hand, when we shall say with David, " We have rejoiced for the days in which Thou hast humbled us, for the years in which we have seen evils." (Ps. 89, v. 15).

LETTER XXXVII.—*Not to Desire Consolations.*

To the same person. Nancy, 21st February, 1735. Desire for consolations a mistake.

My dear Sister,

I have seen the card announcing the death of dear Sister Anne-Catherine de Prudhomme (see note). I could in no way regret the departed whose fate is rather to be envied. At the sight of death fear should be united to confidence, but confidence ought to predominate.

Abandonment is what the Sister you mention should aim at. I refer her on this subject to the letter of B. Paul, who says she is no longer uneasy, as formerly, about the graces necessary during life, and at the hour of death, because she will be encouraged by God whose name of "Father" gives her confidence with resignation. If it is not possible to feel this, even then one must abandon oneself to God, and this abandonment when not felt is of more value since it involves a greater sacrifice.

This letter of B. Paul I use as spiritual reading. After having answered it, it seemed to me that I had understood better from it, and more enjoyed certain very interior things that were both delicate and profound. I do not at all approve of an anxious pursuit after consolations either in spiritual or physical wretchedness and misery. That comes of too much care of oneself. Would that there were souls strong and courageous enough to endure the apparent absences of the heavenly Spouse, who never absents Himself in reality, but only in appearance, to detach us from what is sensible even in the most spiritual things, because the gifts of God are not God Himself. He alone is all, and should be all in all to us. Excessive fear arises from a want of confidence and abandonment; it is on this account that I referred Sister . . . . to this letter of B. Paul. God wills that she, and you too, should remain in such absolute poverty that He has given me nothing for either of you; but I hope that you will both profit by a good long letter written to someone of whom I asked a copy. Will you return me the original as I want to send it to another person, who is precisely Sister . . . . of whom God made me think. I greet most heartily all the Sisters, and particularly Marie-Anne-Thérèse, and with especial respect your Rev. Mother, L. F. de Rosen.

NOTE.—This Sister came of a very noble family of Lorraine, and was professed in the Convent of the Visitation, Sister Marie de Nancy, in the year 1666, at the age of 21. Her principal attraction was that of abandonment to divine Providence. She was perfectly submissive to the will of God by a continual " fiat " for every event, saying on all occasions, " If you, my divine King, my great Monarch, will, or do not will such, or such a thing, that suffices me. May You be praised and blessed for all and in all." Her great confidence in God drew down abundant graces upon her soul. In her last illness she remained always in a state of constant adoration, contrition, faith, confidence, and union with Jesus Christ crucified, of love of God, and abandonment to His fatherly goodness, and always wore a look of peace, joy, and thanksgiving. Her union with God continuing up to her last breath, she quietly expired of simple weakness at the age of 90, with all her intellectual faculties unimpaired. (This extract is from the life of this good Sister, by Rev. Mother L. F. de Rosen.)

THIRD BOOK.

ON THE OBSTACLES TO ABANDONMENT.

LETTER I.—*About Vanity and Infidelities.*

To Sister M. Thérèse de Vioménil. About feelings of vanity and frequent infidelities.

My dear Sister and very dear daughter in our Lord. The peace of Jesus Christ be always with you. You must know that before curing you of vanity God wills to make you feel all the ugliness of this accursed passion, and to convince you thoroughly of your powerlessness to cure it, so that all the glory of your cure should revert to Him alone. You have, then, in this matter, only two things to do. Firstly to examine peacefully this frightful interior ugliness. Secondly, to hope for and await in peace from God alone the moment fixed for your cure. You will never be at rest till you have learnt to distinguish what is from God from that which is your own; to separate what belongs to Him from what belongs to yourself. You add, "How can you teach me this secret." You do not understand what you are saying. I can easily teach it to you in a moment, but you cannot learn to practise it until you have been made to feel, in peace, all your miseries. I say, in peace, to give room for the operations of grace.

Remember the words of St. Francis of Sales : "One cannot put on perfection as one does a dress." The secret you ask for I give you freely; try to understand it so that it may gradually work its way into your soul, which is what you hope.

All that is good in you comes from God, all that is bad, spoiled and corrupt comes from yourself. Therefore put on one side the nothingness, the sin, the evil inclinations, and habits, a whole heap of miseries, and weaknesses, as your share, and it belongs to you in truth. All that remains : the body with all its senses, the soul with its faculties, and the small amount of good performed, this is God's and belongs to Him so absolutely that you could not appropriate any part by the least act of complacency without committing a theft and robbery from God.

That which you so often repeat interiorly, "Lord, You can do all things, have pity on me," is a good and a most simple act; nothing more is required to gain His all powerful aid; keep constant to these practices and interior dispositions; God will do the rest without your perceiving it.

I am thoroughly convinced that, without great unfaithfulness on your part, God will work great things in you by His holy operation. Count upon this and do not place any voluntary obstacles in the way; and if, unfortunately, you recognise that you have done so, humble yourself promptly, return to God and to yourself always retaining an absolute confidence in the divine goodness.

3rd. A lively sense of your misery, and the continual need you are in of God's help is a very great grace and opens the way to all good but especially to the prayer of humility and annihilation before God which is so pleasing to Him.

4th. You do not understand as I do, the effects, and the operations of grace in your soul; if you recognised them you would be too satisfied with them, but your weakness and lack of virtue do not allow you to bear the knowledge. It is necessary that this fruit of grace should remain hidden and, as it were, buried in the abyss of your miseries and beneath a keen sense of your weakness. Under this heap of refuse God preserves the fruits of His grace, for such is the depth of our wretchedness that we compel God to hide from us His gifts as well as the rich ornaments with which He adorns our souls; unless He did so the least little breath of vanity, and of an imperceptible self-satisfaction would destroy or spoil these flowers or fruits. When you are in a state to be able to bear, and to enjoy them without danger, God will open your eyes, and then you will only praise and bless Him without any reverting to yourself, and asribe all the glory of your deliverance to your divine Redeemer. In the meantime follow the guidance given you now by His Holy Spirit, and do not let fear enter your heart. Understand that in all that you actually experience there is no sin, since you endure it with so much pain and would only be too happy to put an end to these wretched effects of your sensitiveness. Maintain yourself in this holy desire, pray for it patiently, above all, humble yourself before God; it is for Him to complete the work He has begun in you, no one else could succeed in it. Understand that this is the little sacrifice that God demands of you before filling your heart with the ineffable delights of His pure love. You will have no rest till this merciful design of God shall be realised because your heart cannot exist without love. Let us pray, then, that this thirst may be satisfied by the love of God alone, that He and He alone may captivate our hearts, that He may sustain, possess, enlighten, and change them.

5th. The abyss of misery and corruption in which God seems to take pleasure in seeing you plunged is, to my judgment, the chief of graces since it is the true foundation of all self-distrust, and of an entire confidence in God, the two poles of the interior life ; at any rate, of all graces it is the one I like best, and that I find most frequently in souls that are far advanced. What you think of yourself, therefore, although terrible, is nevertheless perfectly true and very well founded, for, if God were to leave you to yourself you would be a heap of all that is evil and a monster of iniquity. But God makes this great truth known to very few people, because few are capable of bearing it properly, that is to say, in peace, in confidence, in God only, without anxiety or discouragement.

6th. There is no other remedy for these frequent infidelities than to lament them, peacefully to humble yourself, and to return to God as soon as possible. We shall carry these afflictions and humiliations during the whole of our lives, because we shall always be ungrateful and unfaithful ; but, as long as it is so only through the frailty of our nature, without any affection of the heart, that is enough. God knows our weakness, He knows the extent of our misery and how incapable we are of avoiding all infidelity ; He sees also that we have need of being reduced to this state of misery without which we could not resist the continual attacks of pride, presumption, and secret self-confidence. Be careful not to get discouraged even when you find that the resolutions so often renewed, of belonging entirely to God, fail. Make use of these constant experiences, to enter more deeply into the profound abyss of your nothingness and corruption. Learn a complete distrust of yourself to depend only on God. Often repeat : " Lord I can do nothing without Your help. Enlightened by sad experience I can depend on nothing but Your all-powerful grace, and the more unworthy I feel, the more do I hope, because my unworthiness will more surely draw down Your mercy." You cannot carry your confidence in God too far. An infinite goodness and mercy should produce an infinite confidence.

7th. It is a very subtle and imperceptible illusion of self-love to wish to know how you stand with regard to the mystical death, under the pretext of being able to act so as to render this death more complete in you. You will never know it in this life, neither would it be expedient for you to know it, because even supposing a soul to be entirely dead to self ; if it became conscious of the fact, it would run a great risk of losing this state ; because self-love would be so much pleased, and so satisfied with this assurance that it would rise to life again, and begin a new existence more sensitive and difficult to destroy than the first.

Oh, God! how subtle is this wretched self-love! It turns
and twists like a serpent, and is only too successful in preserving
its life in the midst of the most fearful deaths. This is of all
illusions the most specious. Have a horror of this accursed
self-love, but learn that, in spite of all your efforts, it will not
die completely and radically until the last moment of your life.

8th. The impression of the sanctity of God which throws
you into such a state of confusion and pain, without, however,
causing you trouble is, I am assured, a great grace, more precious
and more certain than the consolation by which it is succeeded.
I can, then, only wish for you that it may continue. Do not
resist it, let yourself be abased, humiliated, annihilated. Nothing
is better calculated to purify your soul, and you could not
approach Holy Communion in a disposition more in keeping
with a state of annihilation to which Jesus Christ has reduced
Himself in this mystery. He will not be able to repulse you if
you approach Him in a spirit of humility and as though annihilated in the profound abyss of your misery. If you have not
the impulse, nor the facility to discover your interior state after
habing begged this grace, you must remain in peace and silence.
Your discouragement is a sign of a want of purity of intention
and is a very dangerous temptation, because you must only
desire to improve, to please God, and not to please yourself.
You must, therefore, be always satisfied with whatever God wills
or permits since His will alone should be the rule, and the exact
limit of your desires, however holy they may be. Besides,
you must never get it into your head that you have arrived at a
certain state, or you will become self-satisfied, which would be a
grievous misfortune. The most certain sign of our progress
is the conviction of our misery. We shall, therefore, be all the
more rich the more we think ourselves poor, and the more we
humble ourselves, distrust ourselves, and are more disposed to
place all our confidence in God alone. And this is just what
God has begun to give you, therefore let there be neither anxiety
nor discouragement. Each day you must say to yourself,
" To-day I am going to begin." I greatly applaud the practice
you have adopted of never upholding your own judgment, and
of allowing yourself to be blamed and criticised even in
circumstances where you believed you had good reasons to
excuse yourself. You sacrifice, you say, the good opinion that
you wish others to have of you, and you keep silence although
until now you would have thought that it would be better to
defend yourself that your conduct might give edification when
that which was said against you was untrue. This is my answer: To endure every kind of blame and unjust accusation
in silence without uttering a single word in justification under

any pretext whatever is according to the spirit of the Gospel, and in conformity with the example of Jesus Christ and of all the saints. Your ideas to the contrary were the result of a pure illusion ; therefore, keep firm to your new and holy conduct. You are right in saying that we carry a fund of corruption inseparable from our nature, and that it resembles muddy stagnant water that gives out an intolerable stench when it is stirred. That is an unquestionable truth, and God has given you a great grace in making you feel is so keenly. From this feeling will come, gradually, a holy hatred and complete distrust of yourself in which true humility principally consists.

LETTER II.—*The Defects of Beginners.*

On the defects of beginners.

I am not surprised at the calmness of the person of whom you speak ; it is the fruit of the humility she practised in opening her heart, in spite of her repugnance to doing so ; and also the effect of the words that God never fails to inspire, in such a case, to those who are acting in His place. Make her thoroughly understand that God has begun to try her like this to punish her, and to cure her of a subtle hidden pride which she has been nursing without noticing it. The greater has been the trouble, the more it has shown the greatness of the vanity which it has disconcerted, and which rebels at the least humiliation, even that which is interior. This person, therefore, must try to divest herself gradually of that self-complacency which is hidden in the most secret recesses of the heart ; whether it be about natural qualities, or about those virtues that she may have, or flatters herself that she possesses. For, without being careful about it, there may be some foolish self-satisfaction in all that ; and without allowing it to herself she thinks herself superior to others in many ways. A subtle self-love feeds on these vanities of the spirit, in the way that worldly pride is satisfied with the beauties of the body; and, as the latter finds pleasure in thinking continually of its beauty and in looking in the mirror ; so, in the same way, the former takes interior delight in all the natural and supernatural gifts which it flatters itself to have received from heaven. The remedy for this diabolical evil (diabolical, because it is the crime of the proud angel) is—

1st. To imitate modest women who never contemplate themselves in the mirror, or who drive from their minds all vain thoughts about their appearance, or exterior accomplishments.

2nd. To force this self-love often to look at its defects, miseries, and weakness, to enjoy abjection, and to feed on contempt.

3rd. To consider what we have been, what we are, and what we should become, if God removed His hand from us. When we neglect to apply ourselves to these humiliating reflexions, God, in His fatherly goodness, feels obliged to take other means to destroy the secret vanity of souls whom He desires to lead to a high state of perfection; He allows temptation, or even falls that throw them into the deepest confusion to cure them of this inflation of the mind and heart. When God makes use of this bitter but salutary remedy, we must be on our guard to prevent our hearts rebelling against it, but submit humbly without vexation, and without voluntary agitation.

4th. We ought not to imagine that by dint of reflexions we shall be able to lessen our troubles, but should remain as if motionless in the bosom of the mercy of God, and let the storm pass without struggling against it, and without interior disturbance which would aggravate the evil instead of lessening it.

5th. We should never ask to be delivered from our afflictions since they have been brought about by the favourable action of Providence, but we must pray for patience with ourselves and others, and for an entire resignation.

6th. Instead of becoming strong-minded, we must become like children by a great simplicity, candour, ingenuousness, and openness of heart towards those who have the task of guiding

NOTE.—This letter was addressed in 1731 to Sister Marie-Anne Thérèse de Rosen by Fr. de Caussade, and was about a person who was making a retreat. There is every reason to believe that it concerned either Madame or Mademoiselle de Lesen whom God had brought back to Himself by the trial of the loss of her property, and who had vowed to become a Religious, but who was obliged to remain in the world for a long time leading a devout life. She made a retreat in 1731 and another in 1732 in the Convent of the Visitation at Nancy, and had Sister Marie-Anne Thérèse de Rosen for her directress. Shortly after she entered the Order of the Annunciation at St. Mihiel in 1733.

LETTER III.—*The Illusions of the Devil.*

To Sister Charlotte-Elizabeth Bourcier de Monthureux (1735). On interior troubles voluntarily entertained and weakness.

My dear Sister,

For several days past I have had so many letters to write, either for this country, or for France, that I have not been able to read your long account. I do not disguise from you that it seemed to me very useless, because God has given me the grace to thoroughly understand your state without my having the trouble to read all this. However, I have read the most essential part, that against which you have put a particular mark, and it has only confirmed the opinion I had formed of you some time ago. Excuse me, my dear Sister, if I insist on the same direction that I have always hitherto given you. Until now you have derived great benefit from having followed it, why then allow yourself to be misguided by the illusions of the devil ? I am not speaking to you at random, but with full conviction, do then believe me, and prove, by your docility, that the confidence with which you honour me is not a vain pretence. If you really have a good will, if you are sincerely and earnestly resolved to belong to God, you ought to make every effort to maintain yourself in peace in order not to give the lie to the message of the angels, " Peace to men of good will." But you must expect that Satan will exert every effort to prevent you acquiring a peace so desirable. I know that, unfortunately, he has but too well succeeded up to now. The greatest evil in your soul at present is that of anxiety, uneasiness and interior agitation. This malady is, thank God, not incurable, but as long as it remains unhealed it cannot but be even more dangerous than painful to you. Interior disturbance renders the soul incapable of listening to, and following the voice of the divine Spirit, of receiving the sweet and delightful impressions of His grace, and of applying itself to pious exercises, and to exterior duties. It is the same with such sick and afflicted souls as with bodies enfeebled by fever, which cannot accomplish any serious task until delivered from their malady. And as there is a certain analogy between them there is also some resemblance between the remedies to be used. The health of the body can only be restored by three means, obedience to the physician, rest, and good food. These are, likewise, the three means of restoring peace and health to a soul that is agitated, sick, and almost in agony.

The first condition for its cure is obedience, a childlike blind obedience founded on the principle that God, having authorised His priests to guide us, cannot allow those souls to be deceived who, on this account, abandon themselves blindly to their guidance. Before all things, therefore, make your virtue consist in the renunciation of your own judgment, and in a humble and generous intention of believing and doing all that your director judges, before God, to be expedient. If you are animated with this spirit of obedience you will never allow yourself voluntarily to entertain thoughts opposed to what has been enjoined you, and you will take good care not to give in to the inclination to examine and scrutinize everything. If, however in spite of yourself, some thoughts contrary to obedience enter your mind, you must reject them, or better still, despise them as dangerous temptations.

The second remedy for your complaint is rest, and peace for your soul. To acquire this, you must first of all desire it ardently, and pray to God earnestly for it, and then work with all your might to acquire it. If you wish to know how to set about this task I will tell you.

Be very careful not to allow any thoughts which would bring about uneasiness, sadness, or depression to remain in your mind. These thoughts are, in one sense, more dangerous than temptations to impurity; you must, therefore, let them alone; without dwelling on them; despise them, and let them fall like a stone into the sea. Resist them by fixing your mind on contrary ideas, and above all by making aspirations suitable for the occasion, with sighs and interior groanings accompanied by acts of humility. But this struggle while being energetic and generous must also be quiet, tranquil and peaceful, because if it were to be restless, unhappy, ill-humoured and wild, the remedy would be worse than the disease. In the second place avoid in your actions, whether exterior or interior, all eagerness, hurry, and natural activity; accustom yourself, on the contrary, to speak, to walk, to pray and to read quietly, slowly, without over-exerting yourself no matter for what, not even to repulse the most frightful temptations. You must remember that if these temptations are displeasing to you that is the best sign that you have not consented to them. As long as the free will feels nothing but horror at, and hatred for the objects presented to the imagination in these temptations, it is evident that it does not in any way consent to them. Keep yourself, therefore, in peace in the midst of these temptations as you have done in other trials.

1st. It only remains then to cure the weakness resulting from the fever which torments a soul in trouble. For that a strengthening diet is necessary—that is to say—to read good books, and to get accustomed to read very slowly with frequent pauses, more to try and take an interest in what you read than to make use of the intellect in reflexions on it. Remember the wise saying of Fénélon, " The words we read are like the bark of the tree, but the interest we take in them is like the sap which feeds and fattens the soul." We must act as regards this spiritual nourishment as gluttons and sensualists act with regard to their feasts which they taste in remembrance, and enjoy after having swallowed them.

2nd. We must only speak on useful and edifying subjects, and with those who are most capable of leading us to God by their holy conversation.

3rd. Never seek consolation from creatures by useless intercourse. This is an essential matter for those who are suffering interior trials. God, who sends them for our good, desires that we should bear them without going elsewhere for consolation, but to Him ; and He claims the right to settle the moment when such consolation should be given to us.

4th. We must apply ourselves, each according to his or her capacity and attraction to interior prayer, but without intense application or strain, keeping very quietly in the holy presence of God, addressing Him occasionally by some interior act of adoration, repentance, confidence, or love. If, however, it is not possible to make such acts, we must be content with the good desire of doing so ; for, whether for good or evil, desire is equivalent to an act in the sight of God. Bossuet, somewhere in his works very truly says : " Desire is, with regard to God, what the voice and words are with regard to men. We ask, and return thanks by the desires we have, which say everything, and make our petitions known to God much more distinctly than any words could do, or even those interior acts which are called particular and formal." This is what gave rise to the saying that a cry uttered only in the depths of the heart is the same in the sight of Him Who sounds all hearts, as a cry that pierces the heavens.

5th. It is necessary to put this manner of praying into practice, not only at morning devotions, but also during the whole day in a quiet, easy, tender, and affectionate manner by frequently raising the heart to God, or by an interior attention to the divine presence. To gain greater facility you might review in the morning nearly every event both interior and exterior, likely to occur during the day, and ask yourself, " If I find myself in such a circumstance, or such a position, what shall I say to God, what act should I make ? " and if, when the time arrives you are prevented from carrying out your good intentions, you can be content to adhere to them, even if only indistinctly, and to lay before God your inability. Finally the best food for the soul consists in willing in all and for all what God wills ; or, in other words to adhere to all the designs of divine Providence in every imaginable circumstance whether interior or exterior, health or sickness, aridity, distractions, weariness, disgusts, temptations, etc., and to accept all this very heartily, saying, " Yes, my God, I will everything ; I accept all, I sacrifice all to You ; or, at any rate I wish to do so, and ask for this grace, help me and strengthen my weakness." In the most fearful temptations say to Him, " My God, preserve me from sin in this matter ; but I willingly accept as much confusion to

my pride, and interior abjection and humiliation as You will and
for as long as You will, I unite my will to Yours."

The most uneasy and enfeebled soul could not fail to recover
its lost peace and joy if it adopted these means for regaining
them.

LETTER IV.—*Interior Troubles.*
To the same person. Interior troubles (1755).

If my letter distressed you, my dear Sister, I will say to you
with St. Paul, that I rejoice not, indeed, at your affliction, but
at the good effect it has produced. It is good to recognise that
one has been culpable in many ways, not in order to reproach
oneself in a hard, bitter, angry, and disturbed manner, but to
humble oneself quietly and peacefully without self-contempt
or bitterness. You do not consider yourself disobedient, you
say, in relating to me quite frankly your fears and doubts.
That is not the question, my dear Sister; but what is, is that
you continue to cling to your fears and doubts; you study them
too much, instead of despising them and abandoning yourself
entirely to God, as I have preached to you for a long time past.
Without this happy and holy abandonment you will never enjoy
a solid peace full of absolute confidence in God alone, through
Jesus Christ.

But, I ask you again, what have you to fear in this abandonment, especially after such evident signs of the very great mercy
of God towards you? You are endeavouring to find help in
yourself and your works, and to satisfy your conscience, as if
your works gave your conscience greater security and stronger
support than the mercy of God, and the merits of Jesus Christ;
and as though they could not deceive you. I pray God to enlighten you, and to give you a change of heart about this matter
so essential to you. You say that I should feel distressed and
surprised if you laid bare to me all that you experience. This
is exactly what people in your state so often say to me, people
with whom I am not so well acquainted as with you. Here is
my answer to you, and to others like you. The keen perception
of faults and imperfections is the grace suitable to this state, and
it is a very precious grace. Why? First because this clear
view of our miseries keeps us humble, and even sometimes
inspires us with a wholesome horror and a holy fear of ourselves.
Secondly, because this state, apparently so miserable and so
desperate gives occasion to an heroic abandonment into the hands
of God. Those who have gauged the depths of their own
nothingness can no longer retain any kind of confidence in

themselves, nor trust in any way to their works in which they can discover nothing but misery, self-love, and corruption. This absolute distrust and complete disregard of self is the source from which alone flow those delightful consolations of souls wholly abandoned to God, and form their inalterable peace, holy joy and immoveable confidence in God only. Oh! if you but knew the gift of God, the value, merit, power, peace and holy assurance of salvation hidden in this state of abandonment, you would soon be delivered from all your fears and anxieties. But you imagine you will be lost directly you think of abandoning yourself; and yet the most efficacious means of salvation is to practise this total and perfect abandonment. I have never yet come across any who have so set themselves against making this act of abandonment to God as you. Nevertheless you will, necessarily, have to come to it, at least at the hour of death; because, without an express revelation and assurance of eternal salvation, no one can be free from fear at the last moment, and therefore, every one is absolutely compelled then to abandon themselves to the very great mercy of God.

"But," you say, "if I had lived a holy life and performed some good works I might think myself authorised to practise this abandonment, and to divest myself of my fears." An illusion, my dear Sister. Such language can only have been inspired by your unhappy self-love, which desires to be able to trust entirely to itself, whereas you ought to place your confidence only in God and in the infinite merits of Jesus Christ. You have never really thoroughly fathomed this essential point but have always stopped short to examine into your fears and doubts instead of rising above them, and throwing yourself heart and soul into the hands of God, and upon His fatherly breast. In other words you always want to have a distinct assurance based on yourself, in order to abandon yourself better. Most certainly this is anything but an abandonment to God in complete confidence in Him only, but, rather, a secret desire of being able to depend on yourself before abandoning yourself to His infinite goodness. This is to act like a state criminal who, before abandoning himself to the clemency of the king, wishes to be assured of his pardon. Can this be called depending on God, hoping only in God? Judge for yourself! And God has for so long a time been calling you to this state of abandonment in filial confidence. And you, instead of responding to this loving call allow yourself to be tyrannised over, and martyrised by a slavish fear. I greatly insist on this matter, because experience has taught me that this is the last battle of grace for souls in your state; the last step to take in forsaking self, and the one that costs the most. But it seems to me that no one has ever offered so much resistance as you. This proceeds from a very strongly rooted self-love, from a secret great presumption and confidence in yourself that, possibly, you may never have found out; for, mark well, that directly you are spoken to about this total abandonment to God you feel a certain interior commotion as though all were lost, and as if you had been told to throw yourself, with your eyes shut, into an abyss. It seems a trifle, yet it is very much the contrary, for the greatest assurance of salvation in this life can only be obtained in this total abandonment, and this consists, as Fénélon says, in becoming thoroughly tired of, and driven to despair of oneself, and made to hope only in God. Weigh well the force of these words which at first sight seem too strong and exaggerated.

However, to bring you to this state of total abandonment God has imparted to you two great graces. Firstly, a powerful attraction to induce you to place all your confidence in His very great mercy and goodness ; secondly, a great knowledge of, and a very penetrating insight into your miseries, weaknesses, perversity, powerlessness to act well, etc. ; as if to say to you : " You see that in this state you neither ought nor can, in any sort of way, depend on yourself, since you are nothing but a heap of corruption. Let Me then, have the care of you, and forsake yourself once for all, to depend only on Me." " But how shall I work out my salvation ? " What ! do you not understand that the most certain way of assuring this is to leave the care of it entirely to God, and to occupy yourself only with Him ; as a man in the confidence of a great king leaves the question of recompense to him, and thinks only of the service and interests of his master. Do you not think that, in acting in this generous manner he would be doing better for himself than others who, more selfish, would think continually of what they might gain or obtain ? But are we not commanded to think of ourselves, to enter into ourselves, to watch over ourselves ? Yes, certainly, when beginning to enter the service of God in order to detach ourselves from the world, to forsake exterior objects, to correct the bad habits we have contracted, but, afterwards we must forget ourselves to think only of God, forsake ourselves to belong to God alone. But as for you, you wish to remain always wrapped up in yourself, in your, so-called, spiritual interests ; and God, to draw you out of this last resource of self-love, allows you to find nothing in yourself but a source of fears, doubts, uncertainty, trouble, anxiety and depression, as though this God of all goodness said by this, " Forget yourself, and you will find in Me only, peace, spiritual joy, calmness, and an absolute assurance of salvation. I am the God of your salvation, and you can be nothing but the cause of your own destruction."

o

But again you say, "In this forgetfulness of self, far from correcting myself of my sins and imperfections, I do not even know them." An error! an illusion! ignorance! Never can you more clearly detect your faults than in the clear light of the presence of God. This is like an interior sunshine, which, without necessitating a constant self-examination, makes us see and understand everything by a simple impression. In this way also, better than in any other, all our defects and imperfections are gradually consumed like straw in a fire. And then how happy is this state at which you should have arrived a long time ago! and of which God has given, and still gives me frequent experience. As the human heart is a bottomless abyss of misery and corruption, the more the light of God penetrates into it the more sad and humiliating are the objects disclosed; but at the same time these fresh disclosures, far from grieving the soul, console it in keeping it in an interior humility which it knows to be the solid foundation of the whole spiritual edifice. Far from disturbing its holy joy, and casting it down they inspire in it a solid confidence which it feels is placed in God alone, and that this confidence, according to Holy Scripture, has never been confounded. I have known, and know now many souls that, following this method, are astonished to find that the more feeble, poor, and miserable they realise themselves to be, the greater becomes their confidence in God. The reason of this is that in proportion to our insight into our own misery and corruption will be our distrust in ourselves and our confidence in God. God then imparts to those souls which have acquired this insight, an absolute self-distrust joined to an entire confidence in Him, from which proceeds total abandonment; these are the two strong springs of the spiritual life, and as long as you are in this state you run no risk of your salvation.

In abandoning all to God, therefore, we regain all in Him alone and with profit to our souls. In this way we are delivered once for all from these foolish self-examinations, fears, troubles, and uneasiness; in one word from these tortures to which those self-engrossed souls condemn themselves who wish to love God only out of self-love, who seek salvation and perfection, not so much to please God and to glorify Him, as for their own interests and eternal happiness.

But, you will say, God commands us to desire our salvation and eternal felicity. Yes, without doubt, but according to, and in submission to the ordaining of His will. Well! this is God's rule, which it is necessary for you to understand thoroughly; God has created us for His own glory and to do His will, and He could not have created us for any other purpose, for He owes his to Himself, and to His own sovereign dominion; but, as He

is also infinitely merciful He has so arranged that His creatures
find their own interests and eternal happiness in doing His will.
But see how this miserable self-love which seeks itself before all
else, reverses the order of things.   We want first and principally
to provide for our own interests, spiritual and eternal, and as for
the glory of God, in our preoccupation we give Him only the
second place.   God sees this subversion with a jealous eye in
souls He has loaded with graces, and by which He desires to be
loved with a pure and disinterested affection! and, in order to
make them return to this right order of things He sends them
troubles, fears and interior agitation, seeking by means of these
secret trials to destroy that self-love so harmful to them.   He
desires to induce them by degrees to think less of themselves and
their own interests, and to occupy themselves quietly with Him
alone by abandoning to Him the care and management of their
salvation ; and this is the meaning of those words of Jesus Christ
addressed to many holy souls.   "My daughter think of Me and
I will think of you, busy yourself for My glory, and allow Me
to occupy Myself with your interests and eternal welfare."

As for us, what are we doing when we always worry, and are
busied about ourselves ?   It is as though we said, " Lord, what
are You saying ?   I shall be lost if I do not continually think
about my own soul, if I am not constantly asking myself how
I stand with You, and what is going to become of me.   This
is what I am obliged to do without ceasing.   As for what concerns Your glory and Your good pleasure I can only think of
them now and then.   I hope I shall be able to occupy myself
with them more habitually by the time I have conquered all
my faults, and it is proved to me that I shall risk nothing by
this constant attention to Your divine interests.   But first of
all I cannot now decide about it for I should consider myself
lost and You wish me before all things to try and provide for
the safety of my soul."   To those of His spouses who address
such language to Him, this is the very clear and concise reply
of our Lord in the Gospel, " Whosoever loveth his life shall
lose it, and he that hateth his life in this world, keepeth it unto
life eternal."   And, in fact, I have never met with souls which
have a greater horror of sin, more strength for the practice of
virtue, or which make greater sacrifices for God when occasions
arise than those souls which seem never to think of themselves
but depend upon Him for everything, including their salvation.
It is in this state that salvation is most certain ; from which I
conclude that not only scruples, but excessive fears, distressing
doubts, spiritual trials and bitterness of heart, are caused by
selfish feelings, a greater preoccupation about personal interests
than about the glory of God and a desire to please Him out of

pure love and all that should take the first place in our hearts. Since He is the sovereign good, love of Him should take precedence of the charity we owe ourselves. And since He has promised to love those who love Him, and to love most those who love Him only, we can be assured that in making use of all our powers to love Him for Himself we shall regain with interest by this pure love all that we seem to have sacrificed ; therefore, far from losing, we gain all in abandoning ourselves entirely to God by love and confidence. The sight of that confused heap of weaknesses, miseries, unworthiness, and of all corruption should never distress you. It is on this account that I say boldly, all is well, for I have never known a soul endowed with this keen insight, so humiliating to it, to whom it was not a most singular grace of God ; nor who has not found in it, combined with a true knowledge of itself, that solid humility which is the foundation of all perfection. I have known, and do know many saintly souls who, for their sole possession, have that profound conviction of their misery, and are never so happy as when they feel themselves, as it were, engulfed in it. They then dwell in truth, and consequently in God Who is the sovereign truth. If you but knew how to walk before Him, your head bowed in this spirit of self-effacement, you would find in it all that makes the spiritual life. It only remains to know how to preserve this spirit of peace and abandonment. Would to God that you had the grace to pass all your time of prayer in this holy interior self-humiliation, engulfed in your misery, but in peace, submission, resignation and confidence. Then I should say to you : stay as you are, and all is well ; God will do the rest, and perhaps without you knowing, or feeling that He is doing it.

You are trembling over your state, and I am blessing God for it. I only wish you changed in one particular, and that is that your self-humiliation should be mingled with peace, submission, confidence, and abandonment, as I have just said. After that I should have no fear for you not even about the laxness of which you tell me, which makes you walk like a crab. God will prevent great laxness and will allow small relaxations to keep you humble. St. Francis of Sales said it was an heroic virtue to rise again unceasingly without ever losing courage.

God be praised in all, and for all.

Letter V.—*On the Love of One's Neighbour.*

To Sister de Lesen.   On the love of one's neighbour.   Nancy, 1735.

I am not at all surprised at the friendship you have for your dear relative, and understand that it is due to her for many reasons.   However, because by your own showing this affection disturbs you, and prevents you giving your whole heart to God, there must needs be some irregularity about it.   If you wish to sanctify it, and to render it altogether supernatural, this is what God demands of you.

1st. That you will not allow yourself to think about this person too often nor to be engrossed by thoughts of her ; there is moderation in all things.

2nd. That in the illnesses and afflictions she has to endure you will submit to them as a sacrifice you must make to God, and abandon yourself to Him so that He may dispose of her, and of you in all things, and about all things according to His most holy will and loving good pleasure.   You must know that in abandoning her thus to the will and care of divine Providence you render her, as well as yourself, the greatest possible service, since by this sacrifice you place her in the hands of God Who is infinitely good, and infinitely powerful.

We must certainly make use of our reasoning faculties in our trials ; but, as a very holy and learned Christian has well said, we must not depend too much on this feeble faculty which is stronger in opposition to what is good, than in overcoming evil. It is religion, and the grace we obtain through humble prayer which can sustain us.   Sadness, depression, interior rebellion when our relatives suffer from various causes, taking rise in a too affectionate disposition, will be a grand occasion of virtue and merit to us, if, endeavouring to raise ourselves by faith above our natural feelings, we understand that all has to be sacrificed to the adorable and most holy will of God.   Do we not know that nothing can happen in this world without His permission, and that He has arranged everything for the greater good of those who submit to Him, or at least who desire to acquire and to practise this submission ?

If we could only understand the value of this virtue ! Of all the means of salvation this is, together with the fulfilment of the divine precepts, the most universal, and the most infallible.. Nothing more is required to sanctify most people and to lighten for them the trials of life.   A wise pagan thought in this way when he said, " If one has a sensitive nature, and is accustomed to foster in oneself what the world calls refined and generous sentiments, it is no easy matter to cure oneself of thinking too much about the family honour, and of taking too great an interest in family affairs, and also of being too much moved by every incident affecting those to whom we are most tenderly attached." It is necessary to pray much about this, and also to reflect how to combat it. Firstly, to reflect on the uselessness of our worries and our feelings, and on the harm they do ourselves, as much to the bodily health, as to the welfare of the soul. Secondly, to combat it by refraining from frequent, lengthy, and earnest thoughts on the subject, and by sacrificing and abandoning it entirely to God in spite of the pangs the heart must endure from the violence of such sacrifices ; consider that, after all, there is only one thing necessary, and that provided that this great affair succeeds everything else must be as God pleases. These feelings are quickly overcome, or rather, they are so trifling and paltry that they pass like shadows, to return no more. Let us act like worldly people when they have to attend to business of the utmost importance on which depend their honour, their life, their property, in fact everything, as they think. They have nothing else in their minds day or night but this important business, and neglect everything else as being nothing in comparison. As Jesus Christ has said, we must learn from the children of this world who are " wiser in their generation than the children of light." Remember that what can help to save us is not exterior solitude, nor retirement, for these can be had even in the world ; but an interior withdrawal and solitude of the mind and heart ; of the mind, by banishing superfluous cares and thoughts and by endeavouring to make God the absorbing occupation of the heart, by lamenting its defects, by humbling it and frequently sighing after God, and by detaching it gradually from the creature to attach it solely to the Creator. He is the supreme truth, and nothing has any reality apart from Him. Consequently purely temporal interests, the business, the honours, pleasures, or sufferings of this lower world are nought but shadows and phantoms ; they appear to exist, but, in reality, are nothing.

LETTER VI.—On *Attachments*.

To Sister Anne-Marguerite Boudet de la Bellière. On attachment too keenly felt.

My very dear daughter in Jesus Christ. I cannot thank God enough for this great desire of giving yourself to Him without reserve that He has bestowed on you with the courage which inspires you to make so many little sacrifices, and to moderate even the most harmless attachments. Oh ! my dear Sister, how thoroughly God has enlightened you about this, and how many dangers you will escape if you are faithful in following this light. We, unhappily, find only too many who, making profession of piety, are caught in this snare, and thus prevented from making any progress. With the excuse that there is no sin in the attachments they allow themselves, they give themselves up to them without scruple, and thus place an impenetrable barrier to the grace, and the communications of God. He desires to fill and inflame their hearts with His ·pure love, but how can He do so as long as those hearts are distracted by foolish amusements, and filled with a miserable love for some creature ? You know what a dangerous snare this was for St. Teresa, and in truth after such an example you cannot be too much on your guard. Go on then, detaching yourself more and more, and I assure you that in proportion as your detachment becomes more complete you will feel more drawn to God, to prayer, recollection and the practice of every virtue ; for, when the heart is empty in this way God fills it, and then one can do everything easily and pleasantly, because all is done out of love, and that, you know, makes all things easy, and sweetens all bitterness.

LETTER VII.—*Personal Attachments.*

My dear Sister,

Allow me to tell you in all sincerity, a fear that makes me anxious about you. It seems to me that your too frequent intercourse with the members of your numerous family, and with other people from outside, raises a serious obstacle to your advancement. Take care that, while trying to do good to others, you do no harm to yourself. Although I am obliged by my vocation to have more communication with the world than you, I assure you nevertheless, that I find it very good for my soul to keep these communications within bounds. Since I came here I have only made necessary visits, and try as much as possible to avoid receiving them. To those who come to me I speak only of God, of salvation, or of eternity. This is the rule laid down by St. Ignatius and one which he declared suited him well. If people like this kind of conversation they will profit by it, and their visit will not have been a waste of time ; if they do not care for it they will not come again, or, at any rate not so often, and then I shall have more time left me for my priestly duties. It is useless to expect to make any progress as long as your mind is filled with news from outside, and your heart preoccupied with temporal affairs. The first condition for

the interior life is recollection. I cannot urge you too strongly
to restrict your communications and to follow the plan of St.
Ignatius about those that you think you ought to retain. This
plan is better suited to a Religious, who is obliged by her vocation
to keep secluded, than to other people. Far from being surprised, people in the world cannot but be edified at the fidelity
with which she conforms her conduct to her vocation. On the
contrary, if by these useless communications with people in the
world she frequented society too much, she would only scandalise
them, and would also lose all those graces which she might have
acquired by her communications with God.

LETTER VIII.—*On Natural Activity.*

To Sister Marie-Henriette de Bousmard.   On natural activity.

I wish, my dear Sister, that you were able to understand well
all the harm that the excessive activity of your nature, unless
completely under the rule and direction of grace, will infallibly
cause you. This is one of those defects that the world mistakes
for virtues, but which is none the less disastrous to the soul in
its progress in the path of sanctity. Natural activity is the
enemy of abandonment, without which, as I have often told
you, there can be no real perfection. It prevents, obstructs,
or spoils all the operations of grace, and substitutes, in the soul
which succumbs to it, the impulsion of the human spirit for
that of the divine Spirit. In fact there is no doubt that the
impetuosity with which we give ourselves up to good works
proceeds from a hidden source of self-confidence, and a thought-
less presumption that makes us imagine that we are doing
or can do great things. How much more modest and reserved
we should be if we were thoroughly penetrated with the undoubted truth that we have nothing of our own, and are utterly
powerless to do anything good, but only powerful for evil. To
cure, and to tear up by the root an evil so fruitful in imperfections,
and even in sins, requires much time and much trouble. These
are the means I most recommend to you.

1st. To be thoroughly convinced, by past and present
experience, of your own weakness and misery, in order to distrust
more and more your own works even to the length of feeling a
kind of horror of them.

2nd. To repress your excessive exterior activity by performing all your actions without eagerness or hurry, quite gently
and quietly, as St. Francis of Sales advises.

3rd. To do the same in all your spiritual exercises, and always
to mortify the initial eagerness with which you start any good

work, no matter what it may be; to undertake it only under the influence of the pure Spirit of God, and by the peaceful impulse of grace.

4th. When you pray and hold intercourse with God interiorly, try to avoid all sensible ardour, all that fiery fervour, and excitement of the imagination characteristic of beginners. To effect this, follow the advice of St. Francis of Sales and manage so that all your interior acts shall flow, and be drawn from, and distilled by, the highest point of the mind, so that you hardly feel that you are praying and making acts. Far from these acts being, on this account, less fruitful, they make a deeper impression on the soul and penetrate more deeply and more pleasantly into the heart.

5th. When you feel, however confusedly, that something is acting in your soul, the stronger this impression is, the more necessary it is to keep quiet and still, and as though in a state of inaction, so that you may not spoil all by interfering unseasonably.

6th. When God makes you experience certain consolations, or strong emotions, instead of giving yourself up to them with a sensual avidity, behave with the reserve and modesty of a mortified person invited to a great feast.

7th. During the day let the principal interior occupation be what is called simple interior waiting, silent, peaceful, and entirely resigned; and do not think that this is idleness, waste of time, or in any way useless, because, as a beggar who waits the whole day long at a rich man's gate, or at the church door, is by no means idle but much occupied interiorly with his own misery, his wants and continual necessities; so, in the same way, a soul in this simple waiting before God is very much occupied interiorly, and in this simple manner is making the following acts; of faith in the presence of God, of adoration before this great God whose infinite power and mercy it acknowledges; of self-distrust, of profound humility in thinking itself incapable of anything; of desire for the holy operations of God, of hope since one does not wait for what one does not expect to receive; and of abandonment to divine Providence in regard to all His gifts or operations. And although these acts may not be accurately performed, specified, nor sensible, yet they are none the less there, at the bottom of the heart; and God, at least, sees them in our desires, and in our state of preparation. Now, as you are aware, our wishes and desires, even if only begun to be formed, are to God what the voice is to our fellow men. He hears them, in fact, far more clearly than men hear our voices, and it is enough for Him that we form these desires; for, as the Psalmist says, He knows even the mere intention and disposition

of our hearts from the first moment that they begin to turn, and
to move towards Him. And this, by the way, is very consoling
to you in the present state of your soul. But a still more efficacious way than any other is to bear patiently darkness, dryness, coldness and weakness. This sad state is the specific
remedy employed by God to suppress natural activity by re-
ducing us to our own nothingness. Without this we should
never be able to overcome it, because the inordinate activity
of our powers cannot be regulated until, by constantly reiterated
efforts, we force them to act only under the influence of the
Spirit of God, and by His grace, and never of themselves, or
by themselves. You see in this how blindly and unjustly we
act when we turn the benefits of God into subjects of affliction and
complaint; for they not only tend to extinguish our natural
activity but to kill our self-love, and to enable us to live the
supernatural life of grace.

LETTER IX.—*On Excessive Fervour.*

To Sister Marie-Thérèse de Vioménil. On excessive fervour
of good desires.

My very dear Sister,

The desire about which you have consulted me is very good
in itself, but I fear lest it may become too strong. If you wish
that it may not be hurtful to you under the appearance of good,
you must manage to be always submissive and resigned about
it, and consequently, peaceful. You know how, in even our
best desires, nature and passion get mixed, making them violent,
restless, hasty and wild. For this reason, and to preserve us
from this danger, and also gradually to purify our desires, even
those that are most saintly, God defers granting them for a long
time. For the wild desires of our natural inclinations do not
deserve to be answered, only those desires formed by the Holy
Spirit deserve to be heard by God, and these are always quiet,
gentle and peaceful. Keep yourself, as much as possible, in a
state of peace and even of a holy joy in order to be fit to receive
holy impressions. You know that grace more easily makes
way in hearts that are calm and free than in those that are full
of uneasiness and trouble, for the latter are more exposed to be
under the influence of the evil spirit.

LETTER X.—*Restraint of Over-Eagerness.*
To the same person.   On eagerness to read good books.

———

I send you the book on " Christian Hope " that I promised
you.   It will prove a real treasure to you, but if you wish to
derive from it all the fruit that I expect, you must restrain your
eagerness to read, and not allow yourself to be carried away by
curiosity to know what is coming.   Make use of the time allowed
by the Rule to read it, concentrate all your attention on what
you are actually reading without troubling about the rest.
I advise you above all, to enter into the meaning of the consoling
and solid truths that you will find laid down in this book ; but
more in a practical way than by speculative reflexions, and, from
time to time, make short pauses to allow these truths time to
flow through all the recesses of the soul and to give occasion for
the operation of the Holy Spirit who, during these peaceful
pauses, and times of silent attention, engraves and imprints these
heavenly truths in the heart.   All this, however, without disturbing your attraction, or violent effort to prevent reflexions,
but simply and quietly trying to make them enter into your heart
more than into your mind.

Take particular notice of certain more important chapters,
of which you are in greater need, in order to read them again
when next you have time.   In general I advise you strongly not to
overload your mind with readings and outward practices, it
is much better to read little, and to digest what you read.   Just
now, too, your soul is in need of unity and simplicity, and all
your readings and practices should tend to a single end, and that
is, to form in you a spirit of recollection.   In time God will give
you this grace if you aspire to it with confidence quietly, simply,
and humbly, without eagerness, trouble, or uneasiness.   Frequently ask God to detach you absolutely from all things, so
that you may love and enjoy Him only, in Jesus Christ, and
through Jesus Christ, in fine, that He may take full possession
of your heart and make it altogether His.   " My God I abandon
myself to You, grant that I may desire only You."

LETTER XI.—*Intemperate Zeal.*
To the same person.   On intemperate and indiscreet zeal.

———

I see, my dear Sister, that a mistaken zeal exposes you to
dangers all the more serious because they are hidden under the
most insidious appearances.   Desire for the perfection of our
neighbour is, doubtless, very good ; the pain that is felt interiorly

at the sight of his defects is good also, provided it proceeds from a pure desire for his perfection. But with all this there must needs be mingled much secret self-complacency, confidence in one's own superior light, and severity towards one's neighbour. Zeal such as this cannot, you must well understand, come from God; it is an illusion of the devil, hurtful to yourself and to others. However, the evil can be easily cured provided you are sincere enough, and submissive enough to recognise the gravity of it, and to apply the remedy. That which I am about to offer you has already produced a very happy result in a soul which was subject to the same illusion. Let us hope it will not be less efficacious in your case.

I advise you, therefore, and command you in the most sacred name of Jesus Christ, and that of His divine Mother, never more to think of practising the virtue of zeal as long as this prohibition is not expressly removed. I exculpate you before God absolutely, and I take upon myself the responsibility of all the ill consequences that may result from this prohibition. If you should get scruples about it, and the devil should put in your mind that you could do some good or avert some evil, say to God, " My God, although charity is the queen of virtues, I may not practise this zeal until You have made me able to do so without detriment to the charity I owe to others and to myself. When I am found to be sufficiently strong, or rather sufficiently humble, to exercise zeal without disturbing the peace of my soul, and with all possible sweetness, compassion, and thoughtfulness for my neighbour, and a helpfulness, kindness and charity which nothing can embitter, a charity which is scandalised at nothing but its own shortcomings ; with all that patience and long-suffering which enables one tranquilly to endure the defects of others, and for as long as You will suffer them, Oh, my God ; and when I am neither troubled, nor uneasy, nor astonished that others are incorrigible, then this prohibition will be removed, and I shall be able to think that I can glorify You in my neighbour. But until then, Oh, my God, I must exercise my zeal on myself, in the correction of my numerous defects."

In fact, my very dear Sister, when humility has dug that deep foundation indispensable to every virtue, I shall be the first to urge you to resume the practice of zeal ; until then think only of yourself. Remember that God, to punish those who have practised this indiscreet zeal, and to correct them, has often allowed them to fall into much graver faults than those which had scandalised them in others.

In the second place I command you never to speak of God, or of anything good, unless in a spirit of humility and meekness, in an amiable and gracious manner, with moderation and en-

couragement, and never with bitterness and severity, or in
a way to wound and repel those who hear you, because, although
you may only say what is in the Gospel and in the best books,
I believe that in your present state of mind you might say it
very badly and in such a way as only to do harm.   Did not
Satan make use of the words of Holy Scripture to tempt our
Lord ?   Truth is the proper relation of things.   It is changed
when pushed to extremes, or wrongly applied.   Your peevish
temper is like a smoked glass, which, if you do not take care will
prevent you seeing things in their true light, or showing them to
others.   Keep always on your guard against this fatal influence,
and feed your mind on thoughts and feelings that are contrary
to those inspired by temper.   Entertain yourself and others
with conversations on the infinite goodness of God, and on the
confidence we ought to have in Him.   Compel yourself to offer
an example in your whole conduct, of a virtue that has no bounds,
and which imposes no restraint on others.   If you have nothing
kind to say keep silent, and leave the care of deciding to others.
They can avoid better than you too much laxness, and will be
exact without being severe.   If exactitude be praiseworthy,
severity is blamable, it does nothing but revolt people instead of
convincing them, and embitter their souls instead of gaining
them.   As much as true meekness, with the help of God, has
power to repel evil and to win to good, so much has an excessive
harshness power to make goodness difficult and evil incurable.
The first is edifying, the latter, destructive.

LETTER XII.—*On Obedience*.

On disinclination to accept the comforts enjoined.

Be careful never to leave off the practice of obedience under
the pretext of mortifying yourself ; and never forget these words
of the Holy Spirit, " I will have obedience and not sacrifice."
Do not, therefore, hesitate to take those little comforts that the
doctors, the superiors, and infirmarians prescribe for you ;
at any rate, you should have much scruple about refusing them.
In this way you will practise a more meritorious self-denial than
any bodily mortification—that which consists in the renunciation
of your own ideas, of your own judgment, and of your own will.
Through ignorance or forgetfulness of this truth certain devout
persons, who are strongly attached to their own ideas, commit
many faults in being obstinately determined in their pretended
self-denial, and extremely unmortified in their mortifications.
How can they delude themselves so far as not to understand

that self-love spoils and corrupts even the most holy practices ? Those who renounce their own will, their own judgment, and their own ideas for the love of God will make great progress in the path of true and solid perfection. Henceforth, do not make any other use of your mind and of your reason than to know what you are ordered to do, and to do it promptly, joyfully, with a great confidence in God, and an absolute abandonment to His mercy. It will be all the easier to practise this confidence when you no longer have any other ambition than to do His holy will. And in fact, could there be a pleasanter task ? Does not this divine Will sanctify all Its decrees ? Follow It then in all things, as much in what gives you pleasure, as in that which costs you most ; in consolations, as well as privations ; working and resting ; in mental and vocal prayer, in the Office, at Mass, in confession and Communion ; in all things. Blind obedience makes no exception, it generally sacrifices its own thoughts, ideas, judgments, inclinations, repugnances, aversions, tempers, in one word all its own will. On this account is this sacrifice more pleasing to God than any other that could possibly be made, and without this sacrifice all else is of little value, and cannot fail to be harmful. The divine Spirit also assures us in Holy Scripture, that the obedient man will gain many victories.

LETTER XIII.—*On being Self-Opinionated.*
On attachment to one's own judgment.

My dear Sister,
At last you are freed from your ties and released from all those engagements by which the world expected to keep you always captive. I do not doubt that you understand the full value of the inestimable grace of a religious vocation, and that you are disposed to accomplish generously all its duties. The longer you have waited for this grace, the greater is the gratitude you owe to Him Who has, at last, bestowed it on you. You must, however, be prepared to encounter many difficulties in your new life, difficulties not felt by those who embrace it earlier ; but humility, renunciation, simplicity, and the holy spiritual infancy of the Gospel will diminish these difficulties considerably and will finish by making them disappear altogether. With the help of these virtues you will be preserved from a very subtle illusion of pride, to which many novices yield, and which is all the more dangerous because it is almost imperceptible. With the excuse of trying themselves better, they always want to do a little more than the rest, or to deprive themselves of those little comforts that the charity of the Superiors offers them. All this

is nothing else but a refined self-love, and a disguised vanity. As for you, my dear Sister, never, I implore you, have any other ambition than to follow the ordinary course in all things ; not one iota beyond that. Accept with simplicity and humility the little comforts and alleviations that the weak are allowed, rejoice at seeing yourself reduced to the level of a small child and treated like one and take good care not to seem strong and courageous. What profound and meritorious humility will you not thus exercise ! delightful in the eyes of God, and more pleasing to His heart than the most austere life chosen by yourself. What an amount of pride and vanity may be concealed in conduct contrary to this ! I do not wish to hide from you what a good long experience has taught me ; that those who were most devout in the world before entering the religious state, have generally given the most trouble to their Superiors and Mistresses. This comes of their having formed certain ideas of virtue for themselves which they will not relinquish. Accustomed to be admired by all who surrounded them, and to be, usually, approved of by their directors, they cling to their own ideas and their own spirit without suspecting that this attachment is the very antipodes of all true sanctity. Therefore it is far more difficult to make those persons practise humility and renunciation, to give up their notions and self-will than in the case of young people of unformed character ; or even of worldly people who have become converted. Nevertheless if we do not become as little children we shall not enter into the kingdom of heaven. I hope, therefore, that you are treated exactly as if you were a young person of fifteen or sixteen years of age, equally unformed physically and mentally, and who is told : " Sister, you must rest to-morrow ; you are dispensed from such or such a thing ; you must take some recreation in the garden," or " My dear Sister, that work is too hard for you, the Mother Superior will dispense you from it," while you, a formed character, formerly most devout, should, without replying by a single word or frowning, carry out all you are told to do, to the letter, in a spirit of humility and simplicity, satisfied to be treated thus, as if you were the weakest and the least of all. Look upon yourself as such, and even rejoice at it, or at least, do your best to do so. Admire the loving charity of the Rev. Mother and the Sisters, and bless God for it. This is what a true interior spirit, and a spirituality that is real and good should teach you, and inspire you with. But, it must be admitted, it is a most difficult matter to reduce these pretended devotees to this. Poor souls ! blinded and deceived, the less they know how to humble themselves the further they are from real greatness. If they would but go to Bethlehem, and there contemplate the God of Heaven become a little Infant in swaddling clothes, in a manger, handled, carried, and taken from place to place, turned and touched by everyone, it might effect their cure. Let this example, my dear Sister, be that which you propose to follow during your noviciate; and it is by becoming like this little Child that you will merit to enter into the Kingdom of Heaven.

LETTER XIV.—*On Reserve with a Director.*

To Sister Marie-Thérèse de Vioménil. On a difficulty in and a dislike to opening one's mind to a director.

Believe me, my dear Sister, it is necessary to struggle with all your power against the repugnance you feel to open your mind, and to regard as a most dangerous temptation the jealous susceptibility you experience when you imagine that someone has revealed your fault. It is the devil who inspires such fear and pain at having your interior miseries made known, because he knows by countless experiences that those souls that have sufficient courage and humility to disclose themselves thus, simply and straightforwardly, are speedily cured, or at least very greatly consoled. He knows, too, that those wounds of the soul most frequently healed by such a disclosure, can become poisoned and inflamed if not shown to the physician. In fact nothing is more evident than that, as long as we are full of self-love, which only dies when we die, we shall be exposed to deceive ourselves as to what concerns us, and to make to ourselves a false conscience. This consideration is calculated to make us tremble, whoever we are. To avoid this danger there is only one means; not to trust to our own light in what regards ourselves, but to allow our directors to guide our conscience, and to them we must make known with great frankness all that might serve to enlighten them. The misfortune is that even in these revelations we risk being deceived by our self-love, and also to mislead those of whom we ask advice. What is to be done to guarantee ourselves against this fresh danger? Well! those who guide us must be enlightened by others about us; and this is just what is so difficult to put up with. There are plenty of people very much inclined to exercise zeal with regard to others, who find it very unpleasant when they are subject to it themselves. This ought not to be. True zeal should say to itself " Think of yourself, and do not trouble about others who are not under your care, and be very thankful that some charitable person has made known to your director what is thought about you, so that he will be better able to guide you in future." This two-fold feeling is only to be found in the most perfect souls, and, perhaps, in some persons of an extraordinary natural sincerity if but of moderate virtue. Usually a zeal for instructing others is accompanied by a great sensitiveness with regard to the persons who desire to render us the same good office by instructing our director thoroughly as to what is thought and said about us. Here again we have that two-fold illusion of all ordinary devotees in the world, and also in the cloister. Examine yourself without any flattery as to this two-fold matter, and enlighten yourself with the considerations I have just given you.

LETTER XV.—*On Discouragement.*

To the same person. On discouragement.

My dear Sister,

At this moment you are suffering from one of the most dangerous temptations that could assail any soul of good will; the temptation to discouragement. I conjure you to resist it with all your might. Have confidence in God, and be convinced that He will finish the work He has begun in you. Your foolish fears about the future come from the devil. Think only of the present, abandon the future to Providence. It is the good use of the present that assures the future. Apply yourself to obtaining attachment and conformity to the will of God in all things and everywhere, even to the smallest things, for in this consist all virtue and perfection. For the rest, God only allows our daily faults to keep us humble. If you know how to gain this fruit, and to remain in peace and confidence, then you will be in a better state than if you had not committed any apparent fault, which would only have greatly flattered your self-love, and have exposed you to the extreme danger of being satisfied with yourself. Nothing, on the contrary, can be more easy than to make use of your faults to acquire a fresh degree of humility, and thus to dig more deeply in yourself the foundation necessary for building up true sanctity. Ought we not to admire, and to bless the infinite goodness of God who knows how to make our very faults serve for our greater good? For this it suffices to dislike them, to humble ourselves quietly about them, and to raise ourselves again with an untiring perseverance after each fall, and to work peacefully to correct ourselves. Submit to the will of God as to your employments, but do not be uneasy or eager about them. Do amiably all that you know you ought to do, and depend on divine Providence for success, without solicitude or anxiety, in order to have a free mind and a tranquil heart in so far as it is

P

possible. If you are faithful in this practice, you will be able to live in peace even in the midst of disturbances, and the involuntary trouble these may occasion you will but increase the merit that is grounded on the conformity of your will to the will of God. May He be blessed by all and in all, now and for ever.

LETTER XVI.—*Fear of Singularity.*

To the same person. On the fear of being deceived, and of appearing singular.

When one begins to wish to belong to God entirely and unreservedly, He increases, by the interior operations of His grace this holy desire which He has Himself inspired ; but the more vehement this desire becomes, the more does the soul feel seized and penetrated with fear lest it should be deceived. This fear is a fresh gift of God, and provided the soul knows how to make good use of it, she will derive great benefit, become more humble, more self-distrustful, vigilant, and eager to obtain the help of God. But precisely because it is a gift of God, the spirit of darkness does not fail to make use of his ordinary tactics, and if he cannot prevent these gifts of God, he sets to work to spoil and corrupt them by every kind of stratagem. This is what he does with regard to the salutary fear of which I speak ; and for this he makes use of two kinds of deception. At first he attempts to make this fear immoderate, excessive, uneasy and vexatious, to unsettle and weaken the soul, and having effected this, to cast it into a state of pusillanimity, and depression. For this, the only remedy is, to turn the laugh against the tempter, and to address him thus : " He who has begun the work will finish it, and since of His own goodness He has chosen me even when I shunned Him, He will take care not to abandon me when I seek Him with my whole heart." Remember, besides, that a good beginning is the best guarantee of perseverance. It is very much easier to continue in the same way than to change it. There never would have been any conversions if attention had been paid to foolish fears. These are the first temptations of beginners. But, another and more dangerous stratagem still is this ; the tempter seeks accomplices, and too frequently finds them amongst good people. In the way of our good resolutions he throws people not wanting in a sort of wisdom, nor in good intention, who find something to carp at in everything that grace inspires in our souls to take them out of the ordinary groove. To listen to these counsellors, who are the more eager to offer their advice the less they are asked for it, one would think that to aim at perfection is to make yourself remarkable in a dreadful way.

We ought never, say they, to exaggerate, nor to undertake a course of life contrary to nature; what is out of the common never lasts, and exaggeration is blamable in everything. I do not hesitate to say that this is one of the greatest obstacles to divine grace that souls called to perfection can encounter. It is human respect in the cloister, which in its way, is as dangerous as that in the world, and no less prevents the conversion of souls from imperfection to sanctity, than the latter prevents the conversion from bad to good.

By what means can these dangers be avoided? By these. We must overcome, courageously, for the love of Jesus Christ, the impressions made on us by a false human respect, and make a generous sacrifice of them to our Lord, begging Him to help and sustain us that we may despise all these foolish remarks. It is enough to compare the maxims of the Gospel with the captious sophisms to which they are opposed, to convince ourselves that they cannot possibly proceed from the Spirit of God but only from human reasons, and that carnal spirit which is reprobated by God. "But those who talk like this are pious people." That may be, but it only proves that some pious people do not always judge things by the pure light of the Gospel, but allow themselves to be deceived by false prejudices, and natural considerations, by interested self-love, error, blindness, or ignorance. They must, in fact, of necessity, be very ignorant and very blind not to perceive that there never has been a true conversion nor real change of heart that escaped notice either in the world or in religion. And why are these conversions noticeable when they are real? It is because they, necessarily, extend to the regulation of outward conduct, and even if there were nothing in the outward conduct that required regulating, the perfect order and heavenly peace restored to the soul would be manifested by infallible signs by which the good would be edified, but which, perhaps, would irritate the jealous self-love of others. One must needs be voluntarily blind not to see that at the beginning of a new life one's conduct may seem constrained and uneasy, for this reason; because neither the person who is changed, nor others, are accustomed to an altered way of acting. In all things ease comes with habitude. Besides, how can a soul which is entirely employed in keeping recollected, in fighting against itself, in compelling itself to do violence in a hundred different ways, both interior and exterior, be expected to appear gay, free, happy, agreeable, and amusing? Truly, if I saw it like this I should have strong doubts as to any interior change whatever. However there are some people who are very interior, and at the same time appear very gracious outwardly. This is when a sufficiently long experience has made the exercise of interior recollection, in a sort of way, natural to them. But when they began they were just like you, my dear Sister, and the same things that are said of you, were said of them. They went their way without taking any notice of the talk, and God at last placed them in a state that is called the liberty of the children of God. Like them you also will attain to this, be assured : the day will come when your recollection will be without compulsion, constant, sweet, agreeable and good-humoured ; then you also will be able to add to the pleasure of others by reflecting exteriorly that abounding peace and joy which is caused in the soul by the pure love of God, and of your neighbour. But no one can arrive at this suddenly, or at once : it is the result of a sufficiently long practice of virtue and of an interior life, which, at the beginning, seems of necessity uncomfortable and rather constrained ; but in the end it will become natural. Then you will be able to resume your light-heartedness and gaiety, for both will be reformed and spiritualised by the holy operations of grace. In the beginning, however, it is impossible to do this without spoiling something.

You see the ignorance of these clever reasoners ? Their judgments and remarks are to be pitied because it is precisely in this way that the world judges and reasons when God by His grace effects one of those great changes that are visible to all. Can it be possible that Religious talk in this way ? It must be the work of the father of lies, who alone could make them speak and reason in such a wrong way. God be praised in all things ! He will procure glory from it in some way or other. As for you, think only of bearing this trial bravely, and encourage yourself with the teaching of faith and the evangelical counsels which these grand reasoners seem to have lost sight of. Rejoice interiorly at this appearance of folly and stupidity which exposes you to their mockery ; for it is a most sure sign of the change that has taken place in you. Say to our Lord with the Psalmist : " I am become like a beast of burden in Your presence, Oh my God ; no one can separate me from You again." In the service of so great a Master can any position be without honour ? Act the part that He has given you at present, of seeming silly and awkward, as well as you can, and with a joyful heart wait patiently for the moment when another change will take place quite different to that which you are going through now. Then your faculties which now seem in bonds will regain their freedom of action ; ease will succeed restraint and the holy liberty of the children of God will drive away excessive fear. The sight of the imperfection of all your works is a great grace of God Who by this, wishes to keep you humble, and with a poor opinion of yourself, but the excessive severity you are tempted to exercise towards yourself about it, the sadness, low spirits, and the idea that you will be lost, are suggestions of Satan who tries in this way to spoil the gift of God in you, and to turn it into poison. Cast them away therefore as diabolical imaginations. For a certain time such thoughts will return again and again without ceasing and will be matter for combats, for victories, and for merit; but, have a little patience, perfection is not the work of a day. At first do not attempt what is the most perfect; that would be trying to fly before you have got your wings, as St. Teresa says. Be content with what God gives you, and what He does for you at present, without desiring anything more until He judges fit to give it to you. In this way you will avoid interior agitation by which the devil succeeds too well in upsetting those souls who seek in the practice of virtue, more the satisfaction of their own self-love than the glory of God. In fact, it is impossible not to recognise the vexation of injured pride in the impatience with which they behold their imperfections and in the pain they feel in finding themselves at the foot of the ladder of sanctity when they wished to persuade themselves that they had arrived at the top.

Do you, Sister, behave in a totally different manner. Love your abjection, allow the good God to carry out peacefully His work in you. Allow Him to place there a solid foundation of humility, and to cement it with frequent experiences of your misery and weakness. We should run too great a risk of losing everything by our vain imaginations if God were to give us, at once, all the perfection we desired. The inordinate love of our own excellence would carry us to as high a flight as Lucifer, but only, like him, to fall into the abyss of pride. God, who knows our weakness in this respect, allows us to grovel like worms in the mud of our imperfections, until He finds us capable of being raised without feeling any foolish self-satisfaction, or any contempt of others.

This conduct of God, full of wisdom and goodness, fills with admiration those who have the guidance of souls, but they cannot help feeling sad when they see souls who refuse to understand the object of these merciful trials, getting out of temper when the ineffable ways of divine Providence are explained to them.

FOURTH BOOK.

THE FIRST TRIALS OF SOULS CALLED TO THE STATE OF ABANDONMENT.

ARIDITIES, WEAKNESSES AND WEARINESS.

LETTER I.—*Aridity and Weakness.*

There is reason to think that this letter was addressed by Fr. de Caussade to Sister Marie-Thérèse de Vioménil, who, to enable her holy director to understand her better, had given him an account of her vocation, and of her spiritual state from the time she had embraced the religious life.

On the trials above-mentioned. General direction.

God has indeed granted you what you told me you had asked of Him, my dear Sister; for, in reading your letter I seemed to be reading your soul, and it appeared to me that I understood your spiritual state as well as if I had been your confessor and director for a long time. Oh! what consoling and instructive things I have to tell you! I hope that the Holy Spirit will enable you to understand and to enjoy them; and that God will deign by the merits of Jesus Christ, and the intercession of His most Holy Mother, of St. Joseph, St. Francis of Sales, and of all the saints of your Order who are now in Heaven, to grant them His holy blessing.

1st. Your vocation seems to me to have the marks of the seal of God; I see in it manifest signs of His divine will, proofs of His gratuitous predilection of your soul, and a solid guarantee of your eternal predestination.

2nd. The attraction you feel to give yourself entirely to Him, and live a wholly interior life in spite of the dissipation of your mind, and the rebellion of nature, is a grace the value of which I would that it pleased God to show you as He has me. It is all the more real in being less accessible to the senses and more completely hidden under contrary appearances.

3rd. Why is it, then, that in spite of this attraction, and of all your pious reading, you seem to remain always at the entrance of the interior life without the power of entering? I will tell you the reason, my dear Sister, for I see it very distinctly; it is because you have misused this attraction by inordinate desires, by over-eagerness, and a natural activity, thus displeasing

God, and stifling the gentle action of grace. Also, because in your conduct there has been a secret and imperceptible presumption which has made you rely on your own industry, and your own efforts. God wishes to humiliate and to confound you by your own experiences, and in this way to moderate that natural ardour that carries you beyond the impressions of grace. Without noticing it you have acted as if you aspired to do all the work by your own industry, and even to do more than God desired. You who would have taken yourself to task for any worldly ambition, have, without scruple, allowed yourself to be carried away by a still more subtle ambition, and by a desire for a high position in the spiritual life. But, be comforted; thanks to the merciful severity of God's dealings with you, so far there is nothing lost; on the contrary you have gained greatly. God punishes you for these imperfections like a good father, with tenderness; and enables you to find a remedy for the evil in the chastisement He inflicts on you. To avenge these infidelities He sends you the sort of trials He is accustomed to make use of to purify and detach those chosen souls called to pure love and divine union.

If you understood this fatherly conduct in your regard, and looked at your trials from the right point of view all your fears would disappear of their own accord. You would not be surprised, for example, that your aridity and interior trouble have increased since you entered religion. I am not by any means surprised, and should have been very sorry on your account had it been otherwise. Has it not been since then, in fact, that you have belonged more entirely to God, and that this divine Spouse has laboured more energetically to purify your soul, and to render it capable of being perfectly united to Him?

4th. As for that state of dissipation of which you complain so much, I agree with you in thinking that it is partly the result of your natural character, of the liveliness of your imagination and, above all, of habit. However, God has only allowed this result to humble and confound you more completely; and the keen pain you suffer is not the least part of the merit of this trial. You see I am very far from believing, as you do, that there is no remedy for this evil or that it is caused by some secret sins.

The fear that this dissipation of mind causes you when you go to prayer, is a temptation, or else simply imagination, and God gives you a great grace in giving you courage to take no notice of it, but to approach Him with confidence in spite of this misleading fear.

5th. In your distaste for your outward occupations and duties I see only another side of your trials and one which can be very meritorious in the sight of God provided that you overcome it instead of allowing yourself to be overcome by it.

The acts that you make in opposition to this feeling, and of sacrifice and self-abnegation are very solid and very good. The merit of these acts is much increased by the renewal of the interior rebellions by which you are crucified; this is another part of the trial.

6th. That which you add about your powerlessness and apparent idleness in prayer, is a consequence of this trial, and naturally follows it; I should have been greatly surprised had it been otherwise.

Be reassured, therefore, for you will have to continue to waste your time in prayer, my dear Sister, and although you might do it more quietly, and this, please God, you will eventually achieve, you will never make any prayer that would be better, more useful, or more meritorious; because the prayer of abnegation and suffering being more crucifying is also more purifying for the soul, and makes it die to self more quickly in order to live henceforth in God and for God. Oh! how much I love such prayer during which you stand before God like a beast of burden feeling nothing and bowed down under the weight of all sorts of temptations! What could be more calculated to humble, confound, and annihilate a soul before God? This is what the soul requires, and to what its apparent miseries lead. Ah! if you only knew how to remain with respect and submission in this humiliating condition, abandoning yourself so entirely to the divine will as to take pleasure in your abjection and annihilation for the love of God, you would become much more pleasing to Him in your inaction and silence than by making the most explicit and energetic acts! No! there is no sacrifice more acceptable to God than a broken and humble heart, this is truly a holocaust full of sweet odours. Prayers that are full of fervour and devotion, or voluntary mortifications, bear no comparison because they cannot come near it.

7th. Your terrors about confession and communion are to be rejected and despised as temptations and imaginations; they are another part of your trial. However, should they continue to trouble you, in spite of your resistance, take no notice, and be patient in this state as in other things. As to the wish to get rid of this trying state, it is not the direct, but the natural result of the trial, and the effect of self-love which cries out, and struggles rebelliously when it finds itself on the point of being pitilessly exterminated. You must not be daunted, nor terrified, but struggle bravely with your free-will against these desires, and persevere with an unshaken constancy in choosing always to accomplish the holy will of God. This point is of the first importance, not only to gather the fruit of the trial, but also to soften its bitterness and to shorten its duration. If, in your case, it has lasted a long time, I have grounds for attributing this to the fact that you have not had sufficient courage to make the entire sacrifice that God demanded of you. Hasten then to make it, and say to Him, " Yes, my God, I accept all, I submit to all without reserve, and for as long as You please."

From all I have just said you will conclude without difficulty that there is but one thing for you to do, which is to let God dispose of you as He pleases, and to keep yourself quietly and interiorly tranquil as far as you can, but nevertheless without effort. Abandonment to God is for you just now the one thing necessary. To effect this thoroughly I give you the following rules :

1st. When you go to prayer you must be resigned to suffer at it, to be tormented and afflicted exactly as God pleases. When distractions, aridity, temptations, and weariness overwhelm you, say, " You are welcome, Cross of my God ; I embrace you with a resigned will ; make me suffer until my self-love becomes crucified and dead." Then remain in God's presence like a beast of burden weighed down with its load, and almost ready to perish, but expecting succour and help from its Master. If you could but throw yourself in spirit at the foot of the Cross of Jesus Christ, humbly kiss His sacred wounds, and remain there at His divine feet steadfast and motionless, and do nothing else but wait patiently in silence and peace as a poor beggar waits for hours at a time at the gates of a great king, or of a generous and rich benefactor, hoping to receive an alms. But before all things do not dream of making any more efforts, either in prayer, or in anything else, trying to be more recollected than God wishes you to be.

2nd. Do not therefore, make any violent efforts to preserve recollection during the day, or to drive away the continual distractions that make you uneasy ; be satisfied to know that this state of dissipation displeases you, and that you have a great desire to be recollected ; but only when it pleases God, and as much as it pleases Him, neither more nor less.

3rd. If the dissipation of mind should sometimes be so trying, and the aridity, troubles, fears, and other vexatious feelings so overwhelming that you cannot make a single interior act, nor even entertain a good thought, do not be cast down. You have nothing to fear, but rather, much to gain if, in this deplorable condition you understand how to remain in the simple interior silence of respect, submission, and adoration of which I have

already spoken, and to bury yourself in the abyss of your own
nothingness. This nothingness, accepted and loved for the love
of God, is your safe refuge in the midst of these storms. It is
there that you must remain, and it is from thence that you must
take pleasure in beholding the fulfilment within you of the will
of God. You must love to see Him, in imagination, raining
down from the heights of Heaven, distractions, aridity, fears,
anguish, and every species of trouble and humiliation on your
soul ; as if He would make of you the plaything of His pleasure
and of His divine love ; just as one sees sometimes, how great
princes will amuse themselves with splashing one of their
favourites with mud.

4th. As to the sacraments take good care never to omit
receiving them. " But," you say to me, " how can I prepare
for confession and communion when my mind is obsessed with
all sorts of fears and difficulties ? " You must despise them,
take no notice, and go straight to God without ever disputing or
reasoning with them either for or against, and having done the
little you could, or knew how to do, quietly, and without effort,
remain tranquil in the perfect interior silence of faith, respect,
submission and confidence often saying, but without words :
" May my sovereign Lord and Master do with me whatever He
pleases. Amen ! Amen ! "

5th. As in all that you tell me there is no sin, or at any rate,
nothing voluntary although it often seems otherwise to you,
keep yourself in a constant state of calmness and tranquillity.
I do not speak of the lower part of the soul, which is all in trouble
and desolation : but of the superior part, of that profound depth
of your soul, which, with God's help, can remain tranquil and
peaceful in the midst of these storms and commotions. Agitation
is, so to speak, only outside the soul in the exterior senses, to
mortify them and cause them to die, as they must in order to be
able to attain to pure love and union with God. It is for you
to prevent this trouble from penetrating to the interior ; and it
is in this, that, up to now, you have not been sufficiently enlightened, nor faithful enough.

6th. In fact, although I can discover no particular sin in
your conduct, yet I perceive a whole host of defects and imperfections in it which might do you great harm if you did not apply
a strong remedy. These are uneasiness, foolish fears, depression,
weariness, and a discouragement not quite free from deliberation,
or at least not combated with sufficient energy, all of which tend
to diminish that interior peace the necessity for which I am
endeavouring to inculcate. " But what can I do to prevent
them ? " This : first, never retain them wilfully ; secondly,
never parley with them, nor yet combat them with effort, or

violence, because that would make them doubly hurtful; but drop them, like one drops a stone into the water; think of something else, speak to God of other things, as St. Francis of Sales advises, then take refuge in the interior silence of respect, submission, confidence, and a total abandonment. " But," you say, " supposing that in these, or in other matters I commit faults, how ought I to behave ? " Well! then you must bear in mind the advice of St. Francis of Sales ; do not trouble yourself about your troubles, do not be uneasy about your uneasiness, do not be discouraged because you are discouraged, but return immediately to God without violence but humbling yourself quietly and tranquilly, even thanking Him for having prevented you from falling into greater faults. This sweet and gentle humility united to confidence in the divine goodness will tranquillise and pacify your soul, and this is, at present, your greatest spiritual need. I forgot to tell you that your great desire of divine love in spite of what you undergo afterwards, is certainly not an imagination, nor a chimera, on the contrary it is very real, very solid and most excellent, and must be preserved, but quietly and gently without giving way to those feelings of fervour, to those transports of the imagination, or to that natural activity that spoils everything. That which you experience, after having been all on fire with these ardent desires, when you try to return to yourself, need not surprise you. I will try and make clear by a comparison what then takes place within you. When you throw a very dry piece of wood that will burn easily, on the fire, the flame seizes it at once and consumes it quietly and noiselessly ; but if you throw green wood on the fire the flame does not affect it except for a moment, and then the heat of the fire acting on the green wet wood makes it exude moisture and emit sighing sounds, and twists and turns it in a hundred different ways with great noise, until it has been made dry enough for the fire to take hold of it ; then the flame spreads and consumes it without any effort or noise, but quietly.

This is an image of the action of divine love on souls that are still full of imperfections and the evil inclinations of self-love. These must be purified, refined, and cleared away and this cannot be achieved without trouble and suffering. Look upon yourself then, as this green wood acted on by divine love before it is able to enkindle it, and to consume it with its flames. Or else as a statue under the hands of a sculptor, or like a stone which is chipped and cut with the chisel and hammer to make it the right shape to take its place in a beautiful building. If this stone could feel, and if, while it thus suffered it asked you what it should do in so much pain, you would, without doubt, reply, " Keep perfectly quiet in the hands of the workman and let him proceed with his work, otherwise you will always remain a rough common piece of stone." Take this advice yourself, have patience and let God do the work, because there is really nothing else for you to do, only say, " I adore and I submit. Fiat ! "

LETTER II.—*On Different States of the Soul.*
To Sister Marie-Thérèse de Vioménil. On interior vicissitudes.

My dear Sister,
The different states that you depict in your letter to me are nothing more than interior vicissitudes to which we are all subject. These perpetual alternations of light and darkness, of consolation and desolation, are as useful, I should say, as indispensable for the growth and ripening of virtue in our souls, as the atmospheric changes are necessary for the growth and ripening of the harvests. Let us learn, therefore, to resign ourselves to them, and to accept with equal love trials and consolations, for all trials, even the most painful, are equally just, holy and beneficial, whether they proceed from the justice, or the mercy of God. Often they are sent to us both by justice and mercy, but while we are on earth justice is never exercised without mercy. I am delighted to hear that your usual occupation during prayer is the contemplation of your weakness, and the realisation of your nothingness ; this is the way to acquire, by degrees, an entire distrust of self, and a perfect confidence in God only ; also in this way you will become perfectly grounded in interior humility, which is the firm and solid foundation of the spiritual edifice, and the principal source of all the graces of God in the soul. You need neither be surprised nor pained at the destruction of all that is dear to self-love ; it would not be self-love if it did not fear this. Only those souls that are already detached from self are free from the fear of this death ; and not only do they not fear it, but they desire and beg it of God without ceasing. For us it is enough if we endure in peace, and with patience the successive blows that are effecting it. It often happens that during the day we experience certain feelings and desires for God or divine things, which do not occur during prayer. God arranges it thus so that we may recognise that He is absolute Master of all His gifts and graces ; that He bestows them when and where it pleases Him. In receiving them thus, at times when we least expect them and in being disappointed at other times when we expect them, we shall no longer be able to persuade ourselves that they are the result of our own disposition, work, or industry ; this is what God intends to prove to us. Therefore if He is prodigal

of His gifts He expects to receive all the glory of them, and would be compelled to withdraw them if He found that we appropriated any part of them through self-satisfaction.

LETTER III.—*Abandonment During Trials.*

To Mlle. de Serre who afterwards became Sister Catharine-Angélique. On the same subject. Abandonment during trials.

Keep steadfast my dear daughter, in the midst of your violent interior afflictions, and never relinquish the practice of entire abandonment to God, and of perfect confidence in His goodness. Encourage yourself with these two obvious and invariable principles : first, that God will never abandon any who have abandoned themselves entirely to Him, and who trust completely in His infinite mercy. Secondly, that nothing happens in this world that is not according to the decrees of Providence who turns all things to the advantage and greater profit of souls that are submissive and resigned. Contrary thoughts and interior combats will only serve, if you remain faithful, to strengthen in your mind, and to root more firmly in your heart, the truths and feelings so necessary for your sanctification. The perfection of the state to which God calls you is, no doubt, beyond your power to attain, neither can you depend on yourself in the very slightest degree for its attainment ; on the contrary you must beware of doing so, and rely on God only, grounding yourself on His succour and the power of His grace, with the help of which so many others weaker than yourself have been able, and are still able to do what seems to you so difficult. You ought, therefore, to repeat continually, " Yes ! considering my weakness and misery, this would be as impossible as flying in the air. But that which is impossible to man becomes possible, pleasant and easy with the assistance of the all-powerful grace of Jesus Christ, and I hope to obtain this grace from His goodness, and through His infinite merits." In this way have many young people, who were naturally feeble and timid, triumphed over cruel tyrants, and braved the most terrible sufferings and outrages and shed their blood in imitation and love of a crucified God.

The weariness, distaste, and dryness from which you frequently suffer are the usual vicissitudes through which all those souls, aiming at union with God, are accustomed to pass. What merit should we gain, and how should we prove our fidelity to God if we were always supported, helped, and consoled in a sensible manner by interior grace ? What is essential is to be faithful in the fulfilment of all our duties, and of those interior

and exterior practices that belong to our state, as much during
dryness and distaste as in sweetness and sensible devotion.
Although then we do nothing without effort and repugnance, the
merit is none the less great.   In this way only is our love of God
completely free from that unhappy self-love which thrusts itself
everywhere, mixes with everything, and spoils everything, as
St. Francis of Sales says.   As there is a sweet and delightful
peace to be felt during prayer, so also is there a dry, bitter, and
sometimes a suffering peace by which God operates more freely
in the soul than by the former which is more subject to the in-
roads of self-love.   Therefore one must abandon oneself to God
in this as in all other things.   We must allow Him to work,
because He knows better than we do what is good for us.   Let
us fear only one thing, and that is to allow our self-will to lead us
astray.   To avoid this danger it only needs to will exactly what
God wills, always, at every moment and for everything.   This
is the safest, the shortest, I even dare to say the only road to
perfection ; any other is subject to illusion, pride and self-love.
For the rest, drop gradually but quietly the lengthy reasonings
which absorb your mind during prayer, and aim, rather, at
affections, aspirations, desires for God, and a simple repose in
Him.   This will not prevent you, however, from pausing a little
over good thoughts, if they are simple, quiet and peaceful, and
seem to come and go of their own accord.

LETTER IV.—*Darkness and Doubts.*

To a Postulant.   On obscurity and weakness.

NOTE : " This Postulant is Madame de Lesen, about whom
Rev. Mother Marie-Anne-Thérèse de Rosen had consulted Fr.
de Caussade, and had undertaken to place in direct communication with him.   She entered the Convent of the Annunciation
at St. Mihiel."

My dear Sister,

All that you describe to me in your letter appears to me so
easy to decide, that God must have kept you in very great
darkness if you have not been able, with the help of His grace,
to find a clue for yourself.   Besides, as you tell me, God does,
occasionally, send you some rays of light to illuminate your soul,
and disperse the darkness of your doubts.   These gleams of
light which enkindle your heart, filling it with a sweet peace and
great courage in the service of God, can come only from Heaven.
Therefore you can follow these lights without fear, and the recollection of them will suffice to sustain and guide you in moments
of darkness.   However, since God has inspired you to apply
to me again, it will be quite easy to satisfy you in each particular

1st.   The snares and subtleties of self-love render you, you say, incapable of seeing things in their proper light.   Then why do you attempt to do so ?   Have you not, in holy obedience, an infallible guide, and in humility and docility sure guarantees that you are not misled in following the decisions laid down for you.

2nd.   After having consulted your Superior or your Mistress with the simplicity of a little child, remain in peace, for this is your security.   If you do not submit to this rule, you will be much to be pitied, and it will be your own fault.

3rd.   To feel so keenly your weakness, and need of sensible support, and as it were, always on the edge of a precipice is, in truth, a very humiliating trial, but a very salutary one, since it leads infallibly to a total distrust of self, and to the most perfect confidence in God.   This is the only way to leave the region of the senses, and to enter the life of pure faith and love which is wholly spiritual.

4th.   The dark dungeon in which you find yourself is a prison into which, I will not say the justice of God, but His very great mercy throws you from time to time to purify you like gold in a crucible.   You have only to stay there as quietly as you can. " But how then shall I practise virtue ? "   In this case virtue consists in suffering, in silent endurance and abandonment, and in humble and loving submission.   You know the great maxim that more progress is made during suffering than in action. " But," you will say, " I commit sin while in this state."   No, there is no sin, the Master of the prison will prevent that.   " But it seems to me that I look upon hell with indifference."   This is a strong way of expressing yourself, but, thank God, I can understand the meaning of it better than you do.   It only expresses the result of that interior operation by which God weakens your self-love.   Take courage, the day will come, and perhaps soon, when you will be able to realise the great good effected in this dark prison ; for the present you must live in this hope without other light than that of faith.

5th.   No doubt, there occur, in your state of interior fever, paroxysms which seem to devour and consume you.   These are caused by what is impure and earthly in the depths of the soul, which is thus consumed and devoured, like the evil humours of the body during the paroxysms of certain fevers.   This is a symptom of cure not of illness.   " But at these times I can neither pray, nor have recourse to God."   No, perhaps not, at any rate not in a perceptible manner ; but the heart prays without ceasing by hidden desires known only to God.   Your conclusion really made me laugh ; " Judge therefore," you say, " how I acquit myself of the obligation of reciting the Office, assisting at Mass and the rest." Very willingly, my dear Sister, would I take upon myself all the evil you commit in these circumstances, if you would concede me all the good that God is effecting in you. That little word, " therefore," has given me an insight into a certain temptation which the subtlety of the evil spirit tries to introduce into your soul. But let us follow your letter, and the thread of my reply. You begin to think, say you, that you were very rash in making a vow to become a Religious, and that the observances of the religious life are far beyond your powers. If I had not had a long experience of the progress made by even the most manifest temptations, when they are given the least encouragement under pretext of examining them, I should never have imagined you capable of succumbing so foolishly to this one. To cut it short I must tell you firstly, that I knew by the drift of your letter that this was the temptation the devil aimed at by all the changes he has rung in your soul. If he can only make you relinquish your prize, what a victory he will gain! what a triumph for all hell! Secondly, I forbid you in the Name of God and by all the authority He has given me over you, either to listen to, or examine into this subject in any way ; and I command you to act about it in the same way as if the devil suggested that you should throw yourself into a well or poison all the Religious. Thirdly, God wills you to embrace the religious life ; this then ought to take place, and will take place in spite of all hell let loose to prevent it. " But the spiritual afflictions ! the bodily infirmities ! " If necessary God will perform miracles about them, and you must expect these miracles when they are required. Now humble yourself, my dear Sister, annihilate yourself profoundly before God, confess to Him that you are weakness and inconstancy itself. This experience should serve for the future to make you feel how necessary it is to distrust self in our boasted courage and apparent firmness in good reso- lutions which come to nothing without God's ceaseless support. How poor, weak and miserable beyond all expression are we not, and liable to go wrong in every imaginable way, and in things we should never have thought possible !

6th. The sensitiveness you feel when being corrected, in this state of trouble, ought to be a subject of humiliation, but not of discouragement ; because it is true that at such times sensi- tiveness is so keen that St. Teresa herself was obliged to be on her guard against a spiteful and fretful temper which she was tempted to vent on the Sisters. It would take too long to tell you the great good God produces in our souls by these feelings and rebellions, provided they are borne patiently.

7th. God makes you feel that Satan is laying traps for you, and that, at the same time His invisible hand bears you up, and holds you back ; what could be more encouraging ? Keep firm, all this will turn to your very great good, and above all will serve to make you thoroughly convinced of your own weakness which you have never hitherto understood such as it is. You require all these temptations and trials to convince you of it, and to tear from your heart every fibre of foolish self-confidence. It is only when we begin to be cured that we recognise the evil.

I finish by repeating that your state, although, in truth, very crucifying, is nevertheless, and indeed on that account, very safe, very purifying and very sanctifying. You need fear no danger, as long as you hold by Fénélon's great rule : despair entirely of yourself, and put not an atom of confidence in anything but God alone, Who, from the very stones can raise up children to Abraham.

LETTER V.—*Distractions in Prayer.*

To Sister Marie-Henriette de Bousmard. On weakness and distractions (1734).

My dear Sister,

1st. Do not regret the consolations and sensible devotion that God gave you formerly, and has now taken away. With the consolations that you experienced were mingled a thousand imperfections. It is true that by the very fact that these consolations were felt they were extremely pleasant to nature which always desires to see, know, and feel ; but the more according to nature is the state, the less is it adapted for the requirements of divine love. This is the reason that God quickly withdraws a soul from this state ; and the more quickly, the more faithfully it responds to His grace. If He did not act towards us, in this respect, with a fatherly strictness, we should always remain feeble, subject to all sorts of defects, and incapable of protecting ourselves against the allurements and illusions of self-love. The soul that has not been enlightened and set free by trials, indulges, almost without perceiving it, in continual self-examinations, and makes its satisfaction and peace depend on feelings, the most unstable things in the world ; if it loves God, it is not only for Himself but much more on account of the consolations it expects from Him, and it remains in a vain self-satisfaction occasioned by the spiritual riches it supposes itself to possess, and God grant that it may not end by worshipping its own imaginary excellence. However, even if the soul avoids this criminal excess, it is to be greatly feared, that being full of itself it remains empty of God. Rather than expose the souls that He loves with a love of predilection to such a fearful misfortune, God sends them all sorts of trials. He strikes them, humiliates them and makes them contemptible in their own eyes. But how superabundantly does He not compensate those who remain faithful during trials, for the privations they have endured! When, by a complete destruction of one's whole spiritual fortune, one finds oneself reduced to nothing, then one suddenly discovers that one has neither vanity, presumption, nor self-esteem, but is filled with distrust, humility, confidence in God and love for Him; and this love is then absolutely pure because self-love has nothing to lean upon, and, consequently, nothing to become attached to, or to corrupt. Therefore I set more value on your present poverty than on all those former beautiful feelings that seemed to you so perfectly pure, but of which your self-love secretly made its most delicious pasture.

2nd. It seems, sometimes, as if one had neither faith, hope, nor charity, and as if one were without religion, without any virtue, as if one had lost all knowledge of God. This happens when He is pleased to withdraw all delight, all unction, and all that is sensible to make it reside in the essence of the soul, and to enable it to advance by the practice of pure faith. Then it is that God is served and adored in spirit and in truth, as Jesus Christ said to the woman of Samaria. This state is even further removed from the senses, and is, therefore, more valuable, higher, more purified and more solid. In it can the pure delights of the spirit be enjoyed; but this is only to be attained by the privation of all sensible pleasure, as sensible devotion can only be enjoyed by the privation of sensual and earthly pleasure. In this state, however, there is always peace, because the soul is then established in God and feels just as you feel; I mean a secret and hidden power proceeding from the inmost presence of God, and this support, imperceptible though it is, makes a soul stronger than when it believed itself ready to endure martyrdom. So remain in peace, and bless God.

3rd. As for the innumerable acts of offering, resignation, etc., without doubt they are suitable for beginners to form a habit of making them; but in your present state they are made by, and in your heart, and almost without your thinking of it. Does not God see all your intentions, even the most secret, without having them explained to Him by what are called formal and express acts? When, in the midst of your good works some secret intention of self-love, pride, or human respect insinuates itself into your heart, far from making express acts you would endeavour to hide from yourself these perverse intentions, convinced that God sees, and will punish them; do you not believe then that He also sees your secret good intentions and that He is as liberal in rewarding as He is strict in punishing?

4th. The wandering of your thoughts is but another trial from God, an occasion of suffering, of humiliation, and an exercise of patience and of merit, and the anxiety it causes you is a proof of the desire you have of being always occupied with God. Besides, God sees this desire, and, in His sight, desires are equal to acts, whether for good or evil. Suffer, therefore, humbly and patiently all the involuntary wanderings of your mind, and take care not to trouble about them, nor to examine anxiously what could have caused them; this would be a simple curiosity of self-love which God would punish with still greater darkness. Remember what St. Teresa said on this subject, " Let the clapper make a noise, provided the mill grinds the corn." She compares the wandering mind to the clapper, and the will tending to God to the mill that grinds the corn. A will fixed on God is what we should hope for above all things. What do you think takes place in the heart of a worldly woman during a fine sermon? Doubtless a hundred good thoughts pass through her mind and imagination while her will and her heart are fixed on the object of her passion; is she any holier for that? With you it is exactly the contrary; why then do you distress yourself? Otherwise what signifies this tranquillity and peace of the soul in the midst of these attacks, these pains, and this torment, and the little desire you have to refer to them? Is not this a great gift of God, and an evident sign that it is He Who, so delicately, and so peacefully wounds the heart? Remain then tranquilly in your state of total abandonment to God, and do not trouble yourself to find out how you form acts; they are formed by the secret and imperceptible movements of your heart that God touches interiorly, and which He moves as He pleases.

5th. I am not surprised at the fatigue and emptiness you experience in making efforts to multiply and reiterate your interior acts. This is because in this way you withdraw yourself from the operation of God to act for yourself, as if you wanted to anticipate grace and to do more than God wished. This is indeed natural activity! Be content to remain at peace in your soul, and keep yourself there as in a prison where God is pleased to immure you, without bethinking yourself of making unseasonable escapes. Thus you will be in that state of holy and fruitful idleness that the saints describe, and thus also you will have many and great occupations without labour. It is self-love only that complains and is in despair at having nothing to do, to see, to feel, nor to hear; but let it groan as much as it likes, by dint of worrying and despairing it will rid you finally of its presence. By cutting off supplies we shall starve it out. Oh! what a fortunate release! I wish it for you as for myself with all my heart.

6th.   The way in which you keep in the presence of God by a simple glance of faith without mental images, figures, or any kind of representation, in a total surrender of your whole self, is the most pure and most perfect way of treating with God.   It is the true prayer of the heart, a quite interior prayer, the sincere prayer of spirit to spirit, and the more simple, free, imperceptible, and removed it is, from all that can be felt so much the more solid, sublime, penetrating and efficacious it becomes, says the holy Mother de Chantal.

LETTER VI.—*Fear of Wasting Time.*

To Sister Marie-Henriette de Mahuet.   On the same subject, and interior rebellion and spiritual poverty.   Alby, 1732.

My dear Sister,

Nothing is more common with souls who have not yet acquired much experience in the ways of the spiritual life, than the fear about which you have consulted me ;   I mean the fear of wasting time in the prayer of the simple presence of God.   But it is easy to reassure such souls, and to reassure you also.   For this it suffices to recall to your mind the principle laid down by the divine Master :   " the tree is known by its fruits."   That which produces only good effects cannot but be good.   Besides, your own experience teaches you, that since you applied yourself to this kind of prayer you have become, interiorly, greatly changed for the better.   You have, then, only to thank God for the favour He has granted you in substituting as He has, the peaceful action of His grace for the agitation of your natural activity. I wish you could accustom yourself always to judge of your progress and the state of your soul by the infallible rules of faith and the counsels of the Gospel.   When you find that your ways, your ideas, and your conduct agree with the teachings of faith, and with the practice of the saints, you may hold them to be good, and perfectly safe.   In this no illusion is possible, as it is when one judges oneself by sensible impressions, which are always deceptive.   To guide one's conduct by these impressions is to take a weathervane, which turns with every wind, for a mariner's compass.   It is impossible to navigate safely unless guided by the sure and infallible rules of faith which make us turn away from sin, love God and our neighbour, detach us from creatures, and lead us to obedience, self-forgetfulness, complete submission to the will of God, abnegation and mortification.   The kind of prayer which produces these effects is, without doubt, the best.

2nd. As those spiritual books which treat of prayer might fall into the hands of all sorts of persons, and consequently not be well understood, authors and preachers do wisely in making use of general terms and in laying down only general rules, in order to avoid giving any handle for illusion; but directors, in speaking to persons they are well acquainted with, make use of a different method to reassure those under their direction who, without cause, would be terrified in reading or listening to sermons. It is because of my knowledge of your state and of God's designs on your behalf that I do not hesitate to reassure you. Go forward without a shadow of fear. No one can experience the fruit of the blessing of God, unless he follow the attraction of God. The deceptions and illusions of the spirit of darkness are made known by their effects and fruits which are contrary to those produced by grace. If I saw you exposed to these illusions I should not fail to tell you of it; and in default of me there are others who would render you this service on condition that you laid bare your mind to them with sincerity.

3rd. The rule of faith must be also taken, by which to form a judgment about the stupidity you have experienced for some time past. If it be only a question of being stupid, dull, and slow, and even insensible to all the things of this world, faith teaches us that this stupidity is true wisdom. But even if this same stupidity should seem to extend, sometimes, to things of salvation, that is no proof that it is a sign of your being at a distance from God if it does not prevent you from fulfilling your duties, keeping the Rule, and carrying out your exercises of piety. You should, therefore, regard it as a trial from God which you have in common with nearly all the saints. Be faithful, and while accepting this apparent stupidity you will find in it a very meritorious exercise of patience, submission, and interior humility. It can only be prejudicial to self-love, which dies gradually and is thus destroyed and annihilated more efficaciously than by any exterior mortification.

4th. When we have to make great sacrifices, nature and self-love, reluctant to do so, excite rebellions in the heart which seem to overthrow the whole soul. Did not Jesus Christ Himself experience the same in the Garden of Olives? It is enough therefore for the superior part of the soul to remain firm and to say with Jesus Christ, "Fiat voluntas tua." These are the interior combats of which St. Paul speaks, and after him all the masters of the spiritual life : this is how the just man truly lives by faith and escapes from the rule of the senses : these are the great victories which will be crowned in this world by peace, and the submission of the lower nature; in the next by the possession of a God.

5th. The last and most efficacious of all the remedies I have to offer you is an entire and total abandonment into the hands of this God of goodness, Who has not ceased for a long time in being beforehand with the blessings of His very great mercy. You must throw yourself into this abandonment with the same courage with which you would cast yourself into the sea if God asked this sacrifice of you; in the same way as, in times past, a holy martyr by a particular attraction, and an especial inspiration threw herself into the midst of the flames without waiting for the executioners. It is this courage, and this holy abandonment founded on faith and love which charms the heart of God, and establishes in the soul a peace that nothing can disturb.

6th. Your conduct in avoiding useless visits, waste of time, and distractions, seems to me excellent. Know that exterior solitude is the rampart of that which is interior which, without it, can with difficulty be preserved. I advise you to add, with regard to the people in the house, the greatest possible silence, never speaking without a reason, nor without some holy motive—such as for a necessary recreation, to refresh yourself a little, for the sake of charity, or religious condescension ; or to overcome yourself about certain persons towards whom you may feel some antipathy. Finally I recall to your mind a maxim that I wish I could engrave on every heart, and especially on the hearts of Religious, and devout persons who are distressed and uneasy at seeing how poor, miserable and destitute they are ; as they say with sighs and groans. This maxim alone can make them tranquil, contented, and even exceedingly rich in their spiritual poverty. You understand what I mean beforehand, that true perfection and consequently the real wealth of the soul consists in conforming our will to the will of God. Consequently every time that, overcome by the sense of your weakness and interior misery, you think that, while avoiding by the grace of God, everything that could offend Him, you are, at the same time very devoid of those gifts and graces by which the saints were enriched, you can and ought to say : " My God, I will all that You will and for as long as it pleases You." " But," you will say, " what resource shall I have if God takes me at my word, and keeps me always in this state of spiritual poverty ? " You will have, my dear sister, only the Will of God, and this resource will take the place of every other. This divine and adorable Will will supply you with all the gifts in which you are wanting, it will become your treasure, and will constitute a spiritual fortune in the very midst of your poverty ; for how can anyone be more rich in the sight of God than by conforming in all things to His most holy will even in those things that are most afflicting ? Can anyone be more certain of possessing pure love, than those

who resign themselves willingly to all that is most mortifying to
that most sensitive form of self-love, spiritual self-love ?   Believe
me, my dear Sister, the soul that regards its poverty in this light
need not envy even those souls which are most greatly enriched
with the gifts of God.

LETTER VII.—*On Darkness and Want of Feeling.*

To Sister Marie-Thérèse de Vioménil.   On darkness and want
of feeling.

My dear Sister and very dear daughter in our Lord.

May the peace of our Lord be always with you.   By what
you tell me I understand that you are in a state of obscurity ;
but far from sharing the alarms that this state—a very ordinary
one in persons of your sex—causes you ; I believe it to be, unquestionably, the most safe because it is less exposed to the
delusions of self-love, to attacks of vanity, and therefore, even
this obscurity is a grace of God ; for, during this life the way that
leads most directly to God is the way of bare faith which is
always obscure.   In spite of this obscurity you are able to
understand your state and to explain it clearly enough to enable
any director with a little experience to guide you.   I will tell you
what I think about your general state and take your difficulties
one by one.

1st.   You say you do not know how to pray.   Experience
has taught me that persons of good will who speak in this way
know better than others how to pray, because their prayer is
more simple and humble, but, on account of its simplicity it
escapes their observation.   To pray like this is to remain by
faith in the presence of God, with a hidden, but constant desire
to receive His grace according to our needs.   As God sees all
our desires, and as, according to St. Augustine, to desire always
is to pray always, so in this consists our great prayer.   Follow
the leading of simplicity in prayer, there can never be excess
of it, for God loves to see us like little children in His presence.

2nd.   As to Holy Communion, the increasing hunger that is
felt for this divine Food, and the strength it imparts are great
reasons for receiving It frequently.   Therefore fear nothing,
but rest on the assurance I give you.

3rd.   Insensibility towards all created things, and detachment
even from relations, are greater graces than you imagine ; it only
remains to become detached from self by renouncing all interior
self-seeking.   Frequent union with Jesus Christ and prayer
will gradually achieve this task, provided you do your share of

the work in forgetting yourself to think only of God, abandoning to Him all your interests, both spiritual and temporal.

4th. It is right that you should realise that all God requires of you is submission and resignation. Ah! my dear daughter, in that is comprised all perfection. To look for it elsewhere would be only error and illusion. Therefore a spiritual person inclined to an interior life, has, truly, but one thing to do, which is to submit with hearty concurrence, to all imaginable circumstances, whether interior or exterior, in which God wills to place him. Therefore when you are ill say "God wills it, very well, I will it also as He wills it and for as long a time." "But what if it should incapacitate me from fulfilling my duties and being of use to the community?" Well, if God wills it, will it also, and accept beforehand, with the pain you suffer, the holy abjection and humiliation which accompany it. "But in this state, perhaps, I give in to myself a little, and do not make all the efforts that I could and should make." If, even so after having consulted your superior and your confessor you follow their judgment blindly, you are then doing the will of God which is also your will. Then rest satisfied in having acquiesced in the divine will in all this, and preserve that interior peace in which God dwells and works. This, my dear Sister, is a clear and safe way; follow it faithfully, and constantly reject all contrary thoughts and ideas as suggestions of the devil, who desires at least to disturb the interior peace in which your soul should be settled, and which forms the solid foundation of the spiritual life.

5th. You have committed a grave fault of disobedience and imprudence in exposing yourself to three months of fever. Hold for certain that to refuse a dispensation in such circumstances is, by no means, an act of virtue, but stubbornness, and an obstinate attachment to your own judgment, and your own will under a pretext of piety. Many devotees and spiritual persons are to be pitied when they act in this manner, and great patience is required to put up with them. Their blindness and illusion are sometimes so strong that an angel from heaven would find a difficulty in making them see clearly. As for you, submit to everything, listen to every advice, suffer with all peace, gentleness, and patience, and do the will of God in all things, in the same spirit, this will be of great benefit to you.

6th. They were quite right to forbid you to think of giving up your post, or of even wishing to do so. I, also, forbid you most strictly. Be very careful not to attempt to escape from the commands of God. "But I am not strong enough." God can very easily make you strong enough. "I am not clever enough." Well! the power of making you clever enough is not wanting to God, and He has already given you the principal qualification, which is, a distrust of your own powers. To know, and to feel one's incapacity is the essential thing, because then one depends entirely on God, applies to Him for everything, and attributes nothing to oneself, but all to God alone; and these graces will by themselves make everything prosper. In fine be at peace, and place your confidence in the God of all goodness; after that you can despair of yourself as much as you like. This humble feeling of your incapacity, weakness, and imbecility is exactly the instrument made use of by God to exalt His glory, and to make it shine forth more visibly.

To have no feeling about the truths of religion is not a bad sign in certain souls; on the contrary, it is often a sign that God desires to lead them by the safest way, that of simple, bare faith without those feelings of devotion that He can give when He pleases. In the ways of God the only violent efforts to be used must be employed against sin, but with regard to everything else there must only be peace and tranquillity. When you find you cannot succeed in making acts say to yourself: "Very well! they are all made in the sight of God since He has seen my desire; He will enable me to make them when He pleases, He is Master. His most holy will shall always be my rule; to accomplish it is the reason I am in the world. It is my wealth, my treasure. May God grant to others all the light, talent, grace, gifts and sensible and spiritual sweetness that are pleasing to Him. As for me I desire nothing but to do His holy will. That is my wealth." This, my dear daughter, is your path, walk in it continually in peace, confidence, and abandonment of your whole self; you are in perfect safety.

7th. In order to advance, endeavour to suffer peacefully all that God wills or permits to happen to you, without going to creatures to complain, or to seek consolation; neither try to find distraction in useless conversations, nor amusement in frivolous thoughts and idle projects for the future, as all this would withdraw you from God, and prevent the operations of His grace in you; so take great care.

8th. To help you to occupy yourself with God easily and uninterruptedly according to your wishes and requirements this is what you ought to do. Firstly, love solitude and silence, for this will do much towards forming an interior spirit of recollection. Secondly, read only choice books that are solid, and full of piety, and read them slowly, with frequent pauses, trying more to enjoy, than to understand or remember them. Thirdly, during the day make frequent aspirations after God, espexially those that occur to you in sufferings, temptations, weariness, disgust, sadness of heart, contradictions, etc.

9th. The prayers you make to God for detachment from all things, are inspired by grace; continue them, and be assured that sooner or later they will be answered. It is but just that we should wait God's time, since we have kept Him waiting so long, and the great graces we ask of Him deserve to be desired and waited for with patience and perseverance.

LETTER VIII.—*On Dryness and Distractions.*

To Sister Jeanne-Elizabeth Gaury (1735). On dryness and distractions during prayer.

My dear Sister,

1st. Your method is very simple, and that which is simple is always best. It goes straight to God, and you must continue it; but do so quietly, without effort, and without eagerness either to preserve it, or to regain it when the perception of it has been lost; that would be to wish to appropriate to yourself the gift of God. In this method of prayer distractions and dryness are pretty frequent, but all the same if these are endured patiently and with abandonment to the will of God, it is an excellent prayer. Besides, although these distractions and this aridity are painful, they do not prevent the constant desire to pray which remains in the depths of the heart, and it is in this desire that heartfelt prayer consists.

If you have been praying in this excellent manner for a considerable time, say for two or three years, it would serve no purpose to take a book; but if these times of powerlessness and aridity have lasted only for seven or eight consecutive days, then make use of a book, but read with frequent pauses; and should you find that this reading distracts you still more, or troubles your soul, leave it off, and try as well as you can do remain peacefully and silently in the presence of God.

You need not be surprised, nor still less troubled that the very same things that used to touch you deeply at one time, should now make not the slightest impression on you; this is one of the vicissitudes that have to be put up with interiorly just as the exterior vicissitudes of weather and seasons have to be borne; and it is only the very inexperienced who do not expect this.

2nd. In this method of prayer resolutions are seldom made, but virtue is practised much more easily than when resolutions were made in meditation; because by the previous operation of the Holy Spirit the heart is disposed to do so when the occasion arises. The interior dispositions of persons following this method might be expressed in the following manner which would be of more value than any resolutions. " Lord make me do good and avoid evil on such occasions, or in such circumstances, otherwise I know by personal experience that I shall do exactly the reverse of what I ought."

The sweetness and efficacy of holy recollection are often the prize and recompense of former sacrifices ; but this sensible pleasure does not, at first, take away all repugnance and interior rebellion, though it gradually diminishes them until, in time, a sensible joy is felt even in the most bitter trials.

3rd.   God permits your slight infidelities to give you a deeper conviction of your weakness, and gradually to destroy in you that unhappy self-esteem, presumption and secret self-confidence which would never otherwise allow you to acquire true humility of heart.   As you know nothing pleases God more than a complete contempt of self, accompanied by an absolute confidence in Him alone.   This God of all goodness, therefore, does you a great favour in compelling you, often against your will, to drink from this chalice so much dreaded by your self-love and corrupt nature.   And to know how to appreciate this favour at its proper value, and to realise your own happiness, are feelings so supernatural that they can only be attributed to the operation of the Holy Spirit.   Another operation of grace is to feel happy in bearing some resemblance to Jesus Christ, but this feeling is not to be greatly depended on, have a fear of meeting with difficult circumstances, and distrust your own weakness.

4th.   There are never any illusions to be feared in repugnance and involuntary rebellion, as they are incompatible with holy prayer by which they are vanquished and overcome.   You are wrong in persuading yourself that you will never be able to acquire true humility nor perfect mortification on account of feeling in yourself such a strong opposition to these virtues. If you had only your own powers to rely upon it would indeed be impossible, but as you very justly add yourself, with the help of God's grace merited for you by Jesus Christ, all becomes easy.   It might happen that even this truth should make no impression on you and I should not be surprised if such were the case, but your remark to me on the subject proves plainly that like all beginners, you attach much too much importance to feelings of devotion.   Nevertheless, it is an understood fact that in the order of supernatural operations of grace what is most sensible is least perfect and least safe, while that which is most spiritual and most hidden is by far the best.   When God deprives you of His sensible presence, and of devotion in recollection, content yourself with having a holy desire and wish to retain it; this will suffice, as it is most pleasing to God and very meritorious.

5th. Any disquiet is an injury to the soul, therefore you should exert all your energy to repel that which you experience on the subject of the divine Office, especially as there is no reason for it, the desire to say it well and the will to do so always remaining in spite of involuntary distractions, and yours are all of this kind. The proof of this is manifest, which is, that you feel a real pain at heart whenever you notice this wandering of the mind. What more certain, or better sign could you have that you have not consented? If you are afraid of distractions, it shows that they are not voluntary in their origin, and especially if you try to practise recollection during the day. Therefore be at peace and accept submissively these involuntary miseries.

6th. You have shown me another subject of uneasiness; one which is of no consequence, and which has its foundation in various illusions, and of which you must cure yourself. The first is the great desire you have of sensible pleasure in Communion, and is an effect of spiritual self-love. The second is the belief that this sensible pleasure is a necessary condition of a good Communion. Alas! my dear daughter what would become of so many holy souls who usually feel nothing but dryness, callousness, and often distaste? In all our spiritual exercises we must approach God by pure faith which is scarcely felt. The less feeling you have in your communions and prayers the more likely they are to be purer and more pleasing to God. This is the way of bare faith and pure love which is never self-seeking. St. Francis of Sales used to say, " Our miserable satisfactions do not satisfy God." Pure love consists in being content with all that pleases God, and will not permit us to will anything contrary to the will of God, even as to our holiest desires and actions; nor, consequently, to act against His holy permissions, even should the cause of certain occurrences be the result of our own fault. This principle is either ignored, or, at least, obscured by the subtlety of our self-love, so ingenious in making out everything that satisfies it, or gives it pleasure, to be good and holy. A good Religious speaking on this subject said that God had gradually taken away all her pleasure, and all the spiritual attractions and feelings in whatever she did, to purify her love, which the first sweetness had left so imperfect and impure.

For communion and the spiritual exercises of the morning and evening follow the method that most attracts you. One short act of your own is worth more than all the long prayers you read. The indifference you feel as to what is thought or said about you is an effect of the operation of the Holy Spirit. Continue as you are doing, never excusing nor justifying yourself, unless you are ordered to do so ; it is the most perfect way of acting. God be praised for all, and in all. Amen.

LETTER IX.—*Passive Recollection.*
To Mother Louise-Françoise de Rosen. On distractions, weariness, and impulses.

My dear Sister. To all the anxieties you express in your letter to me, and to all the doubts you lay before me, I have but one answer. I will say to you in the words of our good Master : " Peace be with you, fear not." What troubles you, ought, on the contrary, to be a subject of joy. Where you believe you see symptoms of laxness I see undoubted signs of solid progress.

1st. This inattention, almost perpetual, this weariness and distaste that you experience at prayer, at the Office, at Confession and Communion, etc., are nothing else but the natural effect of the apparent absence of God. The divine Spouse of your soul, in order to put it to the test and to purify it, withdraws His sensible presence, and then the poor soul suffers acute grief which sometimes affects the bodily health. In this way it is a martyr of grace, and of the Holy Spirit ; for, now that there are no longer any tyrants to make the blood of the martyrs flow in testimony of their faith, the Holy Spirit knows how to make martyrs of divine love by the suffering caused by His apparent absences, and by many kinds of crucifying operations. Those who submit to this spiritual torture do so by practising resignation, blind abandonment, and the same unwearied patience that the martyrs of old practised in the midst of their torments. The same Holy Spirit who filled the souls of the martyrs with divine peace and joy, while their bodies were suffering the most frightful torments, will in the same way preserve the peace of your soul in spite of all the agitation of your mind and senses. But you must, faithfully, co-operate with His action by giving no voluntary consent to the anxieties which assail you. To regain recollection when you think you have, to some extent, lost it, make no violent efforts. Resign yourself with a good grace to being deprived of sensible and active recollection, and be content with passive recollection which subsists at the bottom of your heart, even when the mind seems all astray, for this is the inalienable right of souls that are free from all inordinate love for the things of this world. It is true that in this state God is not always the distinct object of our thoughts, but He is the principle of our life, and the rule of our actions. There is a kind of abstraction during which it seems to us that we do not think of anything, because, on the one hand visible objects do

not occupy us, and on the other we have such a general idea of
God, a notion so dim and obscure, that the mind cannot grasp
it, and loses itself, seeming to have no consciousness, and to
escape control. In this state all that has to be done, being
suggested by the Spirit of God gently, is carried out in peace,
without eagerness or uneasiness. But, directly the activity of
self-love begins to meddle, the Holy Spirit, jealously desirous
of being the only guide of the soul He has raised to this state,
puts a limit to its action, and then there is nothing to be done but
to drop this activity, and to resume and re-enter the state of
passive recollection. This recollection, you must know, is
nothing else but the fruit and the extension of the prayer of quiet
and of silence, which consists in holding one's peace interiorly,
and in leaving off all thoughts rather than in combating those
that come, or in seeking for those that do not present themselves.

2nd. The occasional outbursts to which you give vent, sometimes lasting for a lengthy period, are trials that should prove
equally fruitful. While causing you interior suffering they bring
you infinite riches, purifying, humiliating and diminishing you
so much in your own eyes that you will gradually become like
those little children whom Jesus Christ desires us to resemble
if we wish to enter into His kingdom. You are quite right in
saying that we have a great need of patience and gentleness in
bearing with ourselves ; perhaps more than in putting up with
others, following out the thought of St. Francis of Sales.

3rd. The continual vicissitudes that take place in the soul
are a good sign. By them the Holy Spirit renders us pliant to
all His movements ; for, by dint of these constant changes
nothing of self remains, and we are prepared to take any shape
that is pleasing to this divine Spirit who breathes where He will
and as He pleases. It is, as Fénélon says, like a continual
melting and recasting of the soul, which, in this process, becomes
liquid like water having neither form nor shape but taking any
form or shape according to that of the vessel into which it is
poured.

4th. It will be quite easy for you to guide yourself in these
different situations. You have but one thing to do, and that is
quite simple, it is to notice in what direction the deepest bias of
your heart inclines you, without consulting the mental attitude
which would spoil all. Always act with the same simplicity, in
good faith and uprightness of heart, without looking back or
about you, but straight in front at the present time and moment,
and I will answer for everything. Do you not see that such a
way of acting is to die to self perpetually by the most complete
abnegation, and a true sacrifice of abandonment to God in the
darkness of faith.

5th. You say that you do not experience any interior re-proach, nor any feeling either for good or evil, and that this silence seems to you terrible. It is part of your state. All feeling ought to be taken from you : it is so in the state of pure faith. Again, fear nothing, go on in peace, in simplicity, in total abandonment, without self-examination or particular reflexions : when any should be made God will give them to you, or supply the want of them by an interior feeling or a hidden attraction which will guide you in everything more surely than your own miserable reflexions. Are these, then, so precious that you need regret their loss and the deprivation of them ? Blessed are the poor in spirit for theirs is the kingdom of Heaven. Love this spiritual poverty which strips us interiorly of self, as exterior poverty strips us of goods. It is thus that the kingdom of God is formed within us.

LETTER X.—*The Use of Faults.*

To the same person. On weariness and idleness.

My dear Sister,
I see nothing in your present state that should alarm you. This weariness, idleness, and indolence that we experience oc-casionally in spite of ourselves has no culpability about it, provided we suffer it with resignation, and do not curtail any of our exercises of piety in spite of the disinclination we feel to perform them. If, with this want of feeling about everything else we experience a strong desire for the Sacraments and a great contrition for our faults, it is a sensible effect of the mercy of God Who makes use even of our faults to make us increase in fervour and humility.

There are two kinds of interior peace ; one is sensible, sweet and delightful, and this kind does not, in any way, depend on ourselves, and is not at all necessary. And there is another which is almost imperceptible, which dwells in the depths of the heart in the most hidden recesses of the soul. It is usually dry and unfelt, and can be retained in the midst of the greatest tribulations. To recognise it would require the most profound recollection, you would say it was hidden in a deep abyss. It is there that God dwells, and He fashions it Himself in order to dwell there as in an atmosphere of His own in the inner chamber of our hearts from whence He works marvellous but inscrutable things. These can only be recognised by their effects, as, when, by His beneficent influence you feel yourself capable of remaining firm in the midst of trials, violent shocks, great pain, and un-foreseen misfortunes. If you find that you possess this dry peace and a sort of quiet sadness, you ought to thank God for it ; this is all that is necessary for your spiritual progress.   Guard it as a most precious gift.   As it gradually increases it will one day become your greatest treasure, but this will not be till after many battles and many victories.

I congratulate you on having adopted my favourite motto, " God wills it ! God be praised in all things."   Oh ! what consolation there is in these few words !   St. Francis of Sales said it was a tonic for the heart by virtue of which it would never give way ; a strong potion which would enable us to digest iron, steel, and any other hard or revolting object that we were obliged to swallow, a balsam that could soothe and heal the most poison-ous wounds.   Oh ! my dear daughter ! let us make use of this remedy against the weakness of nature which opposes everything that is contrary to our inclination.   By the use of this simple recipe you will find bitter things become sweet and everything will seem good and pleasant ; nothing could better cheer the heart.

LETTER XI.—*Remembrance of Past Sins.*

To Sister Marie-Antoinette de Bousmard. On weakness, remembrance of past sins, fatigue, and fears. Nancy, 1734.

My dear Sister,

1st. The calmness you enjoy in solitude, and the peace of mind and heart which, emptied of all created things, is no longer occupied with them in any way, are signs of true interior recol-lection. God deprives you of feelings of devotion during prayer, to prevent the desires and eagerness they give rise to.   While you are at prayer remain exactly as you are in solitude.   I do not exact from you an atom more of application or attention. Continue in this thoughtful pensive state without allowing your thoughts to dwell on created things and then you will be in God without understanding how, without feeling His presence, nor even knowing how this can be.   This is a mystery which you will only be able to recognise by its happy effects which are—death to self, and unconsciousness of the things of this world.

2nd. To believe that you do nothing for God, and that the little you try to do is spoilt by an admixture of self-love, is nothing but the truth, and a truth so self-evident that it is extraordinary that it is not seen by everyone, and that we are not all trembling and annihilated before God.   On the other hand, however, this truth is so shrouded in darkness for us, so completely hidden in the folds of our self-love, that we cannot be too grateful to God when He is pleased to allow us to grasp it.

When it pleases God to grant us by His holy grace, this clear knowledge of ourselves, accompanied by feelings of humility; then we no longer expect anything more from self, but everything from Him alone.   No longer do we count on our good works, but solely on the mercy of God and the infinite merits of Jesus Christ; this is that true Christian hope which will be our salvation. Every other state, every other spiritual condition is full of risks to our salvation; but, to hope only in God, to depend only on God, in and through Jesus Christ, is that solid and immovable foundation that neither illusion, self-love, nor temptation can affect.

Oh! how I congratulate you on having arrived at this state! Hold to it firmly, it is the anchor of the vessel in the harbour of salvation.

3rd.   I am glad to find, by your letter, how completely the good God in His mercy is keeping you in the dark.   You attribute to your wickedness the recollections of the past which fill you with horror of yourself; but it is as clear as day that this is one of the most salutary impressions that grace can produce in you; there is, in fact, nothing better calculated to sanctify you than this holy hatred of yourself occasioned by these recollections, and the deep humiliation in which they keep you before God.   These feelings are given you suddenly when you least expect them or are thinking of them, to make you understand that they are an effect of grace.   " But why used you formerly to experience exactly contrary feelings when recalling the past ? " It is because formerly you would not have been able to endure the sight of your imperfections without great despondency.   It was necessary then that hope should predominate in you, but now you require a holy horror of yourself which is a true change of heart.   When God gives you these feelings, receive them quietly and with gratitude and thanksgiving, and allow them to pass away when God pleases, abandoning yourself entirely to all He wishes to effect in you, and do not attach yourself to any of the interior conditions in which He places you, nor regret any of which He deprives you.

4th.   I understand the difficulties of the duty about which you speak, and the strain to tired lungs of sustaining the chant, especially on great feast days.   All this is very painful it is true, but what is also true and extremely consoling is that such is the will of God, and permitted by Him that you may overcome your own will.   In a few words I will suggest to you how to act in this, and in any similar case.   Prayers, frankness, sacrifice, abandonment.   I will explain my meaning.   Having implored light from God, go and explain clearly to your Superior how you feel, and in what state you are, then wait to hear from her

R

mouth what God is pleased to arrange for you, being resolved to sacrifice to Him by perfect abandonment your dislikes, your health, and even your life, never doubting that God Who has never been known to forsake those who abandon themselves to Him, will inspire her who is charged to manifest to you His will, to tell you what is necessary. One of three things will infallibly happen; either you will be relieved of your office, or God will sustain and preserve you in it, or else He will allow you to succumb and will take you to Himself out of this wretched life. Then, I ask you, my good Sister, if you could end your life in a better manner than by a sacrifice so generous, and an act of abandonment so perfect? Whatever happens, then, keep firm after making your attempt. Live or die in peace. We will not speak about it any more, it is God's affair, and no longer yours. He well knows how to make everything turn to your advantage, and to His own greater glory. Oh! my dear Sister! in what a saintly, happy, and generous manner you will be able to act! How good it is to have chosen, once for all, the part of obedience and abandonment in all things! What peace! what a sacrifice! what a grace! what certainty of salvation! and above all, what merit in the eyes of God! What a consolation for me, in such a case, to learn that you have died a martyr to holy abandonment, and that God has permitted you to immolate yourself as a holocaust on the altar of His most holy, most adorable, and divine Will.

5th. Make yourself, therefore, a partaker of the contentment of God; place your happiness in the knowledge that His good pleasure is always accomplished in you; in this way even when you have occasion to be dissatisfied with yourself, you will reflect the satisfaction of God who, as St. Augustine remarks, is never so pleased with us as when we are displeased with ourselves. In this way it is that we constantly practise without even adverting to it the virtue of pure charity which consists in loving, in satisfying, and in willing in all things the good pleasure of God, preferring His holy will to everything that we could possibly wish, however holy our wishes might appear to be. You have chiefly two ways of exercising this meritorious abandonment. The first is, to say to God, "Lord I hate and detest my sins and imperfections, and I will make every effort to correct myself with the help of Your divine grace; as for the pain and abjection they bring me I accept this with all my heart for the love of You." The second way is to say, "My God, I desire to please You, I desire my own salvation and sanctification, the gift of prayer, of mortification, and of all virtues. I ask them of You, and I will exert all my powers to acquire them, whenever You show me an occasion of doing so; nevertheless

in this as in all other things I prefer Your holy will to my own
wishes, I only desire to possess that degree of grace and virtue
that You are pleased to bestow on me, and at the time appointed
by Your divine wisdom even should that be the last moment
of my life ; for Your most holy will is the rule and measure
of my desires, even of those that are most holy and lawful."
These acts, made with the whole heart, are the fruit of that
pure charity which, according to the Doctors of the Church,
is as efficacious as baptism and martyrdom for blotting out all
our sins ; as Jesus Christ said about Mary Magdalen, " Many sins
are forgiven her because she has loved much." Could anything be more consoling, fortifying and encouraging ? You say
that you live in a mean and poor way. " Blessed are the poor
in spirit." By this is intended interior humility and a holy
self-contempt. You live without assistance, that is to say that
you live in spirit, and in pure faith. Oh ! what a happy state !
Yes, happy indeed although this happiness is hidden from the
soul. You go on blindly from day to day. This is perfect
abandonment, you do not feel it, and hardly realise it, but if
you felt and understood it, it would no longer be abandonment,
but the strongest assurance of your salvation that you could
possibly desire. For, what assurance could you have more
satisfactory than the knowledge of being completely abandoned
to God both for time and eternity ? Abandonment is a virtue
the entire merit of which cannot be acquired unless the possession
of it is unrealised. Go on in peace, then, in the midst of your
fears, pains, and obscurities, and put your whole trust in God
above all knowledge, and all feeling, in, and through Jesus Christ.
May He be with you for ever.

LETTER XII.—*How to make use of trials.*

On the use of trials and how to act about them.

Before anything else, my dear Sister, I think I had better
explain what thought was suggested to me by your anxious
doubts, and eagerness to consult me about your soul. I cannot
help thinking that, if we were more attentive to the light given us
by the Holy Spirit, better disposed to receive His holy impressions, and more faithful in following the impulsion of His grace,
nothing more would be required to enable us to attain that
perfection to which we are called ; for I have noticed that even in
the midst of the most profound spiritual darkness, there is ever in
the centre of the soul a certain light of pure faith which is a most
safe guide. Besides this, there are certain moments when the

Holy Spirit makes known to us by a brighter, but very rapid light, that we are in the right way. Add to this a certain settled peace, even during interior storms, a right way of acting, and a regularity in the performance of duties, which, in spite of the frailty of nature, we never deliberately set aside, but follow with perseverance the maxims of the Gospel and the rules of perfection. An obedient and faithful soul ought to find in this a sufficient guarantee for confidently trusting herself with entire abandonment to this interior Spirit who guides her so well. It is often a sign of weakness, and an effect of the workings of self-love that we hanker after more complete assurance. However, there are exceptions to be made, such as the beginning of the spiritual life when the Holy Spirit has not yet acquired full dominion over us, and some extraordinary occasions when the tumult of the storm prevents us hearing His voice. I might content myself with this general reply but will, however, answer you in detail.

1st. This fresh condition of obscurity, dryness and distaste, into which God has permitted you to enter, does not surprise me. This good Master always begins by making Himself known and loved in sensible devotion, and afterwards deprives the soul of these consolations to withdraw it from the earthliness of the senses, in order to unite it to Himself in a far more excellent way, more intimate and solid, by pure faith entirely spiritual. To make this purification complete, suffering has to be added to privation, at least interior suffering, interior rebellion, diabolical temptations, anguish, weakness, and repugnance for all that is good which sometimes rises to a sort of agony. All this serves marvellously to deliver the soul from self-love and to give it some trace of resemblance to its crucified Spouse. All these trials are so many blows that are inflicted on us by God to make us die to self. The more strongly self-love struggles against these blows the harder they seem and the more cruel the agony. Divine love is a two-edged sword, and strikes self-love until it is killed and destroyed. Great sorrow in these trials proceeds from the strong resistance of our cursed love of self which is loth to relinquish the empire it has gained over our hearts, and to allow the love of God to reign in its stead. This love produces only sweetness and delight as long as it finds no obstacles to its divine influence, nor any enemy to resist it.

Do not regret, then, in any way those days that you pronounce happy because you enjoyed sensible devotion in prayer and communion, and because your union with your Beloved was so charming and delightful. How much more precious and of inestimable value are your present days of agony and martyrdom! These are days of the purest love, since in them you are loving God at your own cost, and for Himself alone. You need not fear any mixture of self-love in your intercourse with Him, since there is nothing in this intercourse but what is crucifying to self-love. In such a state our will is united to the will of God, and it is this that we love, and with a love so pure that the senses have no share in it. It is most difficult indeed to love God in happiness without any admixture of self, or of vain self-complacency, but in the time of crosses, and of interior spiritual privations, all that is needful in order to be certain of the purity of our love, is to endure them patiently, and to abandon ourselves sincerely. How truly consoling and encouraging is this certainty for those who understand the value and advantages of pure love. When God makes you understand this you will also understand why so many of the saints preferred privations and sufferings to consolations and joys, how they so passionately loved the former that they could hardly put up with the latter. God may possibly allow you to think that this painful state is going to last you your life-time, in order to give you an opportunity of making Him a more complete sacrifice. Do not waver, do not hesitate for a single moment, sacrifice all! abandon yourself without reserve, without limitation to Him, by Whom you imagine yourself abandoned, and keep yourself always in this interior state which is, at present, the most essential for you. I would almost say it is the only one for you during prayer, at Holy Communion, at Mass, during the Office, and all the day long; but attend to this quietly without effort, and do not even attach yourself to the frequent repetition of formal acts, it will suffice to keep your soul in this habitual condition of total abandonment without any reserve. I forbid you, therefore, voluntarily to desire anything but the accomplishment of the most holy will of God. Ask neither for more nor less pain, God knows better than we do the right measure that is necessary for us. It is very often nothing but presumption and illusion that makes us wish to imitate certain saints who, in their sufferings were especially inspired to say, " More, Lord, more ! " We are too little and too weak to dare to speak thus unless we have a moral conviction that God requires it of us. I forbid you also, all voluntary scruples, troubles, or doubts on the subject of the Office, of Holy Mass, etc. To act with a pure intention, and in simple good faith is enough ; in this respect God asks no more of us, and I daresay you would not be able to do more at present.

2nd. Oh! how glad I am to hear you say that you are insupportable to yourself, that at every moment you are on the point of falling into a state of despondency and trouble, without, by God's grace, actually doing so. That is to say that God, in making you understand all your weakness upholds you invisibly, thus giving you the victory, while at the same time preserving you in humility. You might very likely lose this virtue, either entirely, or to some extent, if you found yourself possessed of courage, or felt some spiritual strength. Learn from this a most important lesson inculcated by Fénélon. It is a pure grace from God, and one of the greatest to suffer in a petty way, to conquer in a feeble manner, that is to say with a sort of spiritual feebleness, humbly and with self-contempt, and to be so discontented with ourselves that we do not believe that we ever do anything well. This discontent with ourselves is very pleasing to God, and His content should be the basis of our own. Nothing could give us any further anxiety if we found our sole satisfaction in pleasing and satisfying God.

3rd. God gives you a great grace also in enabling you while in your present state to faithfully fulfil all your duties and rules. I greatly commend you for having sought no consolation from creatures and for having made no mention of your troubles to anyone even in confidence. Your silence will sanctify you more than any conversation or advice.

4th. Another great grace is to feel neither trouble, nor fear nor anxiety about your present state, nor about the future, just as though you had become callous about everything. This is the fruit and happy effect of your entire abandonment. As you have abandoned all to God, He takes charge of everything, banishing all trouble, fear, and anxiety from your soul. He takes from it all feelings of self-interest, and leaves it alive only to His interests. This disposition is the solid foundation of the most absolute security that a soul could possibly enjoy, it is the greatest happiness this life contains for us, and a sure sign of the friendship of God.

5th. The words that were spoken to you interiorly, and that you heard so distinctly were assuredly from God. I recognise this by the good and immediate effects they produced in you. Only God can impress souls to such a profound extent with whatever He pleases. You see that the divine goodness does not refuse you occasional scraps of comfort and strength to fortify you during the journey He makes you take through the desert.

6th. There is no reason to be surprised that your spiritual afflictions have no influence with regard to your conduct towards your neighbour, nor deprive you of your patience and equable temper, and kindness. As a rule while in this state of trial one is generally more able to help, to console, to comfort, and to serve others.

LETTER XIII.—*The Use of Trials continued.*

To Sister Anne-Marguérite Boudet de la Bellière (1734). The use of trials continued.

My dear Sister,

1st.   Your present state of obscurity is a real grace from God, Who desires to accustom you to walk in the darkness of pure faith which is the most meritorious way, and the most certain road to sanctity.

2nd.   Dryness and powerlessness are graces equally precious, and make you participate very meritoriously in the sufferings of Jesus Christ. " But," say you, " this powerlessness prevents me asking God for necessary helps." At any rate, it does not prevent you wishing to ask for them, and you ought to know that with God, our desires are real prayers, according to St. Augustine. This made Bossuet say that a cry pent up in the depths of the heart was of the same value as a cry that reached the skies, because God sees our most secret desires, and even the first simple movement of the heart. Apply these principles to your own case, whether at prayer, or before and after Communion. Nothing more is required to make our intercourse with God safe, easy and efficacious in spite of aridity, involuntary distractions and powerlessness, because none of these things prevent the desire to pray well, or to sigh and lament before God. His all-seeing eye detects the pure intention and preparation of heart, with all those acts that we should wish to have made ; as He sees the fruits of the trees before the buds of springtime have formed on the branches ; this is the beautiful comparison made by the Bishop of Meaux.

In God's name, my dear Sister, try to enter into this maxim and to make it your own ; it will console and sustain you on a thousand occasions when you feel that you are doing nothing, are incapable of making any effort. The good will is always there, and that is everything in the sight of God even when you imagine it to be absolutely idle.

3rd.   Acquiescence in and submission to the will of God and the union of our will with His are so essential to perfection that it may be said to consist entirely in adhering firmly to them in all things, everywhere, and for everything. To do this is to do all, and without this, prayers, austerities, and works of even the most heroic nature, and all our sufferings, are nothing in the sight of God, because the only way in which we can please Him is by conforming our wills to His. The more involuntary opposition to this complete resignation we feel in ourselves, the more merit shall we gain on account of the greater effort required, and of the more complete sacrifice exacted.

4th. The knowledge and fear of the traps that are laid for us in all quarters both outside and within our own souls is exactly the grace that will enable us to avoid them, especially if, with this humble fear a great confidence in God is united; then we can rely on being always victorious, except perhaps in matters of minor importance where God permits us to fall for our greater good. These lesser falls are very salutary for us, in keeping us always lowly and humbled in the presence of God, distrustful of our own powers, and as it were, nothing in our own eyes.

5th. You must accustom yourself to seek, and to find the peace of your soul in the higher part, that which is furthest removed from the senses; and disregard the troubles, revolts, and uneasiness of the lower and animal part which should be accounted of no importance because God pays no attention to what takes place there. St. Teresa says that it is like the court-yard of the castle of the soul. Take advantage of this teaching which is that of the saints, and behave as a person who, finding the courtyard of her castle full of unclean animals and hideous reptiles does not stop there a moment, but mounts at once to the upper rooms which are well furnished and filled with an honour-able company. Do you also mount into the sanctuary of the soul, and endeavour always to remain there, because it is there that God makes His permanent dwelling.

6th. Yes, you were right to abandon yourself to God in all things, and to cease disturbing your mind voluntarily with the recollection of the frequent experiences you have had of your misery and weakness; in this way the foundation of true humility and a complete self-distrust is laid and consolidated. These valuable dispositions draw down upon us all the graces of God and bring them to us clothed with His power; especially if He finds us convinced of our own powerlessness to do any good. This it was that made St. Paul exclaim, " When I am weak, then am I powerful."

7th. I assure you on the part of God, that usually, indeed nearly always, when you think you are praying your worst, that is the very time when you are praying best. Why ? Be-cause on the one hand the will, and the firm desire to pray is a real prayer of the heart; and because, on the other hand, you pray then without any self-complacency, without any of those vain reflexions which spoil everything; you pray by your pa-tience, your silence, your self-effacement, your submission and abandonment to God; and you leave off praying greatly humil-iated and cast down, and without any of those sensible feelings of satisfaction to your self-love that made St. Francis of Sales say that our own miserable satisfactions were not those of God.

You may judge by this with what contempt you ought to repulse the fears by which the enemy tries to disgust, and to weary you, or at least to throw you into a state of anxiety.

8th. The great and sincere desire you have to be all for God without reserve, and whatever it may cost, St. Francis of Sales calls the firm pillar of the spiritual edifice. This pillar ought to sustain the whole weight. Fear nothing as long as it remains, and it will remain, by the grace of God, in the superior part of the soul; as for the inferior or sensitive part, think nothing about it.

9th. It is quite true that we can conquer self-love, but not without great trouble, and remember that this is far more the work of God than our own. Take advantage of little occasions for combats and victories, and be well assured that when God sees that, in good earnest, you are doing the little that is in your power with the help of ordinary graces, He will at last set His own hand to the task, and finish and perfect the work you could not accomplish. It is on this account that I advise you always to beg of God without ceasing the gift of His divine Spirit with all His holy operations, without which it is possible to spend a life-time in great defects and considerable imperfections from which there is great risk of never rising, but rather of falling ever lower, and even of being lost.

10th. Holy Communion is the true daily bread of our souls. In it alone can we find subsistence, power, remedy, and support. What a difference there is between those who communicate frequently, and those who do so but rarely! Oh! how little do the latter realise the riches, and the treasures of grace of which they deprive themselves!

LETTER XIV.—*Remedies for Troubles.*

To Sister Marie-Thérèse de Vioménil (1734). The use of trials continued.

My dear Sister,

To apply a remedy to the trouble that makes you so unhappy, it will suffice for me to indicate the causes of it, in order to oppose it with the contrary principles. The origin of the evil is first an ignorance of your attraction. It seems to me that you have forgotten that divine grace makes different souls experience different attractions, some sweet, and some exceedingly crucifying. Among people in the world there are those whom God conducts by the way of prosperity; but a far greater number whom He compels to walk in the thorny path of the Cross, of afflictions and difficulties. Thus He apportions, according to

His wisdom, spiritual joys and tribulations to those who lead a spiritual life. The work of salvation and perfection consists in following faithfully the path allotted to us according to the attraction God has given us, whatever this may be.

1st. You seem equally ignorant of this great principle, that usually more progress is made by suffering than by acting, and that to take things patiently is to do a great deal, and especially to be patient with oneself.

2nd. You forget, at any rate in practice, this other incontestable truth, that perfection does not consist in receiving great gifts from God such as recollection, prayer and the spiritual taste for divine things, but simply in fulfilling the will of God in every possible circumstance whether exterior or interior, and in whatever situation Providence may be pleased to place you.

3rd. Your troubles proceed from this ignorance and forgetfulness together with those anxieties and that interior depression which have embittered and doubled your pains, and have deprived you of the peace of your soul which is the foundation of the spiritual life, and have often led you to seek consolation in creatures by confiding your troubles to them when it was God's will that you should have no consolation but that which He was pleased to give you Himself. You must correct this by other rules of conduct and a totally different way of acting.

1st Principle. Often say to yourself, " My way is painful, it is true; it is hard and bitter, but as it is the will of God I must submit, no matter what it costs; firstly, because God is my sovereign Master who has a right to dispose of me absolutely as He pleases. Secondly, because He is my father, and so tender, good, and merciful a Father that He can will nothing that is not for the benefit of the children whom He loves, and makes all things turn to the benefit of those who are submissive to Him. Thirdly, because I shall never find peace, calm, nor repose of heart, nor any solid consolation except in resigning myself humbly and patiently to all that He is pleased to ordain. Fourthly, because I cannot take a single step in the spiritual life unless I follow the path marked out, and decided for me in the eternal decree of my predestination. Can I mark out a path for myself? And if I could, would it not be like the path of a blind man, leading to destruction?

2nd Principle. I ought to desire only that progress and perfection which God wills for me, and to wish to attain them only by those means He wills me to employ." Such a desire can only be calm and peaceful, although at the same time, full of power and energy. There is, however, another kind of desire for perfection, born of pride, and of an inordinate love of one's own excellence. This does not rely upon God for support, and besides, is restless and always in a state of turmoil. The more we have to give ourselves up to the first of these desires, the more strenuously we must resist the second. Therefore every desire for our progress, however holy it may seem, must be suppressed directly it shows signs of eagerness, disquiet or anxiety. These effects can only proceed from the devil, while everything that comes from God leaves the soul tranquil. Why then, my dear Sister, do you desire with such fiery eagerness those lights of the soul, those feelings, interior joys, and that facility of recollection and prayer, and other gifts of God, if it does not please Him to bestow them on you yet? Would not this be to make yourself perfect for your own pleasure, and not for His? To follow your own and not the divine will, to have more regard for your own inclination than for that of God, to wish to serve Him according to your own caprice, and not according to His good pleasure! "Ought I then to be resigned to spending my whole life in this state of poverty, weakness and misery?" Certainly, if such is the will of God. Your poverty, weakness and misery ought from henceforth to be pleasant to you, and preferable to any other state since it is willed for you by God. Henceforth this poverty will be converted into wealth, for to be exactly what God wills is to be very rich indeed, and all perfection consists in this alone. Moreover are you not aware that there is heroic virtue in the patient endurance of misery, weakness, spiritual poverty, darkness and callousness, of fickleness, folly, and extravagance of mind and imagination? It was this that made St. Francis of Sales say that those who aspired to perfection required to exercise as much patience, kindness, and endurance towards themselves as towards others. Let us then bear our own burdens of misery, imperfection, and defects in the same way that God wills us to bear one another's burdens. It often happens however that, in this spiritual tumult the will endures strange commotions, and is on the point of giving way out of all patience. Let us keep firm for in this new battlefield fighting for patience and making fresh sacrifices we shall find fresh subjects for merit and triumph. And if during the first moments the poor will should escape, it must be made to try to regain possession of itself in humbling itself quietly and peacefully before the infinite mercy of God.

"But all these spiritual vicissitudes take off my attention from prayer, Holy Mass, the Office, and Holy Communion, and my spiritual exercises seem useless." No! No! none of them are useless, because merely the will to acquit yourself well of these duties, which you formed at the beginning, will be valid throughout, unless nullified by long continued and altogether voluntary distractions, in a word, by deliberate venial sin. Far from losing anything, you will have gained doubly, because combined with the merit gained by your spiritual exercises will be that of having made them in a most penitential and cruci-fying manner, and also with much humiliation ; in this way, very far from having spoilt these holy exercises by foolish self-examination, and a thousand satisfactions of self-love, to which you would have been exposed in making them with feelings of devotion, you will have fulfilled these duties well by the practice of holy humility which is the foundation and guardian of every virtue. " But this will prevent me from feeling contrite." The efficacy of contrition is not in the feeling of it, it is entirely in the higher part of the soul—in the will. Sensible contrition very frequently serves only as food for self-love and can never be reassuring, since it is not what God requires. " But supposing I have no contrition of the will ? " You should believe and hope firmly that God has given it to you ; but if you should only have had contrition once after having already confessed your sins it would be enough to remit them all, both past and present sins, so great is the mercy of God.

My dear Sister, I will conclude with this consoling assurance; if it had pleased God to make your state known to you as it is to me, you would be thanking Him for it instead of afflicting yourself about it. Remain in peace then in whatever condition you may possibly find yourself : when you have achieved that you will have done all that is necessary. Repeat constantly " Blessed be God for all and in all. I wish only what He wills and nothing more. May His holy will be done in me, and by me. May none of my wishes be accomplished ; they are all blind and perverse. I shall be lost if they are accomplished."

LETTER XV.—*Trials to be Endured Peacefully.*

To the same person. Trials to be endured peacefully.

1st. We are entirely of one mind, my dear Sister, now that you admit with me that your activity and eagerness are defects. Strive against them with all your strength, that is all that I ask. You say that I want you to be faultless and quite perfect. That is true, and has always been the object I had in view for you. At the same time I do not consider it a crime that you have not yet attained this perfection. I realise that this can only be achieved gradually by a great confidence in God, and a great fidelity to His grace. He alone can accomplish in you the work He has begun ; what you have to do is simply to abandon your-self to Him, and to allow Him to act. Do not be one of those of whom Jesus Christ said, speaking to St. Catherine of Siena, that they made hardly any progress in perfection because they talked so much themselves, that they could not listen to Him, and would act themselves, and gave Him no opportunity of acting in them.

2nd. I am delighted to hear that you feel that God supports you in your afflictions ; continue to endure them as peacefully as you can, and in a perfect interior silence. This practice alone will cause you to advance in a calm and peaceful way. God has given you courage and energy ; these are talents that you must profit by. This divine Master asks that, for the present, you will make your courage consist in patient endurance and resignation ; but it is in the depths of your soul, not in feeling, that He wishes to find this abandonment, and, in His infinite goodness, at the same time that He requires it of you, He bestows it upon you. For this grace unite with me in returning thanks to Him, for He could not have bestowed upon you a more precious gift. Perhaps a day will come when this resignation will become sensible, and then it will be as sweet, as now it is bitter, and you will enjoy that heavenly unction which Jesus Christ has attached to His Cross. This is what makes the peace and joy of the saints unchangeable, and it is what those experience who follow generously the path of perfection and a spiritual life, in sacrificing everything for God. You tell me that with your character and temperament it seems to you impossible to acquire a taste for the interior life. So it is, truly : but what is impossible to man is easy to God, and it is on Him alone, and on His grace through Jesus Christ, that you have to depend. In order to compel you to lay a foundation of humility in your soul this God of goodness begins by making you feel most keenly your own weakness ; but, when this feeling depresses you, encourage yourself to hope, for God, as you know, is pleased to make His grace triumph most in our greatest weaknesses.

3rd. The petition you so often make interiorly, " Lord, have pity on me, You can do all things," is the best and most simple prayer that you could possibly make. Nothing more is required to draw down His powerful aid. Keep steadfastly to this practice and to the habit of never expecting anything from yourself but of hoping to obtain all from God. He will do the rest, without your perceiving it, and I feel assured that this will be visibly shown by the result. I am interiorly convinced that unless prevented by great infidelity on your part, God, by His holy operation, will perform great things in your soul. You may count upon this, if you do not voluntarily oppose any obstacle. If you become aware of having unfortunately done so, humble yourself immediately, and return to God and to yourself with a perfect confidence in the divine goodness.

4th. We must only attach ourselves to God and to His holy will by acquiescing in all His arrangements which cannot fail to be for our happiness and profit. If, on our part, there should be nothing else but this blind submission to His good pleasure, we ought to be contented, because in this alone consists all perfection, and the true love of God.

5th. It is a great grace to realise the folly and extravagance of the pleasures that worldly people pursue so eagerly. From this you will derive great good for your soul which, in this contempt for the world, will find a powerful motive for giving itself entirely to a spiritual life. Perhaps you will say that you are still but a novice in this life. I acknowledge that, but you admire it, desire it, ask for it, and are tending towards it ; here are so many different degrees of grace ; the rest will follow in due time. Meanwhile moderate your spiritual vehemence, and your holy ambition.

6th. You are beginning, you say, to be indifferent as to whether people behave well or badly towards you. This is a greater grace than you imagine. But there are times, you say, when sadness and discouragement seem to overwhelm you. This you must put up with as well as you can, and accept the annoyance of finding yourself so weak, for this is most irritating to our spiritual self-love. This is the most meritorious of all the sacrifices by which we must immolate it, as it is the most humiliating., It is quite permissible to expect some sensible help and support in the spiritual life, but we must hope for it with moderation, seek it without excitement, and make use of it without becoming too much attached to it, and lose it when God wishes to deprive us of it, I do not say, without pain, but without being voluntarily cast down and troubled. Above all it is necessary to make God our principal help, to count on Him in default of others, to trust in Him unreservedly, to have recourse to Him in all dangers and for everything, as little children do with their loving mothers. This holy simplicity, this humble and child-like conduct towards God will touch and move His paternal heart, and obtain sooner or later all that we ask, or something else better for us, which is often given us even without our knowledge.

7th. The complaints made by our Lord to St. Catherine of Siena of the exaggerated activity of those souls in saying and doing so much themselves, that they left Him not one moment in which to effect anything, should be understood in this sense ; that in working and accomplishing our duties, we should do so without excitement, and natural impetuosity, and that, during the day we should listen to the voice of divine Wisdom to hear

Him who speaks in the centre of our hearts without sound of words, because His operation is His word. Moreover, that in all our prayers, readings, examens, and thoughts of God we should act quietly, gently, without confusion or effort, seeking only the union of our hearts with God, and for that making use of frequent pauses to give the Holy Spirit of God time to work in us what He pleases, and as He pleases.

8th. All that you tell me about your fear of your faults being rendered greater on account of your realisation of the presence of God is an illusion of the devil who, in this way tries to withdraw our attention from this divine Presence, and to diminish our devotion while we are before the most Holy Sacrament. Continue to follow this exercise without fear; I see the fruits of it, and they will become so sensible that you will see them yourself in course of time.

9th. I congratulate you that God has taken away some of your natural vivacity. The loss of your gaiety will only be temporary. It will return, but completely changed, or rather transformed into spiritual joy, quiet, tranquil and peaceful, because it will be like that of the saints, in God and coming only from God.

10th. I greatly approve of your method of prayer; continue the same, and make acts when you feel inclined. When, during pauses, or interior silence some good thought or inclination should be suggested to you, receive it quietly; and do the same with interior repose, whether sometimes greater or less, as God pleases. In a word, tend always towards that sovereign Lord, more by the affections and desires than by the mind and intellect; and no matter what He gives you be always satisfied. God knows better than we do what is necessary for us; let Him act, but let us be absolutely convinced that the least repose of heart we enjoy in His holy presence is worth more than anything we could say or think ourselves. May this conviction impel you ever more strongly to tend with all your heart towards this holy repose; and when God gives it to you do not interrupt it, for these are the precious moments when the King of Kings admits those souls Whom He honours with His predilection to a friendly audience.

———

LETTER XVI.—*Sensitiveness about Defects.*

To Sister Charlotte-Elizabeth Bourcier de Monthureux. Sensitiveness about defects a sign of self-love.

My very dear Sister,

1st. I thank you for your good wishes, and above all for your prayers. I also pray for you every day at the Holy Sacrifice of the Mass. I thank our Lord for the good effect produced in your soul by my letters, but you must allow me to remark that I find you still very sensitive about the state of misery, poverty, and spiritual weakness to which you find yourself reduced. This can only come from a great amount of self-love which cannot endure a state of nothingness, and abhors the necessity of self-effacement. Nevertheless you must necessarily pass through this trial because your mind has to be emptied of self before it can be filled by the Spirit of God, and He will make you die to your old life, before you are able to begin a new one. What you want is to acquire the one without losing the other; this cannot be: have patience and preserve a certain peace in the centre of your soul during these interior tempests. Your state of obscurity and callousness, to whatever degree it may attain, need not alarm you; all that is necessary is to submit, and to abandon yourself entirely to God. Do not worry yourself to try and feel submissive; feeling has nothing to do with this business; it is enough if you are willing to submit, for this is practised by the higher part of the soul.

2nd. You are wrong in finding your weakness a subject for anxiety. As long as you have confidence in God, He will sustain you as He has done hitherto on the brink of the precipice. Possibly it will be by an imperceptible thread, but, in the hand of God, this slight thread is like a thick rope.

3rd. In the painful positions of which you speak there are only two things to be done; either to throw yourself in spirit at the feet of Jesus Christ, and to kiss those sacred feet, or, if you cannot do that, keep an interior silence of submission and adoration, and content yourself with an exterior sign, such as, raising your eyes to heaven, and then lowering them and bowing your head, remaining thus for a little while in union with Jesus Christ in the Garden of Olives. If possible, remain ever there, by the side of Jesus Christ humiliated, cast down, and annihilated before His Father. I love to see you in prayer taking the position of a beggar, of a beast of burden; but still more do I love that indescribable something which inwardly draws you on without any distinct aim, but with a certain dry repose full of aridity. When you get so far, hold on to this state contenting yourself with waiting in that peaceful expectation of which I have so frequently spoken to you. Again at other times try to make some acts, or to read something as quietly as possible and with frequent pauses to give room for the interior attraction to act. But always remember that you ought to follow the least attraction that draws you interiorly, and to retain it peacefully without too much exertion, and without seeking out distinct thoughts. This repose in the presence of God, this slight recollectedness is of even greater value, and will cause you to make more progress than the most sublime thoughts.

4th. I congratulate you in having, by the help of the grace of God, overcome the rebellion and repugnance you felt with respect to your office. It is by these difficult victories that solid virtue is acquired. All the details you give me about your painful feelings and distastes make me see the goodness of God Who desires to destroy in the centre of your heart that presumption of which you could never be cured without this bitter medicine. These truly diabolical feelings that God allows the devil to produce in your soul are an antidote to that much more diabolical feeling of pride. Learn from this to allow God to act, and to abandon yourself, if it so please Him, to much greater miseries and interior humiliations. If He should condemn you to these, He knows well how to draw you out of them, with great profit to your soul, provided always that you are faithful in calling upon Him with confidence out of the depths of your nothingness.

5th. I think that what you say is true; God wills your humiliation; love this state for yourself because it forms some resemblance between you and your divine Spouse. This love for and desire of humiliations will make you progress more in the ways of God than all the other practices together. Try, therefore, to profit by every little occasion, and feed your mind on the thought and desire of abjection, just as worldly people feed their minds on thoughts and desires of vanity. The profound peace that you have begun to experience in the midst of humiliations, contempt, and rebuffs, is one of the greatest graces of which you have ever spoken to me. If you continue thus a great change will be effected in your soul by this means alone.

6th. As to what regards exterior mortification, follow in everything the rules of moderation, discretion and obedience, but make up for what they refuse to allow you to do, by interior abnegation in refusing yourself the least little desire, the least little pleasure, and the least thought which is not of God and for God, rejecting all that is useless in order to occupy yourself exclusively with Him. Oh! what a joy and triumph for me when I shall see my dear daughters abject like Jesus Christ,

humbled and annihilated! Do you, therefore, follow the grace
of this attraction; it will lead you on. I cannot repeat often
enough that I will never cease praying that God may give you
this holy love of abjection. About evening devotions; I have
neither time nor inclination to enter into the subject. Believe
me you already have too many practices, and must try to
simplify matters that relate to the soul. Just the presence of
God, abandonment to God; just the desire to love God, and
to be united to Him. These are the most simple exercises, and
more definite for souls a little advanced in spiritual matters,
and of far greater importance than any exterior practices.

LETTER XVII.—*Confidence in God.*

To Sister Marie-Thérèse de Vioménil. Confidence in God is
the cure of self-love.

My dear Sister,

When you have neither time nor inclination to read, try to
keep yourself simply in peace in the presence of God, and do not
trouble to practise works of supererogation unless by His special
intimation and impulse, and if they are done with facility. If
you seem to be wanting in courage for many things, compel
yourself at any rate to retain in your heart a determination to be
all for God. Humble yourself with the consideration of the
inefficacy of your own resolutions, and look upon yourself as
having so far done nothing. The less confidence you place in
yourself, the more easy will it become to have entire confidence in
the mercy of God alone, through the merits of Jesus Christ.
This is that solid and perfect confidence which completely
annihilates self-love by withdrawing all those resources upon
which it was accustomed to rely. There could be nothing more
salutary for some souls than this kind of martyrdom.

You say that some sort of sacrifices lead to God while others
do not, but rather lead to revolts against Him. This idea is
a mistaken one, caused by judging of good and evil in matters of
devotion, by the senses. Some sacrifices which do not touch
the heart in a vulnerable spot, always afford consolation, and
thus lead us sensibly to God; but those that wound the heart,
poignantly cause so much pain that we are greatly troubled,
and inclined to break down completely. To the sorrow these
sacrifices entail is joined another very painful suffering; namely,
the fear of being unable to bear it, and of gaining nothing by it.
This it is that produces the false idea that these sacrifices turn
us away from God. Nevertheless it is an assured principle
that the more these sacrifices touch us to the quick, and the more

they make us die to ourselves, and detach us from all consolation, and sensible support, the closer they draw us to God and unite us to Him.   This union is all the more meritorious in being hidden and further out of the range of the senses.   Self-love, therefore, has no share in it, since it cannot feed on what it can neither know nor feel.   May God deign to convince you of the truth of this consoling assurance, which is the teaching of all the Doctors of the Church, and is confirmed by every experience. In order to understand it thoroughly you must remember that in almost everyone there is such a depth of self-love, weakness and misery, that it would be impossible for us to recognise any gift of God in ourselves without being exposed to spoil and corrupt it by imperceptible feelings of self-complacency.   In this way we appropriate as our own the graces of God, and are pleased with ourselves for being in such or such a state.   We attribute the merit to ourselves, not, perhaps, by distinct and studied thought, but by the secret feelings of the heart.   Therefore, God, seeing the innermost recesses of the heart, and being infinitely jealous of His glory, is obliged, in order to maintain it, and to protect Himself against these secret thefts, to convince us, by our own experience, of our utter weakness.   It is for this purpose that He conceals from us nearly all His gifts and graces. There are hardly more than two exceptions to this rule.; on the one hand beginners who require to be attracted and captured through their senses, and on the other hand great saints who, on account of having been purified of self-love by innumerable interior trials are able to recognise in themselves the gifts of God without the least feeling of self-complacency, nor even a glance at themselves.   For my part I can bear witness to this constant action of divine Providence.   God has so completely hidden from those who have appealed to me, the gifts and graces with which he has loaded them, that they cannot see their own progress, nor their patience, humility and abandonment, nor even their love of God.   Then, too, they can hardly help weeping at the supposed absence of these virtues and at their want of generosity in their sufferings.   However, the more afflicted and full of fear are their souls, the less need have their directors to fear and to be afflicted on their account.   This ought to cure you of making so many difficulties for yourself.   You would understand this still better, perhaps, if you were to consider what Fénélon said on this subject.   " There is not a single gift so exalted but that after having been a means of advancement, cannot become, in the sequel, a snare and an obstacle to the soul, by the instinct of possession, which sullies it."   On this account God withdraws what He had given, but He does not take it away to deprive us of it absolutely.   He withdraws it to give it back in a better way, after it has been purified from this malicious appropriation made by us without our perceiving it. The loss of the gift prevents this feeling of proprietorship, and this gone, the gift is returned a hundredfold. All this seems to me to be of such great importance for you that I think you would do well to read it over often although it is rather lengthy. By dint of impressing it on your mind you will, I hope, relinquish those false prejudices, and the many errors that so frequently disturb and destroy the peace of your soul. Without this peace, as you know, it is impossible to make any progress in the spiritual life.

I am acquainted with a spiritual person who is so convinced of the truth of this rule that I have heard her say many times, that after having prayed for certain spiritual favours for a very long time, and after having had innumerable novenas and prayers offered for the same intention she often said to God, " Lord, I consent to be for ever deprived of the knowledge as to whether it has pleased You to grant me these graces, because I am such a miserable creature that when I know I possess a particular grace I immediately convert it into a poison. It is not that I wish to do this, Lord, but such is the corruption of my heart that this accursed self-complacency spoils all my works almost without my knowledge and almost against my will. I feel that it is I who tie Your hands, Oh my God! and who oblige You to hide from me in Your goodness those graces that Your mercy induces You to bestow upon me."

You, my dear daughter, have more need than anyone else to understand these feelings, for I have never hitherto met with anyone who depended so much on what is called the sensible help of direction under the specious pretext of spiritual need. I have always thought, without mentioning it to you, that the time would come when God, desiring to be the only support of your soul, would withdraw from you these sensible props without even allowing you to learn in what way He could supply all that of which He had deprived you. This state I must own is terrible to nature, but in this terrible state, one simple " Fiat," uttered very earnestly in spite of the repugnance experienced in the soul, is an assurance of real and solid progress. Then there remains nothing but bare faith in God, that is to say, an obscure faith despoiled of all sensible devotion, and residing in the will, as St. Francis of Sales says. Then it is, also, that are accomplished to their utmost extent the words of St. Paul when he said, " We draw near to God by faith," and " The just man lives by faith." All this ought to convince you that it is not in anger but in mercy and in very great mercy that God deprives you more than others. It is because He is more jealous of the possession of your whole heart and all your confidence, and for this reason He is obliged to take away everything and to leave nothing sensible either exterior or interior. Therefore, my dear Sister, a truce to reflexions on present or future evils. Abandonment! Submission! Love! Confidence!

LETTER XVIII.—*Sacrifice and Fidelity.*

To Madame de Lesen after she had become a Religious in the Order of the Annunciation. Sacrifice and fidelity are the death of self-love.

My dear Sister,

You ask me several questions, but what can I say in answer that holy books, meditations, preachers, directors, and above all the interior spirit have not told you hundreds and hundreds of times?

1st. Do you not know that it is only very gradually that self-love dies, and that we learn to live only in God and for God? This is effected by a constant fidelity in carrying out those sacri, fices demanded by the interior spirit; sacrifices of the mind, of the will, of every passion and caprice, of every feeling and affection, in fine and above all, the sacrifice of an entire submission in every trial, in the perpetual vicissitudes of the soul and in those sometimes very painful states through which we have to pass in order to be entirely united to God.

2nd. Do you know that the state of pure faith excludes all that can be sensibly felt? In this state of deprivation progress is made without assistance from anything created, but the bare light of faith remains always in the highest point of the soul, and by this light we can not only see what we ought to do, and what to avoid, but we know also that, by the grace of God, we live in horror of evil and fly from it, and in the love and practice of virtue. Therefore it is well to say, "I am living in perfect confidence, and am not risking my eternity." "But suppose I am mistaken, and deceiving others without knowing it?" If you do not know it, then you are in good faith, and this will excuse you in the sight of God Who is as merciful as He is just. "But in spite of all this I still feel very much alarmed." Yes, that cannot be helped; our condition in this life is one of fear, because no one can be perfectly sure. God wills that we should glorify Him by an abandonment full of love and confidence. This is the tribute He most particularly exacts, and as He gives us the means of offering it with greater merit, why should we be alarmed? We should have more reason to be afraid if we had ceased to fear. There is no state that is more suspect than

that which is devoid of fear, even if it should be accompanied
by love and confidence. When, on the contrary, the fear of
offending God is the prevailing sentiment, the considerations
I have explained ought to be sufficient reassurance. They are
perfectly solid, because they rest on the immutable principles
of faith. In default of sensible devotion we should attach ourselves to this bare faith preserved by God always in the centre of
the soul, or the higher point of the spirit.

3rd. Do you not know that the sensible presence of God
is often by its sweetness an occasion of satisfying our self-love,
and that in order to prevent it being dangerous to us God deprives us of it leaving us only bare faith devoid of sweetness,
or any kind of mental images, figures, or representations?
"But," you say, "I do not know if I have this faith." Well!
at any rate you know that you aspire to it continually. This
desire is, in fact, perhaps too vehement in you, since you are so
prone to get excited and vexed when you are disappointed.
Therefore you have, at least, the continual and habitual desire
of this divine presence. This desire is known to God Who sees
the slightest movement of the heart. That ought to be enough
for you. Remain then in peace, confidence, submission, and
abandonment, and in grateful love.

4th. Do you not know that the best preparation for Holy
Communion is that operated in the soul by God Himself?
Approach then with confidence, with complete abandonment to
the state of poverty and deprivation in which it has pleased God
to place you. Remain in it as though sacrificed, annihilated
and unseen like Jesus Christ in His Sacrament, because He
is there in a kind of annihilation. Unite yours to His. Where
there is nothing left that is created, or human, there is God.
The more destitute of all things, and divested of self you become,
the more will you be possessed by God. Make for yourself a
spiritual treasure of this very poverty by a continual adherence
to the will of God. From the time you begin this practice you
will become richer than any of those who possess the greatest
gifts of joy and consolation. You will possess the riches of
the holy will of God without fear of self-complacency, since this
holy will is bitter to nature and humiliating to pride. Sweet and
salutary bitterness which serves as an antidote to the poison
of self-love and the sting of the serpent of pride!

LETTER XIX.—*God Glorified by Sufferings.*

To Mother Louise-Françoise de Rosen. On the use of trials even if they be punishments.

Reverend Mother,

I do not presume to find excuses for the imperfections of the good Sister about whom you ask my advice, and since God has taken upon Himself the punishment of them by sending her the most cruel trials, she seems to me more to be envied on this account than to be blamed for her faults. There is much in these faults that deserves the verdict of the church on the sin of Adam. " Happy fault which merited so glorious a Redeemer ! " This good Sister, you tell me, has acknowledged her faults, and now, overwhelmed by the weight of her trials, is much more inclined to depression than to obstinacy. Therefore you only have to revive her courage and to console her gently. Tell her that she has lost nothing, and that far from being abandoned by God she is much nearer to Him than when all was prosperous with her, and she seemed to succeed in everything. I authorise you to tell her from me that I consider her more happy than before in consequence of her sufferings by which God is purifying her more and more, like gold in the crucible, to unite her more closely to Himself. For you must both take into consideration this great principle : the extent to which the soul is purified in its most secret recesses, is the measure of its union with the God of all holiness. By this you can judge if this poor Sister should not be considered the happiest of all, if she could be persuaded to look upon her state of suffering from this point of view. However, if the violence of this trial prevents her seeing clearly the value and use of it, let her rely on her faith, and let her glorify God by patience and an unreserved submission, abandoning herself entirely to His adorable permissions without relaxing in the least degree any of her spiritual exercises, especially as regards prayer and Holy Communion ; and without giving way to a secret desire suggested by self-love, to shake off the yoke of the cross of God. " But," she will answer, " this comfort would be just if my state were a trial only, but I have every reason to believe that it is a punishment inflicted by God." I acknowledge this, but in this life no punishment is inflicted by divine justice without a loving intention of divine mercy. This is particularly the case with those souls whom God most loves. God often permits their faults in order to be enabled to derive glory from them, and to make them serve for the salvation of these souls. The chastisements He inflicts sanctify while humiliating them, and dispose them to unite themselves more closely to God, at the same time as they become more detached from self. Therefore they are chastisements as well as trials; chastisements inasmuch as they atone for the past evil and satisfy divine justice; and trials because divine mercy makes use of them to prevent future danger, and for the exercise of many very meritorious virtues. You cannot insist too strongly on these truths with souls in trouble and affliction no matter what may be the cause of their anguish. Let all such remember that nothing happens except by the ruling of divine Providence, and by His adorable permission. Give this dear Sister who is so full of pain the most deeply spiritual reading; this is the only means she has to soften and relieve her continual torment, and to make it bearable; to convert her pain into profit, and to recover from it at the time arranged by divine Providence. God has given me in her behalf, all the interest and charity of a spiritual father, and the thought never leaves me that the day will come when she will be my joy and my crown in the presence of God, and even now visibly before men by a most edifying life. I hope she will always keep before her mind the memory of the past in order to humble herself before God, and thus to establish firmly a solid foundation for the spiritual life in which even her faults may prove a guarantee of her perseverance and progress.

———

The Religious in question seems to be Sister Anne-Marguerite de la Bellière towhom Fr. de Caussade had wr ittenseveral times. For having taken too much time and pains to prepare a little oratory where she made her Retreat she became deprived of all that light and consolation that God usually lavished upon her during prayer.

———

LETTER XX.—*The Fruit of Trials.*
To the same person on the fruit of trials, Profound Peace.

———

1st. The deep calm you experience, the profound inner peace with which you are filled and which you find so sweet, is not an illusion but a true operation of the Holy Spirit Who speaks in the centre of your soul. Peace and love, says St. John of the Cross, are one and the same. Peace can be felt, but love cannot be perceived in the same manner, but is very real, nevertheless. I am not surprised that when God deigns to bestow these precious gifts upon you, you no longer feel your usual infirmities. The interior grace in your soul reflects itself in your body, and causes your pains to cease. I know many who find no more efficacious means for the cure of their maladies than this quiet recollection in God, when He is pleased to bestow it upon them; for, as you truly say, it does not proceed from ourselves

2nd. To remain simply in the presence of God, quite abandoned to His love and mercy is also an effect of the Holy Spirit in the soul. You have but to remain humbly and simply in the hands of God, adhering to Him, and giving yourself up to His love, so that He may do with you, and in you all that He pleases. But never make this sweet repose your object; always go further and aim at the possession of Him Who bestows it upon you, and value it only as a means of uniting you more closely to God Who is your centre, your life, and your all. Never forget that you may, possibly, find yourself bereft of everything in the most complete spiritual poverty, and left to the simple practice of bare faith for the extinction of self-love. This death of self hardly ever occurs without a deprivation of all things, and at the mere thought of this one's very nature shudders. It is then that one seems lost indeed, without any support, and left in the most cruel abandonment.

3rd. I am glad that God has lessened the fear of reprobation by which you were tormented. Now you can, without so much difficulty, abandon yourself, by making the following act. " May God do with me whatever He pleases, I wish to belong entirely to Him by loving and serving Him as well as I can. He is the God of my heart, the God of my salvation, and my salvation cannot be left in more secure keeping. I abandon it to Him with the greatest confidence." Abandonment by itself can give us an assurance of security that self-love seeks unsuccessfully from creatures or from self. Our weakness and blindness are much more calculated to make us tremble; and, when we enter into ourselves we find what would cause us to despair unless we remembered with confidence the infinite goodness of God. Therefore we can only be reassured through Jesus Christ, in Him; and we find Him proportionately to the measure in which we abandon ourselves.

4th. The simple " Fiat " you pronounce comprises everything, and the feeling of your continual dependence is one of the greatest of God's graces. The thought of His paternal love and all-powerful aid is the reward of it. When the heart is animated by filial confidence it becomes easy to receive no matter what from the hands of this most merciful Father.

5th. Pure love without any admixture of interest or self-love can only come to you from God, but to acquire a gift of such infinite value the soul is obliged to endure many deprivations and trials. These are so many operations necessary for its purification, because we are always prone to become attached to the pleasure that God allows us unless taught by sad experience to love Him even in the most terrible state of privation. I am delighted to hear that the interior spirit reigns in your community.   If holy recollection does not comprise everything it is, at any rate, the way to acquire all.   You are quite right to leave out all those compliments and ordinary good wishes for the New Year as far as I am concerned.   God sees that they are in your heart where they form a continual prayer on my behalf, just as my wishes for your welfare are as a prayer in the sight of God.   " Our desires," says St. Augustine, " are as regards God, what our speech and words are with regard to men."   He hears them, and, we may hope, will answer them.

LETTER XXI.—*Things Painful to Nature.*

To Sister Marie-Thérèse de Vioménil (1731).   Things painful to nature are good for the soul.

You need not to remind me to pray for you.   I never forget to do so, especially since I became aware that you are in a state so painful to nature, although so good for your soul.   However, I assure you I have never thought of asking God to grant you anything but patience, submission, resignation to His holy will, and total abandonment to His kind providence ; and I do this through the conviction I have of the great grace God is giving you, and of the great need you are in of these virtues ; a need all the greater because you do not acknowledge it.   When this storm is past you will understand these two things so keenly and distinctly that you will not know how, sufficiently, to thank God for having been so good as to put His own hand to the work, and to operate within your soul in a few months, what with the help of ordinary grace would have taken you, perhaps, twenty years to accomplish, namely, to get rid of a hidden self-love, and of a pride all the more dangerous in being more subtle and more imperceptible.   From this poisonous root grows an infinite number of imperfections of which you are scarcely conscious ; useless self-examinations, still more useless self-complacency, idle fears, fruitless desires, frivolous little hopes, suspicions unfavourable to your neighbour, little jokes at her expense, and airs full of self-love.   You would have run a great risk of remaining for a long time subject to all these defects, filled, almost without suspecting it, with vanity and self-confidence without either power or will to sound the profound abyss of perversity and natural corruption that you had within your soul.   It is this collection of miseries that God now makes you feel, not in particular, for if you experienced them in this way one by one, it would not affect you, but by viewing them in general, in a heap, and in a confused manner. This mass of imperfections is like an overwhelming weight. Do not search your conscience, therefore, for the great sin that you imagine must be there; what is actually there is still more alarming, and this is a chaotic mass of interior miseries, weakness, imperfections, and little faults which are almost imperceptible and continual and are produced by that amount of self-love of which I am speaking. God has given you a great grace in giving you light to recognise this, for never would you have been able to discover it yourself, not even from its consequences, being in this respect as blind and callous as are vicious men in regard to certain gross sins the habit of which renders them hardened to their gravity. You also were unconscious of that leaven of corruption that was within you and which spoilt and poisoned all your works, even those which had their origin in grace.

The heavenly Physician has therefore treated you with the greatest kindness in applying an energetic remedy to your malady, and in opening your eyes to the festering sores which were gradually consuming you, in order that the sight of the matter which ran from them would inspire you with horror. No defect caused by self-love or pride could survive a sight so afflicting and humiliating. I conclude from my knowledge of this merciful design that you ought neither to desire nor to hope for the cessation of the treatment to which you are being subjected until a complete cure has been effected. At present you must brace yourself to receive many cuts with the lancet, to swallow many bitter pills, but go on bravely, and excite yourself to a filial confidence in the fatherly love which administers these remedies. Humble yourself under the mighty hand of God, annihilate yourself without ceasing and allow this work to be accomplished. Do not lose sight for one moment of the contempt and horror of yourself with which your present state inspires you. Think only of your infidelities and ingratitude. When you look at yourself let it not be in the flattering mirror of self-love, but in the truth-telling one that God, in His mercy, presents to your eyes to show you what you really are. This sight so frequently presented produces a forgetfulness of self, humility, and respect for your neighbour. " Come and see," the Holy Spirit says to you, which means, come to our Lord and behold by that new light with which He has enlightened you what you have been, what you are, and what you would, infallibly, have become. Be careful never to give up prayer and Holy Communion, for it is in these that you find help and defence.

As for sin, you do not commit any, at any rate, none that are serious. As long as you fear, as you do now, to offend God, this fear should reassure you ; it is a gift from that same hand which invisibly supports you in your trials. Have patience ! you will be consoled in good time, and your consolation will last, while the time of trial passes very rapidly. Poor human nature in its dislike of suffering looks longingly for the end. The important matter is to gather the fruit of the Cross. Let us pray, then, and sigh for that power which we do not possess and should never find within ourselves. This is a fundamental truth of which you have an entire conviction based on your own experience ; and it is for this reason that God prolongs your trial until you become so thoroughly convinced that the memory of it may never be effaced from your mind. You speak of pure love ; no soul has ever yet attained to it without having passed through many trials and great spiritual labour. In order to arrive at this much-desired goal you must learn to love those labours which alone can lead you to it. The more generous you are the sooner the end of these trials will come and the more fruit will they produce.

Continue your way, then, courageously. Rejoice every time you discover a new imperfection. Look forward to the happy moment in which the full knowledge of this abyss of misery completes within you the destruction of all self-confidence and foolish self-satisfaction. Then will it be that, flying in horror from the putrefaction of this tomb you will enter with joyful transports the bosom of God. It is after having completely cast off self that God becomes the sole thought, the only joy ; that on Him alone you will rely, and that nothing will give you any pleasure out of Him. This is the new life in Jesus Christ, this is the life of the new man after the old has been destroyed. Hasten then to die like the caterpillar, so that you may become like a beautiful butterfly, flying in the air, instead of crawling on the ground as you have hitherto done.

FIFTH BOOK.

LETTER I.—*Rules to be Observed in Illness.*
On illness and its uses. Rules to be observed. To Sister
Marie-Thérèse de Vioménil.

My dear Sister and very dear daughter in our Lord,

The peace of Jesus Christ be always with you. Do not fear
that your illness will be a danger to your soul, but, on the contrary, be reassured that you will derive great profit from it,
because :—

1st. To suffer peacefully and patiently without any resistance
is to suffer well, although you may not make any express and
energetic acts of acceptance. The heart by submitting, and by
a humble and simple acquiescence offers them passively.

2nd. Also, my dear Sister, you ought to thank God as for a
grace, in that you suffer in a feeble and small way ; that is to
say without feeling much courage and as if you were overwhelmed
by your illness and on the point of losing patience, of complaining, and giving way to the revolts of nature. Yes, it is a grace
and a signal grace, because to suffer thus is to suffer with humility
and lowliness of spirit ; whereas, if one felt a distinct courage
and strength, a conscious resignation, the heart would swell
with satisfaction, and one would become filled with self-
confidence and spiritual pride and presumption. In your state,
on the contrary, you feel weak before God, humbled and confounded at suffering in so feeble a manner. This is a certain
truth, very consoling, very spiritual, and very little recognised.
Remember it, then, on all occasions when, feeling more keenly
the weight of the Cross and of your sufferings you feel at the same
time your weakness, and submit in peace and simplicity in the
centre of your soul to all that God wills. This way of suffering
is most sanctifying, and is what Fénélon calls becoming little in
your own eyes and humbling yourself with the knowledge of
how wanting you are in courage to suffer. If all people of good
will understood this truth they would be able to suffer in peace
and simplicity, without being distressed and wounded in their
self-love by finding themselves so helpless and with so little
courage to bear their sufferings. You should apply this rule
to all your afflicting trials, and especially to those daily annoyances you experience from the person who worries you, and also
when you have feelings of antipathy towards anyone else.

3rd. As regards the alleviations you might find beneficial; certainly those officious persons who imagine they cannot do better to show their charity to the sick than by raising in their minds all sorts of longings are, as you remark, not to be accounted charitable ; their flattering conversations are so many snares ; at the same time you ought to take, without scruple, humbly and in holy simplicity, all that the doctors, superiors, and infirmarians order. Obedience and giving up our own will which we practise in acting thus are much more agreeable to God than any bodily mortification. This is another truth that many devout persons lose sight of, and are consequently very unmortified even in their mortifications. Do not forget this, because self-love and following your own will would spoil everything, corrupt everything, even in practices that are very holy in themselves. Oh! how happy should we be if we could once for all renounce our own will, judgment and ideas for the love of God !

LETTER II.—*On Different Sufferings.*

On sufferings of different kinds.

My dear Sister,

The sufferings about which you ask my direction are of different kinds. There are great trials, and the vexations of daily occurrence. These, on account of their multiplicity, form the chief part of our treasure if we only know how to take advantage of them. Believe me, inasmuch as it depends on our own efforts it is necessary to bear the little crosses we encounter every day, for by them God will enable us to destroy our self-love. Oh ! how happy should we be if we could but get rid of this accursed vanity which embitters us and irritates us about every trifle, makes us commit a thousand faults, and do ourselves great harm by the constant annoyance and interior trouble it causes us. Even should the occasion present itself of having to endure still greater sufferings, remember that they will pass like everything else, and that when they are over we can have no consolation in having borne them badly, and in having derived no advantage from them. On the other hand what a great satisfaction it will be to have made a virtue of necessity. To do this do not speak more than is necessary about them, and then in as few words as possible ; do not make a fuss about them, or about the pain they cause you ; abandon all to divine Providence who will make everything conduce to your profit if you live by faith. I pray God to make you well understand the great spiritual fruit, and the temporal blessings derived from the holy practice of entire resignation to the holy will of God in all things, and from total abandonment to all that He permits, recognising that without this divine permission not a hair can fall from our heads, nor a leaf in Autumn from all the innumerable trees of the forests. This is of faith. Could Jesus Christ have more clearly expressed than by these words, that there is no event, great or small, in the world which has not been expressly arranged by the sovereign providence of God? Oh my God! how consoling this is, and how easily we could cast off all our cares if, according to Your own words we could learn to look upon You as a loving Father, and upon ourselves as Your children, and to remember that You never show us more love than when You make us take bitter remedies for our cure! Have pity, Father of infinite goodness, on those who are sick, who, in their delirium turn against You, their good Physician, and refuse the medicine which is intended to procure them health and life.

Oh my God! how many blind and senseless people there are in the world who will not even listen to these truths although You have revealed them in the sacred Scriptures for our present consolation and our future salvation!

LETTER III.—*On Public Calamities.*

To Sister Marie-Thérèse de Vioménil. On public calamities and disasters.

The disaster of which you speak is, as you say, a most visible scourge of God; happy will they be who take advantage of it to save their souls. These punishments, borne well, as from the hands of God, are of more value than all worldly prosperity. At the same time they may be made, by a bad use, the occasion to some of eternal reprobation. This will be, however, entirely by their own fault, and their very great fault, for what could be more reasonable, or easier in a sense than to make, as I said before, a virtue of necessity? Why make a useless and criminal resistance to the chastisements of God, who is our Father and Who strikes us only to detach us from the miserable pleasures of this world? Could He do us a greater favour than to deliver us from attaching ourselves to that which would cause us to lose eternal happiness and our own souls! On such occasions it is well to think often and attentively of this passage in the writings of one of the Fathers of the Church. "Such is the goodness of our heavenly Father that even His anger proceeds from His mercy, since He only strikes us to withdraw us from sin, and to save us." Like a wise surgeon He cuts the mortified flesh away from that which is sound to save the life of the patient, and to prevent the infection from spreading. We should accustom ourselves to see everything in the light of faith; and then no event of this life, nor desires, nor fears will have any effect on us. Those strong hopes that so frequently upset the peace of the soul and the tranquil course of life, even those will make very little impression on us. How blind men are! and how much attached to their own ideas! How rarely one meets with anyone who will own that he has been obliged to seek and to take good advice! St. Francis of Sales had good reason to say that we are all wanting in sense. At least let us understand the depth of the misery and blindness into which sin has caused us to fall. Let us learn from this to be always distrustful of ourselves, and to guard against our own judgments and perverse ideas. St. Catherine of Siena was so convinced of the truth of this that she wished she could cry out constantly in a way to be heard by everyone: " Lord help me, come to my assistance and have pity on me! " Do not forget in future that a simple " Fiat " with regard to your present pains, and to those which you fear in the future either for yourself, or for others, will suffice to amass for you a treasure of peace even on earth. If this practice does not bring perfect peace immediately, it will, at least, fill your soul with joy and enable you to taste a solid consolation in all your pains and fears.

LETTER IV.—*Opportunities for Practising Charity.*

On contradictory tastes and characters.

Far from pitying you I consider that you are more to be congratulated on having, at last, an opportunity of practising true charity. The antipathy you feel towards the person with whom you have such continual intercourse, the difference in your ideas and tastes, the offence she causes you by her manners and conversation are so many infallible signs that the charity you show her is purely supernatural and without any admixture of human feeling. This will be a way of amassing pure gold, and it depends entirely on yourself whether or not you will heap up an immense treasure. Be grateful, therefore, to the good God and in order to lose nothing of the inestimable advantages of your present position follow out exactly the rules that I will now give you.

1st. Bear patiently the involuntary feelings of disgust that this Sister's behaviour causes you, just as you would bear a sudden attack of fever or megrim. Your antipathy is really, in fact, an interior fever, with its shivering and paroxysms. This is very crucifying, humiliating and painful, consequently it is more meritorious and sanctifying.

2nd. Never speak, as perhaps the others do, about this Sister unless to speak kindly about her, remembering that she has her good qualities. And which of us is without bad ones? Who is perfect in this world? It is possible that without your will or knowledge you are as great a trial to her as God allows her to be to you. God often polishes one diamond by friction with another, says Fénélon.

3rd. When you have committed some fault in this matter do not distress yourself but humble yourself quietly without voluntary vexation either with her or yourself, without anxiety, annoyance or uneasiness. If we treat our faults in this way they will be to our profit and advantage. God keeps us in a state of true humility by these miseries, and the daily faults by which we discover our own pettiness.

4th. For the rest, unless your duty obliges you, do not meddle in anything that is said or done, let everything go on without speaking or thinking about it. Abandon all to divine Providence. What does it matter if everything goes, if everything perishes, provided that we belong to God and save our souls? But, I almost hear you say, if such or such a thing should happen what shall I do? This! I will take no notice, I will have nothing to do with it, because I should be sorry to lose this happy state of abandonment which makes me live in complete and absolute dependence on God from day to day, hour to hour, moment to moment, without a thought of the future, nor even of to-morrow. To-morrow will take care of itself. He who sustains us to-day with His invisible hand, will sustain us to-morrow. The manna in the desert was only given from day to day, and whoever, through want of confidence, or a false wisdom, gathered it up for the next day, found it spoilt. Let us not in our anxious and ignorant foresight make unnecessary provision for ourselves, when God in His wisdom and fore-knowledge provides for us. Let us depend entirely on His fatherly care and abandon ourselves to it utterly both for our temporal concerns and our spiritual and eternal interests. This is true and total abandonment which binds God to take all under His care with respect to those who abandon all and thus pay that honour to His sovereign dominion, His power, wisdom, goodness and mercy that is due to all His infinite perfections. Amen. Amen.

T

LETTER V.—*Profit to be gained by Patient Endurance.*

You have reason to bless God, my dear Sister, for having preserved in your heart peace, gentleness, and charity for the person whose place it is to wait upon you. He has given you a great grace. Perhaps He may still allow that, either through ignorance, thoughtlessness, or even, if you will, out of caprice, or bad temper, she may give you occasion to practise patience. Then, Sister, try to profit well by these precious occasions which are so adapted to gain the heart of God. Alas! we offend this God of all goodness not only through ignorance and thoughtlessness, but deliberately and maliciously. We want Him to forgive us, and this He most mercifully does, and then we will not forgive others like ourselves. And we recite every day the prayer our Lord taught us, " Forgive us, Lord, as we forgive." We must remember also the words of our God, telling us that He would act towards us as we act towards our neighbour; therefore we ought to bear with our neighbour, and to show him consideration, charity, gentleness and condescension; and God Who is faithful to His promises will treat us in like manner. I am enlarging on this subject a little because it will give you occasion to practise the greatest and most solid virtue every day; charity, patience, meekness, and humility of heart, benignity and the renunciation of your own ideas; and these little daily virtues faithfully practised will procure you a rich harvest of graces and merits for eternity. It is in this way better than in any other that you will be able to obtain the great gift of interior prayer, peace of mind, recollection, the continual presence of God, and His pure and perfect love. This simple cross borne patiently will draw down upon you an infinitude of graces, and will enable you more efficaciously to become detached from self than trials, in appearance much more grievous, and to attach yourself unreservedly to God.

LETTER VI.—*Difficulties.*

To Sister Marie-Thérèse de Vioménil. On different kinds of difficulties.

My dear Sister,

How can you still feel surprised at that of which your experience ought to have convinced you for a long time past? As long as we live upon earth, and do not live among saints we shall always require patience to put up with each other. It is a good thing for us that such is the case, so that we may have more frequent opportunities of practising the most meritorious virtues ; charity, humility, and self-renunciation. Let us then resign ourselves with a good grace to this necessity, let us try to profit by the faults of our neighbour and be indulgent towards them, and by our own faults and rise speedily from them. This is the only way to keep peace. I acknowledge that your habitual position is extremely hard, but then what a fund of merits for Heaven ! what a magnificent opportunity of doing penance, and of practising heroic virtue ! You can hardly fail, if it lasts, to attain in a short time, the grace of an interior life, if you continue to practise abnegation, and self-renunciation by charity, humility, resignation and abandonment to God. These acts of virtue will soon make your heart ready to receive the sweet infusion of divine love ; and therefore I should feel very much disappointed on your account if you were given an easier and more agreeable post. These trials of which you complain were valued and sought for by the saints with eagerness, because they understood their worth and advantages for the reformation of the soul, and for arriving at true union with God. You have, for a long time past, been attacked by a temptation all the more dangerous the less you suspected its danger. This comes from never having rightly understood this truth, which is an article of faith, that everything that happens in the world, with the sole exception of sin, comes directly from God, and the ordinance of His will. Also further, although it is certain that God never wills sin, nor consequently the calumnies, persecutions and injustices of which His elect are the victims, He wills the consequences nevertheless ; that is to say, that He wills that His elect should endure calumny, persecutions, humiliations, and often martyrdom in a thousand different ways. I say the same of the consequences of our own sins. A man, by his own imprudence, or even by more culpable means, falls into poverty, illness, and all sorts of severe afflictions. God, while detesting the sin, wills its consequences, such as poverty, illness and misfortune. This man then can, and ought to say, " Lord, I have thoroughly deserved this, You have permitted it, it happens by Your will, may Your holy will be done, I acquiesce in all. I adore and submit."

It was the knowledge of this great principle which made holy Job say, " The Lord hath given, and the Lord hath taken away, blessed be the Name of the Lord." He did not say, " The Lord hath given, and the devil hath taken away," because the devil has no power to do so without the permission of God, and it was from this principle that he drew his perfect submission, constancy, and peace of mind.

For want of being thoroughly imbued with this great principle, you have never known how to submit to certain conditions and events, nor, consequently to remain in them firmly and tranquilly according to the will of God. The devil has always tempted you, made you uneasy and deceived you by a hundred illusions and false arguments about them. Try then, I beg of you in the interests of your salvation and peace of mind, to put an end to such a mistake; you will, at the same time put an end to the vexations you feel, and to all the rebellious feelings of your nature. For this end accustom yourself to make acts of faith and submission about every event that happens either through the agency of men or the malice of the devil or your own fault, and even your sins. God has permitted it thus. He is Master, may He be blessed in all, and may His holy will be accomplished in all things. Fiat! Fiat!

Your situation is very painful, it is true, but on that account it is very sanctifying and is the best penance you could possibly perform, being assured that it is imposed on you by God Himself. All that the devil presents to your mind to the contrary is an evident illusion to deprive you of the peace of God, to make you sad, uneasy and vexed; always discontented with your present state, and sighing for some other. This is why so many in the world are as unhappy as they are culpable, for want of being able to understand this truth, so important and so consoling, of which I have just reminded you. How many torments would they not spare themselves, and how much merit would they not amass in the midst of their trials if they could but persuade themselves that God makes use of all things for His glory and for the benefit of His creatures; and that it remains for them to derive profit from all by a blind submission which must be total, general, without exceptions and without contrary arguments, at any rate, none that are deliberate. If I could but inscribe this truth on your mind and heart even with my blood! But God will do so Himself gradually I am sure, if you will but co-operate with His grace by rejecting at once all thoughts contrary to it. Once more I entreat you to submit in spite of all repugnance and disgust to the secret decrees of this adorable Providence, and you will become holy and pleasing to God.

———

LETTER VII.—*Rules for Difficult Circumstances.*

To the same person. On the same subject. Rules to be followed.

———

I own, my dear Sister, that there is nothing more difficult than to keep a perfect evenness of temper and an immovable patience amid domestic difficulties and intercourse with those persons of different character by whom we are surrounded. The constant friction makes it almost impossible for us not to forget ourselves occasionally; but if one falls one moment, one can rise immediately. To fall is a weakness, to rise, a virtue. If one loses hold on oneself it is but to gain a firmer hold without feeling annoyed, and little by little God gives all to those who know how to wait patiently. But you want everything with impetuosity and imagine you are going to become perfect at once. You must try to moderate by degrees the turbulence and agitation of these desires which clash with each other at the risk of being broken. However, if you cannot altogether prevent this collision you must try to endure it quietly and humbly, and not increase the misery uselessly by tormenting yourself because you are tormented. The difficulties that are caused you, and the injustice of certain people towards you are, I own, the most revolting thing in the world, my heart is troubled with only reading about it; but what other remedy is there than the one we have already made use of for the cure of many other ills?—to raise our eyes to heaven and to say, "Lord, it is Your will, You permit this to happen, I adore and I submit. May Your holy will be done. Your divine permission will help me to carry this cross in expiation of my sins, and to make me merit heaven. Fiat! fiat!"

If I knew a better remedy I would impart it to you, but as I am certain that this is the most efficacious you must excuse me trying to find others. I own that it is next to impossible not to give way on such occasions to some slight movements of impatience, revolt, and bitterness, at any rate, interiorly; but you must return as quickly as you can to God and to yourself by humbling yourself quietly without too much trouble, and asking earnestly of God the necessary patience.

———

LETTER VIII.—*Annoyances caused by Good People.*

To the same person.   On annoyances caused by good people.

———————

1st.   The annoyances you have experienced must have been all the more painful as coming from people from whom you would least expect them ;   but be assured that you will have gained great merit for heaven by them.   Men's ideas are so different ; they vary according to their interests or temper, and each is convinced of his own sense, and that he has right on his side.   Oh men !   men !   To what have we come ?   What an abyss of humiliation for the whole human race !   It is a good thing to have arrived at the bottom of this abyss, for it will be more easy to place all one's confidence in God.   The mind, enlightened by faith, disposes the heart to submit to the decrees of divine Providence who permits good people to make each other suffer to detach them from each other.   On occasions such as these we can only resign ourselves, and abandon ourselves to God who will support us.   These dispositions will enable us to turn a deaf ear to arguments that might tend to disturb us. Whether we consider ourselves, or the conduct of others towards us there will never be wanting specious reasons for becoming vexed and uneasy.   But there is never any reason for depression and worry.   These irregular emotions are always contrary to reason as well as to religion ; and the peace of which they deprive us is of incalculably more value than that for which we sacrifice it.

2nd.   For the rest it is always allowable to speak in confidence to a director, to obtain consolation, strength, and instruction, but always do so with charity and discretion.   Nevertheless it is better and more perfect to keep silence.   It is to God alone that we should confide our vexations, and tell all as to a friend, or director worthy of our entire confidence.   This is an excellent and easy way of praying, and is called the prayer of confidence, and the outpouring of the heart before God.   By it is gained great spiritual fortitude, and from it proceeds consolation, peace and courage.   If you continue to live as you are doing now, very imperfectly no doubt, but with a sincere desire to improve, and with efforts proportioned to your weakness, your salvation is certain.   Even the fear you feel about it is a gift of God provided it does not go so far as to trouble you, and to prevent you frequenting the Sacraments, practising virtue, or continuing your spiritual exercises.   As for the hardness of heart and want of feeling that you complain about, be patient and offer this affliction to God in a spirit of penance as you offer Him your illnesses and bodily infirmities.   Those of the soul are much harder to bear and consequently more meritorious.

LETTER IX.—*How to Bear these Trials.*

To the same Sister.

I feel keenly, my dear Sister, the painful nature of the trial to which God has subjected you, and the sadness of your heart at receiving these daily wounds. It is true, I own, that it is necessary to be very holy to be able to let such things pass unnoticed, without feeling any kind of resentment; but, if you cannot attain such perfection yet, try at least during these times of trial, first to dismiss as far as you are able, all those thoughts, feelings and that language likely to embitter your mind; secondly if you cannot succeed in doing this, at any rate, say interiorly in the superior part of your soul, " My God, You have permitted this, may Your adorable will and divine decrees be accomplished in all things. I sacrifice to You this affliction and its consequences according to what pleases You. You are the Master, may You be blessed by all and in all things." Then add, " I forgive, Lord, from the bottom of my heart for the love of You the persons who cause my sufferings, and to show the sincerity of my feelings about them I ask for them all sorts of graces and blessings, and every happiness." When the heart is inclined to resist say, " My God, You see my misery, but at least I desire to have all these feelings and I beg this grace of You." Having done this think no more about it, and if uncharitable feelings still molest you be resigned to endure this torment in conformity to the divine Will which permits it, contenting yourself with renewing the offering in the higher part of the soul. This is one of the ways by which we can share the chalice of Jesus Christ, our good Master.

LETTER X.—*To see God in our Trials.*

To the same Sister. On seeing God in our trials.

I am surprised, my dear Sister, that with the help of the rules I have so often given you, you are not even yet able to recognise the hand of God in the misunderstandings that arise among people with the best intentions. " God," you say, " does not inspire anything that brings trouble." That, in one sense, is true, but is it not also true that God has permitted, and often permits His servants to be given to mistakes and illusions which are intended to try them, to exercise them, and, in this way to sanctify them by the trouble they cause each other? We see hundreds of examples of this in the lives of the saints, and again

quite recently in the lives of St. Francis Regis, and the venerable
Sister Marguérite-Marie Alacoque.* Try to judge, not by
human judgment, weak, narrow, and blind as it is, but by divine
judgment which alone is upright, sure, and infallible. In this
way you will improve, and not have the peace of your mind and
heart disturbed.

*N.B.   Canonised in 1921.

LETTER XI.—*To Seek God's Help Alone.*

To the same Sister.   On the deprivation of human assistance.

You think yourself greatly to be pitied, my dear Sister,
because God has deprived you of the helps that up to now He
has contrived for you.   You are indeed to be pitied, but only
on account of your want of resignation to the arrangements of
divine Providence.   Is it not deplorable that a soul chosen by
God, and which He had taken into His service and overwhelmed
with graces, instead of being contented with Him, ardently
sighs after the little helps it receives from fellow creatures?
These helps are all very well if God allows them, but when He
takes them away, how much better it would be to rely upon Him
alone! With what joy a soul that truly loved Him would repeat
over and over again, "My God, You are my all! Lord! I have
only You, but You are enough for me, and I desire nothing but
what You give me." The almighty hand of God will then take
the place of a weak and worthless reed in regard to this soul.
With this certainty how can you possibly consider yourself
unhappy and abandoned? That which terrifies you is, that
in future you can have no advice until too late.   For my part I
must say that, after so much advice and so many letters from the
most enlightened directors you ought to be able to advise others.
Besides, even though in certain circumstances you should have a
serious doubt, is that any reason to despair?   Raise your heart
to God and He will not refuse to guide you when all other
guidance is taken away from you; and then choose, unhesi-
tatingly, what you believe, in good faith, to be the most suitable,
the most useful to souls, and the most in conformity with the
Will of God.   Whatever may be the result, you must believe that
you have acted rightly because, under the circumstances, you
could not have done better.   Do you really think that God demands impossibilities?   No! God, Who is infinitely good, loves
straightforwardness and simplicity, and is satisfied when we have
done all in our power after having asked with confidence for
His divine light.

You tell me that in your isolated condition you can see nothing that is not a subject of trouble and affliction. Oh! what a grace is this! It should have produced, or will necessarily produce in you, a complete detachment from all created things Does not God give such a grace only to those souls He most loves? Oh! daughter of little faith, but daughter beloved of God, complain after this if you dare! "Only God," you say again, "can know all that I suffer." If you are not exaggerating, I congratulate you with all my heart. It was thus that the blessed Mother St. Teresa spoke during her great spiritual difficulties. It is a good sign to find life sad and bitter. Death is terrifying because of the judgment that follows: but unless this terror causes disquiet, it comes from the Holy Spirit. I should fear much for anyone who did not feel this salutary dread.

LETTER XII.—*God Alone*.

To the same Sister.   On the absence of a director.

My dear Sister, I am neither angry nor surprised at what you feel about the departure of your director. If, instead of allowing yourself to be cast down by this feeling, you could master it, it would be the occasion of the most meritorious acts of abandonment to God. Thus you would gradually become detached from creatures, and unite yourself to Him, Who alone is your sovereign good. Oh! what a joy! what safety as to the future life, and unchangeable peace for the present to be in God alone, to have no other treasure, no other support, no other help or hope but God alone! I wish I could send you a beautiful letter that one of your Sisters has written to me on the subject. She says that, for a whole month this thought, "God alone, I have only God," gave her so much consolation and support, that instead of regret, she felt full of peace and an inexplicable joy. It seemed to her that God took the place of director, and that in future He would correct and instruct her Himself. It was to Him I recommended you when I left, and continue to do so. This is the farewell that Mother . . . ¹bid me on the eve of my departure," Father, I bid you farewell as this is the will of God." That same evening she went to console the other Sisters, and the next day held the conference as usual. Since then she has had much to suffer, but has done so with a resignation that was worth more than any gratification, even spiritual.

¹ The Religious of whom Fr. Caussade speaks here seems to have been the Superior of the Refuge at Nancy, founded by Mdme. de Ranfaing.

LETTER XIII.—*Reliance on God Alone.*

To the same Sister.

_____

I acknowledge that a visible guide endowed with all the requisite qualities for so difficult a position, is a grace of God, and a powerful help to the soul. But if Divine Providence should refuse us this assistance, or should take it away from us, if we could say with our whole heart, " My God, I have only You, You are all that I desire," what we should obtain by doing so, would be worth all that we could obtain by means of a director. It is an undoubted fact that God often deprives us of all outside help in order that we may give Him our sole confidence. Oh ! if we would but give it entirely to Him without sharing an atom of it with anyone, whoever it might be ! how well repaid we should find ourselves ! For the want of any help from creatures, we should experience a great liberty of spirit. If, however, you have such contrary feelings it is because you are still very far from having that purity of love which makes us seek God for Himself alone. In fact this is evident, because the extreme sorrow and trouble to which a soul deprived of exterior help abandons itself, can only proceed from an immediate attachment to these human helps.

This attachment excites the jealousy of God, particularly if souls that have been favoured behave in this way, as He desires all their confidence and affection. But take courage ! as God has made you endure the severe trial arising from such an attachment, He wishes in this way and by means of this very pain to moderate it gradually, until finally you are freed from it altogether. Allow Him to effect in you this desirable purification, and compel yourself to fulfil His designs faithfully. This will be an operation of grace as salutary as it is painful. You must endure it patiently as you would endure the suffering of some painful remedy intended to cure certain serious complaints. However, if you cannot at once succeed in becoming completely detached, at least desire with all your strength to become so, and moderate as much as you possibly can, the sorrow of which you cannot entirely rid yourself. God will do the rest when He thinks fit. Offer yourself to Him to do with you as best pleases Him, and show Him simply and humbly all your misery and weakness ; that will suffice ; this good Master asks no more at present, because this is all that you can do. Rise quickly from your frequent falls, which, as far as this matter is concerned are not sins but merely imperfections. For the rest, be satisfied to go to confession for the sake of absolution, then go to Communion as usual ; in other respects your only help will be God.

The rules which have been given you on former occasions will suffice to guide you, provided that you allow God to animate them with His spiritual unction. The more you wish for something fresh, the more tormented will you become, and to no purpose; and you will also commit many imperfections which will impede your spiritual progress just as much as real sins prevent others entering the way of salvation. The fear of not knowing, or of passing over many interior sins is another temptation of the enemy to deprive you of peace, and to disturb you. I command you for God's sake to make yourself quite easy in this respect, contenting yourself with mentioning in confession that which your conscience tells you is the most important. Leave all the rest to the very great mercy of God without worrying yourself at all about it. Thus your confessions will be unconstrained and peaceful, and in this way will also be very fruitful. If we give way to trouble, we derive hardly any fruit from our confessions, and this the devil knows very well. If you have any difficulty in finding positive sins that you know to be such, just mention some particular sin of your past life, and after that be at peace. This is the usual practice of well-intentioned persons, and you will lose nothing by following it.

LETTER XIV.—*Abandonment in Trials.*

To the same person. On abandonment in trials of this nature.

My dear Sister,

1st. I always exhort you to be patient and to abandon yourself to God because you have need of these virtues. God alone is all, everything else is nothing. Attach yourself to Him therefore strongly, entirely and resolutely. He has intentions and designs which are not for us to fathom. For all our ills there is no other remedy; for all our sufferings no other consolation than submission, and complete abandonment. This is the most certain way of amassing a fortune for eternity and of gaining that true life which will never end.

2nd. Look upon your ills and infirmities as a very advantageous exchange for purgatory where you would have to suffer much more severely in the next life, if you did not pay your debts while here on earth.

One simple "fiat" during your exterior and interior pains will be enough to make you acquire true sanctity. Remind yourself of what St. Francis of Sales said to one of his penitents, " My daughter, repeat often during the day, ' Yes, my heavenly Father, yes, and always yes.' " It is a very short and easy practice; nothing further is required to attain perfection. We need not go far to attain it, since we can easily do so without seeking it outside our own souls.

3rd. I am much edified by your holy reflexions about the very small amount of consolation you find in creatures, and I strongly approve of your taking this as a merciful punishment for your over great tenderness and excessive affection for your relations and friends. A trial endured in such a manner cannot fail to contribute powerfully to recall your affections to Him for Whom alone we are created, and apart from Whom we can find no repose.

4th. But I perceive that now, as formerly, the most afflicting trial you have to endure is the deprivation of all outward help for your soul. I have often told you, and again repeat, that although it is true that this help is a grace from God, yet, I maintain that, with regard to some people and certain characters, the withdrawal of this support is in the end a still greater grace, and a most efficacious means of sanctification. Listen to me without interruption. When God honours a soul by being jealous of its love, the greatest favour He can confer upon it is to gradually deprive it of everything that could turn its love away from Him; because never would it have sufficient courage and strength to detach itself. Now, God has seen that for a long time past, after having become detached from all other creatures, you still kept an attachment for and a confidence in your spiritual guide. This attachment was in no way wrong, most certainly, but it was the same sort of feeling that the Apostles had for their divine Master before His Resurrection. This jealous God Who aims at being loved purely and solely for Himself, cannot endure this sort of division, and therefore He has taken away from you the one who shared with Him the affection of your heart. This is truly your heaviest cross, because by it you have been attacked in that most sensitive spot, your heart, which formerly discovered so many ingenious pretexts to render its sorrow justifiable. I can hear you say to yourself that you do not regret this deprivation on account of the consolation of which it has robbed you, but because of the assistance it has given you for your spiritual progress and which is now taken from you. A mistake! an illusion of self-love! One "fiat" uttered in this sort of privation gains more merit in the sight of God than could be acquired by the most beautiful, the most worthy, the most consoling direction in the world. "But," say you, "if one were guided by a connected course of advice one would not commit so many faults." I answer that these faults are less displeasing to God than the smallest little attachment, however pure and innocent it may seem, and really be fundamentally. Therefore, I cannot sufficiently admire the goodness of God Who for many years past has led you by this sort of privation to break off in you all, even the least attachment. At present He is attacking your body by illness to detach you from yourself. He attacks the soul by weariness, disgust, callousness, and other troubles to detach you interiorly from all sensible help and consolation. If you will but allow Him to act freely in you, you will come at last to adhere only to Him by pure faith and in spirit, or, as St. Francis of Sales puts it, by the higher faculties of the soul. Let this God of all goodness act then, for He desires all your confidence. I cannot help adding that the longer I live, the more clearly I see and understand that everything depends solely on God, and that if everything is left to Him, all will go well. No sooner do I make the sacrifice of everything to Him, than all goes perfectly.

5th. You do well to think that there are others who have much heavier crosses than yours, but be careful that the thought of the weight of yours does not prevent you being resigned to God. We might very likely be deprived of a sensible and consoling submission, but that which comes from pure faith and is simply spiritual can never be wanting to us. That which is not spoilt by any sort of vain self-complacency is very much more meritorious. This is why God gives only this last sort of submission to most people, leaving the soul groaning and humbled under the weight of its afflictions. God's gifts are according to our requirements. He bestows especial graces to enable us to bear extraordinary troubles. What we cannot help, patience makes bearable. This is what a pagan philosopher said, enlightened only by human reason; what, then, may not faith and religion make us think and say when we look at the crucifix and think of the eternal happiness in store for us?

LETTER XV.—*The Use of Afflictions.*

On the usefulness of these afflictions.

My dear Sister,

When I consider the infinite value of your present trials I dare not wish them to cease ; what I do wish is that you should keep yourself in a perpetual state of sacrifice and abandonment, or at least to tend that way, and to desire and implore it incessantly of God. With this disposition, and by making good use of crosses and afflictions, you will advance your eternal interests much more rapidly than you would by consolations and success. In a short time everything will have an end for us, and we shall have a boundless eternity in which to rejoice and to return thanks. This thought should completely console us for all our pains both interior and exterior, for these will procure us the joys of paradise. Let us remember that we have but little time to attain to this infinite happiness, and let us try to render ourselves worthy of it, at no matter what cost.

To continue, my dear Sister, I have already pointed out the fruit obtained by your soul in the great trial through which God has made you pass. In spite of the violent tempests it raised in your soul, I have no doubt that it greatly contributed to your spiritual progress. You learnt by it how to remain interiorly crucified, to be wearied of everything earthly, to make many painful and frequent sacrifices to God, to overcome yourself in many ways, to be patient and submissive and to abandon yourself to God. " But how," you will ask, " has all this been done ? " It has been done by means of troubles, reverses, and feelings of utter repugnance ; by the higher faculties of the soul, and often without your knowledge, and without your being able to understand how you had this submission which you possessed without being aware of it. At other times you were persuaded that you did not possess it, and hardly desired to have it, while all the time there it was at the bottom of your heart ! Oh ! how admirable are the ways of God ! If you had known as I did, the depths of your soul, you might, perchance, have spoilt all by secret reflexions and vain self-complacency. Let God do His work. It is through our ignorance, blindness, and obscurity that He can act as He pleases, without having His work spoilt by us. We acknowledge this, even by our humiliation when we believe that all is going wrong, that all is lost; but it ought to suffice for you to know that I see clearly enough the progress you have made to re-assure you, to answer for you, and to encourage you. Oh ! how I wish that you would have more confidence in God, more complete abandonment to His all-wise and divine Providence which arranges even the smallest events of our lives ! He turns them all to the advantage of those who confide themselves to Him, and who abandon themselves unreservedly to His fatherly care. What peace does not this confidence and entire abandonment produce in the soul ! and from what uneasy and vexatious cares without end does it not deliver us ? But as we cannot attain to this all at once, but gradually and by imperceptible degrees, we must aspire after it without ceasing, ask it of God and make frequent acts of it. Occasions for doing so will not be wanting ; let us avail ourselves of them, and repeat constantly, " Yes, my God, since it is Your will and You permit it thus to be, I also will it for love of You, help and strengthen me." All this quietly, without effort, with the higher powers of your soul, and in spite of interior repugnance of which you need take no notice, except to bear it patiently and so make a sacrifice of it. Let us even wish to make these acts in the midst of these repugnances and revolts, since God wills or permits it thus to happen. If we should fail in this respect, let us act as we should after any other fault, try to regain what we have lost by interior humility, but a humility that is sweet and tranquil, without self-contempt, or annoyance with ourselves or others. I repeat, without despondency or voluntary vexation, for the first involuntary movements do not depend upon ourselves, and provided that we do not give our consent to them, they will make us exercise more meritoriously the virtues of patience, meekness and humility. In this miserable exile we find everywhere continual and unavoidable dangers, and there is no other way of safe-guarding oneself, than to take quietly, and without over-eagerness, those precautions that prudence suggests, and then to trust everything to divine Providence. Throw yourself into the arms of God and remain there peacefully and without care, like a little child in the arms of a good and loving mother. Whoever knows how to make use of this practice will find in it a treasure of peace and of merit. Try to act thus about everything and at all times, and to adopt somewhat of this interior spirit. Nothing could be more calculated to pacify and to moderate impulsiveness and natural impetuosity; nothing could better prevent or soften a thousand bitter annoyances, and a thousand uneasy forebodings. The state of P.F. is to be lamented. God wills to sanctify her indeed, since He afflicts her so grievously at the end of her life. At that time it is doubly hard to nature to be neglected, but what a consolation to be able to suffer so much for God before going to appear before Him. Consolations are in truth a great blessing, but not to be compared to sufferings and trials. God preserve me from that sort of blessing. I have no doubt I should like it and find comfort in it. A middling virtue could make good use of the first grace, but it would require heroic virtue to practise, with God's help, the second. I remain yours in our Lord until death and even after, if God will do me this favour. I sincerely hope that He will.

Letter XVI.—*Detachment*.

To Sister Marie-Thérèse de Vioménil. Bitterness mingled with pleasure to detach the soul.

1st. I am not surprised, my dear Sister, at the trouble which the grievous trial to which our Lord has subjected you, has caused. This sort of events affect us all the more keenly in that they wound us in our most intimate affections. But if I am not surprised at this involuntary trouble, at the same time I urge you to supersede it in your heart by an entire resignation to the will of God. How great will be the treasures of grace, of merit, and of peace which such an act will bring to you! It is on this account that I have so constantly inculcated the virtue of perfect abandonment, and still preach it incessantly, wishing you to become as tranquil and as happy as I wish you to be holy. You have not yet attained to this, but with God's help you will.

2nd. God allows my sick relation to remain in the same state, to prove, and to convert the whole family. If they avail themselves of this opportunity, as I have every reason to believe they will, I shall bless God from the bottom of my heart for this happy occurrence which is worth more than all the fortunes in the world.

3rd. I am about to lose the best and dearest friend I had left, one whom I most esteemed, and on whom I could thoroughly rely. God has willed it thus. His holy will be done! Fiat! I commend him to your prayers.

4th. Blessed be God in all, and for all, but especially in this, that He knows so well how to make everything serve for the sanctification of His elect by one another. On this subject the holy Archbishop of Cambray has well said that God makes use of one diamond to polish another. What a useful thought for our consolation! and one that will prevent us ever being scandalised at the little persecutions of one another that good people are given to.

5th. Hail and rain have caused great havoc in many provinces as well as in your neighbourhood. May God grant us grace to derive profit from all these disasters for the expiation of our sins. A simple and sincere " fiat " is worth more than all the superfluities that we desire, because it adds to our treasure for eternity. Once filled with these high thoughts and hopes, we shall feel much less the occurrences of this short and miserable life.

6th. By dint of constantly thinking of death, we shall gradually come to contemplate it without shrinking. Fr. Bourdaloue has very well expressed this when he said, "the thought of death is indeed a sad one, but by dint of considering it as salutary, it will at last appear almost pleasant"; and a Jesuit theologian, Fr. Francis Suarez, said when his last moment came, "I did not know it was so sweet to die."

7th. Sometimes one hears it said, "I have no longer either help to fortify me, or instruction to encourage me." This is an occasion for sacrifice, "fiat, fiat." All instruction, however much it may strengthen us, does not equal in value what we gain by one simple "fiat" uttered in the lack of all extraneous help. The high road to all perfection is pointed out in the "Our Father." "Fiat voluntas tua." Say this with your lips as well as you can; and still more perfectly in your heart, and be assured that, with this interior disposition nothing is wanting to you, nor ever will be. Learn by this to find repose in no matter what difficulties and troubles, because all will come right when God pleases, and according to our desires, if He should will it so, or permit it. Crosses and afflictions are such great graces that the wicked are rarely converted without them, and good people are only made perfect by the same means.

8th. God can easily make up for all, and really does so if we wish for nothing but Him, and expect to receive all from Him alone. It is in order to lead us gradually and by a happy necessity to this beautiful and desirable condition that He frequently deprives us of all human aid and consolation, and in the same way He mingles bitterness with worldly pleasures to disgust and detach the souls of worldly people from them, in order to save them. Fortunate disappointments! happy privations! which come from the goodness of God rather than from His justice. It is thus that we ought to regard them.

LETTER XVII.—*Conduct during Trials.*

To the same Sister. On conduct during trials.

My dear Sister,

Ought you not to be able to overcome your fears, and to check your tears after all the experience you have had of the way in which your mind creates phantoms when anything affects it keenly, making you indulge in idle terrors? If it is impossible to prevent these tiresome wanderings of the imagination, at least endeavour to gain some profit by them, and to make of them matter for interior sacrifice, and an occasion for the exercise of a complete abandonment to all the decrees of divine Providence whatever they may be. I am of your opinion, and have never

U

desired, and still less, prayed for pains and contradictions. Those sent by Providence are quite enough without wishing for more, or inflicting them on oneself. We must wait and prepare ourselves for these ; that is the best way to gain strength and courage to receive them, and to bear them properly when God sends them. This is one of my favourite practices, and suits me both for this life and the next. I offer to God, beforehand, all the sacrifices that occur to my mind without any effort of my own. It is to enable us to acquire the merit of this offering that God tries us by these ideas, and these fears of future evil that He does not intend to send us. When, on the other hand, He sends us consolations whether spiritual or temporal, we ought to accept them simply, with gratitude and thanksgiving, but without clinging to them or taking too much pleasure in them, because all joy that is not in God only serves to feed our self-love. Your solitude in the absence of the person on whom you could most rely, in spite of her having been very tiresome, cannot fail to be very good for you. How many acts of resignation will you not have made in your illness and weakness ! How often will you not have raised your heart to God ! How many holy affections and good resolutions will you not have made ! You will be saved by the good will which God sees in your heart. Each of us has a particular path to follow, according to his light. Try to make use of your present circumstances and of your sadness, to place your whole confidence in God, both for time and eternity. The present calamities of which you paint so sad a picture, will, if only for the sake of your own peace, place you under the necessity of making incessantly, very meritorious sacrifices to God. Public misfortunes are great, but the part you can take about them is great also. The lives of sinful men, and that we all are, ought to be passed entirely in works of penance and mortification, and God shows His mercy by giving us this remedy with His own hand. The chalice is bitter, it is true, but how infinitely more bitter would be the pains of hell, or of purgatory ; and since we must drink this chalice whether we like it or not, let us, as the proverb says, make a virtue of necessity. In this way all our difficulties will be smoothed away. As you say, interior sufferings are much harder to bear, but they are also more meritorious and purifying, and after having been made to endure these purifications and detachments, everything else seems easy. Then it will be much more easy to give oneself up to a perfect abandonment and a filial confidence in God through Jesus Christ. The reflexions you make on this subject are reasonable and true, but too human. We should always revert to abandonment and hope in divine Providence, for what can man do, exposed as he is to continual vicissitudes ?   Let us depend then on God alone, for He never changes, and knows better than we do what is necessary for us, and, like a good father, is always ready to give it.   But He has to do with children who are often so blind that they do not see for what they are asking.   Even in their prayers, that to them seem so sensible and just, they deceive themselves by desiring to arrange the future which belongs to God alone. When He takes away from us what we consider necessary, He knows how to supply its place imperceptibly, in a thousand different ways unknown to us.   This is so true that bitterness and heaviness of heart borne with patience and interior silence, make the soul advance more than would the presence and instruction of the holiest and cleverest director.   I have had a hundred experiences of this, and am convinced that, at present. this is your path, and the only things that God asks of you are submission, abandonment, confidence, sacrifice, and silence. Practise these virtues as well as you can without too violent efforts.

LETTER XVIII.—*The Will of God to be Preferred.*

To the same Sister.

Believe me, my dear Sister, and put an end to all your fears and entrust all to divine Providence who makes use of hidden but infallible means of bringing everything to serve His ends. Whatever men may say or do, they can only act by God's will or permission, and everything they do He makes serve for the accomplishment of His merciful designs.   He is able to attain His purposes by means apparently most contrary, as to refresh His servants in the midst of a fiery furnace, or to make them walk on the waters.   We shall experience more sensibly this fatherly protection of Providence if 'we abandon ourselves to Him with filial confidence.   Quite recently I have had experience of this, therefore I have prayed to God with greater fervour than ever to grant me the grace never to have my own will which is always blind, and often dangerous, but always that His which is just, holy, loving, and beneficent may be accomplished. Ah ! if you only knew what a pleasure it is to find no peace or contentment except in accomplishing the will of God which is as good as it is powerful, you would not be able to desire anything else.   Never look upon any pain, no matter of what kind, as a sign of being far from God ;   because crosses and sufferings are, on the contrary, effects of His goodness and love.   " But," say you, " what will become of me if . . . ? "   This is indeed a temptation of the enemy. Why should you be so ingenious in tormenting yourself beforehand about something which perhaps will never happen ? Sufficient for the day is the evil thereof. Uneasy forebodings do us much harm ; why do you so readily give way to them ? We make our own troubles, and what do we gain by it ? but lose, instead, so much both for time and eternity. When we are obsessed in spite of ourselves by these worrying previsions let us be faithful in making a continual sacrifice of them to the sovereign Master. I conjure you to do this, as in this way you will induce God to deal favourably with you and to help you in every way. You will acquire a treasure of virtue and merit for Heaven, and a submission and abandonment which will enable you to make more progress in the ways of God than any other practice of piety. It is, possibly, with this view that God permits all these troublesome and trying imaginations. Profit by them then, and God will bless you. By your submission to His good pleasure you will make greater progress than you could by hearing beautiful sermons, or reading pious books. If you only understood this great truth thoroughly, you would enjoy great peace of mind, and advance rapidly in the ways of God. Without this submission to His good pleasure no spirituality counts for much. As long as people restrict themselves to exterior practices, they can but have a very thin veneer of true and solid piety which consists essentially, and in reality, in willing in everything what God wills, and in the manner in which He wills it. When you have attained to this, the Spirit of God will reign absolutely in your heart, will supply for all else, and will never fail you in your need if you call with humble confidence for His help. This is of faith, but is known to very few souls who are otherwise pious. Thus, for the want of this disposition we see them kept back and obstructed in the ways of God. What a pitiful blindness ! All the business and complicated affairs in which we are immersed by God's will and by the decrees of His divine Providence, are equal to the most delightful contemplation, if one says from the bottom of one's heart, " My God, this is Your will, and, therefore, also mine." Although this is said only in the higher part of the soul without the will seeming to take any share in it, still the sacrifice is no less agreeable to God, and meritorious for oneself. Keep with a firm determination to this practice and you will soon experience its excellent results. If you could also combine with it a certain peace and quietness of mind, a certain gentleness of manner towards others and also towards yourself, without ever showing signs of annoyance, worry, or vexation, what great and meritorious sacrifices you will have made ! At least humble yourself gently after all your faults, and return to God with confidence as if nothing had happened, as the "Spiritual Combat" teaches. As we can never enjoy happiness or peace in this miserable world except in proportion as we blindly submit to the decrees of divine Providence, I shall continue to speak to you about it untiringly. Believe me and rely on divine Providence alone, and abandon everything to His care absolutely and without reserve. Do with simplicity what you believe you ought to do under the circumstances, so as not to tempt God, but do it gently, quietly, and without effort, trouble, excitement, or eagerness; as St. Francis of Sales advises. Of how many anxieties, disappointments and forebodings should we not rid ourselves, if we could only act in this reasonable and Christian manner.

Letter XIX.—*The Happiness of Resignation.*

On the happiness of souls that abandon themselves to God in their afflictions.

It does not astonish me, my dear Sister, that you find it difficult to understand the ways of divine Providence. Neither do I understand them any better than you, but what I know and what you know as well as I, is that God arranges and disposes of all things as He pleases, and makes use of whom He will to carry out His designs at the time and moment He has decided upon. Let us learn then to resign ourselves in all and everything with submission and confidence in Him Who can do all things, and Who disposes of all things according to His own plans. If we could only attain to this state of holy submission we should wait patiently for things to happen at the appointed time, instead of at the time that, in our impatience, we expect them. Abandonment to God's holy providence binds Him, in a way, to find a remedy for everything, and to provide for and console us in all our needs. Remind yourself of this great saying, "Everything passes away, God alone remains." Abandon yourself and all who are dear to you, therefore, to His loving care. In public disasters as in all others we should, by our confidence, glorify His infinite goodness, and then we shall be able to say with David, "We have rejoiced for the days in which thou hast humbled us; for the years in which we have seen evils." Suffering patiently endured, is the lot and the seal of the elect; let us say also with the same prophet, "I was dumb, and I opened not my mouth, because thou hast done it." There is no greater consolation in our trials than a lively faith in the goodness of Him Who sends them, an expectation of that eternal happiness these trials have merited for us, the remembrance of our sins that they help to expiate, and the contemplation of the sufferings that Jesus Christ underwent for love of us. Impatience would only serve to aggravate the evil, while patience has the great power of lightening them. God has different chastisements for each country and these are like so many different rods with which He threatens us and punishes our sins, but always with a fatherly love, since He only threatens and punishes us in this world in order to be able to save us with greater certainty. May He be blessed for ever !

SIXTH BOOK.

ON THE CONTINUATION OF TRIALS, AND FEAR OF THE ANGER OF
GOD.

LETTER I.—*On Temptations.*

On temptations and the fear of giving way to them.

I acknowledge, my dear Sister, that the trial to which our Lord is subjecting you at this moment, is worse than any through which you have hitherto passed. To a soul that loves God, the fear of offending Him is worse than any other. Nothing is more frightful than to have the mind filled with bad thoughts, and to feel the heart carried away to some extent, against one's will, by the violence of the temptation; but that which is, to you, a subject of cruel anguish is, to your directors, a subject for satisfaction. The stronger are your fears, and the greater the horror these temptations cause you, the more evident is it that your will has given no consent to them, and that, far from doing you harm they only serve to increase your merit. In this even more than in other things you ought blindly to follow the advice of those who direct you. Besides, and I say it without the least hesitation, all these fearful temptations, these interior revolts which agitate you, the discouragement which makes you despond, that kind of despair which seems to separate you from God irreparably; all this takes place in the inferior part of your soul without any express and formal consent of the superior part. The latter also, it is true, is often so troubled, and so blinded that it cannot discern what it has, or has not, done; or whether or not it has consented. It is this that makes this trial so painful; but take courage! it is then that you must cast yourself, as well as you can, at the feet of Jesus Christ crucified, humbling yourself and being overcome at the extent of your weakness, but quietly and without vexation, imploring the help of God through His divine Son our Saviour and our Advocate, through the intercession of Mary our sweet mother, and firmly believe that He Who pursues us when we flee from Him will never permit us to be separated from Him against our will.

LETTER II.—*The Fear of Temptation.*

To Sister de Lesen, a Religious of the Annunciation. On the fear of temptations.

———

My dear Sister,

It is an illusion to have too great a fear of combats. Never shrink from the occasions afforded you by God of acquiring merit, and of practising virtue, under the pitiful pretext of avoiding the danger of committing sin by avoiding the struggle. Do soldiers who fight for their king act in this way ! and do we not know that we are soldiers of Jesus Christ and that our whole life is nothing but a continual struggle, and that only he who has fought valiantly will win the crown. Blush for your cowardice, and when you find yourself contradicted or humiliated say that now is the time to prove to your God the sincerity of your love. Put your trust in His goodness and the power of His grace, and this confidence will ensure you the victory. And even should it happen that you should occasionally commit some fault, the harm it will do you will be very easily repaired. This harm, besides, is almost nothing compared to the great good that will accrue to your soul either by your effort to resist, or the merit resulting from victory, or even by the humiliation these slight defects occasion you. And if your temptations are altogether interior ; if you fear to be carried away by your thoughts and ideas, get rid of that fear also. Do not resist these interior temptations directly ; let them fall, and resist them indirectly by recollection and the thought of God ; and if you are not able to get rid of them in this way, endure them patiently. The distrust that makes you try to avoid temptations that are sent to you by God, will cause others more dangerous of which you have no suspicion, for, what temptation could be more evident and plain than the thought which you express when you say that you will never succeed in the spiritual life. What ! Are not all Religious called to this life and you in particular ? Even this weakness so clearly revealed to you by your trial, and your inability to make any serious progress in perfection, or of enjoying any peace except in this way of life, is not this a magnificent sign that God calls you to it more especially than others ? Open your eyes then and recognise the fact that all these thoughts that discourage, trouble, and weaken you, can only emanate from the devil. He wishes to deprive you of that spiritual strength of which you have need in order to overcome the repugnance that nature feels. I implore you not to fall into this trap, and not to continue to look upon the revolt of the passions as a sign of being at a distance from God. No, my dear daughter,

it is, on the contrary, a greater grace than you can imagine.
Becoming persuaded of your own feebleness and perversity, you
will expect nothing from anyone but God and will learn to depend
upon Him entirely.   God alone ought to suffice to the soul who
knows Him.

LETTER III.—*The State of One Tempted.*

An explanation of the state of a soul in temptation and of the
designs of God in regard to it.

One would imagine, my good Sister, that you had never medi-
tated on those numerous texts of holy Scripture in which the
Holy Spirit makes us understand the necessity of temptation,
and the good fruit derived from it by souls who do not allow
themselves to become disheartened.   Do you not know that it has
been compared to a furnace in which clay acquires hardness,
and gold is made brilliant ; that it has been put before us as a
subject of rejoicing, and a sign of the friendship of God ; an
indispensable lesson for the acquirement of the science of the
saints ?   If you were to recall to mind these consoling truths
you would not be able to give way to sadness.   I declare to you
in the name of our Saviour that you have no reason to fear.
If you liked you could unite yourself to God as much or more
than at the times of your greatest fervour.   For this you have
but one thing to do in your painful state, and this is to suffer
in peace, in silence, with an unshaken patience, and an entire
resignation, just as you would endure a fever or any other bodily
ailment.   Say to yourself now and then what you would say
to a sick person to induce him to bear his pain with patience.
You would represent to him that by giving way to impatience,
or by murmuring he would only aggravate the evil and make it
last the longer.   Well ! this is what you ought to say to yourself.
I greatly approve of the order you have received to go to Holy
Communion without taking any notice of your temptations.
Your confessor is right, and would have made a great mistake
if he had listened to what you said on the subject.   " But,"
you will say, " if I have consented to the temptation, and have
committed a mortal sin, what a misfortune ! "   It is not for
you to judge about it, but to obey blindly ; and this opinion is
founded on the great principle that even should the confessor
be mistaken, the penitent cannot be misled in obeying in good
faith in the sight of God, those who are in the position of guides.
" But," you say again, " I should like to know how my confessor
can understand better than I what takes place in my soul during

temptation ? " Useless curiosity ! It is not a question of knowing how this or that—but it is so, and you must obey without reasoning or replying. Nevertheless, as I wish to be kind and gentle towards souls but little accustomed to the spiritual warfare, I will reply to your unexpressed question, and this reply will teach you some important things. You must know first that in each of us there are, as it were, two souls, or two persons ; one, animal, sensitive and earthly which is called the inferior part, the other spiritual, in which the free will resides, and this is called the superior part. Secondly, that all that takes place in the inferior and animal part, such as imaginations, feelings, disorderly movements, are in us, but not of us, and by their own nature are indeliberate and involuntary. All these can tempt us, but cannot compel the will to give free and voluntary consent without which there can be no sin. When the temptation is not strong it is easy to recognise for oneself and to feel that, far from giving consent to it, one rejects it ; but when God permits the temptation to become strong and violent then, on account of the great involuntary agitation taking place in the inferior part, the superior has great difficulty in discerning its own movements, and remains in great perplexity and fear of having consented. Nothing more is wanting to occasion in these good souls the most terrible trouble and remorse which is a further trial permitted by God to prove their fidelity. Confessors who judge calmly and without difficulty, easily discern the truth ; and the great distress the poor soul experiences, and its excessive fear of having consented, are to the confessor proof positive that there has been no full and deliberate consent. In fact we know by experience, that those who consent and give way to temptation do not suffer from these troubles and fears. The greater the temptation and the pain and fear that result, the more certain is the verdict in favour of the person tempted. I join therefore in the opinion of your confessor, and this is the rule I lay down.

1st. Neither examine, nor accuse yourself as a rule about these things.

2nd. Bear peacefully your humiliation and interior martyrdom which, I assure you, is a great grace from God, but a grace which you will not be able to understand properly till after the trial is over.

3rd. This is the interior petition which you ought to make incessantly to God. " Lord, deign to preserve me from all sin, especially in this matter ; but, as for the pain which mortifies, and ought to cure my self-love, and the humiliation and holy abjection which gall my pride and ought to destroy it, I accept them for as long as You please, and I thank You for them as for a grace. Grant, Lord, that these bitter remedies may take

effect and that they may cure my self-love and vanity, and help
me to acquire holy humility and a low opinion of myself which
will form a solid foundation for the spiritual life, and for all
perfection." I find you very ignorant on the subject of temptation. It is true that it does not come from God, Who does not
tempt anyone, as St. James says. It comes, therefore, either
from the devil, or our own temperament and imagination;
but since God permits it for our good, we ought to adore His
holy permission in all things except sin which He detests, and
which we also ought to detest for love of Him. Be careful,
then, not to allow yourself to get troubled and harassed by
these temptations, for this trouble is much more to be feared
than the temptations themselves.

You tell me that you are travelling along the path that is very
dark. That is exactly what is meant by " the way of pure faith."
It is always obscure, and necessitates a complete abandonment
to God. What could be more natural or more easy than to
abandon yourself to so good and merciful a Father Who desires
our welfare more than we do ourselves ? " But," you add, " I
am always in trouble and extremely afraid of having sinned ; this
makes life very miserable, and prevents me possessing the
peace of the children of God." It is so for the present, I know,
but I also know that by these continual terrors the salutary fear
of God takes root in the soul, and is followed by love of Him.
It is thus that God endeavours to make us disgusted with this
life and with its false goods in order to attach us to Himself
alone. Know that none can enjoy the peace of the children of
God who have not shared their trials. Peace is only purchased by
war, and is only enjoyed after victory. If you could only see as
I do the advantages and good to be derived from the state in
which God has permitted you to be, instead of repining as you
do about it you would be making continual acts of thanksgiving.
You are, you say, as deeply involved as the greatest sinners.
Oh ! my dear daughter, this is just what galls your pride. And
what are we in truth but great sinners ? Do we not carry about
with us an amount of misery and corruption, which, without God's
grace, would lead us into the gravest disorders ? This is what
God wishes to make us understand by personal experience
without which we might live and die without ever attaining to a
knowledge of our nothingness, the foundation of humility. Let
us thank God for having solidly laid this foundation, necessary
for the salvation of our souls, and also for the perfection of our
state.

The thought and fear of the justice of the judgments of God is
a great grace, but do not spoil it by carrying this fear so far as to
be troubled and rendered uneasy by it ; because the true and

right fear of God is always peaceful, quiet, and accompanied with confidence. When contrary effects are produced, reject them as coming from the devil who is the author of trouble and despair. "If I had made myself," you say, "I would have done it in such a way that—" Oh! what are you saying here? One must never wish to be other than what God wills. Do you not know that to be able to bear one's miseries, weaknesses, caprices, spiritual defects, follies, and extravagancies of the imagination, is the effect of heroic virtue? What treasures have not these same miseries enabled a crowd of saints of both sexes to acquire! In using them as subjects and matter for interior combats they have served for victories and for the final triumph of grace. You say again, "Of what use can it be to me for my heart to be emptied of one object if it becomes filled by another, and God has no place in it?" Know, daughter, that the heart is so full that it cannot be emptied all at once. It is a work of time, and as the space is enlarged God fills it gradually; but we shall not experience what St. Paul calls the plenitude of God until we are completely empty of all else. This will take a long time, and will require many trials to accomplish the work. Be patient and faithful. Have confidence and you will see the gift of God, and will experience His mercy.

LETTER IV.—*On Different Temptations.*

To Sister Marie-Thérèse de Vioménil. On different temptations.

I see clearly by your letter, my dear Sister, that in the midst of your interior troubles and trials you have made unknowingly very solid progress.

1st. To understand the value of the interior life, and of peace of mind, and to endeavour to acquire them through all your perplexities and drawbacks, is a good step in advance, the rest will follow in time and will be the result of your gentleness towards yourself and others. Let us accustom ourselves to accept everything in a right spirit from the hand of divine Providence, and to bless Him in all things, and for all things, whatever they may be. If we do this we shall find that what causes us most grief will, in the end, be most advantageous to us. Let us trust God and never be wanting in confidence; if necessary let us make more sacrifices, and thus we shall obtain continually fresh graces from Him, and shall increase our riches in Heaven.

2nd.   Thoughts and feelings against our neighbour, if not consented to interiorly, nor shown outwardly, are matter for merit, and are not sinful.   Guard carefully the virtue of charity and gradually all this will subside and come to an end.   If some interior or exterior fault should escape you, be content to humble yourself before God without trouble, but peacefully, and generously repair whatever pain you may have caused, or bad example you may have given.   You will gain more by this apology than you have lost by the fault.

3rd.   Hardness and want of feeling in the reception of the Sacraments is certainly very painful; bear it with patience and humility; do what is in your power gently in the spirit of pure faith; it is the greatest penance that God allots to any soul to purify it from self-seeking and the satisfactions of self-love.

4th.   Try during the day to make of everything a help for raising the heart to God, but without effort or eagerness. Observe the most filial submission to the different arrangements of divine Providence about everything; you will gain more by doing so than by all the spiritual exercises that you perform to please yourself.   Above all make your perfection consist in willing exactly what pleases God, and in the way it pleases Him. His good pleasure is, in fact, the rule of all good will, and the principle of all perfection whether in Heaven or on earth.

LETTER V.—*On the Fear of Being Wanting in Submission.*
To Sister Charlotte-Elizabeth Bourcier de Monthureux (1734).
On the fear of being wanting in submission to God.

God grant me sufficient grace, I do not say, to cure you, but to help you to make your trouble salutary; and may He give me the necessary light to properly understand it.   This trouble is not a fresh one, and I do not perceive any particular change in the state of your soul.   Also I have no new remedy to give you.   All that I can do is to repeat in a different way what I have said to you before.   I have reduced my advice to rules and practices, and I beg of you in the name of Jesus Christ to read this letter, from time to time, in the presence of God and in a spirit of recollection.   The most suitable time for reading it will be when you are a prey to darkness and mental agitation; for, during the time when the storm rages, no other reading can be of any use.   An angel from Heaven himself could not succeed in giving you either light or consolation.   There is no intelligence nor power in the world capable of wresting from the hand of God a soul He has seized in the rigour of His mercy to purify it by suffering.

First rule. Be convinced that all the trials that God sends us in this life are sent in mercy more than in justice; this is why the prophet says that God remembers His mercy even when He is angry with us.

Second rule. Even as God, for the conversion and sanctification of people in the world often sends them purely temporal afflictions such as illness, loss of goods, reverses of fortune, etc., so, likewise, for the purification and sanctification of the souls that belong to Him more entirely, especially in the Religious life, He sends spiritual trials and purely interior afflictions. It is thus that He acts with regard to you, for, although you are suffering from a bodily illness, your principal sufferings arise from the tortures of your mind which react on your body, and redouble and augment your illness, rendering it more painful.

Third rule. As we help people in the world to sanctify themselves in temporal adversities by preaching patience, submission, and continual resignation, so also to souls in pain and interiorly crucified we preach nothing else but abandonment into the hands of God.

Fourth rule. It is a certain and known fact that when one no longer commits either mortal or deliberate venial sin one makes more progress in the ways of God by suffering than by action; from which I conclude that all you need do to ensure your salvation, and even to attain perfection is to endure as patiently as you can, and with peace and interior resignation, the painful state in which you are, imploring the aid of divine grace with an unshaken confidence in the merits of Jesus Christ. This is your principal difficulty, you say. I admit it, but I have no doubt that this practice will become easy enough in time if you try to accustom yourself to it, and follow the rules I will give you.

1st. To take, as you already do, the word "fiat" for your favourite act, and constant exercise.

2nd. To despise and treat as nothing the continual rebellions you feel in your heart during your troubles, and not to attempt to resist them directly but to content yourself with pronouncing the word "fiat"; or, better still, simply to form an interior act. "But," you will say to me, "how can I despise or count as nothing these rebellions of the heart which prove to me that my submission to the will of God is neither interior nor real?" Listen to me, I beg of you, to the end. I feel that God inspires me for your good, and possibly for your consolation. You deceive yourself, Sister, and it is, no doubt, the most cruel of your trials to think that because of these violent, and to all appearances, voluntary rebellions of the heart, your submission is not real. In this respect you are by the divine permission rather like persons in the world with violent temptations to impurity, hatred, aversion, vengeance, or any other unruly impulse, that makes a strong impression but is indeliberate and involuntary. In these poor souls temptation is sometimes so violent, the accursed pleasure which is called precedent and involuntary seizes them so strongly, the tempter raises such a disturbance and causes so much trouble in the sensitive and inferior part, that it becomes impossible for them to discern if they have consented or not in the superior part. Only the confessor can know and discern by certain signs that they have not consented. In the same way God, for your greater trial does not allow you to distinguish that true submission which resides almost unknown to yourself, in the higher part of the soul as in a hiding place. But, thank God, I recognise, see, and feel that you have this true submission which is purely intellectual, spiritual, and well-nigh imperceptible. "But," you say, "how can you recognise, see, and feel in the depths of my soul what I cannot perceive in the slightest degree myself?" I will tell you, but possibly God may not allow you to understand it, or else only for a single moment so that the knowledge of it may not diminish in any way the pain by which He wishes to purify you by crucifying you.

Let us return to the comparison of the other temptations. A person will tell me of the great interior trouble that these temptations to hatred, impurity, etc., cause her, and will add that the fear of having given way to them makes her feel troubled, saddened, and downcast. Here, I say to myself, is proof positive of a great fear of God, of a great horror of sin, and of a great wish to resist. Besides, theology as well as a knowledge of the human heart teaches me that a soul in this interior condition could not give a free, whole, entire and what is called deliberate consent; that if it did, it would immediately lose that interior state and habitual condition in which it is, and which I recognise in it. At the same time it might happen that on account of the violence and frequency of the temptations there may have been some negligence, some momentary surprise. For example : some slight desire for revenge begins, some feeling of pleasure half voluntary, as theology teaches, but, in this condition of the soul, full, entire and deliberate consent is not possible. Also we find by experience that those who really consent to sin are very far from feeling these pains and troubles, this despondency and fear ; they feel no uneasiness whatever. You have only to apply this reasoning to your own state and you will see, as I do, when your soul has regained its calm, that the more you fear and are in trouble about your want of interior submission the more certain it is that you possess it in the depths of your soul. But

God does not allow you to see it as I do, because the assurance
of this submission, by consoling you and delivering you from
your greatest trouble, would put an end to the state of trial in
which God wishes you to remain for a certain time, the better to
purify your soul in the crucible of affliction.   From this I deduce
a third rule ; you must say the same " fiat " about the apparent
absence of this submission that you so much desire, as you do
about your other trials, because it is probably the most useful
of all.   You have perhaps some reason to fear lest this keen desire
may be a seeking of self-love, which would find consolation for
feeling convinced of having endured them well.   Do not be
surprised then that God, wishing to purify your soul from all
the ingenuities of self-love, refuses you this consolation ; and
doubt not that by so doing He confers upon you a great grace.
Therefore when you feel the greatest sadness on account of your
supposed want of submission or the greatest terror at the
idea of the judgments of God, the only thing to do is to say
" Lord, You do not even wish me to know in what state I am,
whether I have the submission I ought to have, or am deprived
of it.   As You will, fiat, I submit to this also."   You can then,
with the intention of regaining interior peace, and to encourage
yourself, say, " At least I feel that by the grace of my God I
desire this submission with a desire that is, perhaps, only too
great and too strong since the fear of not possessing it throws
me into a state of agitation and despondency, and distresses me
more than anything else.   Therefore, as I have a sincere desire
for it, I must have all the effect and the fruit of it, because a
sincere desire is of equal value to the thing desired and makes
the merit or demerit of our good works."
    When nature and the inferior part are thus distressed and
despair of any remedy, or of any consolation for its interior
miseries, then it is that self-love is in its agony and on the point
of expiring.   Ah ! let it die, then, this wretched love of self,
let it be crucified ! this domestic enemy of our poor souls, this
enemy of God and of all good ! I add some advice which will
form the fourth rule.   Practise a blind submission to those
who guide you, and beware in future of omitting a single communion you have been ordered to make.   " But," say you,
" what about this frightful indifference towards God ? "   This,
Sister, is only superficial and in the inferior part.   The superior
part desires God, and He is satisfied, but does not wish you to
know it.   An evident sign that I am right is that you acknowledge to being upset and saddened during all your exercises to
feel that you do not love God, and that you can only pity yourself and tell Him, " My God, I do not love You ! "   Oh ! how
violent must be that profoundly interior desire if you are so

deeply afflicted at the mere idea of not loving Him! This is a
sure sign that in the midst of your apparent coldness, insensibility and indifference God has enkindled in your soul the fire of
a great love which will go on increasing and becoming stronger
and more fervent even by the fears themselves of not loving Him.
"But," you say, "why does He remain so hidden that I can
neither feel His presence, nor know that He is there." This,
Sister, is the simple effect of God's goodness to purify you and
to make you merit a more perfect love. If you understand it
at present you would be so satisfied with your love of God as to
think more of this love than of God Himself Who ought to be its
sovereign and sole object. It would happen to you to the
injury of this love what Fénélon said about the sensible presence
of God, that often by its sweetness it makes us forget God Himself; that is to say that we attach ourselves to the sweetness and
enjoyment more than to God until we actually forget the object
of it, which is, God realised by faith. You cry out and exclaim,
"What, must I then abstain from asking for this love?" Your
heart asks for it without your knowledge; your fears, troubles
and alarms about it are petitions and prayers most powerful
with God Who beholds to what these fears and your most secret
desires tend, and even sees the most hidden recesses of your heart.
Remain, therefore, in peace and fear nothing. If you are in need
of a director God Himself will direct you, or will find you a suitable person. Sacrifice, abandonment, peace and confidence
in all things! In the meanwhile leave everything to God. He
will care for and provide for all. Amen! Amen!

LETTER VI.—*Fear Caused by Self-Love.*

To Sister Marie-Henriette de Mahuet (1731). How the fear
of displeasing God may be caused by self-love.

My dear Sister,

On re-reading your letter to which I have not been able to
reply sooner, I remarked two things in it: many graces of God,
and many very evident marks of self-love. Your pain and distress are, you say, made worse by your uneasiness. Pain and
distress are graces from God which serve to purify and to elevate
the soul; uneasiness is an effect of self-love which is agitated
and complaining under this interior cross by which God desires
to put an end to it in order that you may live a new life in Him.
You experience a miserable inability to make your mind act,
so that all reasoning and reflexion are a weariness to you.
Another sign that God would have you feel that He wishes to do

away with your own petty and miserable operations and to substitute the divine operation without which your progress would
be very slow and painful. But, at the same time, you are very
much afraid of wasting time. Another effect of self-love always
seeking for certainty on which to place reliance, while God wills
you to rely entirely upon Him. Books and directors say enough
to reassure you completely as concerns those foolish fears of
wasting time, suggested by self-love or the devil, in the position
you hold. You always feel confused and in a state of abstraction
that makes you seem stupid, and on account of this you believe
yourself to be under an illusion. God grant that it may not be a
mistake to believe that you are in that state of abstraction which
is one of the greatest graces that God could bestow on a soul. If
you are actually, as you say, in this state I congratulate you ; far
from being an illusion, what you call abstraction can be nothing
else but a profound recollection leading to everything good by the
constant feeling of the presence of God, and by an intimate union
already formed, or about to be formed in your soul. You are in
great peace : another grace ; but you do not dare to think so :
another effect of self-love. Do you not know that the solid peace
established by God in a soul subject to trials, is always without
sensible sweetness ? and besides, does not God necessarily
deprive a soul of sensible sweetness when it would only make use
of it to nourish its self-love ? Could He do us a greater favour
than to kill this domestic enemy by depriving it of its most
essential sustenance, such as sensible spiritual sweetness. It
would indeed be very unjust to complain of this God of infinite
mercy, Who alone knows how to purify your soul, a thing you
would never have been able to do yourself. Your very complaints
prove that you would never have had the courage to put an
end to your self-love which alone impedes the reign of divine
love in your heart. Bless our Lord then for sparing you the
trouble and because He only asks you to allow Him a free hand
to accomplish this work in you. You fear, you say, that your
past unfaithfulness may prevent the operations of God in your
soul. No, my dear Sister, neither your past infidelities, nor yet
your present miseries, darkness, and weakness ought to terrify
you. The only obstacles to the divine operations are your want
of submission and your voluntary annoyance in times of spiritual
poverty, obscurity and weakness. Poverty, darkness and weakness patiently endured without anxiety would, on the contrary,
only facilitate the divine action. You have nothing to fear
but your own fears. However, if you wish to know how you
ought to act during these interior trials I will tell you. You ought
to keep an attitude of peaceful silent waiting, submissive, and
entirely abandoned to the divine will, as one would wait under

shelter until the storm had passed, leaving to God the task of calming the elements let loose. The difference between outward and inward storms is that patience in the former case could not prevent the greatest disasters resulting, while in the latter case it would produce the greatest good in the soul.

Your excessive fears about your past confessions are another result of self-love which desires certainty about everything. God, on the contrary, wills that we should be deprived of the absolute certitude so pleasing to our self-love. We must then make a sacrifice of it to our sovereign Master Who has willed it so to keep us in humiliation and complete dependence. When you do violence to yourself you imagine that it does not please God on account of the imperfection of your interior dispositions. Another very dangerous illusion of the devil by which he hopes either to prevent you from doing good, or else to throw you into a state of uneasiness and trouble after having done so. In the one case, as in the other, he would deprive you of a great deal of your merit. Do not, I beg of you, be trapped in such a palpable snare.

What causes me pleasure is, that in spite of mistakes caused by your inexperience I find in your soul, by the grace of God, the two dispositions most essential to the divine operations, namely, a firm resolution to belong to God without reserve whatever it may cost you, and a firm and constant will to avoid the smallest deliberate fault. Persevere in these dispositions, keep more on your guard than you have done hitherto against the secret seekings of self-love, and you will find that the reign of God will be re-established within you.

LETTER VII.—*The Want of Good-Will.*

To Sister Marie-Thérèse de Vioménil (1838). On the fear of being deficient in good-will.

Yes, my dear Sister, in spite of the fears which haunt you and cause you ceaseless agitation you should apply yourself with all the energy of which you are capable to the practice of an entire and filial abandonment into the hands of God.

1st. Your greatest mistake as well as your deepest affliction is the conviction that you are wanting in that good-will which is the essential condition of the friendship of God. Yes, doubtless you are wanting in a good-will that you can feel and know that you possess ; but there is a certain settled will that God preserves in the centre of your soul, and which I clearly perceive in you in spite of your contrary opinion. Therefore let my decision tranquillize you. Return thanks to God that in depriving you of those gifts which are sensible, and which would only serve as food for self-love, He preserves in you, by a singular effect of His grace, the far more precious gifts of the Spirit. Your abandonment in the midst of the apparent absence of good-will should serve in a powerful way to purify and to augment this imperceptible good-will which is in your soul. This is quite certain. Keep firmly to this belief and in the end you will be convinced of its truth by your own experience.

2nd. What I have just said about the absence of good-will I say also about the lack of power which forms the other subject of your fears. What is this want of power about? It prevents you from making recognized acts in turning towards God. These acts would give you pleasure; but, from the moment that God does not require them you would do wrong to force yourself ot make them. This is an infidelity for which you pay dearly by a great increase of lassitude and desolation. What then is to be done? What you can do, and for which you will never lack power. This is to form a simple desire of good, for God sees all the actions you would wish to perform in this sincere disposition to act rightly. Cease then to distress yourself and to lament over your weakness. Rather say "Fiat, fiat." This will be of infinitely more value than anything that you could say or do according to your own ideas, or to please yourself. I allow you, however, on account of your weakness, to say to yourself from time to time, "I know that usually I must wish to turn to God, but I am not able to do so. I know also that God sees this desire, and that this desire is all that He requires of me even though it be at once arrested, and as it were, stifled. I ought then to remain in peace and to depend on His love." "But," I hear you say to me, "sometimes it seems as if I had lost this desire," and my answer to this is, "why do you experience so much anxiety about this supposed deficiency?" The privation of an object causes pain only in proportion to the affection you entertain for it; if you had no desire for it you would experience no pain at being deprived of it. Are you in great distress about the want of riches, honours, beauty, etc.? No, because these things do not affect you, and you simply do not think about them. It would be the same about the desire for God if the desire itself were, in truth, absent from your mind. If then this apparent absence afflicts you it shows plainly that it is not a real absence. You are only suffering from this dearth of strength and grace because at present God requires no more from you; but you do not experience any want of good desires, since you feel so much sorrow at being unable to form them. Remain therefore in peace in your great spiritual poverty. It is a real treasure if you know how to accept it for the love of God. I see plainly that you have never understood in what true poverty and the nudity of the spirit consists, by which God succeeds in detaching us from ourselves and from our own operations to purify us more completely, and to simplify us. This complete deprivation which reduces us to acts of bare faith and of pure love alone, is the final disposition necessary for perfect union. It is a true death to self; a death very inward, very crucifying, very difficult to bear, but it is soon rewarded by a resurrection, after which one lives only for God and of God through and with Jesus Christ. Understand then your blindness in grieving for what is the surest guarantee of your spiritual progress. After the soul has mounted the first steps in the ladder of perfection, it can scarcely make any progress except by the way of privation and nudity of spirit, of annihilation and death of all created things, even of those that are spiritual. Only on this condition can it be perfectly united to God Who can neither be felt, known or seen. Oh! daughter of little faith, of little intelligence, and of little courage, who afflict yourself and are in despair about what ought to console and rejoice you! Despise your self-love, tell it that it may despair as much as if it found itself struck to the heart, but that your soul will rejoice in God over its despair, even should it be torn with vexation.

3rd. As to the violent desire you sometimes feel to belong entirely to God, and as to what you feel directly after, as though you were being repulsed by an invisible hand, assuredly you have no reason to conclude from this that you are cast away. These spiritual vicissitudes ought to inspire you with an absolutely contrary conviction because this two-fold feeling is an infallible sign of the action of the Holy Spirit who works in us by this inward crucifixion the death of self. But what am I saying! if God allowed you to understand it as I do this would cease to be a trial, but would be changed into an ineffable joy. Happy daughter that you are without knowing it, cease to increase your distress by reflexions quite contrary to the truth of God.

4th. But what can be done you ask when you can no longer make an act of abandonment? Abandon then even this abandonment by a simple " fiat " which then becomes the most perfect abandonment. Oh! grand idea! how it will charm the heart of God, and what an act of the most perfect love it contains! Earthly lovers sometimes come to this through the excess of their insane love. It is your state of privation and sacrifice which has gradually led you to this holy excess of despairing love, and is precisely what God intends to effect by these privations, sufferings and interior weaknesses.

5th. God almost always allows a soul to imagine that this sort of affliction will never end. Why? In order to give occasion for a more complete abandonment without end, without limit, without measure; it is in this that pure and perfect love consists.

6th. Once more; you are only powerless to do those things that God does not wish you to do and that it would not be expedient for you to do if you were able. God effects then within you something so excellent that if you could understand it you would fall prostrate in thanksgiving. Fortunate weakness which prevents you interfering by your wretched and petty operations with those which the Holy Spirit effects in you almost invisibly, but which I can plainly perceive, and for which I return thanks to God for you, poor blind creature that you are.

7th. It is quite unnecessary to explain your troubles and doubts; they are not sins, but simply spiritual crosses, which it is only necessary to bear with unlimited submission. It is on this account that God has made it impossible for you to speak about them, or even to have distinct ideas about them because nothing sanctifies pain so much as silence both exterior and interior. What a great sacrifice the " fiat " becomes then, especially if it is hidden in a simple desire that can scarcely be discerned! God, however, sees all the greatness and extent of this sacrifice. This desire tells Him all that we wish Him to know without allowing us to enjoy the least consolation, nor giving us any certainty. From this there results a terrible agony which drives self-love to despair and assures in us at the same time the triumph of divine charity.

LETTER VIII.—*The Love of Creatures and of God.*

To the same Sister. On the fear of loving creatures more than God.

I am delighted, my dear Sister, that God has made use of my letter to reassure you and to make you understand the reason of the difference between the love that we have for God and that which we feel for creatures, about which you have been so terrified. It is true that if we were more holy our love for God would be more ardent, and more tender. The want of this sensible tenderness is well calculated to humiliate us but ought not to trouble us. It is another misery in addition to so many others which will become for us a source of grace and merit when we understand how to endure it in peace without any vexed feelings of self-love and pride. For, to regard all these miseries in peace and humility, trying all the time to diminish them with the help of God's grace by perpetual vigilance and tranquil prayer is, so to say, no longer to have them, in the sight of God.

Allow yourself to become thoroughly imbued with this truth, as certain as it is but little known. But I add, this coldness we feel towards God ought not to trouble us, because it by no means proves that we are deficient in real love. Recall the words of our Lord to St. Catherine of Siena : " My daughter, I leave to you and all creatures the love which is tender and sensible, and reserve for myself the love of preference which is purely spiritual." This love resides in the apex of the soul ; that impregnable citadel, the key of which is held by free will which governs the whole. As long as charity has not been driven from this citadel, even if the greatest indifference invades the feelings, nothing is yet lost ; and should this sensible coldness be only a painful trial and not an effect of your own negligence, it will help to increase the merit of this genuine love. As an instance a Christian mother would weep and be inconsolable at the death of her beloved children ; but how great soever her sorrow she would not have them return to life at the price of one single venial sin ; do you not see that for this mother the horror of sin is the more heroic in being in opposition to a love that is more sensibly felt ? It is the same with contrition, and all acts of the love of God. These acts are produced in the higher faculties of the soul, and are spiritually accomplished as if without our knowledge, and it is a great advantage to us that it should be so. During this life we are such miserable creatures that every gift that we recognize is changed into poison by our self-love. This is what in a measure compels God to hide the graces He bestows upon us. If we understood our own interests properly we should look upon this salutary blindness as the most precious of all graces, and like holy Job we should never kiss His hand more lovingly than when it seems to weigh most heavily upon us.

LETTER IX.—*On Displeasing God.*

To Sister Marie-Antoinette de Mahuet. On the fear of displeasing God, and deceiving others.

Madame and very dear Sister,

I can only bless God for prolonging your trial, and for renewing those interior sufferings that you experienced in prayer because I find you are acquiring so much profit therefrom and practising so well the virtues I recommended to you, namely, the complete sacrifice of everything, and a total abandonment to the good pleasure of God.

Far from wishing to see you lose these occasions of amassing invaluable merit, I can only congratulate you and exhort you to persevere. Prayer made under such circumstances is indeed very painful, but at the same time it is the most fruitful and meritorious. If this great fear of displeasing God were anything else but a trial I could very easily dispel it. It will suffice to ask you from whence comes this fear, as your conscience is free from any serious matter, and as you feel and even know that usually to please God you would not hesitate to undertake things that are hardest to nature. You clearly perceive that your terrors are nothing but idle imaginations. Therefore if God does not wish you to be entirely delivered from them, you have nothing to do but to drop them like a stone in the water. Take no more notice of them than flies that pass backwards and forwards buzzing in your ears. Despise them and have patience. It is very surprising that after all I have said to you, and all that you have read you still recur to the interior changes and vicissitudes that you experience. It is just as if you imagined yourself obliged to note down all the variations of the atmosphere, and to make known to me that after a few fine days the weather had become stormy and that a hard winter had followed a very beautiful autumn. It is the rule established by God, and these are merely the vicissitudes of a life in which nothing is stable; it is what all the saints have experienced. In fine weather you must prepare for bad times, and when they come as they infallibly will, you must bear them patiently and let the storms blow over and wait for the return of better weather. Instead of all the violent and forced acts you compel yourself to make it would be much better, as I have already told you, to keep yourself in the presence of God in an interior silence of respect, humility, submission, and abandonment. But self-love is always anxious to feel and to enjoy; this cannot be, however, God does not wish it, so you must give in with a good grace. It occurs to your mind, I am aware, that you are deceiving everybody, but you know perfectly well yourself that you do not intend to deceive, and that ought to be enough for you. If it came into your head to kill yourself or to throw yourself from a height you would say at once, " What folly ! I know well that I shall not do it." Put a stop then in the same way to the follies and absurdities of the human mind and particularly of the imagination. These thoughts are like tiresome flies; put up with them patiently. When these have gone others will come and must be endured in the same spirit of patience and resignation.

I bless God for the holy interior dispositions of sacrifice, abandonment, death to self, and complete annihilation with which He inspires you. How can you for one moment imagine that God, Who is so good, would abandon you, when by such a singular change He accomplishes in you such wonderful operations, and favours you as He favours the saints? Indeed, what could He give you more in conformity with the holy Gospel, more sanctifying, or in any way better. Ecstasies and revelations are nothing compared to these interior dispositions of abjection, because it is precisely in these that sanctity and perfection consist. I can only urge you to let nothing be lost of these precious gifts by contrary acts, but when God is pleased to deprive you, apparently, of them, in taking away all these feelings, allow Him to do it. Let Him give, take away, and give again. Is He not Master of His gifts? His holy name be always equally praised.

LETTER X.—*Fear of Making No Progress.*

To Sister Marie-Thérèse de Vioménil. On the fear of making no progress, and of not doing enough penance.

Do not be astonished, my dear Sister, at making apparently so little progress. One does not ever advance in spiritual as one does in visible works. The business of our sanctification and perfection ought to be the work of our whole life-time. I notice that your natural vivacity and eagerness intrude into everything, and from this proceed anxieties, discouragement, and troubles which lead you astray in causing you distress. Here is the remedy! As long as you feel a sincere good-will to belong to God, a practical appreciation for everything that leads you to God, and a certain amount of courage to rise after your little falls, you are doing well in the sight of God. Have patience with yourself then; learn to bear with your own weaknesses and miseries gently, as you have to put up with those of your neighbour. Be satisfied to humble yourself quietly before God, and do not expect to make any progress except through Him. This hope will not be disappointed, but God will realise probably by a hidden operation which will take place in the centre of your soul, and this will cause it to make considerable progress without your knowledge.

You are uneasy about your penance. Oh! my dear daughter, how could you perform a better penance, and one in which there is less of your own will, than to bear patiently the crosses that come from God? Besides, all our crosses come certainly from Him when they are the necessary, natural, and inevitable consequences of the state in which divine Providence permits us to be settled. These are the heaviest crosses, but also the most sanctifying because they all come from God. Crosses from our heavenly Father, crosses from divine Providence, how much easier to bear they are than those we fashion for ourselves, and embrace voluntarily. Then love yours, my dear Sister, since they have been prepared for you by God alone for each day. Let Him do this; He alone knows what is suitable for each one of us. If we remain firm in this, submissive and humbled under all the crosses sent by God, we shall find in them, at last, rest for our souls. Thus we shall enjoy an unshaken peace when, by our submission, we shall have merited from God to be made to feel that divine unction which belongs to, and is a part of the cross since Jesus Christ died upon it for us. But you ask how the spiritual life can be compatible with this state of trouble and darkness. Ah! my dear daughter, how many are mistaken about this! Do not you share their delusion. The spiritual life, gentle, and tranquil as I have always described it to you to inspire you with a taste for it, is only to be found in two sorts of persons; first, in those who are entirely separated from the world and have nothing to do with its affairs; secondly, sometimes, but more rarely, in persons living in the world, when by dint of having overcome themselves, and detached themselves from everything, they live in the world, but are not of it; that is to say they belong to it outwardly, but not in mind and heart. But this absence of business and of care is far from constituting the essential part of the spiritual life, or from forming its merit. There is another sort of interior life, which, devoid of sweetness, is on this account all the more meritorious, and it is to this that you must conform yourself; the other may follow later. This interior life may also be divided under two heads, first, the generous fulfilment of the divine will whenever manifested to us either by the precepts it has itself laid down for us, or by our Rule, or by the commands or desires of our Superiors; secondly, to receive everything as coming from the hand of God, whether business affairs, adversity, illness, difficulties, or annoyances. Sometimes, however, one forgets oneself. You must expect this to happen. What is to be done then? You know what, return quietly to yourself, regain your tranquillity with submissiveness, humble yourself gently before God, never be discouraged nor disheartened, and above all take good care, according to the teaching of St. Francis of Sales, not to be grieved at having been grieved, nor to be angry at having been angry, nor worried at having been worried, because this would be to go from bad to worse, and would augment still more the interior trouble. This is the rock ahead of lively persons.

LETTER XI.—*On Fears About Confession.*

—————

I can only repeat to-day, my dear Sister, what I have so often told you before. God wishes to make you do penance and to sanctify you by the endurance of personal offences that wound you, by interior crosses, and more especially by troubles of conscience. I only ask you in all these trials for a little submission and resignation such as you practise in the different circumstances of life, such as losses, illnesses, infirmities, etc. I forbid you to dwell voluntarily on the uneasiness that torments you with regard to your confessions. Be at peace. Blind obedience can never deceive you. As for contrition which is the only thing that you might have some reason to fear about ; if you mention in each confession a sin of your past life without going into details you will have absolutely nothing to fear. The best sign of having true contrition is to fall no more into grave sins, and to do your best to get rid of those that are lighter. Therefore remain in peace on this point, enduring patiently the different returns of these troubles. As you are infirm these troubles will do instead of fasting or taking the discipline, or wearing a hair shirt, but with this difference, that whereas in these latter penitential exercises self-love can be met with again and satisfied, in the former penances sent by our heavenly Father to men and women for whose salvation He has a special desire, there is only the pure will of God.

—————

LETTER XII.—*Rules to Free Oneself from these Fears.*

—————

It depends on yourself, my dear Sister, to free yourself once and for all from the fears which torment you on the subject of your confessions. It only requires a grain of faith and of docility in following the perfectly safe rules that I will outline for you.

1st. Never ask to be freed from this trouble, because God has made it perfectly clear to you why He permits it. It is because He wishes to be your only support, your sole consolation, and to have your complete confidence so that no other sensible motive may interfere to spoil the singleness of your love. Finding that you had not the courage to attain to this purity of love by making heroic sacrifices like the saints, He leads you gradually to it by less painful means. Return thanks to Him for so much condescension, and compel yourself to submit to His merciful designs.

2nd. Prepare for your confessions in the following manner.

After a quarter of an hour at the very utmost for the examen, and without taking too much trouble but doing it as you best can, you will say to yourself, " By the mercy of God I live in a state of habitual contrition since I would not commit a mortal sin for anything this world could give me. I even feel a horror of venial sin, although, unhappily, I have not yet left off committing it ; therefore I only have to make an act of contrition as best I can, and as He has put it into my heart by His grace." That will not take long, a few minutes will suffice, and the best way to make acts of contrition is to pray that God will Himself produce them in you.

3rd. " But what if it should be impossible to remember any distinct fault ? " This is what you must say : " Father, I have not light enough to see my ordinary faults but I accuse myself in general of all the sins of my past life, and particularly of such and such a sin of which I ask pardon of God from the bottom of my heart." After that accept tranquilly the penance that your confessor gives you, and do not have any doubt whatever that the absolution he pronounces confers on you all the graces attached to this sacrament.

What on earth, I ask you, could be easier or more consoling ? If you adopt this method you will be delivered from all the anxieties that have so much harassed you up to now. I should like this little rule to be known and practised by most of the members of your community who experience the same difficulty as yourself, and who, like you, could so easily be set right.

LETTER XIII.—*On Fears About Contrition.*

To Sister Marie-Thérèse de Vioménil.

You desire the impossible, my dear Sister, you want to feel what is not perceptible by the senses, and to enjoy a certainty that we cannot possess during this life. True contrition which remits sin is, of its nature, entirely spiritual and consequently above the senses. It is true that with certain persons and on certain occasions it becomes sometimes sensible, and then it is much more consoling to self-love, but is not on that account either more efficacious, or more meritorious. This tenderness of feeling does not in any way depend upon us, neither is it by any means essential for obtaining the remission of our sins. A great number of souls truly devoted to God hardly ever experience this tenderness, and the fear inspired in them by this deprivation is the best proof that they are not responsible for it. The coldness they feel, far from depriving them of true repentance is, on the contrary, one of the best penances they could offer to God.

What I now say on the subject of contrition in general, I say in particular about the sovereignty of this sorrow, a quality that is usually the one least felt. It must be asked of God and you must wait till He produces it Himself in your heart by His grace. To persist in tormenting yourself after this would be to allow yourself to fall into the devil's trap. Nothing should astonish us less than to be sometimes touched and affected, and at others to find ourselves callous and insensible to everything. This is one of the inevitable vicissitudes of the spiritual life. Fiat! fiat! resignation is the only remedy. It is certain that God always gives what is necessary to those souls who fear Him. The gifts He bestows on them are not always the most apparent to the senses, nor the most agreeable, nor the most sought after, but the most necessary and solid; all the more so, usually, in being less felt and more mortifying to self-love; for that which helps us most powerfully to live to God is what best enables us to die to self.

LETTER XIV.—*On General Confession*

To Sister Marie-Antoinette de Mahuet. On general confession.

My dear Sister,

Your fears have no reasonable foundation, and you ought to reject them as dangerous temptations. When, in the course of one's life one has made a general confession in good faith; all the ideas and anxieties that follow are so many idle scruples which the enemy makes use of to trouble the peace of the soul, to make one lose time, and to weaken and diminish one's confidence in God. Do not let us foolishly fall into this trap; let us abandon all the past to the infinite mercy of God, all the future to His fatherly Providence, and think only of profiting by the present. The " fiat " formed in the mind by repeated acts and gradually reduced to an habitual disposition, leads to all that perfection which ignorant and mistaken people seek far and wide in all sorts of ways. For the rest, do not imagine that you tire me by speaking of your miseries. By dint of seeing nothing but poverty and misery in oneself, one is not surprised at finding the same in others. But if, in peace and humility they annihilate themselves before God and ask for grace, working with His assistance to diminish their faults and to overcome themselves, they may be considered, in a way, not to have these faults. This is what Fénelon thought. May it sink deeply into your heart as well as this sentence which I find in the same author, and which I copy for you because I think it is exactly what will console and encourage you. "We are obliged to live and to die in the deepest uncertainty, not only as to the judgments of God about us, but also as to our own dispositions." "We must," says St. Augustine, "have nothing of our own to present to God but our own miseries, but then we have His very great mercy which is our only title to His love, through the merits of Jesus Christ." Often reflect on these beautiful sayings in which you will find peace for your mind, abandonment, confidence, and the greatest certainty in the very midst of doubt.

LETTER XV.—*Different Fears.*

To Sister Marie-Thérèse de Vioménil. On the same subject—Different fears.

My dear Sister,

As neither my advice nor my efforts can deliver you from your fears about your confessions I can see nothing for you but to resign yourself to them. Regard these troubles as a penance sent you by your heavenly Father, but never stop to think about them voluntarily because I am convinced that in your general confession you mentioned everything ; or, at any rate, you had a sincere desire to say everything ; that is enough. I do not hesitate to assure you, before God, that in this confession no omission of any importance could have been made, therefore remain in peace about it.

You are still distressed that certain sublime states that you admire in others, you can neither dare to ask for, nor even to desire for yourself. Here are two remedies to alleviate your trouble and to make you derive advantages from your weakness. Firstly, to humble yourself, and to lament interiorly, but without vexation, at beholding yourself so far from such holy dispositions. Secondly to desire interiorly to have the wish for them. This desire to desire is the first degree from which one passes gradually to a real desire, and this in its turn by dint of being renewed and of dwelling in the heart gets stronger and finally takes root. Try to recall often to your mind this great rule : God has placed me in this world only to know, love and serve Him, and could not have created me for any other purpose, therefore I will attain this end to the best of my power. For the rest He may do with me what best pleases Him, I abandon myself entirely to His holy will which can only will my salvation and eternal happiness in the life to come. It is for this only that He makes me endure so many interior and exterior afflictions. May He be blessed for ever !

LETTER XVI.—*Hatred of Sin.*
On the same subject. Different fears.

My dear Sister,

In all that forms the subject of your letter I see no reason for alarm. You are not pleased, you say, about your want of submission and of patience during suffering. Provided that this discontent does not turn to vexation, trouble, or discouragement, it will inspire you with a sincere interior humility, a profound self-contempt which will please God better and enable you to make more progress than a patience and submission that you felt that you possessed, which would perhaps have only served to feed self-love by almost imperceptible satisfactions. You cannot yet, you say, make known to me anything else but miseries. I can well believe it, since as long as we are in this life we cannot find anything in ourselves but what is imperfect and miserable. Do you want a remedy for all these miseries ? It is this : While detesting the sins that are the cause of them, love, or at least accept their consequences which are the feeling of abjection and a contempt for yourself; but do so without trouble, vexation, uneasiness or discouragement. Remember that God, without willing sin, has made of it a very useful instrument for keeping us always in a state of abjection and self-contempt. Without this bitter remedy we should succumb to the enticements of self-love. Believe me, you must always keep cheerful, steadfast and tranquil in the midst of your miseries, making at the same time efforts to diminish them ; as you advance further you will constantly discover fresh ones. It was this clear knowledge of their own weakness and nothingness, which, becoming ever more distinct, increased the humility of the saints ; but this humility by God's grace is always joyful and peaceful. It goes so far as to make them love spiritual poverty which in this way becomes a real treasure. Learn that under this heap of refuse God hides the gifts He bestows on us to conceal them from the satisfactions of self-love and foolish esteem. I do not blame your tears but I wish that while you are shedding them over your pains you would do so before God and for His sake. In this way instead of feeling their bitterness you would discover in them a hidden sweetness which would tend to increase interior peace by producing an entire submission to the divine will.

As for the supposed want of contrition which distresses you, you need see in it only a trap laid for you by the devil to destroy your peace. Do you not know that an apparently bitter contrition accompanied by torrents of tears is not the best, and that God by no means exacts such from you ? With all these beautiful signs true contrition may be wanting; and, on the contrary, without any feelings of the sort one can have the contrition that justifies. This consists in the will to hate and to avoid sin, and resides in the superior faculties of the soul and consequently is not to be felt as it is purely spiritual. Remain then in peace and do not attend to your self-love which wants to feel and to enjoy this contrition so as to be certain of possessing it. God does not desire this for several reasons, but above all to keep us always in holy humility, and in a certain fear which helps towards our salvation. Enter into His designs, and when you feel no regret for your sins humble yourself profoundly. Offer to God in a spirit of penance this keen dread of not possessing the requisite sorrow ; make a sacrifice of this trouble of mind to God, and abandon yourself entirely to His mercy ; He intends to lead you by the way of obscurity and fear, to Heaven. The greatest saints themselves have no exemption from this law but, more faithful than we, they abandoned themselves entirely to God and, by placing their whole confidence in Him, kept themselves always in peace. As for the review of conscience that souls careful of their state are in the habit of making at least every year, one must remember that it is not a matter of obligation but a work of devotion and humility. Each person gives to this examination as long a time as he desires, with the advice of the confessor, and one can always be certain of saying more than is necessary. At the hour of death there is no necessity to make a general confession. One can accuse oneself of the graver sins in a general way out of compunction, or in a spirit of penance, but without too much introspection. It is much better to occupy the time in making more meritorious acts of religion, of faith, hope, contrition and love of God, of resignation, abandonment, and confidence in the merits of Jesus Christ, and of union with Him. Finally the most solid preparation for death is that which we make every day, by a regular life, a spirit of recollection, of annihilation, of abnegation, patience, charity, and union with our Lord.

I do not like to find you attaching so much importance to the little comforts that are given you in your illnesses, such as getting up a little later, having your bed warmed, eating a little more at the collation. Follow in all this, with the greatest simplicity, discretion and obedience and without thinking too much about yourself, what you feel and judge to be necessary. Provided also that the interior passions are thoroughly overcome, and that you are not wanting in patience, submission and a total abandonment to God, in gentleness and humble forbearance with your neighbour, for these are the most essential virtues and more sanctifying than any exterior mortifications. People who are

rather pious are not wanting in outward practices; usually,
their great mistake is to make their whole sanctity consist in
external works, leaving the enemy, namely, self-love and the
passions, alone. They make a great to-do about having eaten
a few mouthfuls extra on a feast-day but will not attend to these
essential things. Such piety is like that of the Jews who had a
scruple about entering Pilate's house because he was a pagan,
yet thought nothing of putting Jesus to death. Would to God
that these deplorable illusions were never found among Religious.
At any rate do you, my dear Sister, avoid them, and without
neglecting what is external, give your principal attention to the
interior.

LETTER XVII.—*Remorse and Rebellion.*

To Sister Marie-Anne-Thérèse de Rosen. On remorse of
conscience and the rebellion of the passions.

Do all you can to calm your soul on the subject about which
you have consulted me, first because the motives which you
believe you have to make you uneasy have no foundation in
fact. The only danger lies in the uneasiness itself.

When the reproaches of your conscience, however well merited
they may be, throw you into a state of trouble and depression;
when they discourage and upset you, it is certain that they come
from the devil who only fishes in troubled waters, says St. Francis
of Sales. The first care of a soul experiencing these troubles
ought to be to prevent them, to stifle them, or better still to
despise them. Let it say with St. Teresa, "What my weakness
finds impossible, will become easy with the help of the grace of
God, and this He will give me in His own good time. For the
rest, I desire neither perfection, nor to lead a spiritual life, except
as far as it should please God to give them to me and at the time
He has appointed to do so." You must try to acquire a habit
of making these two acts by a constant repetition of them in your
heart. The second will contribute marvellously to reproduce
entire abandonment, which is the special attraction of souls
desiring to belong unreservedly to God.

2nd. The rebellion of the passions, and that excessive sensitiveness which causes one to be put out beyond measure on the
slightest provocation ought not to disquiet, nor to discourage
anyone suffering from them, nor to make her think that her
desire of sanctification is not sincere. This mistake and the
discouragement it occasions are more harmful than all the other
temptations. To get rid of them, or to overcome them we must

w

be well persuaded that these rebellions, and this extreme sensitiveness are sent to us by God to be the ground of our combats and victories; and that these little falls are permitted to help us to practise humility. Looked upon in this light our falls will be incomparably more useful to us than victories spoilt by vain self-complacency. This is a very certain and a very encouraging truth. We must be convinced, thoroughly convinced that our miseries are the cause of all the weakness we experience, and that God, in His mercy, allows them for our good. Without them we should never be cured of a secret presumption and a proud confidence in ourselves. Never should we be able to rightly understand that all that is bad is ours, and that all that is good is from God alone. To acquire a habit of thinking thus it is necessary to pass through a great number of personal experiences, and there is a greater necessity for this the more deeply rooted these vices are, and the greater the hold they have on the soul.

3rd. You must never feel surprised at finding that a day of great recollection is followed by one full of dissipation; this is the usual condition in this present life. These changes are necessary, even in spiritual things, to keep us in humility, and a state of dependence on God. The saints themselves have passed through these alternations, and others still more troublesome. Only try not to give rise to them yourself; but should this, unfortunately, happen, then humble yourself peacefully and without vexation, which would be a worse evil than the original one; then endeavour to regain self-control, and to return to God; doing so quietly without over-eagerness, and by means of a total holy abandonment to God's ways.

4th. Your present method of prayer is good; continue to practise it. The humble feelings of the heart, the submissive attitude of the soul before God are worth more than a multitude of formal acts constantly reiterated; they are acts straight from the heart, stronger and more efficacious with God although not always so sensibly felt, nor as clearly perceived, nor as consoling as the former. God takes from us this multiplicity to give us instead something better, more simple and better calculated to unite us to Him.

5th. The person of whom you speak is not wanting in the love of God. She has as much as is necessary, but God has deprived her of the knowledge of it for fear that she should pride herself on it, and in order to prevent her preferring the sensible pleasure of it, to Him who ought to be its sole object. Let her be consoled about this, while at the same time she should always desire to love Him more without wishing to know it, or to be able to be certain of it.

6th. The opposition and perpetual contradiction between your thoughts and feelings is nothing else than that inner strife spoken of by the Apostle when he says, " the spirit wars against the flesh, and the flesh against the spirit." None of the saints have been exempt from this rule. It is true that this interior war is more violent with some people, and about some things more than others, and also at a certain age, or time or occasion, but whether more or less violent, no harm is done to a soul that fights with a determination never to be beaten nor discouraged. On the other hand, the greater the violence of the attacks the more serious are the combats, and consequently, the more glorious the victories. The greater the merit, the higher the sanctity, and the grander the recompense. These happy results are all the more certain the less they are felt, and especially if a more profound humiliation is experienced.

Oh ! if only this interior abjection were accepted, loved and valued, no one would consent to be without it, because it brings the soul nearer to God. This great God has, in fact, declared that He draws near to those who humble themselves and who love to be humiliated. If it is good for us to be humbled in the sight of others it is no less useful to be annihilated in our own eyes, in our pride and self-love which are put an end to in this way. It is thus, in fact, that they are gradually extinguished in us, and for this purpose does God permit so many different subjects for interior humiliation. It only remains to know how to profit by them, by following the advice of St. Francis of Sales, and practising acts of true humility, gently and peacefully ; and this will drive out false humility which is always in a state of vexation and spite. Vexation and spite under humiliation are so many acts of pride, just as worry and irritation during suffering are so many acts of impatience. Let us not forget this, and let us take good care not to look upon the want of feeling we experience for the things of God as callousness ; it is simply dryness, and a trial as inevitable and ordinary as distractions. If it is constant it is a still better sign, because it is in this way that God prepares the soul to proceed by pure faith, the most sure and meritorious way.

One should repeat continually to anyone in this state," Peace, peace, remain in peace, and keep retired within your soul." Preserve a constant desire of the interior life. This single attraction ought to suffice to make you live within yourself, and in constant communication with God. The results will follow in their own time. Guard above all against anything likely to withdraw you from this good disposition ; avoid all occasions of losing it ; humble yourself when you have failed about it, but do not ever worry yourself, nor distress yourself about anything whatever, nothing could harm you more than that.

_____

LETTER XVIII.—*God Alone can Remove These Trials.*

To Sister Marie-Thérèse de Vioménil. God alone can remove these trials.

_____

1st. To alleviate your troubles and regrets, my dear Sister, I have only two things to say to you. Everything comes from God, and, on our part, all merit consists in acquiescing in the will of God. Whether willingly or by compulsion it will always be accomplished ; let us unite ourselves to it with all the strength of our own will, and thus we shall have nothing to fear. Anguish of the heart, and involuntary rebellion only augment the merit of submission. If you fear lest you do not possess this virtue, ask God to grant it to you, saying to Him interiorly, " Lord, I desire and will to have this entire submission and I offer you the anguish by which I am tormented in union with the agony of Jesus Christ Your beloved Son in the garden."

2nd. Try to avoid all useless reflexions which only embitter the heart. When, in spite of yourself, you feel irritated, bear this trouble patiently, and when you feel impatient, then is the time to make greater efforts to have patience in enduring this impatience itself, and to resign yourself to the want of resignation.

3rd. Read in the book of the " Holy Ways of the Cross," the chapters which bear upon your present state. You will find therein all the instruction, support, and consolation which you can possibly require, but do not expect to find in them what no one on earth can possibly give you. God alone can remove this trial from you, wait His time with patience. You have always counted too much on human help ; God has taken it away from you to compel you no longer to depend on anyone but Him alone, by abandoning yourself entirely to His paternal care. The more painful and violent your trial is, the more certain do I become about your salvation and perfection. You will be able to understand this later just as I do.

4th. As Jesus Christ crucified is our only model, and as He wishes to save us by making us like to Himself, He strews crosses in the path of each one of us in order to keep us in the way of salvation. If we are faithful the reverses that cross our lives will form our riches. And see how great is the mercy of our loving Saviour ; after having passed through the most severe trials, and accomplished the most painful sacrifices, what is left seems hardly to count, and the heaviest crosses begin to seem quite light. Oh! happy experience, as sweet in its effects as, at first, it appeared difficult to nature.

Letter XIX.—*On Relapses.*

To the same Sister. On the same subject and on relapses.

My dear Sister,
The recital you have given me of your troubles, and, above all of your faults and interior revolts, has inspired me with the most lively compassion ; but, as to a remedy I really know of no other than that which I have so often pointed out to you ; each time you have a fresh proof of your misery to humble yourself, to offer all to God, and to have patience. If you fall again do not be any the more disquieted or troubled the second time than the first, but humble yourself yet more profoundly and do not fail to offer especially to God the interior suffering and confusion caused by the revolts and faults to which your weakness has given rise. Even if fresh occasions occur, return each time to God with an equal confidence, and endure as patiently as possible the re-newed remorse of conscience and these interior trials and re-bellions, and continue to act in this way. If you always do so you must understand that you will hardly lose anything, there will be much even gained in these involuntary interior rebellions from which you are suffering. Whatever faults occur, provided you endeavour always to return to God and also to yourself in the manner I have just explained, it is impossible that you should not make great progress. Oh! how little are solid virtue and true interior abnegation known ! If once for all you would learn to humble yourself sincerely for your least faults, and would rise directly by confidence in God with peace and sweetness, that would prove to you a good and certain remedy for the past, and a powerful help, and efficacious protection for the future.

I greatly approve of your keeping away from discussions and arguments, and of your dislike of them. There certainly is, as a rule, a great amount of petty illusions and self-love about such things, for this wretched self-love, says St. Francis of Sales, mixes with everything, intrudes everywhere, spoils everything. This is the effect of human misery to which we are all more or less subject. When we recognise it in others there are two things we have to do ; first we must find excuses for those whom we notice to have been led away by it, and secondly to fear for ourselves and watch over our own conduct so that we may not in our turn be subjects of scandal to our neighbour.

LETTER XX.—*Depression under Trials*.

To the same Sister (1738). On depression during trials, distractions and resentment.

———

1st. You would be mistaken, my dear Sister, to reproach yourself too much for your want of resignation, because I do not consider it at all voluntary. Great afflictions are inevitably followed by a certain depression ; but those souls that are faithful to God rise again quietly by their confidence and filial abandonment to divine Providence. It seems, sometimes, as if it were impossible to do this, or at any rate to do it properly, but one must not be discouraged on this account. Better indeed to make of this weakness itself a subject for renewed acts of resignation to the divine goodness and to remain peacefully and patiently in one's own nothingness. Thus we shall fulfil the designs of God who permits us to fall into this state of depression and weakness to make us better understand and feel our misery. He wills that there should not be in us the least atom of confidence in ourselves, but that we should rely solely on His all-powerful grace.

2nd. I ought to tell you that for a long time past I have remarked in you a great grace to which you pay no attention. You seem to me to become ever more deeply convinced of your miseries and imperfections. Now that happens only in proportion to our nearness to God, and to the light in which we live and walk, without any consideration of our own. This divine light as it shines more brightly makes us see better and feel more keenly the abyss of misery and corruption within us, and this knowledge is one of the surest signs of progress in the ways of God and of the spiritual life. You ought to think rather more of this, not to pride yourself on it, but to be grateful for it. Nothing more is necessary at present but to strive to love holy abjection, poverty, and horror of yourself which begins in this deep knowledge experienced by you. When you have attained this you will have taken a fresh step still more decided towards your spiritual advancement. See then how great is the goodness of God ! He makes use of the sight that you have of your poverty to enrich you. This poverty becomes a treasure to those who understand, accept, and love it, because it is the will of God. This joyful acquiescence in our misery does not exclude, however, the desire of finding a remedy for it, because, if we ought to love the abjection which is the result of our defects, we ought at the same time to hate the defects themselves, and to make use of the most energetic means of getting rid of them.

3rd. Urgent occupations and the interruptions of worldly business are, in the sight of divine Providence who wills and permits them, of equal value as quiet recollection and silence. Instead of the prayer of quiet you then make a prayer of patience, of suffering and of resignation. "But one sometimes loses patience"; well, this is the distraction of this prayer, and you must try to regain it, and to get calm with the thought that God wills or permits what upsets you, and causes you pain; but above all take great care not to lose your temper at feeling impatient, or to get worried at being upset. By humbling yourself quietly you will gain more than you have lost.

4th. I need not enter into minute details as regards the keen pain you describe. I understand all the different distressing thoughts that fill your mind and all the heart-ache they cause, but here again, my dear daughter, is an excellent prayer more sanctifying than any ecstasies, if you know how to make use of it. How can you do so? In this way. (1) Often pray for the person who is the cause of your trouble. (2) Keep perfectly silent, do not speak about it to anyone to relieve your pain. (3) Do not voluntarily think about it but turn your thoughts to other subjects that are holy and useful. (4) Watch over your heart that you may not give way in the very least bit to bitterness, spite, complaints, or voluntary rebellion. (5) Try to speak well of the person, cost what it may, to regard her favourably, to act about her as if nothing had happened. I realise, however, that you will find it difficult in future to treat her with the same confidence without being a saint, which you are not yet. (6) But at least do not fail to render her a service when occasion arises and to wish her all possible good.

LETTER XXI.—*On Humble Silence and Patience During Trials.*

Take courage, my dear Sister, and do not imagine that you are far from God; on the contrary you have never been so near Him. Recall to your mind the agony of our Lord in the Garden of Olives, and you will understand that bitterness of feeling and violent anguish are not incompatible with perfect submission. They are the groanings of suffering nature and signs of the hardness of the sacrifice. To do nothing at such a time contrary to the order of God, to utter no word of complaint or of distress, is indeed perfect submission which proceeds from love, and love of the purest description. Oh! if you only knew how in these circumstances to do nothing, to say nothing, to remain in humble silence full of respect, of faith, of adoration, of submission, abandonment and sacrifice, you would have discovered the great secret of sanctifying all your sufferings, and even of lessening them considerably. You must practise this and acquire the habit of it quietly, taking great care not to give way to trouble and discouragement should you fail, but at once return to complete silence with a peaceful and tranquil humility. For the rest, depend with unshaken confidence on the help of grace, which will not be refused to you. When God sends us great crosses and finds that we sincerely desire to bear them well for the love of Him, He never fails to support us invisibly, and in such a way that according to the greatness of the cross will be the amount of resignation and interior peace, sometimes indeed even greater, so immense is the bounty of Jesus Christ, our Master, and of the spiritual graces He has merited for us. Let us conclude with this—that nearly everything consists in having a good will; and to make our spiritual progress assured God will mercifully do the rest. Knowing the full extent of our weakness, misery, and incapacity for doing anything good, He sustains and fortifies us, working this good in us Himself by His divine Spirit. The practice of accepting at each moment the present state in which God places us, can keep us in peace of mind and cause us to make great progress without undue eagerness. Besides this it is a very simple practice. We should adhere to it strongly but nevertheless with an entire resignation to whatever God requires about it.

A great sign that we are not deceived about our love of God is : Firstly, when we desire all that pleases Him, and secondly when we have a great horror of sin, even the least, and strive never to commit any deliberately. Since God has given you the grace to take my favourite maxims to heart concerning submission, abandonment and sacrifice, be assured that He will enable you to practise them, however imperfectly. But as you are so impetuous about everything, you want to attain at one bound to the highest perfection in these virtues. That cannot be, you must attain to them gradually and even while committing many small faults which will serve to humble you, and to make you realise your great weakness before God. Interior rebellion in these circumstances does not prevent submission in the higher part of the soul. Read often the 57th letter in the third book by St. Francis of Sales. This letter has always charmed me. It will make clear to you the distinction between the two wills in the soul, the exact knowledge of which is an essential point in the spiritual life.

LETTER XXII.—*To Bear with Oneself.*

To Sister Marie-Thérèse de Vioménil. On the realisation of her misery and on exterior difficulties.

I might say to you, my dear Sister, what our Lord said to Martha! Why so much solicitude and trouble? How can you still confound, as you do, the care that God commands you to take about your salvation, with the uneasiness that He reproves? As you try to abandon your temporal affairs to divine Providence while taking care at the same time not to tempt God; do the same for your spiritual progress, and, without neglecting the care of it, leave the success to God, hoping for nothing except from Him. But do not ever dwell on such diabolical thoughts as: I am always the same, always as little recollected, as dissipated, as impatient, as imperfect. All this afflicts the soul, overwhelms the heart and casts you into sadness, distrust and discouragement. This is what the devil desires; by this pretended humility and regret for your faults he is delighted to deprive you of the strength of which you have need for the purpose of avoiding them in future, and of repairing the harm they have done you. Bitterness spoils everything and on the contrary gentleness and sweetness can cure everything. Bear with yourself therefore patiently, return quietly to God, repent tranquilly, without either exterior or interior impetuosity but with great peace. If you act thus you will gradually become calm, and this practice will cause you to make more progress in the ways of God than all your agitations could possibly effect. When one feels a little peace and sweetness interiorly it is a pleasure to enter into oneself and one does so willingly, constantly, without any trouble, almost without reflexion.

Believe me, my dear Sister, and place your whole confidence in God through Jesus Christ; abandon yourself more and more entirely to Him, in all, and for all, and you will find by your own experience that He will always come to your assistance when you require His help. He will become your Master, your Guide, your Support, your Protector, your invincible Upholder. Then nothing will be wanting to you because, possessing God, you possess all, and to possess Him you have but to apply to Him with the greatest confidence, to have recourse to Him for everything great and small without any reserve, and to speak to Him with the greatest simplicity in this way: "Lord, what shall I do on such an occasion? What shall I say? Speak, Lord, I am listening; I abandon myself entirely to You; enlighten me, lead me, uphold me, take possession of me."

I am sorry for the difficulties and worries of which you tell me, but recollect that patience and submission to God in the midst of annoyances that are permitted by His providence will enable you to make more progress than the quietest and most recollected life. The latter always tends to flatter self-love ; the former, on the contrary, afflicts and crucifies it, and thus makes us attain true peace of mind by union with God. When you find yourself in such utter dejection that you cannot make a single act of any virtue whatever, beware of tormenting yourself by violent efforts but keep simply in the presence of God in a great silence of utter misery, but with respect, humility and submission like a criminal before his judge who sentences him to a chastisement he has well merited : and understand that the interior silence of respect, humility and submission are worth more and purify better than all the acts that you, uselessly, force yourself to make, and which only serve to increase the trouble of the soul. The character of the person to whom you allude is very good, I own ; but while praising God for all the good gifts He has bestowed upon her you ought not to despise the share He has given to you. On the contrary, by your submission to, and respect for the designs of God you must wish to be such as He wishes you to be, without, however, neglecting to correct yourself. The greatest improvement I desire to see in you is, that your mind may never get embittered for any reason whatever, and that you always treat yourself gently. Is it not true that you behave thus towards your neighbours ? You are not always reproaching them bitterly and continually about their characters, but you try gently to induce them to reform. Do the same to yourself, and if gradually this spirit of gentleness should take root in your heart you would soon make progress in the spiritual life and without so much trouble. But if the heart is continually filled with feelings of harshness and bitterness, nothing much can be achieved and everything costs great effort. I insist greatly in this matter because it is an essential one for you, and in your place I should apply myself seriously to acquire a great interior and exterior gentleness in all things just as if there were no other virtue to practise ; for this will, in your case, bring all the others in its train. I appeal to your own experience about it. After having worked at it for some time very quietly, without the interruption of those impetuosities and hurries which drive away all sweetness and prevent you gaining the victory, you should be able to recognise the fact, that in this way much more is gained without half the fatigue.

LETTER XXIII.—*On Past Sins.*

To the same Sister.   Alby, July the 23rd, 1733.

My dear Sister, and very dear daughter in our Lord.
May the peace of Jesus Christ be always with you !

1st.   I have never said anything with the meaning that you impute to me, but have only written as to a poor beginner whom God is afflicting in His mercy, in order to purify her and to prepare her for union with Him.   The terrible ideas you have about your past disorders are at present what you are called to and you must bear with them as long as God pleases, just as one keeps to attractions that are full of sweetness.   This keen realisation of your poverty and darkness gives me pleasure, because I know it is a sure sign that divine light is increasing in you without your knowledge and is forming a sure foundation of true humility.   The time will come when the sight of these miseries which now cause you horror, will overwhelm you with joy, and fill you with a profound and delightful peace.   It is not till we have reached the bottom of the abyss of our nothingness, and are firmly established there that we can, as Holy Scripture says, " walk before God in justice and truth."   Just as pride, which is founded on a lie, prevents God from bestowing favours on a soul that is otherwise rich in merit, so this happy condition of humiliation willingly accepted, and of annihilation truly appreciated, draws down divine graces on even the most wretched of souls.   Therefore do not desire any other condition either during life or at the hour of death.   It is in this state of voluntary annihilation that you should have taken refuge, to escape the fears that assailed you during your recent illness.   Do not fail to do so if Satan ever tries to catch you in the same trap.   Self-love desires to have, at the last hours, some sensible support in the recollection of past good works ; let us, however, desire no other support than that given us by pure faith in the mercy of God and in the merits of Jesus Christ.   From the moment that we wish to belong entirely to God this support will be enough for us, all the rest is nothing but vanity.

2nd.   I approve, for the rest, of your interior and exterior conduct during your illness.   I perceive that God, in His wisdom, hid what little good He enabled you to gain from it because unless He had done so, a thousand vain thoughts of self-complacency would have spoilt all.   I know better than you all that took place and I bless God for it.   He supported you well in your weakness ; you have only to thank Him for doing so without reflecting so much as to whether everything has really been supernatural. Leave that to God; only try to forget yourself and to think only of Him.

3rd. What business have you to find so many excuses for your melancholy disposition? Let everyone think what he likes about it, you have only to please God and whatever He permits others to think or to say about you is of no moment to you; therefore do not indulge in reflexions on the subject. All that sort of thing only serves to increase self-love and vanity.

4th. I am charmed that you find peace where you would least expect it; it is a sign that God wills you to enjoy peace only in the accomplishment of His holy will, which is a very great grace. If I have not been able to pity you in your illness it is because I do not look upon the sufferings of the body as real evils since they procure so many blessings for the soul.

5th. You are convinced that you do nothing, that you merit nothing; and thus you are sunk in your nothingness. Oh! how well off you are! because from the moment you are convinced of your own nothingness you become united to God Who is all in all. Oh! what a treasure you have found in your nothingness! It is a state that you must necessarily pass through before God can fill your soul; for our souls must be emptied of all created things before they can be filled with the Holy Spirit of God; so that what troubles you and makes you uneasy is the very thing that ought to pacify you and fill you with a holy joy in God.

6th. Accepting everything without reserve, both present and future, is one of the most perfect sacrifices we could offer to God. This habitual act alone is worth all else that you could possibly do, therefore your best and only practice must be to adhere constantly to all the imaginable arrangements of Providence, whether exterior, or interior. Do nothing but just this, and God will, gradually, operate all the rest in your soul. This is a most simple practice, and exactly in accordance with your attraction.

7th. I am not much affected about the reserved manners of your companion. You must also make this sacrifice to God. She was not so much to blame as you in what put you out so much; but God has permitted this to humble you by making you understand what you really are when He leaves you to your own devices. Humble yourself without vexation or worry. You know what St. Francis of Sales says about such circumstances.

8th. God requires of us the fulfilment of our duties, but He does not require us to find out if there has been any merit in this or not. You think too much about yourself, and under the pious pretext of advancing in the ways of God you are too much occupied about yourself. Forget yourself to think only of Him, and abandon yourself to the commands of divine Providence, and then He will Himself lead you on, purify you and safely raise you, when and as it pleases Him, to the degree of sanctity He wills for you. What have we to do except to please Him, and to desire in all things and everywhere what He wills? We search far and wide after perfection, and yet it is almost within our grasp. It is—to unite our will in all things to the will of God and never to follow our own inclinations. But to arrive at this we must renounce ourselves and sacrifice, if needs be, our dearest interests. This is what we have no wish to do; we want God to sanctify and make us perfect according to our own ideas and tastes. What folly! What pitiable blindness!

LETTER XXIV.—*Results of Imprudence.*

To the same Sister. On the vexatious results of imprudence.

I have already told you very often, my dear Sister, that nothing should trouble you, not even your faults, and certainly far less should you allow yourself to be cast down by those trying consequences of acts which are not sins, although they imply some imprudence on your part. There is hardly any trial more mortifying to self-love, and consequently hardly any more sanctifying than this. It does not cost nearly so much to accept humiliations that come to us from without and that we have not had any hand in drawing upon ourselves. One can resign oneself much more easily to the confusion caused by faults very much graver in themselves provided they do not appear outside. But one simple imprudence that entails annoying results that everyone can see; this is decidedly of all humiliations the very worst; and therefore, as a natural consequence, an excellent occasion for the mortification of self-love. Then it is that we can say over and over again the " fiat " of perfect abandonment; we must even go further and make an act of thanksgiving, adding for this purpose a " Gloria Patri " to our " fiat."

One single trial, accepted thus, causes a soul to make more progress than any number of acts of virtue. I hope I have made this clear to you and that you will no longer distress yourself about the consequences that are likely to follow the mistake of which you have been the innocent cause. Remain in peace with the intention of taking what steps are necessary at a convenient time to bring about peace, and a union of hearts; then abandon to God all the success, whatever it may be. It is well to get accustomed to act in this way in all the troublesome events of this miserable life; thus we shall enjoy peace, and shall have made merit in the sight of divine Providence. Without this submission and total abandonment we can expect no rest during the course of our sad pilgrimage. Think only of pleasing God, of satisfying God, of sacrificing all to God. Let all the rest go, and keep nothing back. Provided that God dwells within you, you will never lose anything. Take good courage and all will go well; do not be so uneasy, nor so surprised at these rebellions of your nature : I assure you that they will be no impediment to the submission of your higher faculties, and that God only hides this submission for your own good. In the most violent attacks try just to say these few words, " It is but just that a creature should be submissive to her Creator, therefore I desire and pray to become so." Read the chapter on "Progress" in the "Interior Life" by Fr. Guilloré; it is an inspired chapter, and I hope you will derive great benefit from it.

For God's sake do not sadden yourself, and try to preserve peace during even the most terrible tempests. If you do this all will go well. In fact I see nothing but good in everything that you have confided to me, but a good that would cease to be so if you saw it as plainly as I do.

When a number of different thoughts enter my head which makes the least thing assume monstrous proportions, I recall to mind the advice I have given to others in similar circumstances. I abandon myself to divine Providence in all things and about all things. When the worst comes to the worst, I defy it like St. Paul, to separate me from the charity of Jesus Christ. I know that without the grace of this divine Saviour I could do nothing; but I know also that with His grace I can do all things; I beg Him therefore to keep me in all my temptations from all sin, from all that could displease Him; but as for the bitterness of soul, the interior crucifixion, the holy abjection and even the confusion before others, I accept them with all their consequences for as long as it pleases His sovereign Majesty. I desire the accomplishment of His holy will, and not my own in all things, and I implore Him not to allow me either to say or to do anything that might place any obstacle to the least thing that He wills. And if, through weakness, error, or malice I should undertake anything of the kind, I implore Him not to allow it to succeed.

I recognise the fact that His holy will is, in all things, not only holy and adorable, but infinitely salutary and beneficent towards those who are humbly submissive; and that mine, on the contrary, is always either blind or ill-regulated. Therefore I subscribe to all that the eternal Father decrees, and would do so a hundred times no matter at what cost to myself. This dear and good Father has commanded it, that is enough, and what have

I to fear? From this, two conclusions can be drawn, firstly that during these tempests and storms often raised by trifles I retain such a profound peace that I am surprised at it myself. Secondly that I consider myself very fortunate to have to endure these interior tortures, temptations and trials. Then I say to myself, this is worth more than all my own miserable arrangements. I feel my soul becoming stronger by this abandonment to divine Providence, so much so, that all my personal desires and attachment to my own will are consumed and annihilated.

LETTER XXV.—*Interior Suffering.*

To Sister Marie-Anne Thérèse de Rosen. Rules to follow during trials.

You know as well as I do, my dear Sister, that in order to raise souls to a state of perfection God is wont to make them bear all kinds of crosses and interior pains to prove their fidelity, to purify them, and to detach them from all created things. The most grievous of these crosses are those in which we may have been to blame ourselves, and where the poor soul severely reprimanded by others, and even more severely by itself, does not hear either outwardly or inwardly anything but a sentence of death. The person of whom you speak is in this state, therefore there is nothing to fear about her; all that you tell me proves on the contrary that God has particular designs with regard to her. When you write to her speak of nothing but patience, submission to God, and total abandonment to divine Providence, as one does to people in the world who are afflicted with temporal necessities. Above all make her try, by means of the most filial confidence in God, to repulse energetically all trouble and voluntary uneasiness. I repeat, voluntary, because the poor souls to whom God sends this trial cannot master the troubles and anxieties by which they are obsessed. This is the subject of their greatest pain, and the most afflicting part of that state of humiliation in which for a certain time God retains them. Therefore they have nothing else to do but to submit to God about these paroxysms of interior suffering as well as about all the rest. Say to this poor soul that her best prayer will be to remain always in silence at the foot of the cross of Jesus Christ, repeating like Him, and with Him, "Fiat." Oh heavenly Father, may Your will, not mine, be done in all things. It is You who arrange all our afflictions for the good of our souls. You would not act thus unless it were for my greater good and eternal salvation. Do with me what You will; I adore and submit. I think that your friend does quite right not to examine her thoughts ; an examination of that kind would only confuse her mind still more. She must leave all to God and despise these thoughts and the pretended cries of her conscience, and go forward without taking any notice of them, directly there is nothing absolutely bad in the act she wishes to perform. These vain scruples are a device of the devil to deprive her of peace, and thus to prevent her making progress in virtue ; for trouble is to the soul a most dangerous malady which makes it too languid for the practice of virtue, as a sick person who is weak and languid is incapable of bodily exertion.

If she succeeds in preserving peace of mind she will gradually recover, just as an infirm and languid person recovers health by taking rest and good nourishment. I will give three methods by which to hasten her recovery.

1st. To repulse quietly from her mind all that troubles her and makes her anxious, looking upon this sort of thought as coming from the devil; because all that comes from God is peaceful and sweet, and helps to establish confidence in Him. It is in peace that He dwells and that He infuses those different virtues that bring souls to perfection.

2nd. Frequently to raise the mind and heart to God, with acts of submission, abandonment, and confidence in His paternal goodness, which only afflicts her at present to sanctify her.

3rd. To choose for her reading those books most likely to contribute to calming her mind and to inspiring her with confidence in God; such as " The Treaty," by Mgr. Languet, the book on " Christian Hope," the " Letters " of St. Francis of Sales. For the rest let her go on as usual without making any change in her conduct, making her confessions and communions as she is accustomed to, because the devil, to deceive her, and to weaken her still more, will very likely use every artifice to inspire her with dislike and an excessive fear of confession, of communion, and of all other spiritual exercises. She ought not to lend an ear to these evil inspirations but always to follow the light of faith and the holy practices of the Christian religion like a true and good daughter of holy Church. Amen.

LETTER XXVI.—*On Different States of Resignation.*

To Sister Marie-Thérèse de Vioménil.   On the same subject Alby, 1733.

My very dear Sister,

1st.   I cannot do otherwise than congratulate you on the efforts you are making to keep always in a state of perfect resignation and of entire abandonment to the will of God.   In this, for you, consists all perfection.   But on this point as on all others you must learn how to distinguish between the appearance and the reality, the feeling of consent and the working of the will.   There are two kinds of resignation; one that can be felt and that is accompanied by sensible pleasure and a quiet repose;   the other unfelt, dry, without pleasure, even accompanied by feelings of repugnance, and by interior revolt.   It is this latter that I understand you to possess.   The first is good, very agreeable to nature, and for this reason rather dangerous, because it is natural to become strongly attached to that which one enjoys.   The second, which to self-love seems absolutely painful and unpleasant, is more perfect, more meritorious, and less dangerous since there is no pleasure to be found in it except through bare faith and perfect love.   Compel yourself to act with these solid motives.   When you have succeeded in doing so your union with God will be proof against every vicissitude, but if you accustom yourself only to act according to sensible attractions you will do nothing when these come to an end.   Besides, we cannot prevent them from often failing us, while the motives of faith never fail.   It is only in order to induce us to act, gradually, from these spiritual motives that God so often takes away sensible devotion and pleasure.   If He were not to act thus we should always remain in a state of spiritual infancy.   You should not therefore be surprised at the weariness and the revolts of which you speak ;   God permits them for your good.   Nevertheless, if you fear that human motives are mixed with the mortifications you inflict on yourself say these two things to yourself (1) "I am not at present in a fit state to judge but will reflect about it when I feel peaceful and calm. (2) If there is still some human element in it, God allows it that He may help my weakness.   When it shall have pleased Him to render me less imperfect I shall be able to act in a more perfect manner."   On this matter be calm, and do not indulge in the least voluntary trouble.

x

2nd.   I can easily understand how your dislike of your duty should materially add to your trials; but consider how the martyrs won their crowns by enduring much worse tribulations than yours.

3rd.   In this state it is usual to feel an inclination for a solitary life, but a life of obedience is of greater value, it is a continual sacrifice, and even if there is more cause for being bored, there are also many subjects for meriting.   Continue as you are with great fortitude and even scruple to utter a word against your state, or that could detach you from the cross of Jesus Christ.

4th.   The best way of bearing these disagreeables is to look upon them as crosses sent by God, just as you do illness and other misfortunes of life.   If God were to send you exterior afflictions that you could feel, you would bear them patiently; bear then with equal patience your interior trials.

5th.   Look upon all these miseries of our earthly existence as so much treasure for the spiritual life, since they afford you such powerful means of acquiring humility and self-contempt.   With this aim in view love every humiliation, and its consequent abjection, as St. Francis of Sales counsels.   You ask me if it would not be better to hide your miseries for fear of causing disedification.   With all my heart.   Try simply and very quietly to manage so that these feelings may not appear externally, but if they should appear and you are not greatly to blame for it, try to accept this little humiliation pleasantly.   Even should it occur by your own fault, then embrace the abjection which it brings you.   In this way you will mortify your self-love very meritoriously, for this seeks to avoid outward faults, not because they are an offence against God, but on account of the humiliation they entail.   Do not dwell on the pain that the difficulty you experience in concentrating your thoughts causes you.   Remind yourself that the habitual desire of re-collection alone will serve equally well, and that all that is necessary is to desire unceasingly to think of God, to please God, to obey God, in order to please and to obey Him in reality.

6th.   You say that the more you desire to learn to pray the less you know how to do so.   This may very possibly be because your desire is not accompanied by a sufficient submission and purity of intention.   Always have the intention of pleasing God when you pray, and not of enjoying sensible devotion.   Pray in a spirit of sacrifice and accept all that God pleases to send you during your prayer; and I must tell you that the prayer of recollection is one of those things that leaves you if you are eager to retain it, and remains if you learn how to keep yourself in a state of indifference about it; this is the doctrine of St. Francis of Sales.

7th. Often recall to mind this great rule, that spiritual poverty recognised, felt, and loved on account of its abjection, is one of the greatest treasures that a soul can possess here below ; because this feeling keeps it in a state of profound humility ; but to imagine yourself lost because you do not find in yourself lively enough feelings of faith and charity, and to be distressed, uneasy, or discouraged about it, is a dangerous illusion of self-love which always wants to see things plainly, and to take pleasure in itself. When you experience this temptation you must say to yourself, " I have been, I am, and I shall be whatever God pleases, but according to my reason and the higher faculties of my soul I desire to belong to Him and to serve Him no matter what happens to me in this world and the next."

8th. You cannot describe to me what you are suffering ; but I will tell you what it is ; it is for one thing all kinds of rebellions, pains, and temptations in the inferior part of your nature, and a perpetual confusion of feelings excited by the devil and your own self-love. On the other hand, in the superior part, a little ray of light and of faith that is almost imperceptible on account of the tumultuous emotions in the inferior part. And with only this slender support you are immovable, because the finest thread in the hands of God is as strong as a cable, and a mere hair is stronger than an iron chain.

9th. It is a temptation and a false humility to keep away from the sacraments. What others do ought never to affect you who know nothing about their ideas nor motives, nor the cause of their keeping away.

10th. You say that God often deprives you of the feeling of being in a state of grace. To whom among His dearest friends has He given continually this sensible support ? Do you aspire by any chance to be more highly privileged than so many saints whom He has deprived of it for a much longer time than you ? What had they to depend upon then save only the light of faith, and of a faith the same as ours which seems like darkness ? And amidst the darkness of their temptations and the tumult of their passions they knew no more than we do whether God was satisfied with them. Faith teaches us that, unless by particular revelation, the saints themselves were not able to be perfectly certain about it ; and you complain because you do not possess this certainty. See how far this unhappy self-love goes. To satisfy it God would have to work miracles. Of all the miseries that humble you so much this is certainly the greatest, and the best calculated to humiliate you.

11th. To wish to be occupied with God and not with yourself, and then to fall back continually on yourself is, I must own, a temptation as troublesome as the flies in autumn ; but then you must drive away this temptation as you have continually to drive away the flies, without ever leaving off this work ; quietly however, without distress or annoyance, humbling yourself before God as you do in other miseries. It is we, ourselves, who compel God to overwhelm us with miseries to make us humble and to increase our self-contempt. If, in spite of this, we have so little humility and so much self-esteem, what would it be if we found ourselves free from these trials ? Believe me, you have appeared to be for some time past so penetrated with the knowledge of your miseries that I believe this feeling alone is one of the greatest graces that God could bestow upon you. Love then everything that helps to preserve it.

I remain yours in our Lord.

I feel very tired of so much writing and before reading to the end of your letter I had the same idea as you, to divide my answers. I do not, however, regret having now placed you in a condition to understand at a single glance the general drift of the direction you ought to follow in order to gather all the fruit of the trial to which God is subjecting you.

SEVENTH BOOK.

THE LAST TRIALS. AGONY AND MYSTICAL DEATH. THE FRUIT
THEREOF.

LETTER I.—*Temptations to Despair.*

To Sister Charlotte-Elizabeth Bourcier de Monthureux. On
spiritual nakedness. Annihilation. Temptations to despair.
Alby, 1732.

My very dear daughter in our Lord. The peace of Jesus
Christ be always with you.

Of all your letters the last is the one that has given me most
consolation before God. You understand nothing about how
you are circumstanced. I, however, by the grace of God, see it
as clearly as daylight.

1st. The state of stupidity and dullness that you depict, the
chaotic mass of misery and weakness, what else can this be
but the gift of God, and this is what has gradually produced in
your soul different spiritual operations of grace. It would be
in vain to attempt to explain them to you, because God would
not enable you to understand them in the state to which He
has brought you, and the knowledge you might gain from reading
my letter would vanish at once. But I can, at least, give you
an assurance which ought to satisfy you.

I acknowledge that, at first, I was somewhat astonished that
God should treat you like one advanced in the spiritual life,
because this state is usually the fruit of long years of combat
and effort. The soul finds itself entering it when God, satisfied
with the diligence with which it has laboured to die to all things,
sets His own hand to the work to make it pass through that death
to which the total privation of all things created leads. He
strips it thus of all pleasure, even to that which is spiritual, of
all inclination, of all light, to the end that, thus, it may become
freed from the senses, dull, and as though annihilated. When
God bestows this grace on a soul, it has hardly anything else to
do than endure in peace this harsh operation, and to bear this
gift of God in the profound interior silence of respect, adoration
and submission. This is your task ; in one sense a very easy one,
since it means nothing more than to act as a sick person confined
to his bed, and in the hands of his doctor and surgeon. He will
suffer quite patiently in the expectation of a complete cure.
You are in the same kind of position, in the hands of the great
and charitable Physician of our souls, and with a better founded
certainty of a cure.

2nd. The violent and almost continual assault of all your passions is the result of the same mortifying and vivifying operation. On the one hand, it causes all these movements to give occasion to repel them and to acquire the opposite virtues ; and, on the other hand, by means of these same attacks it lays a solid foundation of perfection which comprises the most profound humility, contempt, and hatred of self.

3rd. Temptations to discouragement and despair are another consequence of the same state, and possess still greater power of purifying us. I know that there is never any consent because I see that all your voluntary intentions are the exact contrary to those of a soul that would offend God. No, my dear Sister, you do not offend Him at these painful times ; your soul, on the contrary, is then like gold that boils in the crucible ; it is purified, and shines with an added lustre. Never are you upheld in a more fatherly way by the hand of God, and if you were able to see your state as it really is, far from being afflicted about it, you would return thanks to the God of mercy for His ineffable gift.

4th. Your method of prayer is good and will always be so as long as you continue it peacefully in an entire abandonment, and, as St. Francis of Sales expresses it, in a simple peaceful waiting quite resigned to the will of God.

5th. As each ought to follow his attraction in prayer and at other times, do not be afraid to keep yourself always in this great destitution which you find within your soul. Remain therein without any formed thought, quite dull and insensible to all things. Love this state, because with regard to you it is the gift of God, and the beginning of all good. I have never come across any chosen souls whom God has not made to pass through these dry deserts before arriving at the promised land which is the terrestrial paradise of perfection.

6th. Interior reproaches about the slightest faults are an evident sign of the especial care taken by the Holy Spirit for your advancement. With certain souls He allows nothing to escape notice, and about them He has a most fastidious jealousy ; and it is a sure truth that souls which are the objects of this jealousy, cannot, without infidelity, allow themselves to do what other persons can do without imperfection. The fastidiousness and jealousy of divine love are more or less great according to the degree of its predilection. Consider if you have any occasion to pity yourself about the merciful rigour it uses towards you.

7th. You are right to have no particular desire to make a Retreat ; you are no longer in a position to desire, but rather in that of having to abandon yourself unreservedly to all that the Holy Spirit wishes to effect in you. It is for Him to determine the time, the duration, the manner, and the results of His operations, and for you to endure with submission, love and gratitude. Some of these results are extremely severe ; but the most humiliating, the most bitter, are always the most sanctifying. Keep yourself, therefore, very quiet, and allow this good physician who has undertaken your cure to act as seems best to Him.

8th. You can apply to yourself all that I wrote last year to Sister Marie-Antoinette de Mahuet, and derive profit for your own needs ; but you must not be surprised that while you are suffering from this spiritual upsetting neither my letters nor any books will be of any use. God wills it otherwise ; at present He extinguishes all light, all feeling, to operate alone in the depths of your soul whatever He pleases. Now I ask you, is not what God does of infinitely more value than all you could effect by your own industry ? Beg Him to treat you like a beast of burden that allows itself to be led without resistance ; or like a stone which receives the blows of the hammer, and takes what form the architect desires.

9th. The loss of hope causes you more grief than any other trial. I can well understand this, for, as during your life you find yourself deprived of everything that could give you the least help, so you imagine that at the hour of your death you will be in a state of fearful destitution. Ah! this is indeed a misery, and for this I pity you far more than for your other sufferings. Allow me, with the help of God's grace, to endeavour to set this trouble in its true light and so to cure you. What you want, my dear Sister, is to find support and comfort in yourself and your good works. Well, this is precisely what God does not wish, and what He cannot endure in souls aspiring after perfection. What! lean upon yourself? count on your works ? Could self-love, pride, and perversity have a more miserable fruit ? It is to deliver them from this that God makes all chosen souls pass through a fearful time of poverty, misery and nothingness. He desires to destroy in them gradually all the help and confidence they derive from themselves, to take away every expedient so that He may be their sole support, their confidence, their hope, their only resource. Oh! what an accursed hope it is, that without reflexion you seek in yourself. How pleased I am that God destroys, confounds and annihilates this accursed hope by means of this state of poverty and misery. Oh! happy poverty! blessed despoilment! which formed the delight of all the saints and especially of St. Francis of Sales! Let us love it as they loved it, and when by virtue of this love all confidence and hope, all earthly and created support has been removed, we shall find neither hope nor support in anything but God, and this is the holy hope and confidence of the saints which is founded solely on the mercy of God and the merits of Jesus Christ. But you will only attain to this hope when God shall have completely destroyed your self-confidence, root and branch ; and this cannot be effected without retaining you for some time in the utmost spiritual poverty.

10th. " But," you will argue, " of what use are our good works if they may not be for us some ground for confidence ? " They are useful in attaining for us the grace of a complete distrust of ourselves and of a greater confidence in God. This is all the use that the saints made of them. What, in fact, are our good works ? They are frequently so spoilt and corrupted by our self-love that if God judged us rigorously we should deserve chastisements for them rather than rewards. Think no more, then, of your good works as of something to tranquillize you at the hour of death, do not reflect on anything but the mercy of God, the merits of Jesus Christ, the intercession of the saints, and the prayers of holy souls, but on nothing, absolutely nothing that might give occasion to reliance on yourself, nor to placing the least degree of confidence in your works.

11th. That which you say to others, or rather what God gives you to say for their consolation while you yourself are in a state of extreme dryness, does not, in the least, surprise me. God acts thus, often enough, when He wishes to console others, and at the same time to keep oneself in a state of desolation and abandonment. You then say what God inspires you to say without any feeling yourself, but with much sympathy for others ; I do not see any sign of hypocrisy in this.

12th. To avoid relaxation during the fulfilment of the duties you have undertaken through obedience, it is only necessary to do everything quietly, without either anxiety or eagerness, and to do them in this way you have but to do them for the love of God and to obey Him, as St. Francis advises. " Therefore," continues the same saint, " as this love is gentle and sweet, all that it inspires shares the same spirit." But when self-love interferes with the wish to succeed and to be satisfied, which always accompanies it, it first introduces natural activities and excitements and their anxieties and troubles. " Whatever these duties are," you tell me, " I feel sure that they prevent me making any progress." My dear Sister, when one loves God, one does not wish to make greater progress than God wills, and one abandons one's spiritual progress to divine Providence, just as wealthy people in the world abandon to Him all the success of their temporal affairs. But the great misfortune is that self-love thrusts itself everywhere, meddles with everything and spoils all. It is because of this that even our desire of advancing is food for self-love, a source of trouble, and consequently an obstacle to our prayers.

13th.   Another foolish terror! "You fear," you say, "that
your want of feeling is the principle of your peace." Yes, certainly this is true, and it is for this reason that I look upon it
as a gift of God.   I hope that the operations of the Holy Spirit
will lead to a still greater insensibility so as to render you with
regard to all created things like a block of wood, or the trunk of
a tree.   This is what I have already told you, and you ridiculed
the idea.   We are getting to it, by degrees, God be praised!
Without this kind of insensibility we should have neither the
strength, nor the courage necessary in many circumstances to
keep peaceful.   We should require the virtue of blessed Margaret
Mary Alacoque of whom it was related with admiration that in
the midst of all her tenderness she was always mistress of herself.
As for your taste for solitude among all your occupations, I will
say to you what St. Ignatius said to Fr. Laynez in similar circumstances : "Father, if at court where obedience retains
you, you feel this great desire for solitude, it shows that you
are in safety ; if this desire should vanish and you should come
even to love your distracting duties it would be a bad sign."
Preserve, therefore, this love and desire of solitude, but as long
as God keeps you in the midst of the cares and distractions of
your occupations, try to love them for the sake of obedience.

LETTER II.—*Good Symptoms*.

To the same Sister.   Alby, 1732.

My dear Sister and very dear daughter in our Lord.

The peace of Jesus Christ be always with you.   Your letter
reminded me of a saying of Fénélon : "One does not begin to
know and to feel one's spiritual miseries until they begin to be
cured."   It is, therefore, a very good symptom to feel overwhelmed with miseries, provided that this feeling be exempt from
voluntary uneasiness, and joined to a complete interior resignation.

1st.   During this state of obscurity, dryness, coldness, and
spiritual destitution, retain in your soul a firm and sincere will
to be all for God ; this is all that you can do under such circumstances.   Then be comforted and remain in peace in the higher
part of your soul.

2nd.   It is true that this state of which I spoke to you in my
last letter is a great gift of God, and that usually it is kept for
chosen souls who have been tried for a long time in the inferior
degrees of the spiritual life ; but it is also occasionally accorded,
out of pure goodness, to imperfect souls, because God is in no way
subject to laws.   He bestows such graces as He pleases and to

whomsoever He pleases. This is your case I can assure you. You only have, therefore, on your side, to keep yourself continually submissive to the interior dispositions that you experience at each moment, only willing what God wills, and for as long as He wills it. If you are faithful in bearing this trial to the end, you will see in time what will be the result. I rejoice beforehand at the good fruit of which I guarantee you before God.

You are suffering and without merit, without real fidelity. You believe this and it is good for you to think so since God permits it. Remain as long as you like in this belief, but let it be subject to the will of God, and I will answer for you.

3rd. You can see nothing in your present state and still less since you received my last letter than you did before. All the better! I hope that your darkness will increase day by day, for, by the grace of God I see clearly through this darkness, and that ought to be enough for you. Go on therefore through this dark night by the light of blind obedience. This is a safe guide which has never led anyone astray and which conducts with more certainty and more quickly than even acts of the most perfect abandonment.

4th. These acts, however, are excellent, but it may sometimes happen that you find it impossible to make them, and then you will be able to put yourself into a still more perfect condition, which consists in keeping an interior silence of respect, adoration and submission, about which I have so often spoken. This silence says more to God than all your formal acts, and that without reverting to self-complacency, without sensible consolation. This is the true mystical death which ought necessarily to precede the supernatural life of grace. You would never arrive at that entirely spiritual and interior life to which you aspire with so much ardour, if God did not find in you this second death; death to spiritual consolations. These consolations are, in fact, so delightful, that if God did not detach us from them by severe trials we should become more attached to them than to any worldly pleasures, and that would be an insurmountable obstacle to perfect union.

5th. In this state God knows about what you are occupied, and I know also; let that be sufficient for you. It is good for you to believe yourself reduced to complete destitution. Apparently you will never arrive at the happy state of one servant of God who could no longer hold any intercourse with men as he had forgotten the common language. Learn for your support in this trial that what forms your great pain and martyrdom to-day will one day become your greatest delight. When will this happy time arrive ; Only God knows ! it will be when He pleases

6th. The slight distraction and diminution of peace that you experienced directly you left this state of stupidity for a short time ought to have shown you what occupied you without your knowledge in your apparent want of occupation, and what it is that fills this fearful void.

7th. Do not expect to be able to explain this matter to yourself more clearly. With God's grace I see it as plainly as midday. You, yourself, feel at certain moments the fortunate effects of this kind of stupidity. No! No! it is neither melancholia, nor eccentricity, it is the operation of the Holy Spirit.

8th. There are times when everything irritates and wearies you; so they should. Saint Teresa even said that at these times she did not feel that she had strength enough to crush an ant for the love of God. Never could anyone attain to an entire distrust of self and to a perfect confidence in God unless he had passed through these different states of complete insensibility, and absolute powerlessness. Happy state which produces such marvellous effects.

9th. That which you experienced in Retreat was a slight increase of your ordinary state, resembling the paroxysms of a fever. This increase of trouble cannot but have been very salutary for you from the moment you accepted it, as you say you did. Keep quiet; God leads you, His grace works in you, although in a severe and crucifying manner, as is experienced in all violent remedies. Your spiritual maladies had need of remedies such as these; let your good Physician act as He best knows how; He will proportion the strength of the remedy to the power of the malady. Oh! how ill you were formerly without being aware of it! It was then that you ought to have taken the alarm, and not now that your convalescence is secured.

10th. What you experience at prayer is a very good thing although very bitter. Do nothing more, however, than keep firmly an entire resignation in the higher faculties of your soul, as St. Francis of Sales advises.

11th. In the way you made your retreat formerly there was infinitely more sensible devotion, and consequently, more satisfaction for self-love; but your present want of feeling is of incomparably more value, and you will have felt this already by its effects; for you are very different now to what you used to be after those delightful retreats. If you do not recognise this fact I do so instead of you. If you were able to reflect a little you would, yourself, notice how little foundation there is for your fears. How can you explain without a particular operation of grace, that although you passed the whole time of retreat so sadly, yet, nevertheless, the time passed very rapidly and without weariness ? Ought you not to find in this a manifest proof that you were very well occupied while it lasted, without knowing it ?

12th. The terror caused by your past sins is the most hurtful and dangerous of your temptations, therefore I command you to dismiss all these diabolical artifices, in the same way as you would drive away temptations to blasphemy, or impurity. Think only of the present time in order to conform your thoughts to the holy will of God alone. Leave all the rest to His providence and mercy. No ! your stupidity and want of feeling are, by no means, a punishment for some hidden sin, as the devil would like to make you imagine, to disturb the peace of your soul. They are real graces ; bitter, it is true, but which have had, and will continue to have very good effects. Who tells you this ? It is I who assure you of it by the authority of God.

13th. I should have been very sorry to have had the foolish satisfaction of hearing your general confession ; it would have been to allow you to be caught in the devil's trap. What ought you to do then to free yourself from these fears ? To obey simply and blindly him who speaks to you on the part of God who sent him ; and think no more, voluntarily, about it.

14th. Your callousness and indifference towards everything that hitherto gave you the greatest pleasure, is, in truth, one of the greatest graces that God could bestow upon you. But how can this be ? By this frightful void, by this lasting state of stupidity and callousness which seems so bitter to you. Yes, indeed, this remedy is painful, but what fortunate effects are produced by it when you accept it lovingly from the hand of the kind Physician of your soul. Here in a few words is an abridgment of the whole of this letter. Your only spiritual practice will be to continue, as now, in the hands of God like a rough stone to be shaped, cut, and polished, with heavy blows of the hammer and chisel, waiting patiently until the sovereign Architect arranges in what part of the building you are to be placed after you have been cut and shaped by His hand.

Yours always in the Lord.

P.S.—That which you relate to me about the Duke of Hamilton is really wonderful, but does not surprise me at all. We are accustomed to see similar effects of the power and mercy of God. That little conversation was a grace for you. Never forget it.

LETTER III.—*On Interior Oppression.*
To Sister Marie-Thérèse de Vioménil.

My dear Sister,

For the crushing and overwhelming weight which remains ever on your spirit, I have but one remedy : a simple acquiescence, a humble " fiat," which you will perhaps say without feeling it, but which God will hear distinctly, and which will be sufficient to sanctify you and to make of you a martyr of Providence. Besides this, you would never be able to believe how many excellent acts are comprised in the feeling of oppression that this heaviness of heart occasions. It is a much greater grace for you than you can imagine. You will find it a most efficacious means of acquiring a true spirit of penance ; that compunction so much valued by all the saints, and of which God has frequently made you feel the need. Take up your cross, then, and with submission and gratitude, repeat often to God that even in your most holy desires, and those that are most salutary, you wish to take His adorable will for rule and measure, desiring only that degree of virtue and eternal happiness which He intends you to have. Communicate as frequently as you are permitted, and endure with peace and submission all the trials that the reception of this Sacrament will occasion you. Your humility and interior abasement will supply for all the dispositions that you lack ; and the privation of all sensible fruit will be amply compensated for by the courage and abandonment with which you bear yourself in the ways by which God leads you. Your illness and the rule of life it compels you to follow are the best penance you could have. You are afraid of pleasing yourself in this state of suffering by not fasting ? Foolish fear ! rather be afraid of being wanting in interior abnegation while following your own ideas. Obey your doctor blindly : God requires this of you, whereas He certainly does not ask you to fast. Offer Him, as often as you are able, your illness, its consequences, and your fears ; but only in your heart, quietly ; recollecting that you must will all that God wills. Just a thought of, a look at our Lord will be enough.

LETTER IV.—*Purification of the Heart.*

From the bottom of my heart I bless God, my dear Sister, for carrying on His work in you. The crushing weight that you feel on your heart is one of the most salutary operations of that crucifying love which does in your heart what fire does to green wood. Before the flame can make its way the wood crackles, smokes, and gives out all the damp with which it is saturated ; but when it is perfectly dry it burns quietly, diffusing all round it a brilliant light. This will be the case with you after your heart has been purified by many crosses, and particularly by these crucifying spiritual operations. You must therefore endure these operations with courage, with sweetness, avoiding as much as possible worrying, or distressing yourself interiorly. This is the good and sufficient penance that God requires of you. It is of more value than any corporal austerities, although everyone ought to practise the latter according to his strength and health. In what you add I see an evident sign of the good effect produced by your present trial. It seems to you, you say, that you are always waiting for something that is wanting to you. This is because your heart, tired of creatures, and unable to exist without joy and love, feels more keenly than ever a longing for that sovereign good which can alone satisfy it. The greater the void left in the heart by its withdrawal from all earthly affections, the greater is the ardour with which it sighs after the enjoyment of God, and of His holy love. This it is for which you are waiting ; and it is precisely by this waiting and these secret sighs that at last you will obtain this divine love. The waters of life are given to those who thirst for them. Ardent desires are the money with which to buy this sublime and exquisite enjoyment of God ; that heavenly food which alone can appease the hunger and thirst of the soul ; whereas the love for, and even the possession of all created goods does nothing but inflame and irritate, without ever satisfying them.

LETTER V.—*On Emptiness of Heart.*

On Emptiness of heart.

I greatly approve, my dear Sister, of the patience with which you endure the great emptiness you experience in your soul. By this you will make more progress in one month than you would in several years of sweetness and consolation. About this I can only exhort you to go on in the same way. It is necessary to traverse this desert to reach during this life the promised land. I am not at all surprised that this great emptiness seems like a support to you. This is what, in fact, it is, because God is present therein, but in an almost imperceptible manner, just as He was in your trials. Look upon this distaste for all things, and apparent want of feeling towards all that is not God, as a great grace to be carefully guarded and preserved. God will come at the time fixed by His grace to fill the void which He has made in your heart, and the ineffable sweetness of His presence will create a fresh distaste for the miserable pleasures of this world. From this time, therefore, bid a general and final farewell to all creatures ; and rejoice when they forsake you of their own accord ; God permits this as a help to your weakness. As for me, I am delighted at what has happened, and that you have been treated with so little consideration. This conduct has certainly been as salutary for you as it was humiliating. Oh ! if you could gradually become accustomed to love this abjection what progress would you not make !

LETTER VI.—*Fresh Suffering.*

To Sister Marie-Thérèse de Vioménil. On the same subject and the renewal of pain.

My dear Sister,

Since you find my letters consoling and useful, I promise you that, wherever I may be, to the last moment of my life, I will continue to reply to yours faithfully.

1st. The imperfections and even the faults we may commit contrary to entire submission to the will of God, do not prevent that submission from dwelling in the heart, and do not destroy the merit of it. To make up for the harm these faults occasion us, it is sufficient to humble ourselves about them, and to return as quickly as possible to a filial abandonment into the hands of God.

2nd. I understand better than you imagine your anguish of heart and the weight that seems to crush it. For several years I was in the same state and about something, in itself very insignificant, that hurt my pride. I committed many faults, but I tried at once to recover the ground I had lost. Some time elapsed before I recognised the advantages I had derived from this trial. They appeared, eventually, so great and so numerous that I continue to thank God daily for having thus struck me in His mercy by making me pass through this spiritual cleansing. I feel convinced that in due time God will grant you very nearly the same ideas, and that then you will never tire of returning thanks to Him for that which so much afflicts you at present. I have also had similar experiences on innumerable occasions of the increase of trouble about which you speak ; exactly like the paroxysms of a fever.

3rd. At such times, as in severe illness, you can only try to remain as much as possible in silence and peace ; because, as regards express acts, and especially such as are sensible and consoling, one is not then in a fit state to make them. However, God sees the submission that has its foundation in the heart, and that is enough for gaining merit. In this state the less the consolation you enjoy so much the more the spiritual profit you will derive from it.

4th. It is not forbidden to ask God to take away these troubles, especially if they violently afflict the heart. Jesus Christ acted thus in the Garden of Olives ; but you must add as He did and in union with Him, " Nevertheless not my will but Thine be done," and although you may feel very great repugnance to adding these words and do so with much interior rebellion, it does not matter. It is the lower nature that resists and is afflicted. This resistance does not, however, destroy the resignation of the superior part ; on the contrary, it does but increase the merit and hasten the progress of the soul in the paths of solid virtue.

5th. They are doing quite right in making you frequent the sacraments ; you would commit a serious fault if you were to stay away, and nothing could be more dangerous for you. Neither depression, nor discouragement, nor trouble, nor confusion, nor any interior difficulty should ever prevent you going to Holy Communion. Such painful conditions, endured and accepted for God, are worth more than fervour and sensible consolation. The latter often only serve to feed and encourage spiritual self-love, the most subtle and evasive of all the forms of self-love, while the other dispositions tend to its gradual extinction. It is in this destruction of self-love that all true piety and all spiritual progress consist, while for want of real abnegation most devout people have only the appearance of piety. In the unsettled state of your health you should find only another subject for daily sacrifice that is very meritorious. You must submit to all the remedies and even resign yourself to give up fasting, even for a single day. Your worries and scruples about this matter have no foundation. You must make a sacrifice, for the sake of obedience, of these troubles and disinclinations however spiritual them seem to be. If you do otherwise it will be a real illusion which your own good sense should lead you to avoid, but to which I have seen many people, even Religious, give in.

———

LETTER VII.—*Supernatural Fears.*

To Sister de Lesen of the Annunciation. Supernatural fears and pain. (1736)

In spite of the great natural compassion, and the great affection in our Lord that I feel towards the afflicted person of whom you speak, I cannot feel either alarmed at her state, or even pity her very much about it. I have frequently told her that, after the signal favours she has received from God, I was astonished at one thing only, which was, that having received a high degree of the gift of simple recollection she has not been sooner submitted to the usual trials of that state. It will suffice to inform you that when I became aware of the beginning of this trial I could feel neither surprise nor annoyance. Now that I perceive a fresh access of suffering I can but repeat what she already knows, and what God has given her grace to put in practice, in fact, what you yourself have told her. This you know as well as I do. As long as God keeps her in this suffering state an angel from Heaven could not draw her out of it, nor impart to her the slightest consolation. Nevertheless I will, for your satisfaction, willingly explain a few little details.

1st. That which enables me to judge that the state of this dear soul is, at one and the same time, a trial and an effect of her progress in the supernatural life is, first, that this sad condition is the outcome of a sense of faith, of a lively fear of the judgments of God, of death, of eternity, etc. Secondly, that she has been much consoled for a long time by abandoning herself into the hands of God, and uniting herself to Jesus crucified. Thirdly, that this painful access of suffering has come upon her now without any sensible or apparent cause, and without being preceded by any reflexion. Fourthly, even if her natural temperament, character, disposition, and other causes have contributed to produce it, as sometimes happens, the pain, in the end, is none the less supernatural; because it is beyond nature to produce such an effect without sensible or apparent cause. Therefore have no fears on her account for she is certainly in the state that mystical authors call " suffering the crucifying gift of God." As for the fear she has of losing her reason, she is not the only one who has been tormented by such fears. I have known numbers of people who have been impelled to make this great and last sacrifice with an entire abandonment, and full confidence. She will have the whole merit of it without its realisation, I hope, being required of her by God. These are the ways of God with souls. He only asks in in-

Y

numerable similar cases, the sacrifice of the heart without its
completion, as He acted formerly with regard to Abraham.
Therefore let her hope against all hope.   Every trial, borne well,
will turn out for her very advantageous ; be consoled and in
peace about her.   As for the Retreat, I am inclined to think
it would be well to defer it.   But if, however, she wishes to
continue it she has only to do what you have advised her ; her
only meditation to be on confidence in God ; her only reading
such as will nourish her soul with the essence of pure recollection,
almost without thought or reasoning, at any rate none that
requires effort.

2nd.   She should reflect as little as possible about her suffering
and interior distress.   Such reflections while detracting from
the merit only tend to embitter and increase the evil.   Let
her try to forget herself and to think only of God, but gently
and simply without any violent effort.   She should not speak of
her afflictions any more, not even to God in prayer.   Let her
intercourse with Him be on quite different subjects as much as
possible.

3rd.   If solitude has the effect of plunging her more deeply
into anguish in spite of herself, then I advise her to converse about
holy things with you, or any of the other Sisters.   The Rev.
Mother is right to cut off the annual confession.   I forbid it
on the part of God, and prohibit the mere thought of it.

4th.   As you, very rightly, remark, it is certain that this state
of suffering has already produced very good results in this soul.
Nothing ever has, nor ever could do her so much good.   Even
when the extreme pain should have altogether ceased, I foretell
that there will remain for a long time a certain impression of
interior humiliation which will continue to produce marvellous
after-effects.   The fear that this miserable state will return will
make her depend on God with a profound and continual confidence, which will prove for her a very great blessing.

5th.   For the rest, if these supernatural troubles find no
human remedy, nothing is more easy than to point out a way
to derive great profit from them, and to soften them considerably.
Submission, abandonment, peace, patience, confidence in God,
and to allow God to act without interruption by too frequent
interior acts ; in a word, there should only be a humble and
simple interior disposition produced in the soul by the grace of
Jesus Christ, with which it co-operates somehow, but more
passively than actively, or to speak correctly, by making its
activity submissive to the action of God.   Amen.

LETTER VIII.—*On Violent Temptations.*
To Sister de Lesen. (1736)

———

1st. My dear Sister. Each ought to make her prayer, her spiritual exercises, and consequently, her Retreat, according to her attraction, and her needs. Take therefore a spiritual book which suits the attraction which grace gives you at the moment ; and in all your interior occupations let your soul tend above all to a total abandonment to God. Rest an unlimited confidence in the divine mercy, and be strengthened in this feeling with the more energy the more subjects for fear you believe yourself to have. What most delights the heart of God is that you should hope against all hope ; that is to say, against the apparent impossibility of seeing what you hope for realised.

2nd. As to the horrible temptation you have spoken about in your letter to me, I declare that it would be difficult to imagine any more fearful, whether in itself, or in its circumstances. Be very careful not to allow yourself to be overcome by it. To begin with you must know that these trials, which are more grievous than any others, are those which God usually makes those souls whom He most loves undergo. At this time I have under my direction some who, in this respect, are in an indescribable state, the mere account of which would horrify you. The entire interior nature is encompassed with darkness, and buried in mud. God retains and upholds the free will, that higher faculty of the soul, without affording it the slightest feeling of support. He enlightens it with the entirely spiritual light of pure faith in which the senses have no part ; and the poor soul, abandoned, as it appears, to its misery, delivered over as a prey to the malice of devils, is reduced to a most frightful desolation, and endures a real martyrdom. On this subject read that Chapter in Guilloré where he speaks of very great temptations. It is true that we should always fear, but without being anxious or depressed, and always with a tendency to confidence. Never forget that the Almighty who has His plans in these hidden matters, takes possession in the depths of the soul, and sustains it divinely, without allowing it any perception of His presence. In this state God bestows on you a grace that He often refuses to many others ; that of feeling, or at least of knowing and discerning, that you would prefer to be torn in pieces rather than give the least consent.

3rd. Do not be embarrassed as to the way you ought to confess the thoughts and suggestions of the enemy. You must never mention them at all. As to the manner of resisting them, the best, the easiest, and the most efficacious for persons following your way, is that which you have adopted already; I mean a simple look of the soul at its God; an interior movement by which without agitation or anxiety, it turns away from creatures and from itself to turn to its Creator. It is a true conversion of the soul to God. Make use of it always and for everything, whenever in His goodness He gives you this grace. However, you can occasionally form a deliberate act of resistance, but without feeling yourself obliged to do so, and without violent effort. "My God preserve me from all voluntary consent; may I rather die than consent freely to offend You in any way whatever. Yes, death rather than sin, Oh my God! But as for the pain, anguish of heart, spiritual desolation, humiliation, and abjection, I accept them for as long a time as You please."

4th. The terrifying idea of the justice of God, the anguish and interior bitterness which ensue are evidently another trial sent you by God. It is not less evident that the peace and tranquillity which accompany these dreadful feelings arise from the submission that God establishes in the depths of your soul. This peace, with the interior conviction that everything you do is useless for gaining Heaven, is not so difficult to understand as you imagine; not, at any rate, to directors who have had some experience. The peace comes from God, it dwells in the recesses of the soul, or according to St. Francis of Sales in the highest point of the mind. This alarming conviction is nothing else than a vivid impression which the devil is allowed to produce in the lower nature, or, as it were, in the exterior and sensitive part of your soul. It is this diabolical impression which makes a martyr of your soul, and it is the submission which God gives it that produces the peace which is above all feeling. This is certain, I assure you. If you could see it as plainly as I do it would no longer be a trial to you. Be satisfied therefore with the almost imperceptible sight of it which God allows you, and with what I must call some sort of confused feeling which keeps you in peace. For the rest, even if this feeling is lacking obedience ought to suffice you; obedience and abandonment. Repeat without ceasing by a firm, actual disposition of your will: "May God do with me whatever He pleases, but, meanwhile, I wish to love and to serve Him to the best of my power, and to hope in Him. I should continue to hope in Him even if I found myself at the gates of hell." It is of faith that God never abandons anyone who gives himself to Him, and who places all his confidence in Him. Say then, "He is the God of my salvation, never could my salvation be more assured than when placed in His hands, and when confided entirely to His infinite goodness.

If left to myself I could do nothing but spoil everything and lose my soul."

5th. The torment of the lower nature during these attacks would not be able to destroy your peace of mind if your submission to God were perfect. This is called having a solid and not an imaginary peace. With regard to troublesome thoughts, foolish imaginations, and other temptations you must first, as soon as possible, let them fall like a stone in the water. Secondly, if you cannot succeed in doing this, as frequently happens in times of trial, you must allow yourself to suffer as God pleases the maladies of the soul, just as you would those of the body; in patience, peace, submission, confidence, and a total abandonment, willing only to do the will of God in union with Jesus Christ.

6th. Your "fiat," with regard to things of which you disapprove, taking care not to show what you feel, out of charity, is all that God asks of you. Oh! my dear Sister, how happy would be many souls that I know, if God were to give them all the consoling advantages He bestows upon you.

7th. A profound desire for recollection is a very real recollection in itself, although unaccompanied by pleasure. If less consoling than sensible recollection, it is all the more disinterested, and consequently more meritorious. In such a state one appropriates nothing to oneself because one seems to possess nothing at all.

8th. The impatience caused by the feeling of your own nothingness, is only a slight vexation of pride and self-love, and would be a serious imperfection if consented to, because we ought to deplore our misery with a tranquil humility. "Learn," says St. Francis of Sales, "to bear your own miseries as you ought to bear those of your neighbour."

9th. I am not surprised at the increase of your trials and temptations since your Retreat. If you understood, as I do, the good effects they ought to produce in purifying the most secret recesses of your heart, you would bless God for them without ceasing; for this is a great grace, and one that God reserves for those souls whom He wishes to lead to pure love, by detachment from all created things, and especially from themselves.

10th. It is a good thing to do some exterior penance, provided it be done with discretion, but you must not do too much. As long as your present trial lasts you should first of all make your renunciation consist in accepting it with perfect submission. You still have a great deal to do to reach this perfect abandonment, and I should be sorry if you were to lose sight of this kind of mortification to practise others much less necessary,

Your spiritual troubles will only subside when you abandon yourself to all that God wills for you without reserve, without limit, and for ever.

God be praised for all and in all.   Amen.

LETTER IX.—*Death of Self-Love.*

To Sister Marie-Anne-Thérèse de Rosen.   Annihilation and spiritual agony.

My dear Sister,

1st.   Such a lively impression of your nothingness in the sight of God is one of the most salutary operations of the grace of the Holy Spirit.   I know how much suffering this operation entails.   The poor soul feels as if it would become utterly annihilated, but for all that, it is only nearer the true life.   In fact the more we realise our nothingness the nearer we are to truth, since we were made from nothing, and drawn out of it by the pure goodness of our Lord.   We ought therefore to remember this continually, in order to render by our voluntary annihilation a continual homage to the greatness and infinity of our Creator.   Nothing is more pleasing to God than this homage, nothing could make us more certain of His friendship, while at the same time nothing so much wounds our self-love. It is a holocaust in which it is completely consumed by the fire of divine love.   You must not then be surprised at the violent resistance it offers, especially when the soul experiences mortal anguish in receiving the death-blow to this self-love.   The suffering one feels then is like that of a person in agony, and it is only through this painful agony and by the spiritual death which follows it that one can arrive at the fulness of divine life and an intimate union with God.   What else can be done when this painful but blessed hour arrives, but imitate Jesus Christ on the Cross ; commend one's soul to God, abandoning oneself more and more utterly to all that this sovereign Master pleases to do to His poor creature, and to endure this agony for as long as He pleases.

2nd.   For the time that these crucifying operations continue, the understanding, the memory and the will are in a fearful void, in nothingness.   Love this immense void since God deigns to fill it ; love this nothingness since the infinitude of God is there.   Take good courage, my dear daughter, and agree to everything with that holy abasement of spirit of Jesus crucified. It is from Him that we should look for all our strength.   When these agonies begin, accustom yourself to repeat, " Yes, Lord, I desire to do Your holy will in all things, in union with Jesus Christ." What is there to fear in such company ? In the midst of the strongest temptations, cast yourself simply at the feet of your Saviour-God, and your troubles will cease ; He will render you victorious, and aided by His strength your weakness will triumph over all the artifices of the tempter.

3rd. The revolt of the passions without any occasion being given them by you, the interior excitement and involuntary trouble this and a hundred other miseries cause in you, are permitted for two reasons. First, to humble you in an extraordinary degree, to make you realise what a heap of misery, what an abyss of corruption is yours, in allowing you to see what would become of you without the great mercy of God. Secondly, in order that by the interior supervention of fresh operations all these germs of death, hitherto hidden in your own soul, can be uprooted like noxious weeds, which only appear above ground that they may be more easily taken up by the skilled hand of the gardener. It is only after having completely cleared the ground that he can cultivate wholesome plants, sweet smelling flowers, and choice fruits. Let Him do this, give up to Him entirely the task of cultivating this rough ground, which left to itself could bring forth nothing but thistles and thorns. Do not be anxious. Be content to feel yourself greatly humbled and much confounded, remain profoundly abased in this heap of mire, like Job on his dung-hill ; it is your right place ; wait for God to draw you out of it, and meanwhile allow yourself to be purified by Him. What does it signify so long as you are pleasing to Him ? Sometimes princes take pleasure in splashing their favourites with water, then the favourite is happy to be thus treated since it gives his prince pleasure.

4th. When you feel pusillanimous and filled with fears, humble yourself, and say to yourself, " My weakness is so extreme that left to myself I could do nothing, but with the grace of Jesus Christ everything becomes possible and easy. In Him alone will I hope, He will give me all that is good for me."

5th. But what is most trying, but most in conformity with the rules by which privileged souls are guided, is the piercing thought that God rejects you, that He abandons you as for ever unworthy of His favours. Oh ! my dear Sister, you would be only too happy now if you could understand as I do what is even in this, the kind conduct of God in your regard. All that I can say to you about it, and I say it without knowing whether in your state of trial, it will please God to make you understand it, is that never have you loved God so purely as now, and that never have you been so much loved by Him. But this love is so hidden away in the midst of your torments and apparent miseries that your director has need of a certain amount of experience to be able to recognise it. But have patience, this fearful darkness will be succeeded by a clear light, the brilliance of which will delight you. Yes, my dear Sister, you can believe me, even though at present you may not be able to understand, because I do not tell you anything of which God has not given me a certitude. The bitterest part of your trials, those ideas of being separated from God, which plunges you into a kind of hell, is the most divine of all the operations of divine love in you ; but the operation is completely hidden beneath altogether contrary appearances. It is the fire which seems to destroy the soul while purifying it of all self-love, as gold is refined in the crucible. Oh ! how happy you are, without knowing it ! how dear you are without understanding it, what great things God effects in your soul in a manner so much the more certain the more it is hidden and unrecognized. It is our weakness, oh my God, it is our wretched self-love, it is our pride that prevent You giving us great graces without hiding them from us, or, in other words, without our knowledge, for fear that we should corrupt Your gifts by appropriating them to ourselves in foolish, secret, and imperceptible self-satisfaction. This, my dear Sister, is the whole mystery of the obscure dealings of God in your regard. In brief, my dear Sister, fear nothing, keep firm, take courage ; God is with you and in you, you have nothing to fear even if you were in hell in the midst of unchained devils. Nothing can happen to you save by the permission of God, and He will permit nothing that will not turn to your advantage ; therefore you are perfectly safe as long as you confide in the goodness of so faithful a friend, so tender a Father, so powerful a protector, so passionate a lover and spouse. For these tender and loving titles are those which He deigns to give Himself in Holy Scripture, and the significance of which He so perfectly fulfils in your regard.

LETTER X.—*On Mystical Death.*

To Sister Charlotte-Elizabeth Bourcier de Monthureux. Lunéville, 1733. On mystical death. Its use.

My very dear daughter,

I well understand that the state in which it pleases God to place you is very painful to nature, but am rather surprised that you should not yet comprehend that in this way God desires to effect in you a death that will make you live henceforth a life wholly supernatural and divine. You have asked Him a hundred times for this mystical death, and now that He has answered you, the more your apparent misery increases, the more certain you may be that God is effecting that nudity and poverty of spirit of which mystics speak. I recommend to you the works of Guilloré in which you will find your present state very well explained. But you are going to ask me what you should do. Nothing, nothing, my daughter, but to let God act, and to be careful not to obstruct by an inopportune activity the operation of God; to abstain even from sensible acts of resignation, except when you feel that God requires them of you. Remain then like a block of wood, and you will see later the marvels that God will have worked during that silent night of inaction. Self-love, however, cannot endure to behold itself thus completely despoiled, and reduced to nothing. Read and read again what Guilloré says about this nothing, and you will bless God for putting you in possession of this treasure. As for me, I also bless Him for it, and consider yours an enviable lot, for you must know that there are very few whom God gives the grace of passing through a state of such great deprivation. The fear of aridity, of which you tell me, is the ordinary consequence of this extreme nudity. God upholds you insensibly as you experience yourself; and it is proved that this state is from God because of the peace that you possess in it apart from the senses, and because you would be vexed to be deprived of it. You only require patience, resignation, and abandonment, but these dispositions should not be felt. Remember that God sees in the depths of your heart all your most secret desires. This assurance should be sufficient for you; a cry hidden is of the same value as a cry uttered, says the Bishop of Meaux. Leave off these reflexions and continual self-examinations about what you do, or leave undone; you have abandoned yourself entirely to God, and given yourself to Him over and over again; you must not take back your offering. Leave the care of everything to Him. The comparison you make is very just; God ties your hands and feet to be able to carry on His work without interference; and you do nothing but struggle, and make every effort, but in vain, to break these sacred bonds, and to work yourself according to your own inclination. What infidelity! God requires no other work of you but to remain peacefully in your chains and weakness. As for your duties, do outwardly as well as you can, and I will answer for the interior, for God is there in an imperceptible manner to draw you from all that can be perceived by the senses. Just the feeling of your own misery and corruption demonstrates the presence of God, but of God hiding Himself to remain more truly present, and withdrawing Himself to give Himself more completely. About this read

Guilloré again. God has permitted your preliminary imprudence to allow you, without your thinking of it, a necessary consolation, and at the same time to mortify and humiliate your self-love. Oh! happy imprudence! God, no doubt, permitted the second to take you from your occupation. Since you neither spoke, nor acted with this intention, have no scruple about it, and think of it no more, but allow divine Providence to act. Is it not on His side a truly fatherly care which has arranged for you to escape from a false position, with the result that you have been at one and the same time consoled and humiliated, and left to the satisfaction of the thought that you have not contributed in any way to your relief?

Allow your terror of death and of judgment to increase as much as God pleases; do nothing positively either to encourage, or to deliver yourself from it; in a word put yourself in God's hands as if you were a dead body that can be handled, turned, and moved as He pleases.

Finally I see nothing more simple, nor more easy than what you should do at present, since it consists in letting God do everything, and remaining passive yourself. It must be owned, however, that this state of inaction is the most cruel torment for our accursed nature which, living only for itself, fears the loss of its activities as much as death and annihilation.

LETTER XI.—*For the Time of Retreat.*

To the same Sister. Before the Retreat. Nancy, 1734.

The way in which you should make your Retreat is most simple, but cannot fail to be painful on account of the interior state in which God is pleased to keep your soul at present.

1st. Do not forget, my dear Sister, that after having passed through the first degrees of the spiritual life our further progress is effected entirely by the way of losses, destruction, and annihilation. To arrive at a spiritual life it is necessary, by the grace of God, to die to all created things, to all things sensible and human. Consequently you must expect during this Retreat not to enjoy either sensible lights, or spiritual pleasures, or an increased desire for God, and for divine things; but, on the contrary, to fall into a state of greater darkness, an increased distaste, and a more complete apathy. Do not then occupy yourself in any other duty than that of receiving whatever your sovereign Lord and Master chooses to give you; since, after having abandoned yourself entirely to Him, you should regard your soul as ground that no longer belongs to you but to Him alone in which to sow whatever seed He pleases; light or darkness, pleasure or disgust, in a word, all that He pleases ; or nothing at all if such should be His will. Oh ! how terrible to self-love is this nothing ! but how good and profitable for the soul is this grace, and the life of faith. God does not complete His work in us perfectly, unless we become firmly established, by our will, in the conviction of our own nothingness, because the measure of our resistance, and the impediments we place to the divine operations, is the measure also of the acquiescence of our will in this state.

2nd. In this state of despoilment you should never force your inclination by means, or about subjects that do not suit you. Simply meditate, as far as you are able, on the life and mysteries of Jesus Christ. Read the works of St. Francis of Sales, and a few of St. Jane de Chantal's letters ; those which treat of states of suffering and privation. Read especially some of the lives of saints of both sexes that are to the point, or an account of the virtues of your holy Rev. Mother or Sisters. You will derive instruction and consolation from such reading.

3rd. During the day keep yourself spiritually united to God, receiving and accepting from His fatherly Providence all the different circumstances that occur with an entire abandonment and total surrender of yourself. In this way you will practise true recollection in which there is no fear of slothfulness.

When you feel more attraction or facility in forming acts or colloquies with God or our Lord, quietly follow these impressions of grace, but without effort or eagerness. Follow the advice of St. Francis of Sales, who desires that these acts should flow, or be as though distilled by the higher faculties of the soul. The moment it becomes necessary to make some effort to continue these acts leave them off at once and humbly resume your former state.

Keep yourself in repose in the depths of your heart, detached from all thoughts of exterior things, as Fénélon advises ; I mean voluntary thoughts ; as for those that pass through the mind, take no notice of them ; however, if you find that you are obsessed by them in spite of yourself, then have patience, be at peace, and abandon yourself.

Unquestionably you must be very faithful and particular in accomplishing the exercises marked out for the time of Retreat.

If you observe these rules you need not fear wasting your time ; fear only that miserable terror which is the outcome solely of self-love. Do not allow yourself to be distracted from simple recollection by this trouble, but guard and preserve it as a precious treasure however slight, dry, and barren it may be. For with regard to you nothing could be more important than this recollection in God, without which it would be impossible for Him to accomplish in you His divine work. If you keep yourself united to Him you may be assured that He will act in you, although it may be in an imperceptible manner, and the result of His action should be, at this time, to impoverish and despoil you more and more, rather than to enrich and replenish you. When you become, by grace, insupportable to yourself, and find not the least satisfaction in your good works, nothing remains but to put up with yourself and to use towards yourself the same kindness and charity that you employ towards your neighbour; it is St. Francis of Sales who gives us this advice. Happy is he who by dint of having destroyed self-love, which is the false love of oneself, no longer retains any estimation of himself, nor any love except that of pure charity, the same that he has for his neighbour, or even his enemies, in spite of a sort of contempt and horror that he feels towards himself. Many more trials will be necessary before arriving at that degree of perfection in which self-love ceases to exist, and is replaced by the real love of pure charity. I pray God with all my heart to give you this grace.

LETTER XII.—*After the Retreat.*

To the same Sister. After the Retreat. November 4th, 1734.

1st. I must begin by telling you frankly that, although naturally compassionate, I cannot pity you, but even rejoiced interiorly in God while perusing your letter. What I had the temerity to predict when you began your Retreat has come to pass.

2nd. You know what I think about a keen feeling of your weakness and powerlessness. Fénélon says that this is a grace to make us despair of ourselves in order that we may hope only in God. It is then, he adds, that God begins to work marvels in a soul. But usually He performs His work in a hidden manner and without the soul's knowledge, to preserve it from the snares of self-love.

3rd. The way in which God made you pass the feast of All Saints was very hard to nature, but by grace very wholesome. Blind that we are! we must let God act. If He allowed us to follow our own desires and ideas, even those that are, apparently, very holy, instead of making progress we only go back.

4th. You feel as if you had neither faith, hope, nor charity; this is because God has deprived you of all perception of these virtues, and retained them in the highest part of the soul. He thus affords you an opportunity of making a complete sacrifice of all satisfaction, and this is better than anything. Of what then do you complain? It is disconsolate nature which grieves because it feels nothing but troubles, dryness, and spiritual anguish. These are its death, a necessary death to order to receive the new life of grace, a life altogether holy and divine. I am acquainted with some whose souls frequently pass through the most terrible agonies, so that it seems to them, as to you, as if every moment would be their last; just as a criminal on the rack expects the finishing stroke which, while depriving him of the miserable remnant of his life, will put an end to his torments. Courage, patience, abandonment, and confidence in God; these are the virtues you must practise. He accords you a great grace, a signal favour, in allowing you from time to time some slight perception of His help. The different shocks this good Master allows you to experience, the vivid recollection of your sins and miseries, are divine operations, very crucifying, and intended to purify you like gold in the crucible. Why, then should I pity you? I have far more reason to congratulate you, as the holy martyrs in ancient times were congratulated, who considered themselves happy in the midst of their torments and cruel tortures.

5th. The regret that you are tempted to feel as regards the consolations you enjoyed in previous Retreats is only an illusion which you must carefully guard against. Never have you, with God's grace, made such a useful Retreat. This He has made you feel by giving you strength sufficient to enable you to sacrifice sensible pleasure and consolation. "But," you add, "God has rejected this sacrifice." Here again is temptation and illusion. God permits it in order to try you in every way. Fiat! Fiat! If God takes away your peace of mind, very well, let it go with the rest; God remains always, and when nothing else is left to you, you will be able to love Him with greater purity. He alone it is, then, who works in a divine way at our perfection through these spiritual deprivations which are so abhorrent to nature, for they are its death, its annihilation, and final destruction. Have patience. Fiat! Fiat! You cannot follow the path of perfection in reality except through losses, abnegation, despoilment, death to all things, complete annihilation, and unreserved abandonment. We need not be astonished when we experience afflictions, when even our reason totters, that poor reason so blind in the ways of faith; for it is a strange blindness which leads us to aspire after perfection by the way of illumination, of spiritual joy and consolation, the infallible result of which would be to revive ever more and more our self-love and to enable it to spoil everything.

6th. Just the keen feeling of your own frailty has been one of your greatest helps, because by making you realise that you are exposed to the danger of falling at every step it inspires you with an absolute self-distrust, and makes you practise a blind confidence in God; in this sense the Apostle says, " When I feel myself weakest, then it is that I am strongest, because the keen feeling of my weakness invests me, through a more perfect confidence, with all the power of Jesus Christ."

7th. There is nothing more simple than the conduct you ought to follow in order to derive great profit from your painful and crucifying state; an habitual consent from your heart, a humble " fiat," a complete abandonment, and perfect confidence, that is all. From morning to night you have nothing else to do. It will appear to you that you are doing nothing, but all will be done; and so much the better, the more profound the humility with which you remain without the help of those miserable satisfactions which do not satisfy God, but your self-love, as our very dear father, St. Francis of Sales, repeats.

LETTER XIII.—*The Fear of Reprobation.*
On the purification of the soul.

My dear Sister,

While reading your letter I had no sooner arrived at the part where you depicted your suffering state than an involuntary impulse led me to cast myself interiorly at the feet of Jesus Christ to thank Him for it. A thousand experiences convince me more thoroughly every day that interior trials purify a soul in its very essence, and penetrate to its most hidden recesses, and sanctify it more efficaciously than any exterior crosses, mortifications, or penances. I can but bless God, therefore, for the great goodness He shows you, and encourage you to correspond faithfully thereto. For this purpose you have only to observe the following points.

1st. Neither in the present circumstances, nor during the whole time that your trial lasts must you expect to receive any other consolation than it pleases God to give you; for not even an angel from Heaven could draw a soul out of the crucible in which God keeps it, to purify it more and more.

2nd. Moreover, it is certain that the interior crucifixion is so much the greater the greater the degree of love and union with Him to which God intends to raise the soul.

3rd. The fear of being lost does not seem to me at all extraordinary, in fact it is common enough with those good souls whom God designs to raise to a state of perfection.

4th. In this matter God seems to me to give in to your weakness by giving you an abandonment and confidence in Him which He even renders perceptible to you occasionally. How many souls in this state are deprived of such a consolation!

5th. In this matter, as in all others, God teaches you by the spiritual impressions of His grace, that He brings you to practise, exactly, and continually, all that He requires of you, so that I can content myself with saying just two things; first, your present state seems to me the best that you have ever been in during your whole life, and the greatest grace that you have hitherto received. Secondly, God teaches you all that is necessary about it; go on, and be at peace.

However, let us see if, in re-reading your letter God will enable me to clear up, by some explanation, the already perfectly sufficient direction that I am giving you in His name. First, all those thoughts by which God is represented as having ceased to extend to you that infinite mercy which is His attribute, are but the groundwork of your .trial. They are the distinctive features of that deep fear of reprobation that God wills you to endure. This suffering is your martyrdom, and these different suggestions of the enemy are the different arrows that he lets fly by the divine permission. Instead of wounding your body they pierce your heart and your soul, and are none the less meritorious on that account. Secondly, that idea and conviction that the measure of your sins is filled up is decidedly inspired by the father of lies, and not by the Holy Spirit; however, although God is not the author, He nevertheless permits you to be tormented by it, and permits it for your good. Besides this trial being very humiliating, the suffering it causes is like a fire, which cannot fail to purify you the more completely the more intense are its flames, and the more frequently your soul is plunged into the crucible. Thirdly, your supposed lukewarmness, your dryness, and want of feeling, are the results and effects of this unhappy persuasion impressed on your mind; these are the flames which are intended—not to consume, but to purify the victim in order to render it more capable of being consumed by the fire of divine love. Fourthly, I say the same of those efforts of your heart to rush towards God; those efforts to which God seems to make no other reply than to repulse you. These are, in some souls, so violent and painful that they produce what Bossuet calls despairing love—or the despair of love. This movement which is only despairing in appearance is, in reality, the most vehement form of love. This, says this great Bishop, is the way that grace sometimes imitates the effect of the profane love of creatures on those who are carried away by it. Fifthly, it is an additional grace to be able to make the heroic act of St. Francis of Sales, and to say, " If I must be separated from my God for all eternity, at any rate while I live I will love Him and serve Him." This is a help of which many souls are deprived ; make use of it then, but do not depend upon it, because God may take it away from you, or prevent you being aware of it.

6th. It is very wise to multiply your communions in a state in which this support is most necessary. You ought to consider yourself very fortunate in being able to avail yourself of this help.

7th. Faith, abandonment, confidence, hope against hope ; these are the most powerful aids you can have. However if God should deprive you of the consolation of feeling these virtues, nothing remains but to abandon yourself entirely, without limitation, and even without any help that you can feel or perceive. Then will God sustain you in the depths of your soul in an incomprehensible manner ; but the poor soul, being unable to feel any kind of support, and imagining itself completely forsaken, experiences a kind of grief that makes this state a kind of hell. You, however, are, as yet, only in purgatory, but this Purgatory is so purifying, and so filled with treasures of grace, that I pray God not to take you out of it until He has enriched you with treasures for eternity, and rendered you as pure and bright in His sight as so many saintly souls have become by virtue of these same trials.

8th. The peace that you enjoy in suffering is the true peace of God, without fear of any admixture of illusion. Instead of fidelity, courage, strength, and fervour in prayer, you find in yourself nothing but infidelity, weakness, tepidity, and indevotion. This must be. It is what will effect your annihilation before God. Oh! happy state of annihilation ! A holy person told me some days ago that she would be afraid to be taken out of a certain fearful state. " Why so ? " I asked her. " Because, Father," she replied, " I am afraid that I might lose my state of nothingness before God, which is, to me, more delightful than those other sensible, sweet and consoling graces." Here are a few words for your dear Sister, for I notice that with regard to both of you God leaves little for the director to do ; from which I conclude, by the way, that neither of you requires to consult him often. To do so would be a sort of infidelity to the great spiritual Master who wishes to lead you both entirely Himself. To return to the point.

1st. It seems to me that God has, hitherto, made the most of the weakness of this dear Sister. Darkness and aridity are trials in a less painful sense, and yet they are very fruitful because the soul, being unable to perceive anything, has no power to spoil anything, and consequently is led to a more perfect abandonment. Hers increases, she says, in an astonishing manner. This is the acme of grace, because all perfection is to be found in the most perfect abandonment in which our will is lost in the will of God. Love practised like this is the most pure, and is sheltered from all illusion and from all vain recourse to self-love.

2nd. The ineffable consolations experienced by this good Sister before she fell into this state of obscurity and dryness, was only a merciful kindness of grace, intended to gain the foundation and centre of the soul in which God wished to establish His dwelling and from thence to work insensibly. These consolations were a great grace, but the present want of feeling is a much greater one.

3rd. The good Sister should therefore remain as well as she can, in this state of simple surrender, or simple waiting, and not leave it except under the impulse of a movement of interior grace, and only so far as this movement allows : for one must never either forestall attractions, or go beyond them.

LETTER XIV.—*Explanations and Direction.*

To Sister Charlotte-Elizabeth Bourcier de Monthureux. Explanation of certain trials. Direction. Nancy, 1734.

My dear Sister,

As long as you continue abandoning yourself to God as you are doing at present, I assure you in His name that He will never abandon you. The experiences of the past and the present are your guarantee for the future. I acknowledge that the path by which our Lord conducts you is very hard to nature ; but, besides the fact that He is the Master, He allows you to reflect from time to time on the advantages and security of this way, also to consider its necessity. It is the usual way by which God conducts His chosen spouses to the perfection He destines them to attain ; and I have known very few whom He has not judged it necessary to guide along this path when they give themselves up entirely to Him. Why then are there such painful states ? Why this heaviness of heart which takes the pleasure out of everything ? and this depression which makes life insupportable ? Why ? It is to destroy, in those souls destined to a perfect union with God, a certain base of hidden presumption ; to

z

attack pride in its last retreat; to overwhelm with bitterness
that cursed self-love which is only content with what gives it
pleasure; until at last, not knowing where to turn, it dies for
want of food and attention, as a fire goes out for want of fuel
to feed it. This death, however, is not the work of a moment;
a great quantity of water is required to extinguish a great con-
flagration.

Self-love is like a many-headed hydra, and its heads have to be
cut off successively. It has many lives that have to be destroyed
one after the other if one wishes to be completely delivered.
You have, doubtless, obtained a great advantage by making it
die to nature and the senses; but do not dream that you are
entirely set free from its obsessions. It recovers from this
first defeat and renews its attacks on another ground. More
subtle in future, it begins again on that which is sensible in
devotion; and it is to be feared that this second attempt,
apparently much less crude, and more justifiable than its pre-
decessor, is also much more powerful. Nevertheless, pure love
cannot put up with the one any more than with the other.
God cannot suffer sensible consolations to share a heart that
belongs to Him. What then will happen? If less privileged
souls are in question, for whom God has not such a jealous love,
He allows them a peaceful enjoyment of these holy pleasures,
and contents Himself with the sacrifice they have made of the
pleasures of sense. This is, in fact, the ordinary course with
devout persons, whose piety is somewhat mixed with a certain
amount of self-seeking. Assuredly God does not approve of
their defects; but, as they have received fewer graces, He is
less exacting in the matter of perfection. These are the ordinary
spouses of an inferior rank, whose beauty needs not to be so
irreproachable, for they have not the power to wound His divine
heart so keenly; but He has far other requirements, as He has
quite other designs with regard to His chosen spouses. The
jealousy of His love equals its tenderness. Desiring to give
Himself entirely to them, He wishes also to possess their whole
heart without division. Therefore He would not be satisfied
with the exterior crosses and pains which detach from creatures,
but desires to detach them from themselves, and to destroy in
them to the last fibre that self-love which is rooted in feelings
of devotion, is supported and nourished by them, and finds
its satisfaction in them. To effect this second death He withdraws all consolation, all pleasure, all interior help, insomuch
that the poor soul finds itself as though suspended between
Heaven and earth, without the consolations of the one, nor
the comforts of the other. For a human being who cannot
exist without pleasure and without love, this seems a sort of

annihilation. Nothing then remains for him but to attach himself—not with the heart which no longer feels anything, but with the essence of the soul—to God alone, whom he knows and perceives by bare faith in an obscure manner. Oh! it is then that the soul, perfectly purified by this two-fold death, enters into a spiritual alliance with God, and possesses Him in the pure delights of purified love; which never could have been the case if its spiritual taste had not been doubly purified.

But this carries me too far. Let us return to your letter.

What a number of false steps! you say. But do you not know the remedy? To humble yourself gently, rise again, and to take courage. "But," you add, "I do this with so much repugnance, trouble, weariness, and sadness." This is precisely what increases the merit, and makes you acquire solid virtue, because it is only by gaining it at the point of the sword that it is so, says St. Francis of Sales. "Our surroundings are very depressing." I understand that perfectly, and it is precisely on this account that God attacks your heart in its weakest point. "Indeed, my daughter," said St. Francis of Sales, "this is to gain it all for Himself, this poor heart." Well then, give it to Him, at first, perhaps, against your inclination, but later more amiably, when that grace that He has taken away, which was so sweet and alluring, returns again but without being felt. "But I am not sure that I do love, all that I know is that I try to love." Well, that is all that God requires of you. It is a received axiom in theology that God never refuses grace to him who does all that is in his power to acquire it. Try then to love Him, and if these efforts are not the fruit of love, they will obtain for you the grace of charity. God already gives you a great favour in inspiring you with the desire to love Him. Some day, I hope, He will lead you further, and satisfy this desire. Say to yourself, "I should be consoled, even overwhelmed with consolation if I felt towards God what I try to feel, but at present God wishes to take from me all interior consolation, to make me die the second death which should precede that completely supernatural and divine life of His Holy Spirit, of His grace and pure love."

Now I come to a beautiful part of your letter which rejoices my heart before God. You say, "I should like, very humbly, to remonstrate, but instead I will remain on my cross through obedience even if I have to die there." Here indeed the good God gives and inspires you with a great courage. He holds you, therefore, always in His hand; what have you to fear? No, you will not die of it, my dear daughter, except only by a spiritual death more precious than any earthly life. "Yes," you add, "but all the same I should be very glad and much relieved if God would take me out of this state, or these circumstances." The saints in a thousand similar cases would say the same, but the more one would like to be relieved of a position or duty, the more merit there is in being willing to remain in it if such is the will of God. Be consoled, therefore, put your mind at rest and remain in peace. God is with you and a God all goodness, who bears with the weakness, miseries, and frailties of His good friends with a tender compassion even to the extent of forbidding them to distress themselves ; and why ? Because He wishes all whom He loves to enjoy an unalterable peace. Frequent acts of the love of God, or even of a holy desire to love Him, are an excellent remedy for the fear of divine judgments, and for the terrors about predestination. I am not at all surprised at the happy results of this remedy. I much approve, also, of the reply you made to the person who told you that she did not love God with sufficient disinterestedness. This is a visible illusion of the devil, who, under pretext of I know not what self-love, wants to keep this soul back, and to retard its progress. Tell her that self-love (I allude to spiritual self-love which, although not sinful, tarnishes the perfect purity of divine love) is only found in those souls who make of the gifts of God, or of his rewards, a motive to love Him for their sakes. To love God for Himself, and because He is God, and inasmuch as He is our own God, our great reward, our sovereign good, infinitely good to us, is the pure and practical love of the saints ; for to love one's supreme happiness, which is God Himself, is to love God alone. These two terms express the same thing, and it is impossible to love God otherwise than as He is in Himself. Besides, in Himself He is our supreme good, our last end, and our eternal happiness. But, some will say, supposing that God were not our eternal happiness, ought we not to love Him just the same, for Himself ? Oh ! what a strange and pitiable supposition ! It is as much as to say : If God were not God. Do not let us split hairs so much, but go on in a direct and simple manner, broad-mindedly, as St. Francis of Sales advises. Let us love God with simplicity and as well as we can, and He will raise and purify our love ever more and more according to His own good pleasure. As for you, keep to the spiritual condition in which God has been pleased to place you. The fear of death and terrors about the judgments of God and about eternity, were endured by St. Jerome for a longer time and much more severely than by you. Let us be willing to retain these strong impressions for as long as God pleases. Our own will should be ready to die, to be extinguished, and happily lost in that of God, which is always equally loving, perfect and adorable.

LETTER XV.—*Perfect Detachment.*

To Sister Marie-Antoinette de Mahuet. Nancy, 1735.

My dear Sister,

In sending you what is necessary to prosecute the work of charity which I recommended to you, the thought occurred to me to lay before you some of the certain and very consoling truths concerning souls who give themselves up to an interior life.

First Principle. Union with God, the source of all purity, can only be attained according to the degree in which the soul is detached from all things created, which are the source of continual corruption and impurity.

Second Principle. This detachment, which, when it has attained perfection, is called mystical death, has two objects; the exterior, that is to say, creatures other than ourselves; and interior, that is to say, our own ideas, satisfactions, and interests—in one word—ourselves. The proof and sign of the death of all that is external is a sort of indifference, or rather of insensibility with regard to exterior goods, pleasures, reputation, relations, friends, etc. This insensibility becomes, by the help of grace, so complete and so profound that one is tempted to imagine it purely natural; and God permits this to prevent the artifices of self-complacency, and to make us in all things, walk in the obscurity of faith, and in a great abandonment.

Third Principle. Interior privation, or death to self, is the most difficult renunciation of all; it is as though we were torn away from ourselves, or were flayed alive. The excruciating pain experienced by self-love, and the cries it utters, are an index to the power of the links which attach us to the creature, and to the necessity of this renunciation; for, the deeper the knife of the surgeon penetrates to the quick, the keener is the pain; and the greater the vitality one has, the stronger is the resistance to this death. The soul, therefore, cannot arrive at this happy death and perfect detachment except by way of privations and interior renunciation. It requires a proved and heroic virtue to acquire a stripping of the heart in the midst of abundance : and renunciation in the midst of pleasures. It is therefore, on the part of God, a favour and mercy to strip us of all sensible gifts and favours ; just as it is an effect of His mercy to despoil worldly people of temporal goods to detach their hearts from them. What is to be done then while God is effecting this denuding ? This—to allow oneself to be deprived of everything without any resistance, as if one were a statue. But what about interior rebellion ? It must be put up with and no attention paid to it. But if one feels that one is not bearing this state of deprivation properly ? This additional trial must be endured like that of despoilment, peacefully without voluntary trouble. But what if you are not certain that this deprivation comes from God ? As it is now a question of cutting off self-love, which for its own consolation seeks impossible certitude in everything, this is the answer that should be given.

Fourth Principle. 1st, It is certain that without a special revelation God does not let us have any assurance about that which concerns our eternal salvation. Why so ? To make us walk in darkness, and thus to render our faith more meritorious on account of the obscurity in which it leaves the reason. 2nd, To keep us always in a state of the deepest humiliation as a counterpoise to the natural and strong inclination to pride. 3rd, To exercise over us His sovereign dominion, and to keep us in the most absolute dependence and the most complete abandonment to His will, not only with regard to our temporal existence, but also as regards our eternal destiny. This is what makes religion apparently most terrible, but it has another aspect that is sweet and consoling : no sooner do we submit, while trembling, to the sovereign dominion of God, and to His incomprehensible judgments, than we experience the greatest consolation. This is because in His mercy He gives us, instead of certainty, a firm hope which is of equal value, without depriving us of the merit of abandonment, so glorious to God, and for us deserving of so great a reward. On what then is this firm hope founded ? On the treasures of the infinite mercy and infinite merits of Jesus Christ ; on all the graces that have hitherto been heaped upon us ; on the judgment of the directors whose office it is to judge of our state and disposition ; on the clear light of faith which cannot deceive, and which we follow in our conduct ; at any rate, in what is essential, such as overcoming sin, and practising virtue. We see, in fact, that by the grace of God we habitually practise these virtues, and that if we do so very imperfectly we at least desire to practise them better. But in spite of all this there is always some fear remaining. If it is that fear which is called chaste, peaceful, and free from anxiety, then it is the true fear of God which must always be retained. Where there is no fear, there will assuredly be an illusion of the devil ; but should this fear be uneasy and wild, it must then be caused by self-love, and for this we must lament and humble ourselves.

But when one has accomplished this total destitution, what then ?

Remain in simplicity and in peace, like Job on his dung-hill, often repeating " Blessed are the poor in spirit, he who has nothing, in possessing God possesses all things." "Leave all, strip yourself of all," said the célebrated Gerson, and you will find all in God. God, felt, enjoyed, and giving pleasure, is truly God; but He bestows gifts for which the soul flatters itself; but God in darkness, in privations, in destitution, in unconsciousness, is God alone, and as it were, naked. This, however, is a little hard on self-love, that enemy of God, of our own souls, and of all good; and it is by the force of these blows that it is finally put to death in us. Shall we fear a death that produces within us the life of grace, that divine life? But it is very hard to have to pass one's life in this way! What does it matter? A little more or less of sweetness during the short moments of life? It is indeed a small matter for one who has before his eyes an eternal kingdom. But I suffer all this destitution so imperfectly, so feebly! Another unfelt grace; God preserve you from suffering with great courage, and a strength that can be realised. What an amount of secret complacency, of idle reflexions about yourself, would result to spoil the work of God! An invisible hand supports you enough to render you victorious, and the keen sense of your weakness makes you humble even in victory. Oh! how advantageous it is to endure feebly and patiently rather than to suffer grandly, powerfully, and courageously. We are humiliated and feel our weakness and littleness in this sort of victories, while in the other kind we feel that we are be- having grandly, strongly, and courageously, and without per- ceiving it we become inflated with vanity, presumption, and self-satisfaction. Let us admire the wisdom and the goodness of God, who so well knows how to mix and proportion all things for our profit and advantage; whereas if He arranged matters to our liking all would be spoiled, corrupted and, possibly, lost.

LETTER XVI.—*Explanation of Apparent Despair.*

To Mother Louise-Françoise de Rosen (1735). Explanation of apparent despair.

My dear Sister,

One must never take the extreme expressions made use of by orthodox writers quite rigidly, but enter into the meaning and thought of the authors. One ought, without doubt, to prevent good souls from making use of expressions, coolly and with pre- meditation, which seem to savour of despair; but it would be unjust to condemn those who, driven almost out of their senses by the violence of their trials, speak and act as if they had no hope of eternal happiness. It does not do to feel scandalised at their language, nor to imagine it actuated by a real despair. It is really rather a feeling of confidence hidden in the depths of the soul which makes them speak thus ; just as criminals have been sometimes known to present themselves before their sovereign with a rope round their neck saying that they gave themselves up to all the severity of his justice. Do you imagine that it was despair that made them speak in this way ? or was it not rather an excess of confidence in the prince's goodness ? And, as a rule, they obtain their pardon by the excess of their sorrow, repentance, and confidence. Will God then be less good with regard to souls who abandon themselves to Him for time and for eternity ? Will He take literally expressions which, in the main, only signify transports of abandonment and confidence ? It is for want of a just appreciation of these ideas that you thought it necessary to erase similar expressions in the book " *Interior Christian.*" For my part when I find such expressions in good authors' books, far from being scandalised, I feel much edified. I admire the strength of abandonment and discover an excess of confidence, so much the more meritorious as it is less perceptible, in a soul which utters these sentiments in a moment of excitement. These extraordinary states are, in the order of grace, what miracles are in the order of nature. They raise the soul above ordinary laws, but without destroying them. Far from appearing to me contrary to the wisdom of God, they make me admire His power.

LETTER XVII.—*Abandonment in Trials.*

To Sister Charlotte-Elizabeth Bourcier de Monthureux. On the practice of abandonment in the midst of trials. Nancy, 1734.

My dear Sister,

I must thank you for the charming letter of which you have been so good as to send me a copy. I have read and re-read it frequently with great edification. My experience regarding yourself is something that has hardly ever occurred to me before ; it is, that after having read your letter several times and implored the help of God, I cannot remember either what you have said, or what I have written to you in reply. About this, three considerations have presented themselves to me. Firstly, if God wishes to withdraw from a soul all sensible support, He does not permit it to find any, even in its director, unless in a very passing way. Thus He reduces it to find help in this thought alone ; my state is a good one, since the guide appointed for me by God finds it so. Secondly, what does God find it necessary for me to say after the letter which I judged before God to suit you perfectly, and to fully suffice? Thirdly, in spite of your darkness, want of feeling, and stupidity, your faith does not lack an immovable, although unfelt, support; since, following the example of Jesus Christ, you have a great desire to abandon yourself to the very One by whom you believe yourself to be abandoned and forsaken. This is an evident sign that in the midst of your supposed destitution and apparent abandonment, you recognise by pure faith interiorly that you have never been, in the main, less forsaken, nor less friendless than now. Does not the spiritual affliction which the fear of not being able to abandon yourself in all things, nor as well as you desire, occasions you, prove the deep and hidden intention which is rooted in your heart, of practising this total abandonment and abnegation that are so meritorious? Does not God behold these desires, so deep and so hidden, and do they not speak for you to God more powerfully than any words you could utter? Yes, certainly, these desires are acts, and better acts than any others, for if you were allowed to practise abandonment in a manner that you could feel, you would find consolation, but would lose, at least somewhat, the salutary feeling of your misery, and would be again exposed to the imperceptible snares of self-love, and to its fatal satisfactions. Remain therefore in peace and wait for our Lord. This peaceful and humble expectation ought to keep you recollected, serve as subject for meditation, and occupy you quietly during your exercises of piety.

LETTER XVIII.—*Fruit of Death to Self.*

To Mother Marie-Anne-Sophie de Rottenbourg. On the fruit of complete death to self. 1739.

May God be praised, Reverend Mother, for the signal graces He has been pleased to bestow upon you! Henceforth your principal care should be to guard with a vigilant humility these precious gifts.

1st. Your rest in God during prayer comes, without any doubt, from the Holy Spirit. Be careful not to forsake, by any inopportune multiplicity of acts, this simplicity, which is the more fruitful the more closely it resembles the infinite simplicity of God. This way of uniting yourself to Him by a total self-abnegation is based on the great principle that God, who is Almighty and goodness itself, gives to His children on all occasions and always what He knows will be best for them; and that all perfection consists in a constant adhesion of the heart to His adorable will. By this simple and humble behaviour all our desires are gradually absorbed by the will of God into which it becomes completely transformed. When we have reached this point we shall have attained perfection.

2nd. If God does not permit you to derive any other fruit from your illness than the recognition of the continual loss of grace sustained by a soul which pays but scant attention to its interior movements, I should still cry, "Oh! happy, thrice happy illness!"

3rd. Speak then to your dear daughters without ceasing of the great duties imposed upon them by the divine love, and of the priceless advantages of the spiritual life. Oh! how few there are who understand this, and fewer still who practise it. Now-a-days hardly any exercises are understood and valued but those that are exterior, yet God is a pure spirit whom we must adore, as Jesus Christ teaches, in spirit and in truth. Where then, Oh my God, are to be found those who fulfil this precept?

4th. To feel no surprise at one's miseries is a good beginning for a humility founded on self-knowledge; but to feel no trouble at the keen and habitual recollection of them is a very great grace, and the source of a complete distrust of self, and of a true and perfect confidence in God.

5th. Your devotion to the Sacred Heart of Jesus Christ, and the practices you have adopted with regard to it, are a real spiritual treasure which will serve to enrich yourself, and your dear daughters. The more you draw on this treasure the more there is left for your enrichment, for it is inexhaustible.

6th. What you have learnt from the venerable Fr. de Condran about the spirit of sacrifice is indeed a most excellent practice; but it cannot be continual, nor constant, except in the spiritual life, which alone enables us to attend to, and to be faithful in everything.

7th. The humbling of the heart and soul concerning all faults, known and unknown, appeases God, and draws down fresh light and renewed strength, so that the whole subject resolves itself into knowing how, thoroughly, to humble oneself, that is to say, how to remain before God always in a state of spiritual humiliation, with a contrite heart, and sorrow for sin. Then it is that we walk before God in truth and justice, according to the holy Scriptures. In any other state we should be in error and falsehood, and, consequently, far from God who is the sovereign truth.

8th. It is a beautiful gift of heaven to be able to govern in a spirit of meekness and moderation; this will prove more efficacious and salutary both for yourself and others, and make you avoid those faults into which a bitter, indiscreet, and too active zeal would make you fall. When you have to direct the aged, your conduct ought to be full of wisdom and humble charity; and with young Religious of good will, but still rather weak and not sufficiently courageous, you should be doubly gentle and condescending, and act with moderation and prudence.

I end where I began, by blessing God for the graces He has bestowed upon you, and by begging Him to continue them to you. On no account, Reverend Mother, leave off this total self-forgetfulness to which I have so often exhorted you, and which the divine goodness has effected in you. In fact, why should one be so much engrossed in oneself? The true self is God, since He is more completely the life of the soul than the soul is the life of the body. God created us for Himself alone; let us think then of Him, and He will think of us, and provide for us much better than we can for ourselves. When we fall, let us humble ourselves, and rise again, and go on our way in peace, and think always of our true self which is God, in whom we should lose ourselves and be engulfed, in the way in which we shall find ourselves absorbed and engulfed in Heaven during the infinite duration of the great day of eternity. Amen! Amen!

Printed in the USA
CPSIA information can be obtained
at www.ICGtesting.com
LVHW090952010923
756952LV00005B/35

9 789354 212468